JFK
REVISITED

JFK REVISITED

THROUGH THE LOOKING GLASS

JAMES DIEUGENIO

Introduction by Academy Award–winning Director

OLIVER STONE

Skyhorse Publishing

Skyhorse Publishing books may be purchased in bulk at special discounts for sales promotion, corporate gifts, fund-raising, or educational purposes. Special editions can also be created to specifications. For details, contact the Special Sales Department, Skyhorse Publishing, 307 West 36th Street, 11th Floor, New York, NY 10018 or info@skyhorsepublishing.com.

Skyhorse® and Skyhorse Publishing® are registered trademarks of Skyhorse Publishing, Inc.®, a Delaware corporation.

Visit our website at www.skyhorsepublishing.com.

10 9 8 7 6 5 4 3 2 1

Library of Congress Cataloging-in-Publication Data is available on file.

Poster art designed by Sean Dunkerley
Poster and art copyright: Camelot Productions
Cover design by Kai Texel

Print ISBN: 978-1-5107-7287-8
Ebook ISBN: 978-1-5107-7288-5

Printed in the United States of America

Contents

Introduction by Oliver Stone 1
Foreword by James DiEugenio 7
Preface to the Transcripts 13

JFK Revisited: Through the Looking Glass
(Annotated Transcript of Two-Hour Film) 15

JFK: Destiny Betrayed (Annotated Transcript
of Four-Hour Film) 86

Chapter 1 86
Chapter 2 119
Chapter 3 155
Chapter 4 191

Afterword by James DiEugenio 222

Preface to the Interview Excerpts 230

Interview Excerpts 232

Jefferson Morley 232
Aaron Good, PhD 237
Barry Ernest 241
Professor Bradley Simpson 245
Brian Edwards 252
Cyril Wecht MD, JD 259
Dr. David Mantik 264
David Talbot 273
Dr. Gary Aguilar 280

Dr. Michael Chesser 292
Douglas Horne 299
James Galbraith 315
Jim Gochenaur 320
John Newman 331
Judge John Tunheim 341
Lisa Pease 351
Dr. Henry Lee 365
Paul Bleau 370
Dr. Philip Muehlenbeck 375
Thomas Samoluk 383
Dr. Robert Rakove 390
Professor Richard Mahoney 397
Robert F. Kennedy Jr. 406
Edwin Lee McGehee 414
Debra Conway 421
Dr. Donald Miller 428
Dr. Randy Robertson 434

Bibliographic Essay 446
Bibliography 449
Index 453

Introduction by Oliver Stone

More than three decades ago, I met a woman named Ellen Ray at a film festival in Havana. She and her husband, Bill Schaap, ran a publishing company called Sheridan Square Press. She told me words to the effect: *Do I have a book for you!* Little did I know the impact that meeting in Havana would have on my life.

The book that the late couple had published was Jim Garrison's *On the Trail of the Assassins*. Jim's memoir was about his investigation and prosecution of the murder of President John F. Kennedy. Garrison was the district attorney of New Orleans at the time of Kennedy's assassination. Lee Harvey Oswald had lived there in the summer of 1963, before heading back to Dallas, allegedly through Mexico City. On November 22, 1963, with startling alacrity, Oswald was accused of killing Kennedy, wounding Governor John Connally, and then murdering a local policeman, J. D. Tippit. By nightfall, Oswald's pro-communist activities in New Orleans and his purported trip to Mexico were being used to convict him in the public mind. That drumbeat continued on Saturday and through Sunday morning. At that time, an event almost as shocking as the assassination of President Kennedy occurred. It was the first live murder on television: the shooting of Oswald by local bar owner Jack Ruby. As Dallas FBI agent James Hosty commented, it was as if the world had gone mad.

It was because of that live TV killing and the seeming loosening of America from its moorings that certain people in the Power Elite, like columnist Joseph Alsop, convinced the new president, Lyndon Johnson, that he needed to create the Warren Commission. What was happening in Texas seemed like a Wild West show. Therefore Johnson appointed seven seemingly august men to act as a substitute tribunal for the trial Oswald could not have. The Commission worked in secret, with one exception—attorney Mark Lane—who wanted to represent Oswald's interest—demanded his interview be open to the public. Can one imagine such a scenario unfolding today? The press would scream at the top of their lungs that the American people were being deprived of their constitutional right to know what was happening. There would be lawsuits galore. But yet, in 1964, when the Commission began to hold hearings, no one said anything about the closed doors surrounding the investigation of this momentous triple homicide.

But it was even worse than that. Because once the report was issued in late September 1964, the mainstream media accepted it without qualifications. In fact, as we note in our documentary, *JFK Revisited*, there can be little doubt that CBS television cooperated with the Commission in advance. After all, they showed a two-hour special the night the Warren Report was issued which fully endorsed the Commission's conclusions. One might ask: how could CBS read nearly nine hundred pages and put together a 120-minute program about it in one day? The obvious answer is they could not. As our film shows, CBS let it be known that they would cooperate with the Warren Commission. For that homage, they were allowed to interview witnesses of the Commission's choice.

CBS was not alone. NBC broadcasted a one-hour program on that same day. And the *New York Times* printed a supplement to their newspaper which contained almost the entire report. As author Barry Ernest states in our film, the Warren Report is a convincing volume until one reads the twenty-six volumes of testimony and evidence it is based upon. And here is the almost overwhelming irony. Those volumes would not be published until almost two months later! Therefore, how could one judge the Warren Report unless one read the accompanying volumes? Because that is where the raw data was located. What this all meant was this: Oswald had been convicted in the public mind the weekend of the assassination; he was then shot and killed in the arms of the Dallas police on live television; ten months later he was now being officially convicted by the seven-man panel that Johnson had appointed to oversee his case. All done without an attorney to present his side of the story.

As we demonstrate, the idea the Commission was unanimous in its verdict was always a myth that was sustained by a lazy and obedient press. As time went on, we learned that Senator Richard Russell, Representative Hale Boggs, and Senator John Sherman Cooper all had grave doubts about the Warren Report. They were particularly suspicious about CE 399, which Mark Lane later termed the "magic bullet." As we show, President Gerald Ford, formerly a member of the commission, later revealed to French President Valery Giscard d'Estaing that they felt an organization was behind Kennedy's murder, one they could not locate. With the true dispositions of those four people revealed, the Commission becomes a minority report.

The reason that did not really matter is that the most active member of the Commission—the one person who did not have a job at the time—was Allen Dulles. Due to his personal circumstances, Dulles could devote more time than the others to the internal workings of that body. And he did. As Walt Brown proved in his study of the Commission's activities—*The Warren Omission*—no one asked more questions and no one attended more meetings than Dulles did. But further, why did Johnson choose Dulles for the Commission anyway? He must have been aware that Kennedy relieved him of his coveted duties as director of the CIA because Dulles had lied to him about almost every aspect of the Bay of Pigs invasion.

There was something else happening—and going unnoted—at about the time the Commission volumes were published. Just fourteen weeks after their release, the first combat troops landed at Da Nang in South Vietnam. As we prove in the film, not only was this a drastic alteration of Kennedy's policy, but Johnson *knew* he was changing Kennedy's policies. Further, the new president was doing this at the same time he was saying he was *continuing* Kennedy's program. This was after he had campaigned for the presidency by saying he would not send American boys to do a job that Asian boys should do. There is no other way to say this: in more than one way, Johnson was lying his way into direct American involvement in Indochina. Yet no one seemed to notice what now seems obvious. In just one year after he was elected, Johnson had inserted 170,000 combat troops into Vietnam. On the day Kennedy was killed, there were none there. This was the beginning of what became an epic tragedy for both America and the countries of Indochina.

When Zachary Sklar and I wrote the script of the 1991 film *JFK*, we made this issue one of the main pillars of the film. I also directed that picture and I sought help on this story angle from two military advisers, Colonel Fletcher Prouty and Major John Newman. Between them I could back up everything the film said about the matter. But somehow that was not enough All three of us—four of us including Mr. Sklar—were savagely and relentlessly attacked over the thesis that Kennedy was withdrawing from Vietnam at the time of his death.

In 1997, the Assassination Records Review Board (ARRB) proved that we were correct about this. They released documents that forced mainstream newspapers like the *New York Times* to admit that Kennedy had a plan to get out of Vietnam, and he was enacting it in 1963. In *JFK Revisited*, with commentators Newman and James Galbraith, we go even further in this regard. But we go further than just Vietnam. We show the same pattern in other places around the globe: Congo, Indonesia, Latin America, and the Middle East. There has been much good scholarship done in other areas of Kennedy's foreign policy, and we used some of these authors in our documentary: Richard Mahoney, Brad Simpson, Lisa Pease, Philip Muehlenbeck, and Robert Rakove. We also tried to trace how Kennedy's reformist ideas in foreign policy originated and how they were then implemented once he was in office. His ideas on foreign policy were different than those who preceded him and those who came after him. This implementation had been a conscious decision on his part. It was also a conscious decision by Johnson to revert back to the old positions.

As the reader who views *JFK Revisited* will realize, this documentary could not have been made without the ARRB. We interviewed three people who worked for that body: Chairman John Tunheim, Deputy Chairman Tom Samoluk, and Military Records Analyst Doug Horne. The Review Board was created due to the yearlong controversy over *JFK*. At the end of that film, we attached a caption that stated that the last inquiry into Kennedy's death, the House Select Committee on Assassinations, had classified their files until the year 2029. This outraged many people who saw the film. Capitol Hill was flooded with letters, phone calls, and faxes expressing that outrage. From this, the Board was created.

The ARRB was an extraordinary agency of government. As many who work in the JFK field know, the Freedom of Information Act had not always been effective in releasing documents from executive intelligence agencies. But the Review Board had been given remarkable powers in that regard, powers that reversed the burden of proof in these cases. Under the old law it was the private citizen who, sight unseen, had to show why a document should be released. With the Board, it was the CIA or FBI who had to show why it should not be released after the Board had seen it. This new standard allowed the declassification of around two million more pages of documents on the JFK case.

But an odd phenomenon repeated itself in the wake of the Board closing its doors in 1998. The media was silent back in 1964 when the Warren Commission released its twenty-six volumes of evidence and testimony, which was supposed to support its conclusions on the murders of Kennedy, Tippit, and Oswald. Pretty much the same thing occurred with the ARRB. As John Tunheim and Tom Samoluk state in *JFK Revisited*, the press coverage for this unprecedented government body was rather sparse. It was not for the Board's lack of effort. They issued scores of press releases in their attempt to alert the media about the things they were declassifying or discovering. That effort had little effect.

It fell to our film to try and tell the public about the work the Board had done. In addition to the fact that no one else would do so, the Review Board's work altered the calculus of the JFK case. No objective viewer who watches *JFK Revisited* can deny this fact. And the impact of the Board's efforts were relevant in the basic forensic aspects of the case. To mention just three areas: with the provenance of CE 399, in relation to Oswald's alibi, and the Board's inquiry into the almost unbelievable facts surrounding Kennedy's autopsy. This includes the disclosure in the film that the pictures in the National Archives, purportedly of Kennedy's brain, are very likely not of his brain. In itself, this should be enough to reopen the case.

A case that, fifty-eight years later, is not over. The Review Board could not finish its task in four years. But according to the law establishing the Board, all documents designated as relevant to the JFK case should have been declassified in October 2017. At that time, President Donald Trump tweeted that he was looking forward to releasing them. But on the day he was to do so, he suddenly changed his mind. Only the president was allowed to stop release in 2017. And Trump did so. He delayed the process for six months at first. Trump later announced a second delay for an uncalled-for three years.

That second delay continued over into President Joseph Biden's presidency. In October 2021 he could have announced that all papers on the JFK case were now going to be finally released. He did not. He himself has announced two delays so far, one until December 2021 and a second into December 2022.

Question: If the Warren Commission was correct back in 1964, then why is there still this dispute going on over secrecy over a half century later? As we show in *JFK Revisited*, part of the reason is that the Commission was not correct. In our film, we disclose the Warren Report's failure in detail and with an abundance of new information and with experts familiar with that new record.

Why Jim DiEugenio, Rob Wilson, and myself had to do this instead of the mainstream media is a question that goes to the heart of not just the Kennedy case, but to the legitimacy of our republic.

—Oliver Stone
December 14, 2021
West Los Angeles, California

Foreword by James DiEugenio

JFK Revisited could have only been made through the discoveries of the Assassination Records Review Board (ARRB). That body was created by congress through the JFK Records Collection Act. They operated from 1994 to 1998. The Board was created due to the national furor over Oliver Stone's 1991 film *JFK*.

Stone's film was the first major media presentation that encapsulated much of the nearly thirty years of research that independent writers had created on the JFK case. For the first time, the critiques of authors such as Cyril Wecht, Richard Popkin, and Mark Lane—which rendered dubious the conclusions of the Warren Report—were assembled in one place before a wide audience. Added to this were the discoveries of New Orleans DA Jim Garrison concerning the activities of Lee Harvey Oswald in New Orleans in the summer of 1963. The New Orleans information brought into serious question the portrait of Oswald as the sociopathic loner the Commission was at pains to draw up. The combination of these two streams of information created a huge controversy about the mainstream media's embrace of the Warren Report. And since the film was so well made—in every aspect—it made the impact even more potent. In fact, the film was the first in the history of cinema to be attacked seven months before it premiered. (This phenomenon is well captured in *JFK: The Book of the Film*, 1992, Applause Books.)

That yearlong national debate caused congressional hearings to be convened. At the end of the film, Stone alerted the audience to the fact that the files of the House Select Committee on Assassinations had been classified until the year 2029. Consequently, the question became: If Lee Harvey Oswald was the lone assassin, why were hundreds of thousands of pages of documents still being withheld from the public? As a result of those congressional hearings, the JFK Records Collection Act was passed. After an attempted delay by President George H. W. Bush, the ARRB was finally constructed in 1994 and began declassification of these secret records. The ARRB was composed of five persons appointed by President Bill Clinton from public life. They worked together for four years and ended up declassifying sixty thousand documents amounting to approximately two million pages. But they did not have the time to complete their task. To this day, there are literally thousands of pages that have yet to be fully declassified. And a group of attorneys is trying to force the courts to act in order to finally free the last of the records on the haunted JFK case.

One of the main reasons that we made *JFK Revisited*, in both the two hour and the four hour versions, was because the mainstream media had all but ignored the powerful revelations disclosed by the ARRB. A perfect example of this took place during the fiftieth anniversary of President Kennedy's assassination. In 2013, Dealey Plaza was sealed off by about two hundred policemen, and names had to be submitted to the Department of Homeland Security to gain entry into the area. This had never happened on any anniversary before. In fact, members of the critical community had been allowed to pull permits from the city for commemoration services in Dealey Plaza. But the local leaders in Dallas knew there would be a huge media throng on hand for the fiftieth anniversary. And they wished to control the message that was presented to both the American and international media on hand. They accomplished their goal.

Another example occurred in the run-up to what was supposed to be the final release of the ARRB records. This occurred in October and November 2017. President Donald Trump had announced that he was looking forward to the opportunity of releasing the last of the documents related to the murder of President Kennedy on October 26, 2017. This was deemed by law as the last day that any document could be withheld on the JFK case. And only the president could delay it further.

He did delay it further.

But for approximately two weeks the media was abuzz about these records. The amazing thing about this fortnight binge was this: everything the ARRB had done prior to that time was virtually ignored. The broadcast media, especially cable TV, trotted out people like Philip Shenon, Larry Sabato, and even Gerald Posner as alleged experts on the JFK assassination. None of them mentioned the discoveries the ARRB had disclosed prior to this time period, or the investigation that Chief Counsel Jeremy Gunn and Military Records Analyst Douglas Horne had made into the autopsy and medical evidence while working for the Board. Many of these new disclosures had a real evidentiary impact on the official story first parceled out back in 1964.

As we show in *JFK Revisited*, particularly the four-hour version, the media abandoned their traditional role of investigating, questioning, and presenting facts about important and controversial events to the public in the JFK case. The Warren Commission worked in secret. Only Mark Lane's testimony was made in public, and that was because he insisted on it. (Walt Brown, *The Warren Omission*, p. 244) But, as we make clear in the film, it was evident that certain parts of the media, like CBS, were given access to information and witnesses in advance of the public release of the Warren Report in late September 1964. We prove that in the film. But it was obvious at the time. How could anyone, or any team of people, read the nearly nine hundred pages of the Warren Report, comprehend it, and put together a one-hour (NBC) or two-hour (CBS) program on the day it was released? That is simply not possible. As we show, there was a channel of communication between the Commission and CBS that went on for months in advance (Florence Graves, *Washington Journalism Review*, Sept.–Oct. 1978).

But what was shocking about the media in this case was something that author Barry Ernest expresses in the film. The true nature of the Warren Report was exposed when, about two months later, the twenty-six volumes of testimony and exhibits were published. As Barry states, when one reads those volumes, the reader sees that the conclusions in the Warren Report do not always match up with the evidence presented in the volumes. Yet no comparison review by any major media operation was made.

When the House Select Committee on Assassinations (HSCA) was convened in late 1976, it had much ballast behind it. As the viewer can see from our film, Senator Richard Schweiker and the Church Committee had exposed many interesting aspects about the way the Warren Commission worked, or more precisely, how it did not work. Schweiker labeled the Commission a house of cards, one designed to feed the American people pablum while an enormous cover-up about Kennedy's murder was erected. This plus another event we show in the film—the first national screening of the Zapruder film—caused a sensation which gave birth to the HSCA. That second major federal inquiry into Kennedy's murder ended up publishing only twelve volumes of evidence, while classifying over 400,000 pages of documents. It was also a disappointment. So much so that, as Douglas Horne has related, Representative Louis Stokes visited the ARRB shortly after it was sworn in. He requested that they do an inquiry into the autopsy and medical evidence in the Kennedy case. He said no one was satisfied with that part of the HSCA investigation.

That inquiry was conducted by Jeremy Gunn and Horne. It quite literally opened Pandora's box. And this is why *JFK Revisited* spends much time on this aspect of the case. Without the ARRB, we would have never heard of people like Saundra Spencer and Robert Knudsen. Or understood why FBI agents James Sibert and Frank O'Neill were not examined by the Warren Commission. And we would have never been exposed to the flimflammery around the false photos of President Kennedy's brain which, in itself, justifies a reopening of this case.

The fact that the general public had to wait until *JFK Revisited* was released to be exposed to the very important discoveries that the Review Board made tells us a lot about the state of the mainstream media in America today. For the fact is, the ARRB closed its doors in 1998, well over twenty years ago. This strongly indicates that there is a collective media memory of how poorly they performed back in 1963–1964. It's a failure they do not want to acknowledge.

They also do not wish to acknowledge the tremendous impact that Kennedy's murder had on history. As James Galbraith and John Newman show in our film, Oliver Stone and Zachary Sklar were correct back in 1991. Kennedy was pulling out of Vietnam at the time of his death. There are no ifs, ands, or buts about it today. It is amazing that almost no one in the mainstream media made this connection at the time. Namely that no matter what President Johnson said he was doing, he had visibly reversed Kennedy's Vietnam policy, with disastrous results. In fact, there is no other way to say this:

along with Lyndon Johnson, reporters David Halberstam and Neil Sheehan did all they could to conceal the schism between Kennedy's policy and Johnson's. Today, due to the declassification of documents about Vietnam, work by other scholars—Gordon Goldstein, David Kaiser and Howard Jones—has further certified this reversal as a fact.

The impact of that historical fact cannot be overstated. At the time of Kennedy's death, there were no combat troops in Vietnam. By the end of 1965, there were more than 170,000 in theater. This happened under the president who said during the campaign of 1964 that he would not send American boys to do a job that Asian boys should be doing. Thus began what was later termed the Living Room War, one that would continue for a decade and result in the quick collapse of the Saigon government in 1975. That ugly and unnecessary war would erode the public's confidence and belief in government to a point where the polarization became irreparable. As David Kaiser eloquently wrote in his book *American Tragedy*, in 1965 Johnson had a 65 percent approval rating, *The Sound of Music* was the most popular film of the year, and *Time* had announced that American youth was on the brink of a golden age.

He then added, "No one knew that a whole era of American history was over" (p. 483).

Preface to the Transcripts

In the scripts that follow, much of the archived material in the two-hour version is described. For purposes of space, this practice was not followed for the four-hour version.

JFK Revisited: Through the Looking Glass

Annotated Transcript of Two-Hour Film

John Kennedy: I have therefore chosen this time and place to discuss a topic on which ignorance too often abounds and the truth too rarely perceived, and that is the most important topic on Earth, peace. What kind of a peace do I mean and what kind of a peace do we seek? Not a Pax Americana enforced on the world by American weapons of war.

Not the peace of the grave or the security of the slave. I am talking about genuine peace, the kind of peace that makes life on Earth worth living. The kind that enables men and nations to grow and to hope and build a better life for their children, not merely peace for Americans, but peace for all men and women. Not merely peace in our time, but peace in all time.

This is JFK's famous "peace speech" of June 20, 1963 at American University. It was made under the influence of *Saturday Review* editor Norman Cousins, who had visited with Nikita Khrushchev in April (James Douglass, *JFK and the Unspeakable*, pp. 346–47; see also the documentary film *JFK: A President Betrayed*).

Talk show guest: That straight, sleek look that it should have, and very often you'll find a zipper hidden in the arm. And . . . [interrupted]

Reporter: Good afternoon, ladies and gentlemen. You'll excuse the fact that I'm out of breath, but about ten or fifteen minutes ago, a tragic thing from all indications at this point has happened in the city of Dallas.

Walter Cronkite: This is Walter Cronkite in our newsroom.

Reporter: Here's a piece of copy that was rushed to me and was torn off from the United Press. President Kennedy has been shot in Dallas along with Governor Connally of Texas. They've been taken to Parkland Hospital there, where their condition is, as yet, unknown.

Reporter: And just now we've received reports here at Parkland that Governor Connally was shot in the upper left chest, and the first unconfirmed reports say the president was hit in the head. That's an unconfirmed report that the president was hit in the head.

Police began chasing an unknown gunman across the railroad tracks. Would you see if they need some coffee or something? These people are often shaken up. They were in the line of fire.

Witness: The President's car was some fifty feet when we heard the first shot. And then as the car got directly in front of us, a gunshot from the top of the hill hit the president's side of the temple.

Reporter: Where did the shots come from?

Witness: The shots came from the hill.

Reporter: From the hill?

> This is most likely a reference to what came to be known as the Grassy Knoll. Many witnesses said they heard shots from that area, and photos depict scores of witnesses running in that direction (Robert Groden, *Absolute Proof*, pp. 68 and 75).

Reporter: Give me just a moment, John. There was just word from the hospital that they had dispatched to call for a neurosurgeon.

Man on the street: All we can do now is pray for him, and that's about all we can do.

Reporter: President's wife, Jackie Kennedy, was not hurt. She walked into the hospital.

Reporter: A priest has been ordered. Emergency supplies of blood also being rushed to the hospital.

Reporter: Just a moment. We have a bulletin coming in. We'll now put you directly through Parkland Hospital, and KBLX news director, Bill Hampden.

Bill Hampden: Two priests, who were with President Kennedy, say he is dead.

Boy #1 on street: Just, two priests announced it.

Boy #2 on street: Yes. But it's not the truth, is it?

Walter Cronkite: The flash, apparently official, President Kennedy died at 1:00 p.m. Central Standard Time, some thirty-eight minutes ago.

Boy talking to reporter: I just can't see why anybody would want to shoot Mr. Kennedy for all the things he's done for us. He tried to keep us from getting into war and everything.

Malcolm Kilduff: It's a simple matter, Tom, of a bullet right through the head.

Police chief: All the information that we have received now indicates that it did come from the fifth or fourth floor of that building. We're checking it out now. 10–4 now, and 112. We found empty rifle hulls, and it looked like the man had been there for some time.

Dan Rather: Police made a systematic search of the building. They found no weapon.

Reporter: We just got the word. Lyndon B. Johnson has been sworn in as the president of the United States just prior to a takeoff to return to Washington.

Reporter: Behind the casket is Mrs. Jacqueline Kennedy. They are helping her down. Now, new President, Lyndon Baines Johnson.

LBJ: We have suffered a loss that cannot be weighed.

Reporter: At Bethesda Naval Hospital, the autopsy team has completed work. Now the body of the slain president and his widow are at last brought home to the White House.

Reporter: Who do you think would do something like this?

Man on street: It could have been communists, I think.

Woman on street: Probably some segregationist crackpot or something. Just . . . they had it all planned out. I really believe that his blood will be on their hands.

Man on street: All I know, whoever catches him, they deserve the worst.

Reporter: Here is the suspect. Can we roll it please?

Oswald: These people have given me a hearing without legal representation or anything.

Reporter: Did you shoot the president?

Oswald: I didn't shoot anybody. I emphatically deny these charges.

Oswald never made any admission of guilt in the Kennedy case or the murder of Patrolman J. D. Tippit during his nearly two days of detention by the Dallas Police.

Dan Rather: This is twenty-four-year-old Lee H. Oswald. He answers the description of a young man sighted at the Book Depository building.

What Rather is telling the public is not borne out by the record. Even today no one knows where the rather generic description of an armed assassin on the police radio at 12:44 came from (Henry Hurt, *Reasonable Doubt*, p. 163; Joseph McBride, *Into the Nightmare*, p. 435; Warren Commission, vol. 6, pp. 322–23).

Reporter: Police chased Oswald into a movie theater. Police said he fired at them, killing Patrolman J. D. Tippit. A rifle was found in a building where he worked.

Although our film does not deal with the murder of Tippit, it is highly unlikely Oswald was the killer. See James DiEugenio, *The Tippit Case in the New Millennium* at Kennedysandking.com; for a much longer treatment, see McBride.

Dan Rather: Police refused to say whether they have any fingerprints from that weapon as yet. The man obviously was an excellent shot or very lucky, in that witnesses said three shots were fired, at least two of them found their marks.

Reporter: At the Capitol Rotunda, there will be three short speeches before the public is allowed to start viewing the body.

Reporter: Chief, do you have any concern for the safety of your prisoner?

Police Chief: No, because necessary precautions will be taken, of course.

Reporter: Is there any doubt in your mind, Chief, that Oswald is the man who killed the president?

Police Chief: I think this is the man who killed the president.

Oswald: I'm just a patsy!

Reporter: So great is the crush outside the Capitol, that people who have not been in line can't possibly. We are now switching to Dallas, where they are about to move Lee Oswald and whether—

Reporter: He's been shot! There's a man with a gun.

Walter Cronkite: Lee Harvey Oswald, the man who Dallas police say killed President Kennedy, himself is dead. The man that Dallas police seized at the scene, and are holding, has been identified as Jack Ruby. He is being held by the Dallas police. Now, back to Washington.

Reporter: Fifty-three countries are represented in all today. There are a dozen members of ruling royal families, thirty foreign ministers.

Reporter: Will the nation be all right in the few months ahead?

Eisenhower: I'm sure the … entire citizenry of the nation will stand faithfully behind the government.

Walter Cronkite: This bizarre sequence of double killings raise great questions. Who actually fired the shots that killed Kennedy? Was there a conspiracy?

Robert MacNeil: The first wound described, as a wound in the back of the head and would seem to indicate a shot from behind. But the doctors also said there was a wound in the throat at the front, which seemed to indicate a shot from the other direction.

Walter Cronkite: The new president, Lyndon Johnson, appointed a commission of seven prominent Americans to investigate the whole affair. Earl Warren, chief justice of the United States. Richard B. Russell, senator from Georgia. John Sherman Cooper, senator from Kentucky. Hale

Boggs, representative from Louisiana. Gerald R. Ford, representative from Michigan. John J. McCloy, presidential adviser. Allen W. Dulles, ex-head of the CIA.

Reporter: Are you convinced that he was shot from the School Book Depository?

Allen Dulles: Well, I think we better leave all that, you know, the evidence, the report will cover all of that.

Hale Boggs: The Warren Commission had at its disposal the complete resources of the FBI, the Secret Service, CIA. The only direction to the commission was to find the truth. And I, by my own conviction is that we found it.

Reporter: The Warren Commission makes these major findings. Lee Harvey Oswald assassinated President Kennedy. He did it alone. He was not a part of any conspiracy, either domestic or foreign.

Reporter: Some other details will be of interest mainly to historians and others having some special interest.

Walter Cronkite: But there is one further piece of evidence that the public cannot see. Abraham Zapruder's film of the actual assassination.

TV host: This murder now is the most thoroughly documented crime in American history. And for those who care to pursue it down to the last detail, it's all there.

Title card: DALLAS, TEXAS — Fifty-five years later

Oliver Stone: This is Dealey Plaza. To this day, it remains a crime scene. In the years since the Warren Report, many significant reinvestigations were made into the murder of President Kennedy. Each one revealed new facts and evidence that shed more light on what really happened here that day.

Starting in 1975, after the Watergate scandal, Senator Frank Church conducted an investigation into the abuses and crimes of the FBI and CIA. During that time, the public learned of the CIA plots to assassinate foreign leaders like Patrice Lumumba of the Republic of Congo and Fidel Castro of Cuba. Plots orchestrated under Director Allen Dulles. But the Church Committee didn't stop there. Senators Richard Schweiker and Gary Hart were tasked to reexamine the roles of the CIA and FBI as the chief investigators for the Warren Commission, and look for signs of conflicts or cover-ups.

The assassinations are dealt with in the interim report *Alleged Assassination Plots Involving Foreign Leaders*; the Schweiker/Hart Report is Book 5, *The Investigation of the Assassination of President Kennedy: Performance of the Intelligence Agencies.*

Senator Richard Schweiker: J. Edgar Hoover writes, yes, we did have a relationship with Mr. Ruby and he acted as our informant. Now, who said that at the time of the Warren Commission report? Did anybody ever imply that, that Jack Ruby was a confidential informant for the FBI? Nobody breathed that. That was classified.

See Gerald McKnight, *Breach of Trust*, pp. 94–95.

Oliver Stone: Faith in what the American public was told by the Warren Commission was starting to unravel.

Richard Schweiker: The intelligence agencies did all the wrong things if they really were looking for conspiracy or to find out who killed John Kennedy.

Oliver Stone: The search for real answers gained momentum.

Then, twelve years after the assassination, the most iconic piece of evidence was leaked and finally shown to the public.

The first national showing of the Zapruder film took place March 6, 1975, by host Geraldo Rivera on his program *Good Night America*.

Geraldo Rivera: The film shot by the Dallas dress manufacturer Abraham Zapruder. And it's the execution of President Kennedy, and Bob and Dick, would you please narrate what we're seeing as we show this film?

Robert Groden: Now, before he goes behind the sign, the president is waving to the crowd. When he comes out from behind the sign, he is shot. Then Governor Connally is shot.

Geraldo Rivera: He's already been hit.

Robert Groden: He's already been hit. And now, at the bottom of the screen, the head shot.

Geraldo Rivera: That's the shot that blew off his head. That's the most upsetting thing I've ever seen. We'll talk about it in a minute.

Oliver Stone: Seeing the shock and brutality of the actual assassination caused a public outcry. The government formed the House Select Committee on Assassinations. The HSCA reinterviewed witnesses and took new testimonies that exposed massive inconsistencies with the original Warren Report.

HSCA member: Has any other scientist to date linked the so-called pristine bullet to the injuries?

Vincent Guinn: Not that I'm aware of, no.

HSCA member: The Pentagon has destroyed its Kennedy assassination file, and we don't know why that was done.

Oliver Stone: But at the end of that investigation, what the HSCA learned was considered too damaging to be made public. And close to a half-million records were to remain sealed until 2029, a fact that we made clear at the conclusion to our 1991 film, *JFK*. The media controversy that accompanied the film forced Congress to do something about the secrecy that still surrounded these classified files. Hearings were held on Capitol Hill.

Stone testimony before Congress: Most Americans did not believe or support the verdict of the Warren Commission initially. And now more than three in four, according to all recent samplings of public opinion, think some conspiracy was involved.

Oliver Stone: Then in 1992, the John F. Kennedy Records Collection Act was passed.

Senate hearing: Clerk will report the title.

Clerk: Senate 3006, an act to provide for the expeditious disclosure of records relevant to the assassination of President John F. Kennedy.

Oliver Stone: This act provided funding and formed the Assassination Records Review Board. The public wasn't going to have to wait until 2029. Declassification was to begin now. The board was given a budget and time line of four years to declassify and make public as many documents and records as possible. They managed to collect over two million pages of declassified records and artifacts. They are all housed at the National Archives in Maryland, and since then the public has been free to view, study, and investigate. There is now so much more that we know, and with those facts in hand, we will go back and piece together what really happened that day, and discover the reasons why. Let's begin.

Reporter: Something has happened in the motorcade. Stand by, please.

Narrator: The JFK case was such a mass of confusion. For example, the Warren Commission was limited to only three shots, because three shells were found on the sixth floor of the School Book Depository.

J. Edgar Hoover: On that floor, we found the three empty shells that had been fired, but they had characteristics on them so that our ballistics expert was able to prove that they were fired by this gun.

LBJ: Any of them fired at me?

J. Edgar Hoover: No, there was never any. . .

LBJ: All three at the president?

J. Edgar Hoover: All three at the president, and we have them.

This conversation took place on November 29, 1963. One of the ARRB's aims was to declassify Johnson's phone calls after the assassination.

Narrator: The FBI concluded that all three bullets struck inside the car. He was hit by the first and the third. The second shot hit the governor. The third shot tore a large part of the president's head off.

This is contained in Commission Document 1, which was not published as part of the Warren Commission volumes (McKnight, p. 183).

Dr. David Mantik: The Warren Commission put itself in a straitjacket. They could not possibly allow more than three shots, because four shots or more would have clearly indicated conspiracy. And they were not going there.

James Tague: I was standing down by the underpass. On the curb there was a very visible mark where a bullet had struck. Either a fragment, or the bullet, scratched my face.

For the Tague strike see McKnight, pp. 228–33.
The FBI made strenuous efforts to keep it out of the report. Perhaps because no copper was discovered in their analysis. According to the

Commission the bullets used in the assassination were copper coated (Hurt, pp. 130–38).

Narrator: Records show the first shot had missed its target completely, and the final shot hit Kennedy in the head. So, how does one account for one bullet hitting two victims, and doing all this damage? Arlen Specter was a Yale Law School graduate working in the Philadelphia district attorney's office when he was asked to serve on the Warren Commission.

The Commission never decided on a shot sequence. They simply laid out three shooting scenarios, depending on which shot missed. See Warren Commission Report, pp. 110–17.

Dr. Cyril Wecht: Aha! What if one bullet made all seven wounds? Arlen Specter, he is the one that gave birth to the single-bullet theory. What if one bullet went into Kennedy's back and came out his neck, and then went into Connally's back, piercing the lung, destroying four inches of the right fifth rib, exiting from the front of his chest, going into the back of the wrist, shattering the distal of the radius, and in a 6-foot-4 guy like Connally, that's a big heavy bone, comminuted fracture, exits from the front of the wrist goes into his left thigh. Whatever you want, whatever you need. This bullet happily and readily obliges you. It is indeed a magic bullet.

No staff attorney was more involved with the bullet trajectories, ballistics evidence, or the autopsy doctors than Specter. For example it was Specter who questioned all three of the autopsy doctors for the Commisson (See Warren Commission, vol. 2, pp. 347–84). At the Duquesne JFK conference in 2003, Specter called this trajectory, "his theory." See the DVD of that conference, *Into Evidence*.

Dr. David Mantik: CE 399 was the magic bullet, and all government investigations so far have treated that bullet as absolutely foundational to this case.

Mantik is referring to the Warren Commission and House Select Committee on Assassinations. Both built their cases around Oswald firing Commission Exhibit 399.

Oliver Stone: How important is chain of custody in a legal proceeding?

Brian Edwards: Chain of custody basically refers to the integrity of evidence. If I pick up a piece of evidence and I transfer it to somebody else for holding or processing, my name is the first name on this list. The second person who touches this and takes possession of it is next. And if you don't do that, there's no way to prove that the evidence you collected on day one is the same one you get on day twenty-five when you go to court.

Oliver Stone: Can you walk us through the magic bullet's chain of custody from the Parkland employees, to the Secret Service, to the FBI?

Dr. David Mantik: Well, the magic bullet was supposedly found on a stretcher at Parkland Hospital, and went through several hands before it got to the Secret Service. Richard Johnsen was the first Secret Service agent to handle it, and he carried it back to Washington, DC. When he got back to Washington, DC, he gave it to the chief of the Secret Service, who was James Rowley. And at the White House, James Rowley gave it to Elmer Lee Todd, and Todd then took it to the FBI lab and gave it to Robert Frazier.

The most thorough discussion of this chain is Ray Marcus's pamphlet *The Bastard Bullet*. For a short synopsis, refer to Josiah Thompson's *Six Seconds in Dallas*, pp. 155–56.

We have interesting information produced by John Hunt, a private citizen who went to the archives on four or five occasions to track down the story about the magic bullet, and what he found was truly astounding.

Deborah Conway: He practically moved into the National Archives in Washington, DC. They allowed him to set up a desk with a computer and his own scanner. And he also did something different. He didn't interview policemen and FBI people, and he wasn't swayed by their excuses. He went straight to, this is what you told and you signed your name.

Narrator: Working with the FBI, and Warren Commission documents, John Hunt asked the most basic question. Was CE 399 in evidence, the same bullet that was found on the stretcher?

Dr. David Mantik: At 7:30 at night, this is the day of the assassination, November 22nd, 1963, a bullet appears in the record, and it's signed for by Robert Frazier, who is the main investigator at the FBI lab. And it's not just one document. There are multiple documents that indicate that Frazier signed for a bullet at 7:30 that night. Now, here's where things get interesting. Elmer Lee Todd received the bullet at the White House from the chief of the Secret Service, James Rowley. And Todd documents, very clearly in writing, that he got this bullet at 8:50 p.m. How is that possible? How can Robert Frazier receive the bullet in the lab at 7:30 from Elmer Lee Todd, when Todd didn't get the bullet until 8:50?

Deborah Conway: You would think that they would have handled it, you know, like it would have been gold going to the bank. There it is in the record, someone is lying about when they got the bullet.

Dr. David Mantik: It gets worse, though. Todd initialed that bullet, the one that he got at 8:50, and everyone else who touched the bullet after that initialed it too, including Robert Frazier. I went to the archives to look at this bullet. And specifically, what we want to know is, do we see Todd's initials on this bullet? He said he initialed the bullet. It is not there. Todd's initials are not on the magic bullet.

Hunt's landmark essays "The Mystery of the 7:30 Bullet" and "Phantom Identification of CE 399" are housed at both Conway's *JFK Lancer* and the Mary Ferrell Foundation's websites.

Dr. Gary Aguilar: I was very interested in finding out what the Review Board would show us about this. So, we began scouring their evidence, and we found out something very interesting. We found out that the Warren Report had from an FBI report saying that the guys that found the bullet later identified that as the bullet they'd seen. The internal record didn't show that at all. The internal record said this bullet didn't look like that bullet at all. But the FBI had reported to the Warren Commission that it did. It lied.

We then talk to the FBI agent that was supposed to have carried that bullet around. His name was Bardwell Odum. I got Bardwell Odum on the phone. I sent him the documents that said that he had done this. He said, "I never had that bullet. I never showed any bullet to anyone. If I'd had the bullet, there'd be a 302. I would have filed a report, particularly in that era. Everybody was very uptight about getting everything right." So, we scoured for 302 reports. His name appears nowhere in the record. This is just something that the FBI invented.

Aguilar's work, done with the aid of Josiah Thompson, is written about in *The Assassinations*, edited by James DiEugenio and Lisa Pease, pp. 282–84.

Dr. David Mantik: It's conceivable that some mysterious bullet showed up from who knows where. Todd did not initial it, and it ended up in the FBI lab as the magic bullet.

Dr. Gary Aguilar: One can only surmise that somewhere in the FBI they realized they had to close the loop on Oswald's guilt. And so they just switched it out. Because, none of the four people, either the guys at Parkland, or the two Secret Service agents, could identify the bullet. The guy who is supposed to have gotten confirmation that they did identify the bullet said he never did it. And the record supports that. So, there's good reason to be very suspicious about the magic bullet.

Dr. Henry Lee: The chain of custody doesn't start from the laboratory. It starts from the crime scene. Each piece of evidence should be photographed, documented, and preserved properly. From the scene, evidence is collected, sent to the laboratory. We have to keep the chain of custody when they enter the lab. Who examined? Who did the further analysis? And each step has to be maintained until you submit to the court. If this chain is broke, then my evidence becomes inadmissible.

Lee was a police captain in Taipei City, Taiwan, chief criminalist for the state of Connecticut, and also their Commissioner of Public Safety. In those functions, he supervised scores of criminal cases.

Narrator: The other problem is the lack of damage to the bullet, after going through two men, smashing two bones, and making seven wounds. Dr. Joseph Dolce was a much-honored battlefield surgeon during World War II. He worked for the Warren Commission.

Dr. Joseph Dolce: And so they gave us the original rifle, the Mannlicher-Carcano, plus one hundred bullets, 6.5 millimeters. And we went, and we shot the cadaver wrists, and in every instance, the front, or the tip of the bullet was smashed. Under no circumstances, do I feel that this bullet could hit the wrist, and still not be deformed.

Narrator: Dolce came to believe that two bullets had struck Connally. Since Arlen Specter prescreened the medical witnesses for the commission, Dolce's name is not in the Warren Report, and his testimony is not in the volumes. And even Connally refused to accept the single-bullet theory.

For Dolce's work on the Warren Commission and what Specter did to it, see McKnight, pp. 186–89; 196–97.

TV host: Former Senator John Sherman Cooper is the first member of the Warren Commission to agree to talk on television about what went on inside the deliberations.

John Sherman Cooper: Yes, there were disagreements. I think the most serious one when it comes to me the most vividly, of course, the question of whether or not the first shot went through President Kennedy and then through Governor Connally.

Narrator: Although it never specified the order of the shots, the Warren Report had one bullet going through Kennedy and Governor Connally, another missing the car, hitting a bystander on Commerce Street, James Tague, and the final shot hitting Kennedy in the head.

John Sherman Cooper: I could not convince myself that the same bullet struck both of them, although. . .

TV host: You mean that you yourself didn't . . . weren't convinced about the single-bullet theory, which. . .

John Sherman Cooper: No, I wasn't convinced by it. Neither was Senator Russell.

For this dialogue, see the 1978 BBC Documentary, *The Assassination of President Kennedy.*

Narrator: Senator Richard Russell of Georgia did not want to serve on the commission. After he attended the first meeting, he quickly became disenchanted with the proceedings. Particularly the roles of J. Edgar Hoover and acting attorney general Nicholas Katzenbach. His personal papers at the University of Georgia Library contain a memo written after the initial December 5th, 1963, executive session. "Something strange is happening. Warren and Katzenbach know all about the FBI and are apparently planning to show Oswald as the only one considered. This to me is an untenable position."

His papers reveal that he wrote a dissenting opinion for the presentation at the final commission meeting of September 18th. On that day, he shared his concerns with President Johnson.

LBJ: Well, what difference does it make which bullet got Connally?

Richard Russell: Well, it don't make much difference, but they said that the committee, the commission believes that the same bullet that hit Kennedy, hit Connally. Well, I don't believe it.

LBJ: I don't either.

Richard Russell: Of course, if the fellow was accurate enough to hit Kennedy right in the neck on one shot, knock his head off with the next one, according to that theory he not only missed the whole automobile, but he missed the street. Well, if a man's a good enough shot to put two bullets right into Kennedy, he didn't miss that whole automobile. And so, I couldn't sign it, and I said that Governor Connally testified directly to the contrary, and I'm not gonna approve of that.

Narrator: He also thought that Oswald did not act alone. Russell was strongly influenced by the Zapruder film, and by the testimony of Governor Connally.

> The best work done on Russell and the Commission is a master's thesis by Dani E. Biancolli in 2002, *The First Dissenter: Richard B. Russell and the Warren Commission.*

John Connally: I understand there's some question in the minds of the experts about whether or not we could both have been hit by the same bullet, and that was the first bullet. I just don't happen to believe that. I don't believe that I will believe it.

> In private, Connally went further than what he stated in public. In 1982 he told reporter Doug Thompson he never for a second believed the conclusions of the Warren Commission (McBride, p. 418.).

Narrator: This forced the other commissioners to include Connally's dissent in the report. And as a result, they could not absolutely deny the possibility of a conspiracy. Russell became the first commissioner to criticize the Warren Report in public. He was followed by commission members John Sherman Cooper and Hale Boggs. But then Walter Cronkite interviewed John McCloy during a four-night special cohosted by Dan Rather.

For Boggs's eventual disagreement with the Commission, see the Bernard Fensterwald and Michael Ewing book, *Coincidence or Conspiracy* (p. 96).

Walter Cronkite: Are you satisfied that as much effort was put into challenging that case as into establishing it?

John McCloy: I'll answer that in just a moment. If I may just say one thing, I would I'd like to say in the first place, I had some question as to the propriety of my appearing here as a former member of the commission to comment on the evidence of the commission…

Narrator: McCloy never answered Cronkite's question. But even worse, CBS employee Roger Feinman later discovered internal documents showing McCloy consulted extensively on the series through his daughter, Ellen, an administrative assistant to CBS President Richard Salant. In 1992, reporter Jerry Policoff confronted Salant and Ellen McCloy with the documents revealing John McCloy's instructions for the content of the show. Only then did Salant admit to their concealment.

McCloy's secret role in the making of the series was first revealed by Jerry Policoff and Robert Hennelly in the *Village Voice* of March 31, 1992. The compromising of that series was further explored by James DiEugenio in the article "How CBS News Aided the JFK Cover-up" at *Consortium News* on April 22, 2016. The late CBS employee Roger Feinman supplied the information in both instances.

CBS, NBC, and the *New York Times* continued to support the commission's finding and never publicly reviewed the twenty-six volumes of supplemental evidence.

Interviewer: Mr. Dulles, let me put some of the criticisms to you.

Allen Dulles: Surely.

Interviewer: Some of the papers and some of the documents that are in the archives are there but are withheld from public view by the FBI, the CIA, an organization with which you have some experience. Is there anything in those which years from now when they may be released will upset apple carts?

Allen Dulles: Oh, no, I don't think so. No, I think everything that really is vital insofar as forming a judgment as to what really happened has been made available.

> Today, with the final work of the ARRB, there are nearly five million pages of material at the National Archives on the JFK case. The Board itself declassified two million pages.

Narrator: The Warren Commission was aware of something else that was wrong with their evidence.

Tom Brokaw: All kinds of ballistic tests show that the bullets, in fact, came from that rifle. That was his rifle. You took a picture of him with it. His palm prints and fingerprints are all over the School Book Depository.

Marina Porter (Oswald's widow): You have been misinformed. The ballistics tests did not prove anything at all.

Reporter: This is the weapon that was used. A rather well-worn military rifle.

Arlen Specter: We know that Oswald had possession of that rifle because we have him photographed with it. And we have his wife saying that it was, quote, "fateful rifle of Lee Oswald."

Oliver Stone: Is the rifle in evidence today the same rifle the commission said Oswald ordered through the mail?

Brian Edwards: The rifle that Lee Oswald allegedly ordered under an alias of Alex Hidell was obtained through Klein's Sporting Goods store in Chicago, it was a mail order, got it out of *American Rifleman* magazine. He wrote on the coupon he wanted a thirty-six-inch model, Mannlicher-Carcano, 6.5 millimeter, for nineteen dollars, ninety-five cents. Robert Frazier was one of the examiners, and he was a firearms expert for the FBI. And he testified that he did measure it, and the measurement was 40.2 inches in length, from barrel to stock. There's a 4.2 inch difference in the one he ordered, versus what they found in the Book Depository.

> The questions about the provenance of the rifle are stated in the article "Ordering the Rifle" by Martha Moyer in *The Assassination Chronicles*, March 1996; see also *The JFK Assassination: The Evidence Today* by James DiEugenio, pp. 80–87.

Narrator: Klein's may have indeed delivered a different Mannlicher-Carcano model to Oswald, but there are other anomalies to the story. The model that Oswald ordered showed these strap attachment points on the bottom of the barrel and stock.

Brian Edwards: In the photograph is Lieutenant Carl Day with the Dallas Police Department bringing a rifle out of the Book Depository. One of the straps at the back of the gun is on the left side of the stock embedded in the stock. That's clearly not the rifle that was ordered, or that at least appears in the Klein's Sporting Goods store.

Narrator: The straps shown in the so-called backyard photos are on the bottom and not on the side of the stock.

Brian Edwards: Marina Oswald took backyard photographs of Lee Oswald holding a rifle, and a pistol on his hip. And in that first photograph, that she took three of, Commission Exhibit 133A, and 133B, show a ring on the ring finger of the right hand. [In] 133C, the ring appears on the left hand. In fact, the Dallas police showed Lee Oswald one of the pictures while he was still in custody. He said, that's my face, but I don't remember ever having that picture taken of me.

During the making of *JFK Revisited*, the producers had Debra Conway mail a letter from Dallas at the main Ervay Street post office to Michael LeFlem in Chicago, who lived a mile from where Klein's used to be. Including a Sunday, it took six days for the letter to arrive. The Warren Report says the entire transaction, sorting the funds at Klein's by check, money order or cash,, and then depositing the money order into the bank, took one day. There were no zip codes at that time (Warren Report, p. 119).

Narrator: But after all these questions are asked, the underlying mystery remains, why would anyone use a rifle in an assassination knowing there was a paper trail that would lead right back to them?

Oliver Stone: Was there a palm print found on the rifle?

Brian Edwards: The foremost fingerprint expert the FBI had, Sebastian Latona, took that rifle and attempted to lift prints off of the rifle, the stock and/or the barrel. He testified to the Warren Commission that he found no usable prints anywhere on that rifle, on the metal or the stock. But yet, Lieutenant Day in Dallas before the rifle went to Washington, said he found a partial palm print on the trigger guard on the left side and a partial print underneath the stock on the barrel. But Sebastian Latona said there was no evidence that a lift had even been attempted.

For Latona's testimony see Warren Commission, vol. 4, pp. 20–23. See also Hurt pp. 106–9; for an exposé of the PBS presentation of this evidence in 1993, see Pat Speer's essay "Unsmoking the Gun" at patspeer.com

Oliver Stone: No partials at all?

Brian Edwards: Nothing that he could use in court. There has to be eight points of identification. He found nothing that would match that.

Operator: J. Edgar Hoover on 2192.

J. Edgar Hoover: Yes, I've seen the reports on this investigation. This man, Oswald, he had fired three shots. He then threw the gun aside, and he apparently had come down the five flights of steps. A stairway from the fifth floor.

LBJ: He went walking through there?

J. Edgar Hoover: Oh, yes. Oh, yes, they can prove that.

LBJ: Did anybody hear, anybody see him?

J. Edgar Hoover: Most of the employees were down on a lower floor, but he was stopped at the second floor, by a police officer. And some workers, some managers in the building, told a police officer, well, he's all right, he works here. He needn't hold him, so they let him go. That's how he got out.

Officer Marion Baker: From the time that I heard those shots, I ran into that building and made it up to the second floor. It was approximately a minute and a half to two minutes.

Walter Cronkite: In possibly less than two minutes . . . Investigators came to the schoolbook building with stopwatches and critical eyes. Not only police and government agents traced that route, Chief Justice Warren, and some other commission members did it for themselves.

Barry Ernest: I was interested in finding a specific witness to the assassination, which was Victoria Adams. She worked on the fourth floor of the Texas School Book Depository, and she knew Oswald. I went to the National Archives searching for her original testimony. I was told that the tape containing her testimony was missing. And later I learned that that tape had been destroyed by the Warren Commission. And so I finally ended up finding her and getting her side of the story. Vicki Adams was twenty-two at the time of the assassination, and she testified that immediately after the assassination, she ran down the back stairs to get outside to see what was going on. If that were true, she would have seen Oswald on the back stairs. But she testified that she saw and heard no one. She had realized that something was wrong, because no one was believing her. So she asked David Belin, who was questioning her, [to] interview Sandra Styles, a coworker who went down the stairs with me. This became a rather serious problem for the Warren Commission, because discrediting one woman was easy to do. But discrediting a corroborating witness that may have been a little bit tougher. So Belin said, we don't need Sandra Styles, we have you.

Allen Dulles: We've had Mr. Belin here with us too, one of our counselors who's been here several times, and . . . He knows this city now, as very few people do.

Barry Ernest: According to Vicki's original FBI testimony, she left the window on the fourth floor within fifteen to thirty seconds of the assassination. The Warren Commission elevated that time to one minute. She said she arrived on the first floor within sixty seconds of the assassination. The Warren Commission elevated that time to several minutes. So what the Warren Commission did was successfully deceive the public into thinking that Vicki was just another confused witness. Case closed.

Walter Cronkite: Reenactments prove, the report says, that Oswald did have time, just enough time to fire the shots, secret the rifle, and get down to the second-floor cafeteria.

Barry Ernest: But in 1999, I found a document in the National Archives that had been suppressed for thirty-five years, it was a letter written by Assistant US Attorney Martha Jo Stroud. It was a transmittal letter forwarding Vicki's signed testimony to J. Lee Rankin, the head honcho of the Warren Commission's investigation at that point. In the last paragraph of that letter, almost as an afterthought, we're introduced to a woman by the name of Dorothy Garner. Garner was Vicki's immediate supervisor who had stood at the window with Vicki. The letter quotes Garner as saying that she saw Vicki go down the stairs before she saw Officer Baker and Roy Truly come up.

When I found and interviewed Dorothy Garner, she confirmed everything. She said that she had been at the window with Vicki, that Vicki had left the window immediately, that she actually followed Vicki outside the office and to a point where she could see her going down the stairs. And during that whole time, she never saw Oswald. So the Stroud letter became a very dangerous document for the Warren Commission.

Narrator: Without the Review Board's declassification process, we would never have learned of the corroborating testimony of three witnesses that provide powerful evidence that Oswald was not on the sixth floor at the time of the shooting.

For a short synopsis of the Adams/Styles episode, see McKnight, pp. 113–14, but the Barry Ernest book, *The Girl on the Stairs*, is the complete chronicle.

Title card: Parkland Hospital—Today—Dallas, Texas

Dr. Cyril Wecht: Legally speaking, the autopsy should have been done in Dallas, and there was a forensic pathologist, Earl Rose. He was there to assume jurisdiction and to do the autopsy. He was pushed up against the wall and threatened, hands on guns, a lot of expletives and so on. He followed them out of the driveway and they took the body illegally out of Dallas in violation of the laws in the state of Texas.

For accounts of this confrontation, see *Trauma Room One*, by Charles Crenshaw, pp. 89–90, also *The Death of a President*, by William Manchester, pp. 297–304.

Narrator: After Air Force One left Dallas for Washington, two of the key doctors who had tried to save Kennedy's life at Parkland Hospital held a press conference. They were Dr. Malcolm Perry and Dr. Kemp Clark.

Oliver Stone: What were the two major points of evidence revealed by Kemp Clark and Malcolm Perry at the press conference?

Dr. Gary Aguilar: Dr. Perry performed the tracheotomy to help Kennedy breathe, and at a press conference right after the failed resuscitation efforts in Dallas, he was asked, they said, well, where was the bullet? He said the bullet looked like it was coming at him. He had an entrance wound in the throat.

Douglas Horne: Kemp Clark was the head of neurosurgery at Parkland. He said that the president had a gaping wound in the occipital parietal area. That's, you know, in the right rear of the head. And so the description he gave of that was entirely consistent with an exit wound. We have a transcript today of what they said at the press conference. So it's White House transcript, 1327C. That's a very important historical document, because the Secret Service confiscated the videotapes from the local TV stations.

This transcript is available online at the Mary Ferrell Foundation website. The commission did not publish this transcript. James Rowley, chief of the Secret Service, told the commission he could not find either a transcript or video of the press conference. This was false. The Secret Service was in receipt of a transcript time-stamped November 26, 1963 (Doug Horne, *Inside the ARRB*, vol. 2, p. 647). For the seizing of the videos by the Secret Service, see Mark Lane, *Rush to Judgment*, p. 53, and Horne, op. cit.

Narrator: There is, however, a surviving clip of Dr. Perry recorded not long after the press conference.

Dr. Malcolm Perry: Arriving at the emergency room. Dr. [Charles "Jim"] Carrico had placed a tube . . . in the president's trachea to assist his breathing. But there was a neck wound, anteriorly, and a large wound of his head, in the right posterior area.

Narrator: What Clark and Perry both revealed that day would indicate an assassin from the front. And Assistant White House Press Secretary Malcolm Kilduff's statement seems to support this conclusion.

Malcolm Kilduff: It's a simple matter of a bullet right through the head.

Narrator: The day after the shooting, Dr. Perry was seen by Nurse Audrey Bell, who had been with him in the operating room.

Audrey Bell: Saturday morning, when I got over there, Dr. Perry came up to the office. I said, you look awful. Did you get any sleep last night? He said, well, not too much, between the calls from Bethesda, that came in during the night. I said, what about? He said, oh, whether that was an entrance wound or an exit wound in the throat. He said, they were wanting me to change my mind.

Dr. Gary Aguilar: In his Warren Commission testimony he basically retracted what he had said and they forced him to back down and intimidated him on the witness stand. It was really quite embarrassing for me as a physician to see how someone else who was telling the truth was basically forced to recant his own opinion.

Interviewer: Did it occur to you at the time or did you think was this an entry wound or was this an exit wound?

Dr. Malcolm Perry: Actually, I didn't really give it much thought and I realize that perhaps it would have been better had I done so. But I actually applied my energies, and those of us all did, to the problem at hand. And I didn't really concern myself too much with how it happened or why.

> This story is even worse today since, in an interview with reporter Martin Steadman, Perry admitted he was getting phone calls during the night. In notes discovered by writer Rob Couteau, he further admitted the pathologists threatened to take him before an examining board if he did not recant. (See "The Ordeal of Malcolm Perry" by James DiEugenio, at Kenendysandking.com.)

Dr. Donald Miller: In 1975, Dr. Shires hired me on the faculty at the University of Washington in the cardiac surgery division. So I got to know Malcolm when I joined the faculty. We developed a professional relationship and we would operate together on complex cases. And I was particularly interested in Dr. Perry's position with the JFK assassination because he did the tracheotomy on him after he was shot. The problem is that Malcolm categorically refused to ever discuss the assassination, and he wouldn't answer my questions about that neck wound.

And then one night after we had operated together for many hours on a complex case, we were sitting in the surgeons' lounge alone, drinking coffee, and I once again asked him about that neck wound. And this time he said it was an entrance wound, unquestionably an entrance wound. One of the main reasons Dr. Perry changed his testimony and publicly agreed it was an exit wound is a Secret Service agent put the pressure on him and that person was Elmer Moore. In 1970, Elmer Moore was the head of the Secret Service office in Seattle and a graduate student named Jim Gochenaur became friends with him, and he admitted to Gochenaur that he regretted putting pressure on Dr. Perry.

James Gochenaur: So I asked him directly. I said, Mr. Moore, did you pressure Dr. Perry? He stopped for a minute. He says, well, I was ordered to do that. He expanded on it. And he said that Inspector Kelly had ordered him to talk with Perry and convince him that it could be either [an] exit or an entry wound, not an entry wound. And I thought it was pretty interesting that he would admit to something that's pretty close to a felony.

Dr. Donald Miller: Elmer Moore was also in charge of getting the doctors at Parkland to change their testimony, and agree that there was no big hole in the back of Kennedy's head.

The role of Elmer Moore in the Warren Commission inquiry is one of the key finds of the ARRB. See for example Rick Anderson's November 17, 2017, online article at *Crosscut*. See also *The JFK Assassination: The Evidence Today* by James DiEugenio, pp. 166–68. Jim Gochenaur has stated that Moore told him he and fellow Secret Service agent Roger Warner visited the Parkland doctors and tried to enlist them in supporting the official autopsy report by James Humes.

Narrator: Charles Crenshaw, a third-year resident, was in the emergency room at Parkland that day. He later said in public that he felt the wounds in Kennedy originated from the front.

Dr. Charles Crenshaw: From here through.

Dr. Gary Aguilar: Charles Crenshaw wrote a book, *Conspiracy of Silence*, in the wake of the film, *JFK*, saying, look, I was at Parkland Hospital. I saw Kennedy, I was involved in the treatment, and Kennedy's wounds were not consistent with a shot from above and behind because he had a defect involving the right rear of his head.

ARRB interviewer: Using the most precise medical terminology that you can use.

Audrey Bell: OK, let's see, it was on the right rear and he shifted the head, a little bit, to the left, lifted up the, well, kind of the matted area, the flap. And you could see the hole, and there was brain and spinal fluid dripping down out of it. Then I noticed it was dripping, you know, down into a bucket.

> This ARRB interview took place on March 20, 1997, and is available at the History Matters website, history-matters.com.

Oliver Stone: As early as 1981, copies of the autopsy photos were leaked and distributed among JFK researchers. The image of Kennedy's head wound contradicted what was witnessed by the Parkland doctors.

Doctor: I recall the injury being right along in this area.

Dr. David Mantik: It's as if the autopsy materials were designed to hide what was really happening, as opposed to what they should usually do, they're supposed to reveal the full extent of things.

Narrator: The evening of the assassination, the body of President Kennedy was returned to Washington. The autopsy was performed at Bethesda Medical Center, a naval institution.

Dr. Cyril Wecht: All of the top forensic pathologists in the United States were within one hour drive or flying time from DC. Not one of them was called upon.

Dr. Gary Aguilar: There were two Navy pathologists, Commander James Humes and his associate, J. Thornton Boswell.

Dr. Cyril Wecht: These two military pathologists who had never done a single gunshot wound autopsy in their entire careers. This is something that really has to be emphasized to every American. I don't care, Democrat, Republican, liberal, conservative. This is your president and you've got multiple gunshot wounds to determine angles, trajectory, range, sequence. And then you've got to correlate with the multiple gunshot wounds in Connally. This is a formidable task that would have required two or three major forensic pathologists to undertake. So they called Humes and Boswell.

> In the four-hour version *JFK: Destiny Betrayed*, Dr. Wecht revealed that the most celebrated forensic pathologist of that time, Milton Helpern of New York, had packed his bags expecting the call.

Dr. Gary Aguilar: They realize they were over their head. They called in an expert from the Armed Forces Institute of Pathology, a guy named Pierre Finck. Dr. Humes and Boswell started the autopsy before their forensics consultant even got there, but they realize they're in over their head. So they asked to have a medical examiner because Dr. Finck, who is a forensic pathologist, wasn't doing autopsies. He hadn't done one in more than two years. So they asked for permission to bring in somebody who knew what they were doing. Permission was denied.

For the request for outside help see Charles Crenshaw's *Trauma Room One*, p. 179.

Douglas Horne: There were a lot of people at the Bethesda morgue. The latest count by all the researchers that I know of is about thirty-three people. There was a gallery, bleachers. Apparently all three rows were filled with people.

Dr. Gary Aguilar: These three autopsy pathologists were given a body, told here's the body, he was shot from behind. He fell forward, which they wrote in their autopsy report, figure out how the wounds fit the known circumstances of the shooting. But what this really speaks to is the fact that the autopsy was not in the control of the surgeons that were charged with doing it. It was in the control of people who were there, who were telling them what they could do and what they couldn't do.

That part of the autopsy report is labeled Clinical Summary. (See Warren Report, p. 539.) The military control over the autopsy was first revealed by pathologist Pierre Finck at the trial of Clay Shaw in 1969 (James DiEugenio, *Destiny Betrayed*, second edition, pp. 300–6).

Dan Rather: Let's talk about those two wounds, Captain. You examined this whole area of the back.

James Humes: Yes, sir.

Dr. Cyril Wecht: So on the night of the autopsy, Humes and Boswell said, "Hey, we got a bullet hole in the President's back," which they examined with their finger, then with an instrument, then took X-rays, then took out the lungs. No bullets. In a murder case, that is a very serious problem for them. So where did that bullet go? Well, just like you say, a work of fiction. A call came in from the FBI in Dallas. A bullet was found. Darrell Tomlinson, a maintenance man at Parkland Hospital, trying to get to the men's room, passing by the ER, found the stretchers blocking the way, bent down, moved the stretcher, and there was a bullet. How did that bullet get there?

Humes and Boswell came up with this totally absurd conclusion that when the president lay on the stretcher, supine position and pressure was applied to his chest for cardiopulmonary resuscitation, that pressure applied—anteriorly forced the bullet, which had gone deeply into the tissues, back out through like a tunnel. In and out, a car in reverse. And what's very important to note is bullets don't go in and out like that. The bullet becomes encased. But that was their conclusion. Keep in mind, they did not know that there was a bullet hole in the front of the president's neck.

> The probing of the back wound was confirmed by Humes and pathologist Thornton Boswell for Josiah Thompson in his book *Six Seconds in Dallas*, p. 39. As per the cardiac massage idea, see HSCA vol. 7, p. 17, also the Warren Report, p. 88.

Dan Rather: Commander, now Captain Humes, how many autopsies have you performed?

James Humes: Approximately one thousand.

> Humes had a very hazy memory of how many *gunshot wound* autopsies he had done. One can only deduce it was very few, if any. (ARRB deposition, 2/13/96, p. 22.)

Dr. Cyril Wecht: It wasn't until the next morning when Humes decided, "Hey, maybe we ought a talk with the surgeons at Parkland Hospital." Earlier that day, the doctors at Parkland Hospital had determined that a bullet had fortuitously ripped through the trachea. So they enlarged that bullet hole. And now they learned, for the first time, that there was a tracheostomy superimposed upon a bullet wound. "Aha!" said Humes and Boswell. "Now we know!" The shot fired from the rear, entered the back, moving around two thousand feet per second, comes out, then stops, sees the starched white collar, gets frightened to death, plops into the front of his clothing. And that's where the bullet came from, found by Tomlinson on the stretcher.

Four or five months later, under Arlen Specter's single-bullet theory, that bullet has been rejuvenated, it's been revitalized. That bullet has now gone through Kennedy, through Connally, and now, as of April of 1964, the stretcher bullet, Commission Exhibit number 399. The hero of the Warren Commission report is now from Connally's left thigh. How is that possible? It's unbelievable.

For the discarded idea that the bullet was lost in the gurney, see Warren Commission, vol. 2, p. 368. For the commission's explication of the single-bullet theory, see the Warren Report, pp. 95–109.

James Humes: Which is scientific evidence that the wound was made from behind and passed forward.

Dr. Gary Aguilar: Dr. Humes destroyed his original autopsy notes. Now, Dr. Humes, the chief autopsy pathologist, and what we all know as doctor's notes taken while you're doing something are much more important, and are likely to be closer to the truth than anything you write later. And he admitted that he destroyed autopsy notes.

Dr. Cyril Wecht: You destroyed your original notes in a medical legal autopsy? And remember, that night Oswald is still alive. You're going to be asked, Doctor, at some point in time under oath to give sworn testimony. Why did you destroy those notes, Doctor? Doesn't a pathologist keep his notes?

Dr. Gary Aguilar: And he said, "Well, I destroyed my own autopsy notes because they were splattered with the president's blood and I didn't want them to become objects of morbid curiosity." The third doctor, Dr. Finck, who was there, also wrote some notes and complained bitterly about the fact that his notes disappeared, too.

For these disappearing notes, see McKnight, pp. 158–60. See also Doug Horne in vol. 1, p. 95 of *Inside the ARRB*. As per Finck's lost notes, the ARRB secured the affidavit of his friend Dr. Leonard Saslaw dated May 15, 1996.

Douglas Horne: He was so upset because he had to go home and reconstruct all of his notes from memory. The two FBI agents at the autopsy, Frank O'Neill and James Sibert, they reported what they heard during the autopsy, what they heard the pathologists say, specifically Dr. Humes. They were interviewed by Arlen Specter in early 1964. He proceeded to write very unfavorable comments about them in a summary memo for the record. We know with confidence why he didn't like what they had to say, because they were providing evidence that the single-bullet theory could not be true.

This issue is discussed by Horne in *Inside the ARRB,* pp. 673 and 680. He refers to Specter's Commission memo about the two men dated March 12, 1964. Horne concludes Specter wanted to keep secret the difference between the FBI version of the shooting and the Commission's version. There was no magic bullet for the FBI.

Narrator: Neither Sibert nor O'Neill were asked to testify for the Warren Commission, and their written notes became classified. In 1997, their depositions were taken by the Assassination Records Review Board.

Douglas Horne: Both Sibert and O'Neill were shown the photographs of the back of JFK's head. The autopsy photographs that are the most controversial. And they both said that they didn't see anything like that at the autopsy. O'Neill had said, "It looks like it's been doctored. I don't mean the photo has been doctored. It looks like the head has been put back together, you know, by embalmers and then photographed." That was what he said under oath. Sibert did not remember drawing a diagram of the wound for the House committee. So he drew a new one for the review board. And it's one of our most important wound diagrams. And it shows what could only be an exit defect in the right rear of the skull.

James Sibert: There was a piece about the size of a three-by-five card that was missing.

Sibert testified for the ARRB on September 11, 1997, and O'Neill the following day. Their testimony above is extracted and reproduced in Horne, pp. 691–92.

Narrator: This new evidence, combined with the review board's declassification of forty witnesses who saw a hole in the back of Kennedy's head, constitutes powerful evidence of a shot from the front.

The chart of the more than forty witnesses was compiled by Gary Aguilar from the declassified files of the HSCA, then combined with the testimony of witnesses from Parkland Hospital.

Oliver Stone: Who was the autopsy photographer?

Douglas Horne: John Stringer. He was a Navy civilian. He was widely respected. He had written a textbook on medical photography for the Navy. So he was the photographer of record. He photographed the autopsy itself and also photographed the president's brain.

Oliver Stone: The autopsy photos of the President's brain are housed at the National Archives. These photos cannot be scanned or reproduced, but are only available to be viewed on-site by researchers authorized by the Kennedy family.

Douglas Horne: Half of the brain photos are taken of a brain from above, superior views, which is what Stringer said he shot of the complete organ. But the other half of the brain photos in the archives are taken of the bottom, called basilar views.

Now, we were very careful to question Mr. Stringer about all the photographs he took, and ask him what kind of film he used for black and white, what kind of film he used for color. Jeremy Gunn showed Stringer the color positive transparencies of the brain, and Stringer immediately noted, "Well, these aren't Kodak. These might be Ansco." He said, "I don't see the name of the manufacturer on here, but these don't have the right notches in the corner." So Jeremy Gunn said, "Did you use this film with these notches in it?" Stringer said "No." "Did you take basilar views when you shot the brain?" And he says, "Not as far as I know."

When Stringer saw the official photos there were four crucial discrepancies which surprised him and made him question their authenticity. They were 1.) the brand of film used 2.) the technical process used which left numbers on the film 3.) the angle the shots were taken from, and 4.) the intact cerebellum. These are contained in his ARRB deposition, pp. 216–26. He also recalled sectioning of the brain, photos not in the Archives today.

Narrator: Doesn't this all lead to the question if Stringer did not take these photographs then who did? Robert Knudsen was a Navy photographer who was detailed to the White House in 1958. If you read his obituaries in the *New York Times* and the *Washington Post*, you will see that he is credited with photographing Kennedy's autopsy, except officially he was not.

See *Washington Post*, 1/29/89, *New York Times* 1/31/89.

Douglas Horne: Robert Knudsen was not interviewed by the Warren Commission. So they finally found Robert Knudsen in 1978. And to its credit, the House Select Committee did a deposition of him. To their discredit, they never published it. They buried it for fifty years and it got released in 1993. And I know why they buried it, because everything he told them about autopsy photography contradicted what they thought they knew in the official record. After his death in 1989, his wife was interviewed by the Assassination Records Review Board.

Jeremy Gunn: And did he describe for you the wounds that he saw?

Gloria Knudsen: He told me that his whole . . . top of his head was just . . . gone.

Douglas Horne: He told her that one photograph in particular, presumably the back of the head had been severely altered.

Jeremy Gunn: Where was the wound covered?

Knudson's son: Someone had . . . drawn in the hair covering up the wound.

Jeremy Gunn: In one sense, probably worth saying that what you're saying is very different from what the United States government has said for a long time. And why didn't he say something to somebody?

Gloria Knudsen: Well, you have to remember that he was a Navy man, and he had Top Secret clearance. That's a way of life. You don't go around blabbing. He worked at the White House and he stayed because he never opened his mouth.

> The May 10, 1996, ARRB interviews were of the Knudsen survivors: his wife, Gloria, and children, Terri and Bob. They are housed at the History Matters website.

Douglas Horne: John Stringer is still the autopsy photographer of record, I think they both took pictures, and I personally think that many of John Stringer's pictures never made it into the official collection. And a lot of the ones we're looking at are Robert Knudsen's pictures.

Dr. David Mantik: Saundra Spencer worked at the Anacostia facility, a Naval Photographic Center, which was quite separate from the Bethesda lab. That weekend, she received film. The photographs that Saundra Spencer developed, which never made it into the official record. The only evidence we have of them is her testimony.

Douglas Horne: Saundra Spencer was visibly upset when she looked at the official autopsy photographs because she said, "I developed pictures of him and his family for almost three years and he never looked like this." She said, "He looks terrible in these photographs." She started to cry.

Oliver Stone: In front of the Review Board?

Douglas Horne: Yes, she started to cry in front of Jeremy and I and the person from the archives, and she said, "He did not look this bad in the photographs I developed on Sunday." He was very cleaned up. It was very respectful. And in one of the photographs she developed, there was a brain, an intact brain sitting next to the body, the nude body of the president. Strange, first of all, that it's intact because FBI agent Frank O'Neill told the review board that over half of the mass of the brain was missing.

In his HSCA interview on August 11, 1978, Knudsen said he delivered film to the Anacostia lab and he mentions Spencer working there. These were given to him by George Burkley. (See pp. 5, 6, 14.) The striking thing about Spencer is that the autopsy photos she saw differ from what is in the official collection. She was quite frank about this in her interview with William Law (*In the Eye of History*, revised second edition, p. 431). George Lardner wrote an article about the ARRB evidence of missing notes, Knudsen's role, Spencer and Stringer (*Washington Post*, August 2, 1998).

Dr. David Mantik: So the brain autopsy or autopsies, there were probably two such events, occurred later and were not done on November 22nd.

The official supplementary autopsy report which includes a description of the brain, but no serial sectioning, is dated December 6, 1963. But the date is handwritten. The ARRB uncovered evidence that there was probably a previous examination and this likely included serial sections. This constitutes further evidence that the brain in the official pictures is not Kennedy's (Horne, pp. 788–801).

Dr. Gary Aguilar: Anybody that's seen the Zapruder film can see Kennedy's head explodes and debris flies all over the place. Jackie Kennedy climbed out onto the trunk of the limousine, picked up a chunk of the president's brain, had it with her, took it in and gave it to one of the doctors at Parkland Hospital. And when you look at the autopsy photographs of the brain, which I've seen the originals of, you can just see that the brain is disrupted, but very little of the tissue is missing. Then we look at the autopsy report of the brain, what they call the supplemental brain examination. The brain in evidence that's weighed there weighs 1,500 grams.

Dr. Michael Chesser: Fifteen hundred grams is above average weight of an adult male brain. There was one report of eight thousand autopsies and the average weight of an adult male brain was 1,336 grams. So they're saying that President Kennedy's brain was well above the average weight.

The Supplementary Report is Commission Exhibit 391, and is in the Warren Report on page 544. Chesser is referring to a Dutch study published in June 1994 in the academic journal *Der Pathologe* and is available online.

Dr. Gary Aguilar: Where did all that brain tissue disappear to? That flies around Dealey Plaza, that Jackie has in her hand, that everybody is picking off of their clothes?

Dr. Michael Chesser: There are two photographs of the brain at the archives. I viewed those in 2015. The brain looked to me to be distorted. My first thought was that the brain had been sitting in a jar of formaldehyde for a long time.

Douglas Horne: The review board had a consultant. A renowned forensic pathologist. He looked at the brain photographs and he said, "This is a very well-fixed brain. It's all gray. It's not pink at all. It's been fixed for two or three weeks in formaldehyde. It's been fixed at least two weeks, maybe as long as three weeks." I looked at Jeremy Gunn and he looked at me and the hair stood up on the back of my neck, because I knew that JFK's brain was examined less than three days after he was killed.

See Horne, *Inside the ARRB*, pp. 790–791. On the chart on page 791, Horne collects the testimony of five witnesses who corroborate this earlier examination.

Dr. Gary Aguilar: One can only imagine that they wanted the damage to the brain to be consistent with the hypothesis that Oswald had done the shooting. So if you had a defect going all the way to the back of the head, like so many witnesses testified to, it might raise questions about whether that huge defect could have been caused by a single shot to the head as Oswald is supposed to have done.

Dr. Michael Chesser: At a teaching hospital, there was no shortage of brains. Autopsies were very frequent. Frequently, the brain was saved for teaching medical students, so it would not have been difficult to find a brain for replacement. This is just one more reason why this cannot be President Kennedy's brain in the photographs that we have stored at the archives.

Douglas Horne: What we have here is evidence that impugns the authenticity of the brain photographs in the National Archives. If there was a trial today, these brain photographs would not be admissible as evidence.

For a synopsis of this evidence see James DiEugenio, *The JFK Assassination: The Evidence Today,* pp. 160–65, where the author points out twelve witnesses who saw a severely damaged brain.

Clip from *JFK*:

Jim Garrison: I'd hate to be in your shoes today. You have a lot to think about. You've seen much hidden evidence the American public has never seen. You know, going back to when we were children, I think that most of us in this courtroom thought that justice came into being automatically. That virtue was its own reward, that good would triumph over evil. But as we get older, we know this just isn't true. Individual human beings have to create justice and this is not easy, because the truth often poses a threat to power and one often has to fight power at great risk to themselves.

Narrator: The one physician present at both Parkland Hospital and the Bethesda morgue was George Burkley, Kennedy's personal doctor. Arlen

Specter did not depose George Burkley, but Burkley did an interview with the JFK Library in 1967, and was asked this question.

Interviewer: Do you agree with the Warren Report on the number of bullets that entered the President's body?

Dr. George Burkley: I would not care to be quoted on that.

This interview was on October 17, 1967, and the quote is from the transcript, page 18.

Interviewer: I see.

Dr. Donald Miller: The reason he didn't say anything was that he was intimately involved in the cover-up.

Narrator: Burkley signed the autopsy descriptive sheet with a bullet in the back at the level of T-3. And he also signed Kennedy's death certificate, which also placed that wound in the back. That death certificate is not in the Warren Commission volumes, and the descriptive sheet in the Commission volumes does not have Burkley's signature.

In 1977, through his lawyer, he wrote a letter to Richard Sprague, chief counsel of the House Select Committee on Assassinations. He said he had information indicating that others besides Oswald must have participated in the assassination. He was willing to talk about it at this time. Sprague, who made clear his intention to fully investigate the CIA's involvement, was forced out two weeks later. Dr. Burkley submitted a written statement to the House Select Committee, but there is no official record of him being deposed as a witness.

The date of this letter is March 18, 1977. It was from Burkley's tax lawyer, William Illig, to Sprague.

Douglas Horne: In 1982, he told JFK researcher Henry Hurt, "I know there was more than one gunman," and when Henry Hurt, tried to recontact

Burkley for more details, Burkley cut him off at the knees: "I don't want to talk about it anymore." The very next year, Burkley talked to Michael Kurtz, another JFK researcher, told him that he knew there was a conspiracy to kill the president and that he recalled an exit wound in the back of President Kennedy's head.

Now, that's a very significant statement. That the only doctor we know of who was present at both Parkland for treatment, and at Bethesda during the autopsy, told Michael Kurtz in 1983 that Kennedy had an exit wound in the back of his head. When Kurtz tried to recontact Burkley, Burkley cut him off at the knees. "I don't want to talk about this anymore."

See Henry Hurt, *Reasonable Doubt*, pp. 48–49; Horne, vol. 3, pp. 927–28; and the brief essay "The Missing Physician" at the Mary Ferrell Foundation website.

Dr. Burkley was deceased by the time the Review Board was impaneled. So then Jeremy decided, well, we can ask the executor of his estate, his daughter, to sign a waiver so that we could go to the law firm that Mr. Illig used to work for, because he was deceased also, and see if there were any records in the file of Mr. Illig that would have revealed what it was he wanted to tell the HSCA in detail. And she said she would do that. And then Jeremy called her on the phone. She had completely changed her mind and adamantly refused to sign it and terminated the phone call.

Dr. Donald Miller: The face sheet for the autopsy, where it shows the front and back silhouette of the body, where you mark scars and bullet wounds and things, the face sheet showed the bullet wound in the back at the level of Thoracic vertebrae T3, which is five and a half to six inches below.

Narrator: That location coincided with what Sibert and O'Neill wrote in their report. And in order to make the facts fit the single-bullet theory, of one bullet doing all this damage, the doctors needed an exit point for the back wound. The Warren Commission raised the wound in the back so that it would align with the alleged exit wound in the front of

Kennedy's neck. Commissioner Gerald Ford did this simply via the stroke of a pen, changing the description in their report from back, to back of the neck.

See Sibert-O'Neill Report, p. 5, at history-matters.com.

Dr. Cyril Wecht: As I recall, they said about Gerald Ford that he could not chew gum and walk at the same time. Now, all of a sudden, he becomes a forensic pathologist, and a photographer, and criminalist, and an expert, and he knows where the bullet hole was and he moved it up.

This was revealed by the ARRB in the drafts of the report as given to them by Chief Counsel J. Lee Rankin's son. (*New York Times* story of July 3, 1997, "Ford Made Key Changes in Kennedy Death Report").

Narrator: But then in 1979, the House Select Committee moved it lower in the back because they had pictures from the autopsy. It is conceivable that, at the time, the Warren Commission thought no one would ever see the autopsy photos. When the Review Board declassified the notation showing what Ford had done, the former commissioner replied that it had nothing to do with a conspiracy theory. He was only trying to be more precise. This is directly contradicted by a conversation Ford had with French President Valery Giscard d'Estaing. Ford told him the assassination was not the work of one person. "It was something set up. We were sure it was set up, but we were not able to discover by whom."

For Ford's reply see a July 3, 1997, story in the *Seattle Times* by Mike Feinsilber. Ford's talk with the French president was in the November 21, 2013 issue of *Le Parisien* magazine.

Oliver Stone: With all the documents declassified by the review board, we can see this scene in a new light. In regards to the JFK assassination, conspiracy theories are now conspiracy facts. The forensics show evidence of multiple shooters, with Oswald not even at the sixth-floor window at the time of the assassination. And his fingerprints not found on the supposed murder weapon. Still, there was no trial for Lee Harvey Oswald.

Lee Harvey Oswald: These people have given me a hearing without legal representation or anything.

Reporter: Did you shoot the president?

Lee Harvey Oswald: I didn't shoot anybody, no sir.

Oliver Stone: Attorney Mark Lane tried to represent Oswald in the proceedings, but was denied by the Warren Commission.

Mark Lane: The commission has functioned in a fashion which totally disregards the rights of the accused. I don't know if anybody's innocent. I know that the case which has been presented against him is full of falsehoods, and contradictions. I know that right now in the office of the Dallas district attorney, there's a paraffin test which shows that Lee Harvey Oswald did not fire a rifle on November 22, 1963. I know that because I have a photostatic copy of that document.

> Commission Exhibit 2033 contains a reply by Chief Counsel J. Lee Rankin to Lane denying his request to represent Oswald. The paraffin test was used widely at that time. But it was later found to be fallible, with about a 75 percent effective rate. (See *Journal of Forensic Science.* January 1967; and Pat Speer's essay "Casts of Contention" at patspeer.com.)

Walter Cronkite: Did the accused man get a fair trial?

Robert Tanenbaum: I can tell you from my experience as having tried several hundred cases to verdict, and being responsible for thousands of cases as head of the criminal courts and running the homicide bureau, that I don't believe there's any courtroom in America where Oswald would have been convicted on the evidence that was presented before the Warren Commission.

Tanenbaum helmed the Homicide Bureau in New York City and served as chief of criminal courts. At trial, he never lost a felony case.

Oliver Stone: Instead of a jury of twelve American citizens, judgment was passed by a panel of seven appointed wise men and career statesmen. A judgment perpetuated by the media at that time. Looking at the declassified documents, we see there's even more mystery behind Oswald to uncover. A man who was, in his own words, a patsy. Murdered on live television.

Reporter: This was the dreary funeral of Lee Harvey Oswald, alleged murderer of President Kennedy. Burial was in an otherwise empty plot in Rose Hill Cemetery outside Fort Worth. A plot that we were told was bought long ago by Oswald's mother. No one was on hand for the funeral as mourners, except the family of the dead man.

TV narrator: Oswald spent his early years in an orphanage. At the age of seventeen, he joined the US Marine Corps. A year later, he was sent to one of the most secret US bases in the world, Atsugi in Japan. From here, the CIA operated spy flights over communist China using U-2 reconnaissance planes.

Narrator: During the 1975 Church Committee investigation of US Intelligence Activities, committee member Richard Schweiker remarked about Oswald, "that everywhere you looked with him, there are fingerprints of intelligence."

See Henry Hurt, *Reasonable Doubt*, p. 192

Richard Schweiker: Many people said he was a forthright, upstanding American as a young person, and yet later depicted him as a Castro-loving, Cuban-loving, Russian-loving person.

Jefferson Morley: In the spring of 1963, Oswald started handing out pamphlets for the Fair Play for Cuba Committee. A pro-Castro, pro–Cuban Revolution group that was popular on college campuses. And some of them, he stamped 544 Camp Street, which was an office in downtown New Orleans near where the CIA's offices were, right across the street, in fact. There was also the home of the Cuban Revolutionary Council, which was the leading anti-Castro group. Why would a pro-Castro activist put his headquarters in the same headquarters as the leading anti-Castro group in the country? Because he was a provocateur.

According to the HSCA, The Cuban Revolutionary Council was at 544 Camp Street in 1961 and early 1962 (see HSCA, vol. 10, p. 123). But the ARRB declassified a letter from the owner of that building, Sam Newman, dated March 9, 1962, asking CRC headquarters in Miami for rent in advance. Newman originally told the FBI on November 25 he rented out to the CRC in March 1963 for three or four months. The HSCA did not do a thorough job on this issue. (See DiEugenio, *Destiny Betrayed*, second edition, p. 113.)

Richard Schweiker: This gets back to being an agent or a double agent, because he played both roles. Here was Oswald, who had two associations. One, he had a group of anti-Castro Cubans at the same time he was handing out leaflets for the Fair Play for Cuba committee with the other side of the fence. So the two groups that had the most motivation to assassinate the president, he was dealing with.

In early August 1963, Oswald had approached Carlos Bringuier of the CIA-backed DRE, or Student Revolutionary Directorate. Oswald said he wanted to help train Cubans and overthrow Castro (Hurt, p. 293). This was around the time he was handing out leaflets for the pro-Castro Fair Play for Cuba Committee.

Narrator: And not surprisingly, many of these groups were known, and in some cases, supported by the US government. In the spring of 1963, Oswald began associating with men who, it would be revealed, had clear connections with these government efforts. One of these men, David Ferrie, had been with Oswald in the Civil Air Patrol back in 1955, and was known as an extreme anti-Communist. He was also a trainer and a pilot for the CIA in its secret war against Cuba. Oswald was involved with these Cuban exile training activities with Ferrie.

For information on Ferrie and Oswald see William Davy's *Let Justice Be Done* (pp. 3–10, 25–33). Information on Oswald being at a training camp is on p. 30; that information is also noted in Dick Russell's book *The Man Who Knew Too Much* (p. 329). Ferrie's activities are sketched in *Deadly Secrets* by William Turner and Warren Hinckle (pp. 232–33). Ferrie's life and career is also written about in HSCA, vol. 10 (pp. 105–14).

William Gaudet: I do know that I saw him one time with a man by the name of Guy Banister. And what Guy's role was in all of this. I really don't know.

See HSCA Final Report, p. 219.

Narrator: Banister was an extreme right-winger who was close to the FBI, the CIA, and the American Nazi Party. Banister gave Oswald his own office at 544 Camp Street. Oswald now began to use his office to print up and stamp pro-Castro literature. After the assassination when the FBI questioned Banister, a former FBI agent himself, they did not ask him about Oswald.

Banister and his relations with Oswald are described in *Deadly Secrets* (pp. 229–36). They are also reviewed in *Let Justice be Done* (pp. 37–43) and in HSCA vol. 10 (pp. 123–32).

John Newman: At some point, the FBI, I think probably after the assassination, decided they wanted to disconnect Oswald from the FBI, and of course, Banister, who's associated with the FBI, would have to be disconnected as well. The problem with that, many of those handbills had the 544 Camp Street address on them. There was a message from New Orleans to the bureau written by Special Agent [Harry] Maynor, who actually mentioned pamphlets that had the 544 Camp Street address on it. And before that message was sent, it was scratched out.

The Maynor incident is from Newman's *Oswald and the CIA* (p. 310). For more information on how the FBI tried to separate Oswald from 544 Camp Street, see DiEugenio, *Destiny Betrayed*, second edition, pp. 102–3.

Narrator: The Warren Commission pushed the idea that Oswald was a staunch communist, citing evidence of his defection to the Soviet Union in 1959.

Richard Sprague: His trip to Russia raised a number of questions that we wanted to get into. For example, when any American went to Russia and renounced his American citizenship, and subsequently changed his mind and wanted to come back to this country. Upon returning to this country, there was a thorough debriefing by the CIA: with one exception, as far as we could ascertain, Oswald.

Richard Schweiker: That smacks of an intelligence relationship.

Reporter: Did you kill the president?

Lee Harvey Oswald: No, they're taking me in because of the fact that I lived in the Soviet Union.

Narrator: State Department Intelligence Officer Otto Otepka had noted the marked increase in the number of Americans defecting to Russia at the time. He also noted that some of them came from the military. He therefore suspected that some of these men were fake defectors. They had been assigned by the CIA to garner intelligence behind the Iron Curtain.

He sent a letter to the CIA asking which ones were real, and which were their agents. Oswald was one of the names on Otepka's list. Otepka's request was forwarded to James Angleton, chief of counterintelligence. He instructed that there be no research done on Oswald, but Otepka continued to work on the Oswald case.

Lisa Pease: The thing of significance was that he was really interested in Lee Harvey Oswald before the assassination, and he actually had a study of these defectors in his safe. Well, things got worse. His office was not only bugged, they planted people in his office to spy on him. They started putting confidential documents in his burn bag, and then tried to blame him in saying he's burning confidential documents. The guy has gone, you know, wacko.

Narrator: As a result, he was formally removed from the State Department on November the 5th, 1963, just seventeen days before the assassination. So you will not see Otepka's name in the Warren Report. And he was not called as a witness before that body. In fact, Angleton, the man who had access to all the Oswald files at the CIA, coordinated the agency's response to the Warren Commission's requests.

For information on Otepka's request and the CIA, see Newman's *Oswald and the CIA*, pp. 170–72. For a book-length treatment of Otepka and his security problems, see William J. Gill's *The Ordeal of Otto Otepka*. For Angleton taking over the CIA's responses to the commission, see *The Assassinations*, edited by James DiEugenio and Lisa Pease, p. 183.

TV narrator: The CIA deputy director of plans, Richard Helms, swore to the Warren Commission that the agency never had or contemplated any contact with Oswald.

See Warren Commission, vol. 5, p. 121.

Jefferson Morley: The line that the CIA fed the Warren Commission [was] that they really didn't know anything about this guy. We now know that that was complete nonsense. Oswald was a figure of intense interest for four years before the assassination. And a dozen senior CIA officers were very well acquainted with him. Everything he did, where he went, what his politics were, his family life. I mean, remember, they were reading his mother's mail. That's how closely they were watching him right up until Kennedy was killed. And then Kennedy was killed. Oswald's arrested. And they say, "We know nothing about this man."

Narrator: In fact, ARRB records show that Angleton and the CIA were receiving reports on Oswald up until one week before the assassination.

See Jefferson Morley's biography of Angleton, *The Ghost,* p. 140.

Jefferson Morley: So, you know, the whole investigation would have been totally different if the public and the investigators had known just how much the CIA knew about the alleged lone nut.

Narrator: One of the places Oswald leafleted in front of was Clay Shaw's International Trade Mart. Shaw, who was arrested by New Orleans DA Jim Garrison on charges that he was part of the conspiracy to kill President Kennedy, always denied he was associated with the CIA.

TV interviewer: You have never yourself had any CIA connection?

Clay Shaw: None whatsoever.

TV interviewer: Any association with the organization?

Clay Shaw: Not a one.

Narrator: The Review Board has shown these denials to be false. Shaw was both a highly valued contract agent and had a covert security clearance for a project code named QKENCHANT. New Orleans attorney Dean Andrews had worked with Oswald in May of '63 in an attempt to upgrade his military discharge from its "undesirable" status. After the assassination, a man calling himself Clay Bertrand phoned Andrews and asked him to consider going to Dallas to defend Oswald.

Under oath, Clay Shaw denied that he was Clay Bertrand, and Andrews claimed that because of the medication he was on, he had only imagined the phone call. But today, because of the work of the Assassination Records

Review Board, we now have evidence and twelve people who confirmed that Shaw used this name as an alias. Andrews later admitted that Shaw was Bertrand to author Harold Weisberg, but made him promise not to reveal this until after Andrew's death.

For the new CIA information on Shaw, see Davy, p. 195; Joan Mellen, *Our Man in Haiti*, pp. 54–55. For the declassified files about Shaw as Bertrand, see Davy, pp. 190–94 and DiEugenio, *Destiny Betrayed*, second edition pp. 387–88. This Shaw/Bertrand information was known to the FBI, and the DOJ, and according to researcher Ed Tatro's source, it was widely known throughout the French Quarter, which is where Garrison and Joan Mellen discovered their sources. The revelation by Andrews to Weisberg is in the unpublished manuscript, *Mailer's Tale*, chapter 5, p. 11. For another listing, see "The Unprecedented Debate over JFK Revisited" by James DiEugenio at Kennedysandking.com.

John Newman: In the FBI, a "stop" or "flash" was placed on Oswald's files, which meant that no one could ask for a document in those files, or no one could even add a document to those files without going through the FBI's espionage division. And that lasted for four years. It was essentially a blinking red light on Oswald's files at FBI. On 8 October, 1963, an FBI agent whose name was Marvin Gheesling took that status off of Oswald's files. What that action did was to lower Oswald's threat profile at the FBI just weeks before the Kennedy assassination, and what that would mean is there was no reason to put Oswald's name on the Security Index.

One thing about the Security Index, is when you have a presidential motorcade going through a particular route, anybody who's on that index has to be removed from where they are. They cannot be on the parade route. And, of course, that exposes the president to a dangerous situation that he shouldn't have been. That action at the FBI didn't happen in isolation. The same thing happened at CIA at exactly the same time.

For a full discussion of the situation at the Agency, see Newman's *Oswald and the CIA*, pp 398–405; for a concise review of both the FBI and CIA circumstances, see DiEugenio and Pease, *The Assassinations*, pp. 222–23.

Oliver Stone: Who was the CIA's liaison they chose to work with the House Select Committee in 1978?

Jefferson Morley: George Joannides. He was the case officer for the Cuban students who had a series of encounters with Oswald before the assassination. And then thirteen years later, when Congress reopens the investigation, the CIA calls Joannides out of retirement and make him the point person to deal with the congressional investigators who are looking into the CIA's possible role in the assassination.

The HSCA knew nothing about this, and I went to Bob Blakey, the head of the HSCA investigation, and I said, "Bob, did you ever know this guy Joannides?" And he said, "Yeah, you know, we dealt with him a lot. He was the liaison." And I said, "Did you know what he was doing in 1963?" And he said, "He wasn't doing anything in 1963. We had an agreement with the CIA that nobody who was operational at the time of the assassination would be involved in the investigation." And I said, "Bob, Joannides was running those Cubans who were in touch with Oswald. He was running the Cubans who were blaming Castro for the assassination. He was Dick Helms's handpicked man in Miami, controlling the group that had the most to do with Oswald before and after the assassination. And then he came along and he stonewalled you."

The reason why they brought Joannides in to do it was to hide the connection to Oswald. He was definitely shocked because he saw just how clever they had been. They had gone right to the heart of his investigation, and figured out how to paralyze it. I remember that he said, you know, "I'll never believe anything the CIA tells me again."

Morley published much of this information in the *Miami New Times* on April 12, 2001, but more of it is in his e-book, *Morley v. CIA*.

Narrator: Even the Assassination Records Review Board had trouble getting documents from government agencies.

Oliver Stone: What were some of your difficulties working with the CIA?

John Tunheim: One of the censors at the CIA was at a meeting with us, and there was a document that we put up on the screen and said we were prepared to release it. And I asked him, you know, tell us why we shouldn't release this record. And it was silence for about two minutes. And he finally said, "I know there is a reason, I just can't think of what it is."

Narrator: In late 1992, a month after the Records Act was passed, the Secret Service began its compliance plan. But by January of 1995, it had begun destroying important documents.

Thomas Samoluk: The destruction of records is actually referenced in the Assassination Records Review Board final report. Very, very disappointing. They were records that related to trips that President Kennedy had taken in the fall of 1963 prior to him going to Dallas.

John Tunheim: There were many threats made to President Kennedy's life during the year 1963. They're called threat sheets. And the Secret Service fought us on release of those records. They even enlisted Vice President Gore's wife to help them, because she had a very legitimate concern for mental health records. And the idea was that this might disclose the names of people who had mental health problems. In the end, when we required agencies to disclose, to swear under oath that they had located all assassination records, had turned everything over to us, the Secret Service refused to sign the document under oath. I think that was telling.

See The ARRB Final Report, p. 149; for a longer, more detailed treatment, see Horne, vol. 5, pp. 1451–58.

Narrator: Few people knew that there had been at least two prior plots to kill President Kennedy in 1963. One was in Chicago on November 2nd. The second was in Tampa on November 18th.

Oliver Stone: Kennedy ended up not going to Chicago. Tell us about that plot.

Paul Bleau: An informant on October 31st, an informant named Lee, gave a warning to the FBI stating that four Cubans were headed to Chicago to shoot Kennedy. The following day, a landlady reported to the Chicago police that she had rented a room to four people that had rifles with telescopic sights and a sketch of the motorcade. The FBI passed that on to the Secret Service. And the Secret Service botched the surveillance of these four individuals. Two of them escaped, but they actually picked up two of the snipers, and they detained them. They were stonewalled by the snipers. They didn't get any information out of them.

While this was going on, there was another threat coming in from another alternate patsy named Thomas Arthur Vallee, who was making open and loud threats that he would assassinate Kennedy. They only picked him up when Kennedy canceled his trip on November 2nd at 10:00 in the morning. What you found in Vallee and the whole Chicago plot, is so many similarities to what eventually happened in Dallas that it can't be considered coincidental.

Vallee, if we compare him to Oswald, is an ex-Marine. He had been posted like Oswald in the Far East on a station that was linked to the CIA because there were U-2 surveillance planes on it. It was easy to portray him as disgruntled, anti-Kennedy, a loner, armed. He had another intelligence link that he shared with Oswald. He trained Cuban exiles for combat, which was a CIA responsibility. And Oswald, we know, at least offered to do that. He most likely did train Cuban exiles, but we know he tried to. Oswald, as we know, was moved from New Orleans to Dallas in October. To be there just at the right time . . . for the motorcade. And he's placed in a tall building, where he gets a job. He's adjacent to the perfect kill zone.

Now, if we look at what happened to Vallee, he's moved like a pawn in August, from Long Island to Chicago to be there in time for the motorcade. And where does he get a job? In a tall building adjacent to the motorcade with a perfect view of a kill zone. It would have forced Kennedy's motorcade to do a sharp turn, slow down, and be in a point where you could have had perfect triangulation of fire.

The seminal review of the Chicago plot was Edwin Black's "The Plot to Kill JFK in Chicago: November 2, 1963" in the *Chicago Independent*, November 1975; see also Jim Douglass's *JFK and the Unspeakable*, pp. 202–207, 213–18 and Abraham Bolden's book *The Echo from Dealey Plaza*, e-book version, pp. 54–55.

Oliver Stone: And what about the trip to Florida?

Paul Bleau: On November 18th, Kennedy was scheduled to do a twenty-seven-mile long motorcade in Tampa. Secret Service was very nervous about the Floridian Hotel where the motorcade would have gone by. It would have forced a sharp turn. Nobody fired away at him. But in this case, the patsy would have been a Gilberto Policarpo Lopez. He was a Cuban exile. He attended Fair Play for Cuba Committee meetings.

Oliver Stone: And what do you think was the relevance of it?

Paul Bleau: Well, if he had been assassinated in Tampa, Lopez—he would have been the potential patsy. If they had to admit to a front shot, because Oswald was behind, there were rumors that he had assisted Oswald in the assassination in Dallas.

The Lopez case is discussed in Larry Hancock's *Someone Would Have Talked* (pp. 14–15); Hurt, pp. 420–21; and HSCA Final Report, pp. 118–21.

Oliver Stone: Had anyone, anyone tried to speak to the Warren Commission about these incidents?

Paul Bleau: Abraham Bolden was the first black Secret Service agent assigned to the White House detail, and he was handpicked by Kennedy. He was in Chicago when this plot went down. So he was there when the Secret Service was briefed about the four snipers, and he witnessed how much the security was lax for Chicago. And he also witnessed, after the assassination, the steps that were taken to keep the Chicago plot completely secret. No paper trail, compartmentalized. Agents ordered to keep silent about it. This information did not make its way to Secret Service agents that were protecting Kennedy for future motorcades, including Dallas.

Douglass details the cover-up and the setting up of Bolden, pp. 214–15.

Narrator: Secret Service Agent Elmer Moore was aware of Agent Bolden and the Chicago plot.

James Gochenaur: I met with Elmer three times face-to-face, several phone calls, very short, one very long one. I first asked him, "Did you ever interview Thomas Arthur Vallee?" And he says, "Oh, Washington wouldn't let me see the files on that." I said, "Oh, well, what about a man, a Secret Service agent by the name of Abraham Bolden?" His demeanor completely changed. He stood up from his chair, he pulled out his revolver and he put it on the table right in front of me. He leaned over the table and he says, "Jim, tell me right now, who are you working for?" I said, "I'm an independent researcher." He told me . . . in a very loud voice . . . and with a very stern look on his face, "We finally got him."

Paul Bleau: Abraham Bolden was one person who did try to say what he knew to the Warren Commission, but they blocked him. He was blocked from talking and eventually railroaded into some phony crime and put into jail for a number of years.

Bolden's attempt to contact the Warren Commission and the strange, trumped-up charges against him are dealt with at length in his book. (See pp. 61–84 of the e-book version.)

Oliver Stone: The National Archives is home to forensic evidence of Kennedy's assassination and government files regarding Lee Harvey Oswald. But the Review Board also declassified many documents regarding Kennedy's plans for withdrawal from Vietnam, and how he planned to shape his progressive, new American foreign policy. A policy that, if put in motion, would completely derail plans secretly already set up by the Pentagon and the CIA.

Clip from *JFK* (1991)

Jim Garrison: I never realized Kennedy was so dangerous to the establishment. Is that why?

Mr. X: That's the real question, isn't it? "Why?" The "how" and the "who" is just scenery for the public. Oswald, Ruby, Cuba, the Mafia, keeps 'em guessing like some kind of parlor game. Prevents 'em from asking the most important question: Why? Why was Kennedy killed? Who benefited? Who has the power to cover it up? Who?

Narrator: In his first year in office, Kennedy must shape his own policy as president, sometimes in conflict with what his predecessors have done, especially in foreign policy. And by the fall of 1963, Kennedy had made many enemies. He was working on an American withdrawal from Vietnam, an upcoming state visit to Indonesia in '64. An independent, unified democracy in the Congo. Through [Gamal Abdel] Nasser, a balanced policy in the Middle East, normalization of relations with Cuba, and a détente with Russia. Even going so far as to offer them a joint mission to the moon.

But back in April of 1961, the first stain on his administration asserted itself. Kennedy, who had campaigned as a strong anti-Communist, signed off on the Bay of Pigs invasion plan, because the approval of the plan contained two distinct limitations. America would supply arms and equipment, but there would be no Americans in the landing force. Second, after preliminary air strikes by Cuban exile pilots, there would only be further strikes after the invasion secured an airfield. Dulles believed that Kennedy would, like Eisenhower, support the operation with direct US military intervention if needed. All the while assuring him it would not be necessary.

John Kennedy: Well, first, I want to say that there will not be, under any conditions, an intervention in Cuba by the United States armed forces.

Narrator: The invasion was a disaster.

John Kennedy: Victory has one hundred fathers and defeat is an orphan. Further statements, detailed discussions, are not to conceal responsibility because I'm the responsible officer of the government—

Narrator: In public, Kennedy accepted the blame. In private, he and his brother suspected they had been lied to by the CIA.

David Talbot: Allen Dulles confessed that the mission was bound to fail as it was planned by the CIA, without military support. He confessed this while preparing an article for *Harper's Magazine* with the young editor, Willie Morris, that he couldn't have done this with his small group of exiles, his Cuban brigade. He needed the Marines and the Air Force to go in, and he thought Kennedy was going to be young and pliable, and that in the 11th hour, Kennedy would be forced to send in the full might of the US military.

Narrator: While drafting the article in 1965, Dulles told his editor, "That Kennedy—he thought he was a god."

David Talbot: Jack Kennedy did stand firm. He did not send in the military. He did not make it an even bigger global crisis than it already was. Kennedy is just furious. He knows he's been lied to, deceived by his senior military, and intelligence advisers. He announces that the agency is going to be downsized. And he vows famously, he tells friends he's going to shatter the CIA into a thousand pieces, and scatter it to the winds.

See DiEugenio, *Destiny Betrayed,* second edition, chapter 3, and Talbot, *Brothers,* pp. 43–51. The origin of this quote is likely a *New York Times* article of April 25, 1966 about the CIA, and it is attributed to Kennedy by a high official.

It wasn't just the Bay of Pigs that angered President Kennedy when it came to the CIA. In that same month, in April of 1961, he was also being lied to about a coup in France, a military coup that was aimed at overthrowing President Charles de Gaulle, one of our strongest allies.

Narrator: Allen Dulles, who had a long history of antagonism with de Gaulle, falsely reported to Kennedy that the vast majority of the French military was staunchly opposed to de Gaulle's support of Algerian self-determination. What he didn't tell him was that as far back as 1959, the CIA had discussed his overthrow. This coup attempt orchestrated by four French generals was quickly put down. And several news reports pointed to Allen Dulles's hand in supporting the episode.

David Talbot: JFK assures the French ambassador, "I have nothing to do with this. I stand in full support of President de Gaulle." But he says something very, very alarming. He tells the French ambassador, President Kennedy, that "I'm not in full control, though, of my entire government. I'm not in control of the CIA and I can't speak for what's happening there." That's a stunning admission for a US president to make.

David Talbot, *The Devil's Chessboard*, pp. 412–19. See also Andrew Tully, *CIA: The Inside Story* (pp. 48–49, 53). Tully used sources from *Le Monde* and *l'Express*. But see also *London Observer,* May 2, 1961. American sources are *The Nation*, 5/20/61, *Washington Post* 4/30/61, and *New York Times* 4/29/61. Tim Wiener criticized our film on the grounds the CIA was not involved in this subterfuge. He appears to be wrong.

Narrator: In 1960, the Congo had been granted its independence from Belgian colonial rule and carried out a democratic election. In the disorder of the transition, the Belgians, backed by England and France, sought to eliminate its charismatic prime minister, Patrice Lumumba. Eisenhower and CIA Director Allen Dulles favored the European nation in this colonial conflict.

Richard Mahoney: Eisenhower gave the go-ahead to have Lumumba assassinated. Kennedy never knew this. He gets elected the following November of 1960, and he heads in the opposite direction.

John Kennedy: To those new states whom we welcome to the ranks of the free, we pledge our word that one form of colonial control shall not have passed away merely to be replaced by a far more iron tyranny.

For the Lumumba assassination plots, see Mahoney, *JFK: Ordeal in Africa*, pp. 69–74; John Newman, *Countdown to Darkness*, pp. 223–26; Church Committee, *Alleged Assassination Plots Involving Foreign Leaders*, pp. 13–16.

Narrator: But events are already in motion. With the backing of British and US intelligence and arms, Col. Joseph Mobutu's forces captured President Lumumba at the beginning of December 1960.

Richard Mahoney: Dag Hammarskjöld, the UN secretary-general, calls JFK, who's the president-elect at this point, and asks him to intercede to get Lumumba released from prison. When Kennedy intervenes to save Lumumba, that's a signal directly to the CIA that they have to dispatch this guy immediately. And so forty-eight hours before Kennedy takes the oath of office, Lumumba is delivered into the hands of his enemies. He's taken out and shot in the head. Kennedy doesn't know this until months later.

Kennedy's policy on Congo was a clear break with Eisenhower's and was influenced by Hammarskjöld. The CIA felt that, if enacted, it would lead to the release of Lumumba (Mahoney pp. 64–69). JFK found out about Lumumba's death about one month after it happened.

David Talbot: Who finally tells him? The CIA? No, they still keep it a secret. He's informed by his UN ambassador, Adlai Stevenson. His face crumbles, he's holding his hand, he's grimacing in anguish, hearing about the assassination of Patrice Lumumba.

Narrator: Within a very short period of time after the assassination, Hammarskjöld died in a mysterious plane crash. The photographs show his body as the only one not burned or charred, and he had a playing card, reportedly the ace of spades, stuffed into his shirt collar above the knot of the tie. There are controversial documents that indicate Allen Dulles was involved in the sabotage of the plane.

> Susan Williams's book *Who Killed Hammarskjöld?* is the best long treatment of this subject. She discusses the controversial documents. *The Guardian* ran a series of articles on Hammarskjöld's death in January 2019. *Cold Case Hammarskjöld* is an interesting film treatment about Hammarskjöld's accident not being an accident.

Lisa Pease: John Foster Dulles and Allen Dulles, they felt, you know, what they had to say was good enough for the rest of the world, that they knew more than the president. There were things they didn't tell Eisenhower that they were doing under his administration.

> As the CIA Inspector General Report on the subject makes clear, although the plots to kill Castro began under Eisenhower, neither he nor Kennedy ever approved them (pp. 132–33).

David Talbot: And actually, Jack Kennedy does move to decapitate the top of the CIA. He lets it be known that Allen Dulles, as well as his two top advisers, Richard Bissell, who is also very involved with the Bay of Pigs, and General [Charles P.] Cabell, who was the right-hand man to Allen Dulles. So the top three people in the CIA, Kennedy forces 'em out before the end of the year.

TV interviewer: Have you ever committed any act of violence in your life?

Allen Dulles: No.

Narrator: The existence of communism so close to American shores kept Cuba on Kennedy's plate, and the Joint Chiefs of Staff presented a plan to Kennedy called Operation Northwoods, whereby the CIA would secretly perform terrorist acts in the United States and blame them on Castro to justify bombings and an invasion of Cuba.

John Newman: And you see all these plans being sent to McNamara and to Kennedy.

Douglas Horne: Fake an attack by Cubans against the Guantanamo Bay sentries. Sink a US ship in Guantanamo Bay and blame it on Cuba. The one that scares me the most was very sophisticated. Take an airliner and fly it as a drone over Cuba without any people in it, with a tape recording that would play, "We're under attack by Cuban aircraft! Oh my God, they're going to kill us!" Blow up the airplane. Blow up this huge drone and use that to start a war.

Narrator: The president declined the recommendation.

Douglas Horne: The Northwoods plan was our big find in the way of military records. They are universally recognized today for their importance. It's one of those releases that the Review Board members, the board members themselves were justifiably proud of that came out of the JFK Records Act.

> The Northwoods documents were written about at the time of their release by Jim Wolf for Reuters on November 18, 1997, by Mike Feinsilber for the *Seattle Times* on the same day, and Tim Weiner in the *New York Times* the next day.

Oliver Stone: In addition to the problems with the CIA, Kennedy's own military advisers started pressuring him to send troops to Vietnam. A country that Kennedy had visited ten years earlier as a congressman, and witnessed firsthand how the French were losing their war against the Viet Minh in the fight for independence. Once he became president, Kennedy wanted to avoid the same trap.

John Newman: The Vietnam decision is finally arrived at, which is NSAM 111, where Kennedy says no combat troops but will increase the advisers. And that was his decision in the Kennedy presidency never to cross that line.

> For Kennedy's visit to Saigon in 1951, see Mahoney, p. 108; for Kennedy's November 1961 decision, see chapter 3 of *Virtual JFK* by

James Blight, and John Newman, *JFK and Vietnam*, 2017 edition, pp. 138–41.

Narrator: Near the end of his first year in office, Kennedy received a report from Walt Rostow and General Maxwell Taylor, his foreign policy and military advisers, that called for increased training of South Vietnamese troops, increased bombings of the North, and the use of US combat troops. The influence on Kennedy's reluctance to committing ground troops was his ambassador to India, John Kenneth Galbraith.

James Galbraith: My father went to see Walt Rostow. He went in to talk to him. Rostow gestured on his desk to the pile of papers. The Rostow-Taylor report was plainly visible. My father asked to see it. Walt said that his security classification wasn't sufficiently high. My father did not think that Walt Rostow's security classification was higher than his. At a given moment, the phone rang. Walt turned to answer the phone and Dad picked up the report and walked out of the office and read it.

Narrator: Kennedy sent Galbraith to Saigon to write a report that would differ in its recommendations from what Taylor and Rostow had given to him.

James Galbraith: Kennedy knew what he wanted and he knew what my father would deliver, which he did, which is a very detailed and skeptical report about the efficiency of the South Vietnamese government, about the capacity of any military force to prevail in the security situation that existed in South Vietnam at that time.

Narrator: Kennedy told Galbraith to deliver his report to Defense Secretary McNamara, and he, in turn, gave instructions to begin the withdrawal to General [Paul D.] Harkins, the commanding General of all forces in Vietnam. The Pentagon dragged its feet on formulating plans, and McNamara called for a meeting in May of 1963. One of the most important finds of the review board are the notes from this meeting.

See "Galbraith and Vietnam," *The Nation*, February 24, 2005.

Douglas Horne: McNamara said, "It's not fast enough. I want you to accelerate it." He says, "I want to pull out one thousand men in December by the end of the year. And I want you to pull out complete units, not just individuals." He wanted units to come out.

See Douglass, p. 126; Blight, pp. 288–90. The records of the 5/6/63 meeting in Honolulu are also in Foreign Relations of the United States, vol. 3.

Narrator: After the withdrawal plan was approved, Kennedy sent Secretary of Defense McNamara and General Taylor to Saigon in September of '63. He planned on using their report as the basis to formally order the withdrawal to begin. Kennedy controlled the report, since it was actually being written under the supervision of Bobby Kennedy.

John Newman: Three days later, that leaks out into the newspapers. Then his opponents find out. And McGeorge Bundy says to Kennedy, "Hey, look, you know, if they're talking about it in the newspapers, we might as well put it on paper." And they put it and it was NSAM 263. And that's how it was actually written and why.

Well, here's one of the things McNamara said in the secret debrief. He said, "We had agreed, the president and I, that we had trained them, we had given them everything we could. And if they couldn't win, too bad. We had to get out even if they were going to be defeated." So McNamara and Kennedy had decided that they were willing to pull out of Vietnam in a losing scenario. That's very important. But later in that month, McGeorge Bundy, who's the national security advisor, puts together a memo based upon the truth about the war, which is going terribly. And he does it in a way to try and make sure that Kennedy would be able to go along with it.

For the information about Bobby Kennedy, see Newman's *JFK and Vietnam*, p. 408; about making NSAM 263 public, Newman p. 435; about McNamara, see *Vietnam: The Early Decisions* edited by Lloyd C. Gardner and Ted Gittinger, pp. 164–67.

Narrator: This is reflected in the National Security Action Memorandum: NSAM 273.

John Newman: The way Bundy writes the first draft of 273 is to say, "Look, we need to intensify the war effort against the Communists. But the way we're going to do it is to increase South Vietnamese forces." There's not a word about American forces or Americanizing the war.

While Kennedy's body is still in the casket in the rotunda over in the Capitol building, is when Johnson changes NSAM 273 to a new version. And when it comes to the key paragraph, paragraph seven, which just talks about how we're going to intensify the war instead of changing a few words, there's two big hash marks through that paragraph, and it's completely re-written. And I said, I asked Bundy in an interview, I said, "Who told you to do that?" He said, "Johnson did."

> These changes are dramatically illustrated with documents and described in detail in chapter 23 of the 2017 edition of *JFK and Vietnam*.

Narrator: These changes allowed the US to unilaterally engage in combat in Vietnam rather than simply supporting and advising South Vietnamese troops.

John Newman: And within days, we're talking about sending out the DESO-TO missions. These naval excursions along the coastline of North Vietnam that ends up with the *Maddox* and the so-called Tonkin Gulf attacks. And then the resolution in Congress opening the door to intervention in Vietnam.

> Edwin Moise dates the start of these joint OPLAN34A CIA/Pentagon operations from December 15, 1963 (*Tonkin Gulf and the Escalation of the Vietnam War*, pp. 5–7). See also David Kaiser, *American Tragedy* (pp. 293–94).

Narrator: In the Review Board's declassifications, there's evidence that Johnson was fully aware of Kennedy's Vietnam withdrawal plans, disagreed with them, and worked on Robert McNamara to make him renounce them.

LBJ on phone to McNamara: "I always thought it was foolish for you to make any statements about withdrawing. I thought it was bad psychologically. But you and the president thought otherwise, and I just sat silent."

> The book *Virtual JFK* contains a documentary section which includes this February 20, 1964 transcript, and others, which show how LBJ turned McNamara around on this issue (pp. 305–10). See also Gordon Goldstein, *Lessons in Disaster* (pp. 105–6).

Robert McNamara: In retaliation for this unprovoked attack on the high seas, our forces have struck the bases used by the North Vietnamese patrol craft.

Narrator: And as declassified memos have revealed, by autumn of 1964, during his campaign against Barry Goldwater, Johnson had already decided that he was going to escalate the Vietnam War. In fact, the directive that would become the Tonkin Gulf Resolution, had been written before the Tonkin Gulf Incident itself. Three months before the election, Johnson had already planned for an extensive air war. It was to begin after his inauguration.

> The Tonkin Gulf Resolution was drafted in May and June of 1964 (Moise, p. 27). As per Johnson's 1964 decision for direct American intervention, see Moise, pp. 26–27, Goldstein, pp. 108–116, and Fredrik Logevall, *Choosing War*, p. 129.

LBJ: We intend to convince the Communists that we cannot be defeated by force of arms. Or by superior power.

Lisa Pease: When news came of Kennedy's death all over the planet, people were mourning and crying and going to embassies. In Latin America, people just lit candles because they didn't even have electrical power, but they wanted to honor his killing. In the Yucatán Peninsula, peasants cleared an area, and planted a peace garden.

Philip Muehlenbeck: Nasser learned of Kennedy's death in the middle of the night. He got up, dressed, went down to his office, and then realized, "Well, there's nothing I can do about this." According to his son, Nasser went into a great state of depression after Kennedy's death. Relations with Egypt gradually deteriorated, and they increasingly shifted their allegiance towards the Soviet Union as well.

Robert Rakove: A mass was held in the leading Catholic Church in Cairo, which has a capacity of six hundred. They somehow fit four thousand people into that church. Algeria, which had special feeling for Kennedy, declared a state of mourning for a week. Flags were flown at half-mast. The US ambassador to Egypt said that he thought the Egyptians had seen in Kennedy the best of what they saw in Americans. That Kennedy had represented a kind of ideal of America to ordinary Egyptians.

One of the best descriptions of this worldwide outpouring of grief is at the end of Thurston Clarke's book *JFK's Last Hundred Days.* But also see the article, "The Shot Felt 'Round the World," at the Association for Diplomatic Studies & Training website.

Narrator: Castro got the news of Kennedy's death while discussing détente with the French journalist Jean Daniel. He then exclaimed, "This is bad news. Everything is now going to change." When Khrushchev paid his respects to President Kennedy at the American embassy, he was reportedly holding back tears. Robert Kennedy knew that after his brother's death, relations with the Soviet Union hung in the balance.

The Daniel story was first printed by him with the title "When Castro Heard the News" in *The New Republic* of December 7, 1963. For Khrushchev's reaction to JFK's death and his disbelief in the Warren Report, see William Taubman's *Khrushchev: The Man and his Era,* p. 604.

Robert F. Kennedy Jr.: My father, he wanted to convey a message to Premier Khrushchev saying that our family knew that the Soviets were not involved in the assassination. That it was a right-wing plot from our own country.

David Talbot: In other words, the CIA, or forces aligned with the CIA.

Robert F. Kennedy Jr.: The day that his brother died, my father's first phone call was to the CIA desk officer at Langley and he asked them, "Did your people conduct this horror?"

David Talbot: We know from how Bobby operated that terrible day, November 22nd, 1963, at his home in McLean, Virginia, that he immediately suspected there was not a lone gunman. Why do we know this? Because he was being told by his closest aides, people like Kenny O'Donnell and Dave Powers, who were in the limousine immediately behind President Kennedy's limousine. They were both World War II veterans. They knew what gunfire sounded like. They reported it to him that gunfire had not just come from the rear, it had come from different sides. There was gunfire from the front as well. It was a crossfire.

> The letter from RFK to the Kremlin is in *One Hell of a Gamble* by Tim Naftali and Aleksandr Fursenko (pp. 344–46). Perhaps the best chronicle of Bobby Kennedy's reactions to his brother's death is in David Talbot's *Brothers* (pp. 2–12).

Robert F. Kennedy Jr.: I was in the East Room, with my dad and with Jackie and a couple of my siblings, and Lyndon Johnson came in, and told the adults in the room that Lee Harvey Oswald had been killed, and that a man had shot him. And I said to my dad and mom at that time, "Why did he shoot him? Did he love our family?" And the way that they acted was that this only compounded the tragedy.

Narrator: Many people at home felt that after Kennedy's death, a period of depression and cynicism overtook the country, and that America was somehow changed forever. Our overwhelming disbelief in the Warren

Commission's findings contributed to increased skepticism of all our foundational beliefs about government.

David Talbot: But I think Allen Dulles's appointment to the Warren Commission is one of the greatest frauds of American history.

> Larry Sabato's *The Kennedy Half Century* did a poll on the issue of the impact of Kennedy's death on America. An amazing 91 percent of the respondents said JFK's murder changed the nation "a great deal" Sabato writes , "In a real sense, the Kennedy assassination presaged and psychologically prepared America for numerous devastating events to follow during the decade."(p. 416).

Allen Dulles: I don't think that even if you had ten more commissions, you'd never get away from the idea that maybe there was a plot. We just didn't find any traces of it.

David Talbot: What really happened with Allen Dulles was the CIA lobbied to have him put on the Commission, because they needed to have one of their own on the Commission to make sure that certain doors remained closed. I think there's a direct thread between the events of 1963 and the kind of horror show that America is having to endure right now. And I think once you kill a president in broad daylight on the streets of an American city, and everyone knows that powerful forces did it, that sends a signal not only to the American people, but to the American media, to American future leaders. And if America really wants a democratic society, then we should get to the bottom of this traumatic crime that continues to reverberate throughout American history.

> For the lobbying to get Dulles on the Commission, see Talbot, *The Devil's Chessboard,* p. 573–74.

Robert F. Kennedy Jr.: They poll historians, they poll the American people, and they said, "Who were the most popular presidents?" Well, one metric that you can use to objectively—at least judge the foreign policy, is how many boulevards are named after that president in foreign countries? How many hospitals, how many colleges, how many schools? How many statues are standing of that president in capitals all over the world? And in that sense, President Kennedy beats every other president, hands down.

Narrator: Although many of Kennedy's progressive and unprecedented goals and changes in policy were undone after his assassination, a few powerful ones remain.

Martin Luther King Jr.: I think Mr. Kennedy has done some significant things in civil rights, and I would include the attorney general. I think both of these men are men of genuine goodwill. And I think there is a necessity now to see the urgency of the moment.

Nicholas Katzenbach to Gov. George Wallace: I'm asking from you an unequivocal assurance that you will not bar entry to these students, and that you will step aside peacefully, do your Constitutional duty.

Narrator: In showdowns using federal troops, the Kennedy administration won admission of black students to the last public colleges in the south. George Wallace made it clear that this fight was not over.

> This was at the University of Mississippi and Alabama in 1962 and '63. One of the best treatments of Kennedy's civil rights program is in Irving Bernstein's *Promises Kept*, pp. 44–117.

George Wallace: And the South this year, next year will decide who the next president is, whoever the South votes for will be the president. And you're going to see that the South is going to be against some folks.

Narrator: That night, Kennedy addressed the nation in what many consider the finest presidential speech on civil rights since Abraham Lincoln.

John Kennedy: And that the rights of every man are diminished when the rights of one man are threatened. If an American, because his skin is dark, cannot enjoy the full and free life which all of us want, then who among us would be content to have the color of his skin changed? One hundred years of delay have passed since President Lincoln freed the slaves, yet their heirs, their grandsons are not fully free. And this nation, for all its hopes and all its boasts, will not be fully free until all its citizens are free. We face, therefore, a moral crisis as a country and a people, and this is a matter which concerns this country and what it stands for. And in meeting it, I ask the support of all of our citizens. Thank you very much.

JFK: Destiny Betrayed

Annotated Transcript of Four-Hour Film

Chapter 1

Reporter: Shortly before the dawn of Saturday morning, John Fitzgerald Kennedy comes home to the White House. He had been the nation's thirty-fifth president for a period of two years and ten months.

Oliver Stone: I'm Oliver Stone and this is Dealey Plaza, the place where John Kennedy was assassinated on November 22, 1963. Back in 1991, I made a film called *JFK*. That movie tried to explore the mysteries that enshrouded this place and that day. We also tried to explore the reasons why President Kennedy was killed. At the end of our film, we alerted the public that almost thirty years after Kennedy's assassination, tens of thousands of documents were still being kept secret about his murder and his policies. *JFK* created a yearlong sensation in the media. Some quarters praised the film. Others attacked it.

> This controversy is captured in *JFK: The Book of the Film,* published in 1992 by Applause Books.

Oliver Stone: But at the end of that unprecedented controversy, a new agency of government was formed. It was called the Assassination

Records Review Board. The board went to work declassifying this immense amount of material. Yet the public has not been made aware of what, in fact, constitutes a new factual record of who Kennedy was and the real circumstances of his murder. In this series, you will be informed for the first time what was in many of the most important of these files. We have to do this. We have to keep doing this, because democracy, and our freedom from fear, dies when there is no longer trust between the people and their government.

Why the Board was created and how it worked is dealt with in its Final Report, pp. 1–10. A key aspect of the JFK Act was that, unlike the Freedom of Information Act, the plaintiff did not have to explain to a judge why a certain document he had not seen should be declassified. The FBI had to explain to a citizens' board, who had already seen the document, why it could not be made public.

Narrator: After his brother's murder, without hesitation, Attorney General Robert Kennedy began investigating a domestic conspiracy.

Robert F. Kennedy Jr: My father's first phone call was to the CIA desk officer at Langley and he asked him: "Did your people conduct this horror?"

David Talbot: We know from how Bobby operated that terrible day, November 22nd, 1963, at his home in McLean, Virginia, that he immediately suspected there was not a lone gunman. Why do we know this? Because he was being told by his closest aides, people like Kenny O'Donnell and Dave Powers, who were in the limousine immediately behind President Kennedy's limousine. They were both World War II veterans. They knew what gunfire sounded like. They reported it to him that gunfire had not just come from the rear, it had come from different sides. There was gunfire from the front as well. It was a crossfire.

Bobby Kennedy's immediate questioning about JFK's murder is captured in Talbot's book *Brothers.* For the conversation with O'Donnell, see p. 3, for Bobby's talk with CIA Director McCone, see pp. 6–7.

Robert F. Kennedy Jr.: I was in the East Room with my dad and with Jackie and a couple of my siblings, and Lyndon Johnson came in and told the adults in the room that Lee Harvey Oswald had been killed and that a man had shot him. And I said to my dad and mom at that time, "Why did he shoot him? Did he, did he love our family?" And nobody really answered the question, so I didn't know whether we were supposed to be happy that he got shot. And the way that they acted was that this only compounded the tragedy, that it was not a good thing. But I didn't really understand it. I did immediately have that question: "Why would this man shoot in public, in a place where he knew he was going to get caught, why would be make that sacrifice of his own life to kill Lee Harvey Oswald? Did he love our family?" And within a couple of years, right, it was very clear to everybody—he did not love our family. He was a mobster.

David Talbot: When Bobby, you looked at the phone logs of who Jack Ruby was talking to on the phone before he went into the Dallas basement of the police station, he said it read like the witness list of the Senate Rackets Committee. In other words, all mob guys.

> For the Mob angle being inquired into by Bobby, see Talbot, *Brothers*, p. 21.

Robert F. Kennedy Jr.: My father at that time was not aware of the level of involvement between the CIA and the Mafia—that they essentially were a seamless organization.

> The cooperation between the Mob and American intelligence goes back to Operation Underworld, where the OSS made an alliance with Lucky Luciano to maintain security and break strikes on New York docks while also aiding in the invasion of Italy in 1943. Luciano also helped the newly formed CIA in 1947 in preventing a communist strike on the docks of Marseilles, France. The latter allowed Luciano to begin a lucrative drug trade. (John Ranelagh, *The Agency,* p. 203; Alfred McCoy, *The Politics of Heroin,* rev. ed., chapters 1 and 2.)

Narrator: In 1961, the FBI had discovered secret CIA-Mafia plots to assassinate Castro. And when Attorney General Robert Kennedy was told about them, he requested a full briefing from the CIA. They admitted to the plots, but claimed that they had stopped, when in fact they were still ongoing, run by CIA officer William Harvey and Chicago mobster Johnny Roselli.

This is described in the CIA Inspector General Report on the CIA/Mafia plots to kill Castro, declassified by the ARRB (p. 133).

David Talbot: And who was the third party that he suspected in the assassination of his brother? The CIA, the Mafia—anti-Castro exiles. In fact, he calls up somebody who's involved with the Cuban exile community and says bluntly, one of your guys did it. That's Harry Ruiz Williams. He doesn't accuse him of doing it, but he says one of your guys did it.

This phone call is written about by Talbot, in *Brothers* (p. 10).

Oliver Stone: Did Robert Kennedy ever stop inquiring into his brother's assassination?

Robert F. Kennedy Jr.: The day that his brother died he lost virtually all the investigative capacity at the Justice Department. He had thirty thousand employees at the Justice Department, half of them were FBI employees who ostensibly worked for him. Traditionally, however, and in reality, they worked for J. Edgar Hoover. He couldn't investigate it. And so his posture, first of all, he was shattered, so the first year, he wanted, nothing could bring Jack back. He didn't want to hear about it. He told Nick Katzenbach, "I'm not going to testify before the Warren Commission, I'm not going to have anything to do with it," and he tried as little as possible to comment on it. When he did comment on it privately, he would say they did a shoddy job. But publicly he would never say anything. But he knew what it was. It was a commission. And commissions in this country have a tradition of essentially anointing orthodoxies.

The closest Bobby Kennedy came to appearing before the commission was sitting next to Jackie Kennedy when she testified before Earl Warren and J. Lee Rankin at her home in Georgetown on June 5, 1964 (Warren Commission, vol. 5, pp. 178–81). It was Katzenbach who attended the first meeting of the commission on December 5, 1963. Hoover took out RFK's private line to his office after JFK was killed. RFK decided he would resign in 1964 after he helped pass the civil rights bill his brother had submitted (Arthur Schlesinger, *Robert Kennedy and His Times*, p. 657–58).

David Talbot: He knew whatever investigation was under the control of the White House, Lyndon Johnson's White House and the FBI, was going to be a bogus investigation. I have talked to many of Bobby Kennedy's close aides—Dick Goodwin, Frank Mankiewicz, Adam Walinsky—all of them told me that Bobby Kennedy did not believe the Warren Commission, believed that it was a fairy tale, a convenient cover-up. And Bobby Kennedy was determined to get the truth and to bring up a new official inquiry to look into his brother's murder as soon as he was back in the White House.

Talbot's *Brothers* has these examples throughout: for Goodwin (p. 305); for Walinsky (p. 306); for Mankiewicz (p. 358).

Narrator: The Warren Commission was not Lyndon Johnson's idea. Johnson had been in favor of a Texas state investigation into Kennedy's murder. The concept of an independent panel was strongly suggested to the White House, first by Eugene Rostow, dean of the Yale Law School, and brother of Walter Rostow. On Sunday, November 24th, Rostow told Johnson's assistant, Bill Moyers, they had to appoint a blue-ribbon panel because America and world opinion had been so shaken by the murder of Oswald and the performance of the Dallas police that the public was not believing anything. The *Washington Post* was also in favor of the idea. Publisher Kay Graham and editor Al Friendly were going to run an editorial endorsing the concept on November 25th, the day of JFK's funeral. And powerful columnist Joseph Alsop used all his techniques of persuasion.

Archive phone call: "And have Moyers call Friendly or Kay, I'm sure that you will have the strongest possible support. It will be thought that everything has been done that needs doing."

These phone calls to the White House were declassified by the JFK Act in 1993. Professor Donald Gibson wrote an essay based on their contents. See *Mid America: An Historical Review*, "Creation of the Warren Commission," Fall 1997.

Narrator: Johnson began moving forward, appointing an extraordinary federal panel.

Oliver Stone: In regard to the Warren Commission, who do you think was the most puzzling appointment to this commission?

David Talbot: Allen Dulles's appointment to the Warren Commission, I think is one of the great frauds of American history.

Allen Dulles interview clip: "Have you ever committed any act of violence in your life?" "No."

David Talbot: Lyndon Johnson went around telling people that Bobby Kennedy, of all people, lobbied to have Dulles put on the commission.

Allen Dulles interview clip: I don't think that even if you had ten more commissions, you'd never get away from the idea that maybe there was a plot. We just didn't find any traces of it.

For a refutation that it was Bobby's idea to nominate Dulles, see the article "Hardway on Dulles, RFK and the Creation of the Warren Commission" at the website *JFK Facts*, October 26, 2015. For how the Dulles camp lobbied for him to be on the Commission, see David Talbot, *The Devil's Chessboard* (pp. 573–74).

David Talbot: What really happened with Allen Dulles was the CIA lobbied to have him put on the Commission because they needed to have one of their own on the Commission to make sure that certain doors remain closed. He also names Gerry Ford, the young congressman from Michigan, to the commission. Ford is very close to J. Edgar Hoover and the FBI.

Ford's informing to the FBI on the Commission was reviewed by the AP and carried, for example, in the *Denver Post* of August 9, 2008. The story was based on documents from his FBI file. For background on his prior association with the Bureau, see Gerald McKnight, *Breach of Trust*, pp. 42- 47.

Narrator: Not everyone was as eager to serve on the commission as Dulles was. Johnson conjured up images of atomic annihilation to intimidate Earl Warren into chairing the commission. Johnson did the same with Senator Richard Russell.

LBJ phone call: We got to take this out of the arena where they're testifying it's Khrushchev and Castro did this and did that and kicking us into a war that can kill forty million Americans in an hour.

This call was made by LBJ on November 29, 1963. Johnson informs Russell that he also told Earl Warren that there might be a war with the Russians unless he took the position. Johnson said this reduced Warren to tears. This tape is available at "Walkthrough: Formation of the Warren Commission" at the Mary Ferrell Foundation website.

Narrator: Even before Oswald was killed, Cliff Carter of Johnson's White House had called the Dallas police and told them not to indict Oswald as part of a communist conspiracy. Why? For fear of a confrontation with the USSR.

See Walter Pincus and George Lardner's November 14, 1993, *Washington Post* article, "Warren Commission Born Out of Fear."

Narrator: Johnson's nuclear warning was based upon CIA reports that Oswald had been to Mexico seven weeks before the assassination and visited the Cuban and Soviet consulates. FBI director J. Edgar Hoover understood this information was not accurate. Hoover also added that the case, as it stood, was not strong enough to obtain a conviction of Oswald. The FBI would do approximately 80 percent of the investigation for the Warren Commission, and Hoover would keep his doubts about the Oswald case concealed. With that and much more kept secret, stories were leaked to the press that the alleged assassin, Lee Harvey Oswald, would be found guilty by the Commission.

> The Warren Report relates Oswald's journey to Mexico City based on a combination of CIA and FBI reports (pp. 730–36). The Commission says he was there from September 26 to October 3rd, but J. Edgar Hoover told President Johnson that neither the picture nor the tape the CIA sent to the FBI corresponded with Oswald. And the case against Oswald was not very strong (phone conversation of November 23, 1963). The statistical amount of work by the FBI and Secret Service is derived from the Warren Report (page xii). For examples of leaked stories, see *Time*, December 13, 1963, p. 26; *Newsweek*, December 16, 1963, p. 26; and *New York Times*, December 10, 1963. That last story was titled "Oswald Assassin Beyond Doubt FBI Concludes."

Narrator: The commission worked in almost complete secrecy. There were only a handful of investigatory articles published about the JFK case while they were in session. Yet, even though almost no one knew what the commission was doing, on the day the 888-page Warren Report was released, the press accepted it without reservations. In fact, the night it was issued to the public, both NBC and CBS News aired specials propagating its conclusions, but not asking questions about how those conclusions were arrived at.

TV Clip: In three hundred thousand words of lean and orderly language, the Warren Commission makes these major findings. Lee Harvey Oswald assassinated President Kennedy. Lee Harvey Oswald himself was killed by Jack Ruby in full view of millions of Americans.

Some examples of the early questioning of Oswald as the assassin would be "Oswald Innocent?—A Lawyer's Brief" by Mark Lane on December 19, 1963, in *National Guardian*; "Seeds of Doubt" by Staughton Lynd and Jack Miniss in *The New Republic* of December 12, 1963; "Oswald and the FBI" by Harold Feldman in *The Nation* of January 27, 1964; and "The Oswald Affair" by Leo Sauvage in *Commentary* of March 1964. The Warren Report was issued to the public on September 27, 1964.

Narrator: It was later revealed that NBC approached the FBI and told them they would reveal nothing in their reporting on the Kennedy case that would contradict their findings. It was also discovered that some members of the press cooperated in supporting the Commission's findings in return for access to witnesses. In 1978, producer Bernie Birnbaum of CBS admitted that sources on the commission leaked its contents, and his program was in production for months in advance.

See "JFK Unit Reportedly Didn't Seek CBS Film" by Larry Kramer, *Washington Post,* September 17, 1978. For more on the Birnbaum admission, see article by Florence Graves in *Washington Journalism Review*, Sept.–Oct., 1978.

Gary Aguilar: The *New York Times* got its version out of the Warren Report within forty-eight hours and in an introductory essay, you have Anthony Lewis saying—right there with the release of the Warren Report, he said the Warren Commission released all the documents and all the evidence it had acquired, except for the names of a few sensitive people and withheld nothing else, all the documents released. The irony of this is the Commission, Warren Commission documents were not released for two or three months later. They finally came out in November. So here you have the *New York Times* assuring the public that all the documents have been released and that no question remains unresolved, in the absence of having seen any of the twenty-six volumes of supplementary evidence.

> The *New York Times* featured almost the entire report as a supplement to the September 28, 1964, edition and cooperated on three releases of the Warren Report: A Book of the Month Club hardcover, a Bantam Books softcover, and later a highlights version also published by Bantam titled *The Witnesses*. (See Jerry Policoff's essay in *The Realist*, October 1972).

Barry Ernest: If you read the Warren Report, you get a very convincing picture that Oswald did it and he did it alone. And that report, as you know, was sent worldwide with a lot of publicity. What wasn't sent worldwide with a lot of publicity was the twenty-six volumes of evidence. And that is where you begin to see that the evidence they use in the Warren Report does not always match up with the evidence that was given to them during the commission's investigation.

Narrator: The commission published those volumes at Allen Dulles's suggestion.

> See "The Warren Commission in Its Own Words" by Tad Szulc, *The New Republic*, September 27, 1975, p. 27.

Allen Dulles film clip: Here's the Commission Report. I keep it by my right hand here. And here are the various volumes, twenty-six of them.

Narrator: In a private conference, Dulles said, "No one reads anymore. They'll be a few professors who will read the record, but the public will read very little." But still, the commission classified tens of thousands of pages of documents. These included FBI reports, Secret Service reports, and hundreds of their own internal memoranda.

> See the Review Board's *Final Report*, p. 2. In 1992, with the passage of the JFK Act, there were still three thousand pages—not documents—of Commission pages withheld.

Narrator: In 1967, the Warren Report was under attack from several books and magazine articles. Walter Cronkite interviewed Warren Commissioner John McCloy during a four-night special cohosted by Dan Rather.

Walter Cronkite clip: "Are you satisfied that as much effort was put into challenging that case as into establishing it? In other words, did the accused man get a fair trial?" "I'll answer that in just a moment. If I may just say one thing, I'd like to say in the first place I had some questions as to the propriety of my appearing here as a former member of the commission to comment on the evidence of the commission. There seems to be some question and I think there is some question about the advisability of doing that."

Narrator: McCloy never answered Cronkite's question. But even worse, CBS employee Roger Feinman later discovered internal documents showing the network had violated its own journalistic code of ethics. McCloy had consulted extensively on the series through his daughter Ellen, an administrative assistant to CBS President Richard Salant. In 1992, reporter Jerry Policoff confronted Salant and Ellen McCloy with the documents revealing John McCloy's instructions for the content of the show. Only then did CBS admit to their concealment. CBS, NBC, and the *New York Times* continued to support the commission's findings for decades afterwards and never publicly reviewed the twenty-six volumes of supplemental evidence.

The secret guidance by McCloy of the 1967 CBS four-night special was first revealed by Jerry Policoff and Robert Hennelly in the *Village Voice* of March 31, 1992. The compromising of that series was further delineated by James DiEugenio in an article titled "How CBS News Aided the JFK Cover-Up" in *Consortium News* of April 22, 2016. In both instances, the information and documents were supplied by the late Roger Feinman, a former CBS employee. Technically, CBS never admitted this ethical breach, but Salant did to Policoff.

Gary Aguilar: By the time the Assassination Records Review Board came along in the mid-1990s, there were still three thousand pages of Warren Commission documents withheld.

Narrator: In 1959, Fidel Castro had come to power by overthrowing the corrupt and brutal despot Fulgencio Batista. During Batista's twenty-five-year hold on power, he was closely allied with American big business and organized crime, allowing him to accumulate a personal fortune reportedly worth $300 million. When he fled the country, it took three cargo planes to transport his holdings to Portugal.

The US-Cuba relationship is summarized in chapter 2 of Morris Morley's *Imperial State and Revolution*. For his escape to Portugal, see the article "Fulgencio Batista" at the PBS website *American Experience*.

Narrator: In June of 1959, Castro's systematic land reform, which limited the size of property holdings, went into effect in Cuba. This law caused many American businessmen to petition the White House for action to be taken. And so, in 1960 under Eisenhower, the CIA created the Cuban Project in their effort to oust Castro. Kennedy, who had campaigned as a strong anti-communist, signed off on the Bay of Pigs invasion plan in April of 1961. Kennedy's approval of the plan contained two distinct limitations: America would supply arms and equipment, but there would be no Americans in the landing force.

Second, after preliminary airstrikes by Cuban exile pilots, there would only be further strikes after the invasion secured an airfield. Dulles believed that Kennedy would, like Eisenhower, support the operation with direct US military intervention if needed, all the while assuring him it would not be necessary.

For the land reform law, American business reaction to it and the creation of Eisenhower's Cuba Project in March 1960, see Morley (p. 81–85). For Kennedy's restrictions on Americans in the Bay of Pigs invasion, see James Douglass, *JFK and the Unspeakable* (p. 13); for the secured airfield restriction see Peter Kornbluh, *Bay of Pigs Declassified* (pp. 126- 27). For Dulles's optimism about the plan see Arthur Schlesinger, *A Thousand Days* (p. 249) and Trumbull Higgins's *The Perfect Failure* (pp. 104–05).

John F. Kennedy speech: Well, first, I want to say that there will not be under any conditions, an intervention in Cuba by United States armed forces.

Narrator: The invasion was a disaster and became the first stain on his administration.

John F. Kennedy speech: Victory has one hundred fathers and defeat is an orphan. Further statements, detailed discussions are not to conceal responsibility because I'm the responsible officer of the government.

Narrator: In public, Kennedy accepted the blame. In private, he and his brother suspected they had been lied to by the CIA.

David Talbot: Allen Dulles confessed that the mission was bound to fail as it was planned by the CIA without US military support. He confessed this while preparing an article for *Harper's Magazine* with a young editor, Willie Morris, that he couldn't have done this with his small group of exiles, his Cuban brigade. He needed the Marines and the Air Force to go in. And he thought Kennedy was going to be young and pliable and that at the eleventh hour, Kennedy will be forced to send in the full might of the US military.

Narrator: While drafting the article in 1965, Dulles told his editor, "That Kennedy, he thought he was a god!"

> Dulles's notes containing his hidden agenda were discovered by scholar Lucien Vandenbroucke in the Dulles archives at Princeton. He wrote about them in the Fall 1984 issue of the academic journal *Diplomatic History* (pp. 365–75). The CIA's knowledge that the invasion would fail without Pentagon support is in an internal memo that Talbot writes about in his book *Brothers* (pp. 47–48). The quote by Dulles about Kennedy is in Willie Morris's book *New York Days* (p. 36).

David Talbot: Jack Kennedy did stand firm. He did not send in the military. He did not make it an even bigger global crisis than it already was. Kennedy, after the Bay of Pigs debacle, is just furious. He knows he's been lied to, deceived by his senior military and intelligence advisers. He announces that the agency is going to be downsized. And he vows famously, he tells friends he's going to shatter the CIA into a thousand pieces and scatter it to the winds. And actually, he does move to decapitate the top of the CIA. He lets it be known that Allen Dulles, as well as his two top advisers, Richard Bissell, who is also very involved with the Bay of Pigs and General Cabell, who was the right-hand man to Allen Dulles. So the top three people in the CIA immediately know their days are numbered. And he forces them out before the end of the year.

For the reduction in force, see Talbot, *The Devil's Chessboard* (p. 411). For the Kennedy quote and the terminations see Douglass, *JFK and the Unspeakable* (pp. 15–16).

David Talbot: It wasn't just the Bay of Pigs that angered President Kennedy when it came to the CIA. In that same month in April of 1961 he was also being lied to about a coup in France, a military coup that was aimed at overthrowing President Charles de Gaulle, one of our strongest allies.

Narrator: Allen Dulles, who had a long history of antagonism with de Gaulle, falsely reported to Kennedy that the vast majority of the French military was staunchly opposed to de Gaulle's support of Algerian self-determination. What he didn't tell him was that as far back as 1959, the CIA had discussed his overthrow. This coup attempt, orchestrated by four French generals, was quickly put down and several news reports pointed to Allen Dulles's hand in supporting the episode.

For the many tensions between Dulles, the CIA, and de Gaulle, see Talbot, *The Devil's Chessboard*, pp. 414–21. Also Andrew Tully, *CIA: The Inside Story*, pp. 48–49, p. 53; *The Nation*, May 20, 1961; *Washington Post*, April 30, 1961; and *New York Times*, April 29, 1961. In his eager attack on *JFK Revisited* in *Rolling Stone*, Tim Weiner appears to have been wrong on this point. He should have been fact-checked.

David Talbot: JFK assures that French ambassador, I have nothing to do with this, I stand in full support of President de Gaulle. But he says something very, very alarming. He tells the French ambassador, President Kennedy, that I'm not in full control, though of my entire government. I'm not in control of the CIA. And I can't speak for what's happening there. That's a stunning admission for US president to make.

Talbot writes about this conversation in *The Devil's Chessboard*, p. 418.

Narrator: Beyond a coup, in fact, there were at least six attempts to assassinate de Gaulle by the OAS and others that continued even after he agreed to grant Algeria its independence. In one of these plots, there is evidence that French dissidents and the CIA conspired to poison de Gaulle.

William Blum writes about these attempts by the rebel OAS to kill de Gaulle in *The CIA: A Forgotten History* (pp. 165–69). The poisoning attempt was a page one story from the *Chicago Tribune* of June 15, 1975.

Narrator: Allen Dulles was the only commissioner who did not have a regular job. Therefore, he became the single most active member of the commission. He asked the most questions—a remarkable 31 percent of the total, and he attended the most hearings—even more than chairman Earl Warren. Yet, in spite of this, he never revealed to the commission the CIA plots to kill Castro or why Kennedy had fired him over the Bay of Pigs. Behind the scenes, he tipped off the CIA about certain questions the commission would ask regarding Oswald and he rehearsed with them the precise wording of their denials of any contact with the alleged assassin.

The data on attendance and questioning is from a series of charts in the book, *The Warren Omission*, by Walt Brown, pp. 83–87. The cooperation between Dulles and the CIA is outlined by Peter Grose in *Gentleman Spy*, pp. 547–48

Narrator: Contrary to media reports, the Warren Commission was not unanimous in its beliefs. Senator Richard Russell of Georgia did not want to serve on the Commission. And after he attended the first meeting, he quickly became disenchanted with the proceedings, particularly the roles of J. Edgar Hoover and acting Attorney General Nicolas Katzenbach. His personal papers at the University of Georgia Library contain a memo written after the initial December 5, 1963, executive session: "Something strange is happening. W [Warren] and Katzenbach know all about the FBI and are apparently planning to show Oswald as the only one considered. This to me in [an] untenable position."

Narrator: His papers reveal that he wrote a dissenting opinion for presentation at the final Commission meeting of September 18th. On that day, he shared his concerns with President Johnson.

> The best source of information on Russell's thoughts and writings is Dani E. Biancolli's master's thesis, "The First Dissenter." For the quote used above, see Biancolli (p. 47). For his dissenting opinion, also see Biancolli (pp. 49–55).

LBJ phone call: "But we got you a pretty good report." "Well, what difference does it make which bullet got Connally?" "Well, it don't make much difference, but the Commission believes that the same bullet that hit Kennedy, hit Connally. Well, I don't believe it." "I don't either."

Narrator: He also thought that Oswald did not act alone. Russell was strongly influenced by the Zapruder film and by the testimony of John Connally, who himself did not believe the first shot that hit Kennedy also went through him.

> The phone call is from September 18, 1964. For Russell's thoughts about Oswald and coconspirators, see McKnight (pp. 296–97). Biancolli writes that Russell wrote his dissenting opinion on September 16 and relied on Connally's testimony and the Zapruder film for his disbelief in the single-bullet theory (Biancolli, p. 55 ff).

Narrator: This forced the other commissioners to include Connally's dissent in the report and as a result, they could not absolutely deny the possibility of a conspiracy.

Warren Report, p. 22 for the qualification; for Connally, see pp. 49–50.

Oliver Stone: Is there a transcript of that final meeting of the Warren Commission?

Brian Edwards: At that meeting, he was gonna probably voice his opinion and his dissent against the single bullet striking both men and coming out as pristine as it was. Richard Russell probably thought the only female in the room was a stenographer because apparently she was over there doodling or writing or whatever. But there's no record of, no official record of that session.

Narrator: In 1968, author Harold Weisberg told Senator Russell that the National Archives had no transcript of the final meeting. Russell was beside himself and had his assistant confirm what had happened. Russell became the first commissioner to criticize the Warren Report in public.

Narrator: He was followed by Commission members John Sherman Cooper and Hale Boggs.

For the lack of any transcript of the September 18, 1964 final executive session meeting, and Weisberg's informing Russell of that fact, see McKnight (pp. 294–97). For his public dissent, see the *Washington Post* story by Don Oberdorfer, January 19, 1970. In 1978 Cooper said he disagreed with the magic-bullet concept for the British documentary *The JFK Conspiracy*. Before he passed away in 1972, Boggs strongly criticized Hoover's inquiry. Author Bernard Fensterwald quoted him in his 1977 book, *Coincidence or Conspiracy*, cowritten with Michael Ewing (p. 96ff).

Narrator: The years of dissent are over, and Kennedy must now shape his own policy as president, sometimes in conflict with what his predecessors have done—especially in foreign policy.

John F. Kennedy speech: To those new states who we welcome to the ranks of the free, we pledge our word that one form of colonial control shall not have passed away merely to be replaced by a far more iron tyranny.

Narrator: The Congo is the second largest country in Africa. In 1960, it had been granted its independence from Belgian colonial rule and carried out a democratic election. In the disorder of the transition, the Belgians, backed by England and France, sought to eliminate its charismatic prime minister, Patrice Lumumba. Once again, Eisenhower and CIA Director Allen Dulles favored the European nation in this colonial conflict.

Richard Mahoney: And Lumumba, in order to stop that, had invited Russian advisers into the Congo to secure the country. At that point, Eisenhower gave the go-ahead to have him assassinated.

John Newman: Eisenhower got very impatient with Allen Dulles. He had told him to get rid of Lumumba and it wasn't happening. And so he got very frustrated in the middle of an NSC meeting and just blurted out, you know, an order to kill, not to anybody in particular, but blurted out to everybody assembled there to kill Lumumba.

For a good summary of Eisenhower's policy, see John Newman, *Countdown to Darkness* (pp. 220–27).

Richard Mahoney: Kennedy never knew this. He gets elected the following November of 1960, and he heads in the opposite direction.

For Kennedy's immediate changes in Congo policy, see Mahoney (pp. 63–69).

Narrator: But events are already in motion. With the backing of British and US intelligence and arms, Colonel Joseph Mobutu's forces captured President Lumumba at the beginning of December 1960.

Richard Mahoney: Dag Hammarskjöld, the UN secretary-general, calls JFK, who's the president-elect at this point, and asks him to intercede to get Lumumba released from prison. When Kennedy intervenes to save Lumumba, that's a signal directly to the CIA and the Belgian secret police that they have to dispatch this guy immediately. And so forty-eight hours before Kennedy takes the oath of office, Lumumba is delivered into the hands of his enemies. He's taken out and shot in the head. Kennedy doesn't know this until a month later.

The story of how Lumumba was captured and assassinated is told by Newman in *Countdown to Darkness* (pp. 280–96). See also Mahoney (pp. 69–71).

David Talbot: Who finally tells him? The CIA? No, they still keep it a secret. He's informed by his UN ambassador, Adlai Stevenson. His face crumbles. He's holding his hand. He's grimacing in anguish, hearing about the assassination of Patrice Lumumba.

See Talbot's *The Devil's Chessboard* (p. 387). The famous picture of silent pain on Kennedy's face was shot by Jacques Lowe.

Richard Mahoney: Kennedy would say in meetings about the Congo, "The one way to keep the US out of the Congo is to keep the UN in the Congo." And Kennedy backed Hammarskjöld in terms of getting a government of national unity in Leopoldville.

UN secretary-general Dag Hammarskjöld had sent in a small force in July 1960. It was only after Lumumba's death that it became a larger force capable of major operations (Mahoney, p. 76).

Narrator: Hammarskjöld died in a mysterious plane crash in September of '61 as he was working on a peace treaty between the breakaway state of Katanga and the Congo.

Richard Mahoney: The reason why Katanga seceded was because it was an extremely rich province in a wide range of very valuable minerals. And the Belgian company, a colonial company called Union Miniere, convinced the Belgian government to use Belgian military and paramilitary forces to encourage the province to secede. So the province secedes from the Congo and announces itself as an independent country supported by British and Belgian imperial interests.

For this military connection between Belgium and Katanga, see Mahoney (pp. 53–55). Allen Dulles was aware of the Belgian plan for Katanga succession two months before it happened (Newman, p. 153).

John F. Kennedy UN speech: Dag Hammarskjöld is dead, but the United Nations lives. His tragedy is deep in our heart. But the task for which he died are at the top of our agenda.

Richard Mahoney: The US ambassador and close friend of President Kennedy, Edmund Gullion, sent a cable home saying, contrary to the official explanation for this tragic incident, this was an assassination.

Narrator: The photos of Hammarskjöld show his body as the only one not burned or charred. And he had a playing card, reportedly the ace of spades, stuffed into his shirt collar above the knot in the tie. Now, due to Susan Williams's book and new evidence offered by Desmond Tutu and the Union of South Africa's Truth and Reconciliation Commission, there are controversial documents that indicate Allen Dulles was involved in the sabotage of the plane. The project was called Operation Celeste and was to be carried out through a secret white supremacist group called SAIMR.

For the Gullion cable, see the story at CBC News by Melissa Kent dated June 21, 2015. For information on Operation Celeste, see the Williams book and the documentary *Cold Case Hammarskjöld.* For a more concise treatment of Celeste, see the June 20, 2019, story in *The Guardian* by Emma Graham-Harrison.

Richard Mahoney: Kennedy understood pretty early in his administration that the Central Intelligence Agency had an agenda that was completely their own.

Kennedy said words to this effect to the French ambassador in Washington in late April 1961 during an attempt by the OAS to overthrow Charles de Gaulle (Talbot, *The Devil's Chessboard*, p. 418).

Narrator: Kennedy now conveyed to Prime Minister [Harold] MacMillan of England that he would not be backing European imperialism in the Congo. And he allowed UN Ambassador Adlai Stevenson to vote for a use-of-force resolution to expel all foreign mercenaries from the breakaway region. At the end of 1962, Katanga's forces fired on a UN helicopter and outpost. Kennedy approved a UN military attack, codenamed Operation Grand Slam. One month after combat operations, Katanga was defeated and the Congo was one country again.

For the disagreement with England, see Mahoney (p. 112). For Kennedy's approval of UN intervention and Operation Grand Slam, see also Mahoney (pp. 152–56).

Richard Mahoney: Kennedy came back to the United Nations a year after that to reiterate the fact that the peacekeeping operation is working, we have a democratic government and we still do not accept Belgium's role in the secession of this province called Katanga.

John F. Kennedy UN speech: Today, the clouds have lifted a little so that new rays of hope can break through. The pressures on West Berlin appear to be temporarily eased. Political unity in the Congo has been largely restored.

A neutral coalition in Laos, while still in difficulty, is at least in being. The integrity of the United Nations Secretariat has been reaffirmed.

Film Clip of Senator Frank Church: Today we are here to review the major findings of our full investigation of FBI domestic intelligence.

Narrator: After the Watergate scandal, in 1975 Senator Frank Church conducted the first full-scale investigation of the abuses and crimes of the CIA and FBI. Many secrets were revealed for the first time to the public. For example, the FBI's programs to destabilize the Black Panthers and to harass and intimidate Martin Luther King into perhaps taking his own life. The public was also made aware of the CIA plots to kill foreign leaders like Patrice Lumumba and Fidel Castro.

> The declassified CIA Inspector General Report on the plots to kill Castro stated the Agency had no presidential authority for these actions (see pp. 132–33).

Narrator: Former Warren commissioner Gerald Ford was president at this time. Prior to the formation of the Church Committee, Ford had appointed his own commission headed by Vice President Nelson Rockefeller to investigate domestic CIA activities. On January 16, 1975, at a luncheon with executives and editors of the *New York Times*, President Ford, in explaining why he appointed such a conservative panel to investigate these CIA crimes, said that they needed to guard the national interest. Editor A. M. Rosenthal asked, "From what?" Ford blurted out, "From things like assassinations."

> See Daniel Schorr, *Clearing the Air* (pp. 143–44).

Narrator: When CIA director William Colby turned out to be honest and open with the Rockefeller and Church Committees, he was replaced by George H. W. Bush, who, during his confirmation hearing, hid his relationship with the CIA. As part of the Church Committee, Senators Richard Schweiker and Gary Hart set up a subcommittee to investigate the Kennedy assassination and how the Warren Commission had been served by the

FBI and the CIA. That report severely criticized the Warren Commission's lack of independence and their overreliance on government investigators for their findings.

For the controversy around Bush see Joseph McBride's articles in *The Nation*, July 16–23 and August 13–20, 1988. The Schweiker-Hart committee report is in Book V of the Church Committee volumes.

Sen. Richard Schweiker clip: After a lot of prodding and pressuring from the Warren Commission counsel, J. Edgar Hoover writes Mr. Rankin and said, "Yes, we did have a relationship with Mr. Ruby and between March 11th, '59, October 2nd, '59, on some eight, nine occasions, he acted as our informant or something to that effect." Now, who said that? Who said that at the time of the Warren Commission report? Did anybody imply that Jack Ruby was a confidential informant for the FBI? Nobody breathed that. That was classified.

Narrator: The Church Committee had access to the internal CIA report on their plots with the Mafia to kill Castro, which began in 1960 under Director Allen Dulles. In that report the Agency admitted it had no presidential authorization for the assassination attempts. Yet during his nearly ten months' service on the Warren Commission, Dulles never told his colleagues about this Mafia connection. Senator Schweiker was infuriated by both the alliance and the attempted assassination of a foreign leader.

Schweiker Clip: I think the Warren Commission has in fact collapsed like a house of cards. And I think that the Warren Commission was set up at the time to feed pablum to the American people for reasons not yet known and that one of the biggest cover-ups in the history of our country occurred at that time.

Narrator: While working as a technician at a film facility, Robert Groden had come into possession of a copy of the famous 8 mm Zapruder film. In six years he had shown it in public only three times. In 1975, television host

Geraldo Rivera heard about this and scheduled Groden and comedian/social activist Dick Gregory on his ABC program *Good Night America*.

Film clip from *Good Night America*:

Rivera: This film shot by the Dallas dress manufacturer Abraham Zapruder, and it's the execution of President Kennedy.

Groden: Now before he goes behind the sign, the president is waving to the crowd. When he comes out from behind the sign, he has been shot and Governor Connally has been shot.

Rivera: He has already been hit.

Groden: He's already been hit.

Groden: Now at the bottom of the screen is the head shot.

Rivera: That's the shot that blew off his head.

Groden: Now, the Warren Commission said that all the shots were fired from behind by Lee Harvey Oswald, a lone assassin firing at the president. And as you can see clearly, the head is thrown violently backwards, completely consistent with a shot from the front.

Rivera: Right. That's the most pathetic thing I've ever seen. We'll be back in a minute.

Narrator: Due to public outrage, that national viewing caused the creation of the second major inquiry into President Kennedy's murder. This was called the House Select Committee on Assassinations.

> The HSCA was created after a year of lobbying, especially by Congressmen Henry Gonzalez of Texas and Tom Downing of Virginia.

Downing was the first chairman (*The Assassinations*, edited by James DiEugenio and Lisa Pease, pp. 53–54).

Cyril Wecht: When one considers all the things that happened and did not happen, missing pieces of evidence and documents that were destroyed, and so on, I have no idea what might have happened in Dallas that day.

Oliver Stone: What's the situation with the HSCA files in 1979?

David Mantik: After the House Select Committee on Assassinations closed up shop, they sealed many of the witness reports. These were not available to the public.

John Tunheim: Close to half a million records which were segregated. They were concealed under House rules at the time until 2029. Some of them had leaked out, some were a part of the report on the House Select Committee on Assassinations. But most were not released.

Narrator: But then in 1991, due to the uproar over the film *JFK*, hearings were held on Capitol Hill.

Clip of Oliver Stone before Congress: Most Americans did not believe or support the verdict of the Warren Commission initially. And now more than three in four, according to all recent samplings of public opinion, think that some conspiracy was involved.

Narrator: At the end of that film, the public was made aware that the House Select Committee had classified the vast majority of their materials until 2029.

Oliver Stone: Of course, we did not go further than we could, because many of these files as you know, are sealed to the American public in the 1960s. They were never open, and the Warren Commission information was always compromised by the fact that the CIA and the FBI and military intelligence never gave any significant information to the Warren Commission members.

And, in fact, the Warren Commission was chaired—one of the members of the Warren Commission—was Allen Dulles, who had been fired by President Kennedy as chief of the CIA. There seems to be the element of the fox investigating the chicken coop here.

Narrator: Because of the massive media controversy that accompanied the film, Congress was forced to do something about the secrecy still existing thirty years after Kennedy's death.

> These congressional hearings on declassification went on during the summer and early autumn of 1992. The act was then passed in October. But President George H. W. Bush faltered in creating the Board. It was finally constructed under President Clinton and began work in 1994.

Oliver Stone: Judge Tunheim, what was the concept behind the JFK Records Act?

John Tunheim: The President John F. Kennedy Records Collection Act of 1992, as it was called, was created largely to clear up all the questions that people had about the assassination of President Kennedy. There was a frustration that the agencies themselves were never going to release the information, and people wanted to know. And I think the people had the right to know and that's what underlines the entire act.

Oliver Stone: What were some of your difficulties working with the CIA?

John Tunheim: One of the censors at the CIA was at a meeting with us. And there was a document that we put up on the screen that we were prepared to release it. And I asked him, "Tell us why we shouldn't release this record?" And there was silence for about two minutes and he finally said, "I know there's a reason, I just can't think of what it is."

Narrator: Over five million pages of collected records and artifacts are housed at the National Archives in College Park, Maryland, and most may be viewed in person.

Tom Samoluk: The Review Board had an unbelievable task to get at the bottom of the assassination. Not as a reinvestigation. But to make the record of the assassination as robust as possible. And that included really pressing federal agencies on records that they may not have thought about as assassination records. But also state and local government. Obviously Dallas was important, New Orleans was important.

Oliver Stone: What about the Oswald KGB file?

John Tunheim: The National Security Council in September of 1998 refused to allow the issue to be raised in the Clinton-Yeltsin meeting. We went to Moscow to try to negotiate release. We got some records, not very much. We got no help from the Department of State. In fact, we weren't even allowed to go into the United States embassy in Moscow. They claimed later it was just a mix-up. But we could have used some diplomatic help.

These pursuits are described in the ARRB *Final Report*, pp. 139–42.

Oliver Stone: How much media coverage did the ARRB get?

John Tunheim: We issued a hundred or more press releases. We didn't get really too much attention. We were followed most closely, probably, by the *New York Times*, because they had writers that focused on intelligence and intelligence issues.

Thomas Samoluk: I wish there had been more attention. It seemed like the American public today, even twenty years after the review board was in business, is still as interested as they were then and the day of the assassination.

John Tunheim: It very definitely should have been an open-ended process. I think there was some thought probably among the agencies that they could just wait us out. You know, if they didn't respond and delayed, eventually we wouldn't be in office as a review board anymore and they wouldn't have to turn over records.

Oliver Stone: How did you obtain the Zapruder film for the National Archives?

John Tunheim: You know, it's the most important piece of evidence of one of the most shocking crimes of American history. We tried to get the family to donate the film to the United States, the original. They could keep the copyright, they can sell, you know, the rights to use it. They can do whatever they want with it. But we wanted the original and the arbitrators, in a two-to-one vote, voted to award what was really, I think, an excessive sum. I think it was around sixteen million dollars.

Thomas Samoluk: A hard one to swallow as far as the amount. But I think that there would have been criticism if that film was not part of the official JFK collection.

Doug Horne: The Zapruder family, after getting all this money, after this windfall profit, they decide to donate the copyright to the Sixth Floor Museum. So if you want to publish a book or do a documentary about the Zapruder film, you have to get the permission of the Sixth Floor Museum.

On the sale, see *New York Times* story of August 4, 1999, by David Johnston. On the donation, see UPI story of January 26, 2000, "Zapruder family donates JFK film."

Narrator: The Sixth Floor Museum to this day insists that Oswald shot Kennedy from that sixth-floor window. And virtually everything in the museum is dedicated to that proposition.

Narrator: The Zapruder film shows Kennedy being knocked violently backwards as he was hit in the skull. His body goes back and to the left. Yet this shocking moment is not discussed in the Warren Report.

Commission attorney Wesley Liebeler admitted to this curious fact on *The Louis Lomax Show* on KTTV in Los Angeles on October 27, 1966.

Narrator: One of the most serious problems the Warren Commission had was in placing Oswald on the sixth floor at the time of the shooting. They said he was there at 12:30, firing shots. They then had him stow the rifle between boxes, and run down the single set of stairs in order to flee the crime scene. The problem was, there were other employees in the vicinity of his alleged escape path. And the testimony of three of them conflicted with what was in the Warren Report. Barry Ernest went looking for one of these employees.

> The Warren Report largely relied on two witnesses to place Oswald on the sixth floor at the time of the shooting. Charles Givens, who was inside the building, and Howard Brennan, who was a spectator outside (WR, pp. 143–45). Givens' testimony was dissected and shown to be almost certainly false by Sylvia Meagher in her essay, "The Curious Testimony of Mr. Givens," first published in the *Texas Observer,* August 13, 1971.
>
> Brennan's testimony was just as problematic, since he was supposed to have described the assassin's height and weight, yet the window was not from the floor to ceiling. Also, he failed to identify Oswald at the police lineup (see Gerald McKnight's *Breach of Trust,* pp. 109–11).

Barry Ernest: My focus was on finding a specific witness to the assassination, which was Victoria Adams. This would have gone on from when I returned from Dallas in late '68 until probably 2000. There was not much written about her, even in her testimony.

But one thing she did say was that she graduated from high school in San Francisco. I finally ended up with a school called Presentation High School, and it had her name in it. And I wrote to them the alumni office to try and find out if I could get an email address or a telephone number for this woman. I never received a response. But the state police officer who I knew said let me handle it. And within a week, he had written to Vicki Adams and asked her if she was the woman who once worked in Dallas and had been a witness to the JFK assassination. She had replied to him: Yes, that's me. Vicki worked on the fourth floor of the Texas School Book Depository. She testified that immediately after the assassination, she ran down the back stairs in an effort to get outside to see what was going on.

Barry's search for Victoria is chronicled in his book *The Girl on the Stairs,* see especially pp. 235–40. Adams's testimony is in Warren Commission, vol. 6 (pp. 386–93). She mentions the specific timing on p. 392.

Narrator: According to the Warren Report, Oswald was seen in the second-floor lunchroom within ninety seconds of the shooting by Dallas police officer Marrion Baker and Oswald's supervisor, Roy Truly, as they went up the stairs to the sixth floor.

This incident is described in the Warren Report (pp. 149–52).

Narrator: For Vicki Adams to have reached the first floor within sixty seconds and not have seen or heard Oswald, or Baker and Truly, on the wooden stairs was in conflict with the Warren Commission's assumption that Oswald was on those stairs at that time.

Barry Ernest: So what the Warren Commission did was successfully deceive the public into thinking that Vicki was just another mistaken or a confused witness. The whole case based on the Warren Commission is Vicki was wrong because she went down the stairs later than she thought, and she saw two men there who couldn't have been there unless she had come down the stairs later.

This adjustment is located in the Warren Report (p. 154). It is easily juxtaposed with her actual testimony mentioned above.

Narrator: Employees William Shelley and Billy Lovelady had been on the front steps of the building, watching the motorcade pass. According to their statements, after the shooting, they then went to the railroad tracks beside the grassy knoll, returning to the Book Depository within several minutes. The Warren Commission, needing to keep the stairs clear for Oswald's descent, claimed that Vicki had come down after Baker and Truly had passed the fourth floor on their way up, and late enough to see Shelley and Lovelady return from the railroad tracks.

> The Warren Report left out the facts that neither Shelley nor Lovelady mentioned crossing the street to the railroad tracks in their first-day testimony to the FBI or Dallas Police (Gerald McKnight, *Breach of Trust*, p. 114).

Barry Ernest: According to her testimony, she left the window on the fourth floor within fifteen to thirty seconds of the assassination. The Warren Commission elevated that time to one minute. She said she arrived on the first floor within sixty seconds of the assassination. The Warren Commission elevated that time to several minutes. When Vicki was giving her Warren Commission testimony, she felt that David Belin, who was questioning her, did not believe her. And so she asked Belin if she could be a part of the reenactments that were going on. Belin refused. When she then said, "Interview Sandra Styles, a coworker who went down the stairs with me," Belin said, "We don't need her. We have you." Sandra Styles, when I interviewed her, she corroborated everything Vicki had said. She came down the stairs with Vicki, she didn't see or hear anyone on the stairs, and she didn't see Shelley and Lovelady on the first floor. In light of that, I went to the National Archives searching for her original testimony. I wanted the original stenographer's tape that was made by the court reporter, the only other person in the room when David Belin interviewed Vicki Adams. But when I asked about Vicki's tape, I was told that the tape containing her testimony was missing. And later, I learned that that tape had been destroyed by the Warren Commission for no apparent reason.

> Barry's interview with Styles is in *The Girl on the Stairs*, pp. 258–63. He discovered that there were two slightly different versions of Adams's testimony at the National Archives, with two different declassification dates (Ernest, pp. 278–81). Adams always insisted to him that, unlike her WC testimony, she never said she saw Shelley or Lovelady on the first floor, and Styles agreed with her. Barry's attempt to clarify these issues was thwarted by the destruction of the stenographer's tape (pp. 278–81).

Oliver Stone: And Vicki named three people who could corroborate her. And the commission had an affidavit from one of them.

Barry Ernest: The three people were Elsie Dorman, who was a coworker, happened to be filming the motorcade from the fourth-floor window. Sandra Styles and Dorothy Garner, Vicki's immediate supervisor, and had stood at the window with Vicki. Not a one of them was called as a commission witness. In 1999, I found a document in the National Archives that had been suppressed for thirty-five years. It was a letter written by Assistant US Attorney Martha Jo Stroud. It was addressed to J. Lee Rankin, the head honcho of the Warren Commission's investigation at that point. It was a transmittal letter forwarding Vicki's signed testimony. In the last paragraph of that letter, the letter quotes Garner as saying that she saw Vicki go down the stairs before she saw Officer Baker and Roy Truly come up. Now, this is in direct contradiction to the Warren Commission's conclusion that Vicki was on the stairs much later than all this had occurred. When I found and interviewed Dorothy Garner, she confirmed everything. She said that she had been at the window with Vicki, that Vicki had left the window immediately, that she actually followed Vicki outside the office and to a point where she could see her going down the stairs. And it was only after that that Baker and Truly came up the stairs, according to her. And during that whole time, she never saw Oswald. Garner was putting Vicki on the stairs exactly when she said. So the Stroud letter became a very, very dangerous document.

Adams mentions the three witnesses in Warren Commission, vol. 6, p. 388. The Martha Joe Stroud letter is in *The Girl on the Stairs*, p. 298. The date of the letter is June 2, 1964. Meaning that, at the time of its sending, the Commission would be in session for over three more months. Barry's interview with Garner is on pp. 269–70 of his book.

Narrator: The Warren Commission concealed the Stroud document. Without the Review Board's declassification process, we would never have learned of the corroborating testimony of three witnesses that provides powerful evidence that Oswald was not on the sixth floor at the time of the shooting.

Oliver Stone: So all of the records were supposed to have been released in 2017. What happened?

John Tunheim: President Trump tweeted that he was excited to release all of the remaining records of the assassination and what they might disclose. And then at the last minute, after meeting with the CIA, he decided to postpone release until some future time. It's 1960s-era material and there are redactions that we put in because we felt in the 1990s there was still a reason to keep them from being released. But that's changed. This is fifty-six years after the assassination. There's no reason to protect this information anymore.

See Katie Reilly's *Time* magazine story of October 26, 2017, about Trump backtracking on his tweet to release all the JFK files at that time. He then delayed the release again in April 2018, see story by Ian Shapara on April 26, 2018 in the *Washington Post.*

This was now delayed until 2021. On April 30, 2019, Jefferson Morley reported at the website *Just Security* that more than fifteen thousand documents are still redacted in whole or in part.

John Newman: It's a certainly against the spirit of the JFK Records Act and technically now against the law, because the mandate was to get everything out by 2017.

Attorney Mark Adamczyk has concluded that President Trump did break the law since the JFK Act required that he supply specific reasons as to why he was holding back certain documents past 2017. He did not. See "JFK Records Release: Why the Redactions" at Kennedysandking.com, October 27, 2019. President Biden released about 10 percent of these in late 2021 but delayed release of the rest until October 2022.

JFK: Destiny Betrayed

Chapter 2

Narrator: The evening of the assassination, the body of President Kennedy was returned to Washington. The autopsy was performed at Bethesda Medical Center, a naval institution. And there has always been a question about the practices of the men who performed what was one of the most important and confusing autopsies of the twentieth century.

Oliver Stone: Would Milton Helpern in New York have been a good choice to do the autopsy?

Cyril Wecht: I know this directly from Milton, this is not hearsay. He had his bag packed. And he had already contacted two other top forensic pathologists to see if they would be available. All of the top forensic pathologists in the United States were within one hour drive or flying time from DC. Not one of them was called upon. The autopsy should have been done, legally speaking, in Dallas. And there was a forensic pathologist, Earl Rose, he was there to assume jurisdiction and to do the autopsy. He was pushed up against the wall and threatened. Hands on guns, lots of expletives and so on, and he followed them out to the driveway and they took the body illegally out of Dallas, in violation of the laws of Dallas and the state of Texas.

> William Manchester described this confrontation with Rose in *Look* magazine, February 21, 1967. See also his *The Death of a President*, pp. 297–305.

Gary Aguilar: There were two Navy pathologists, Commander James Humes and his associate, Jay Thornton Boswell.

Cyril Wecht; These two military pathologists who had never done a single gunshot wound autopsy in their entire careers. And this is something that really has to be emphasized to every American—I don't care, Democrat, Republican, liberal, conservative. This is your president. And you've got multiple gunshot wounds to determine angles, trajectory, range, sequence. And then you've got to correlate with the multiple gunshot wounds in Connally. This is a formidable task that would have required two or three major forensic pathologists to undertake. So they called Humes and Boswell.

> In his ARRB interview Humes said he had done "two gunshot autopsies" at Tripler Army Hospital in Hawaii and these may have been accidents. His memory was remarkably hazy on this point (February 13, 1996, p. 22). He did not mention this before the Warren Commission (vol. 2, p. 348). According to Dr. David Mantik, Boswell had never done a gunshot wound autopsy. See the introduction to his online essay on Boswell's ARRB deposition at *The Mantik View* website.

Gary Aguilar: They realize they're over their head. They called in an expert from the Armed Forces Institute of Pathology, a guy named Pierre Finck. Dr. Humes and Boswell started the autopsy before the forensics consultant even got there. They took the brain out. Obviously, some key clues would've been lost by doing that. But they realized they were in over their head, so they asked to have a medical examiner because Dr. Finck, who is a forensic pathologist, wasn't doing autopsies. He had done one in more than two years. So they asked for permission to bring in somebody who knew what they were doing. Permission was denied.

Before the ARRB, both Boswell and Humes admitted they needed a forensic pathologist, since neither one of them qualified (Humes, ARRB interview, February 13, 1996, p. 18; Boswell interview February 26, 1996, p. 24). For the denied request of an outside consultant, see *Trauma Room One* by Charles Crenshaw, p. 179.

Narrator: After Air Force One left Dallas for Washington, two of the key doctors who had tried to save Kennedy's life at Parkland Hospital held a press conference. They were Dr. Malcolm Perry and Dr. Kemp Clark.

Oliver Stone: What were the two major points of evidence revealed by Kemp Clark and Malcolm Perry at the press conference?

Gary Aguilar: Dr. Perry performed the tracheotomy to help Kennedy breathe. And at a press conference right after the failed resuscitation efforts in Dallas, he was asked, he said, well, where was the bullet? He said the bullet looked like it was coming at him. He had an entrance wound in the throat.

Doug Horne: Kemp Clark was the head of neurosurgery at Parkland. He said that the president had a gaping wound in the occipital parietal area—the right rear of the head. And so the description he gave of that was entirely consistent with an exit wound. And he made that clear in the press conference.

This transcript is available online at the Mary Ferrell Foundation website. Perry's and Clark's comments are on page 5, but Clark further defined the rear head wound in contemporaneous notes made that day. (Crenshaw, p. 200).

Narrator: What Clark and Perry both revealed at that press conference would indicate an assassin from the front, but no news footage has survived. Although Assistant White House Press Secretary Malcolm Kilduff's statement that day seems to support this conclusion.

Newsreel: Dr. Burkley told me a simple matter of a bullet right through the head.

Doug Horne: We have a transcript today of what they said at the press conference. So it's White House transcript 1327c. That's a very important historical document because the Secret Service confiscated the videotapes from the local TV stations.

Narrator: The Secret Service also lied to the Warren Commission about there being no recordings or transcripts of the news conference. There is, however, a surviving clip of Dr. Perry recorded not long afterward where he confirms having seen a large wound in the back of the head.

> The Secret Service subterfuge about the transcript and tapes is proven in Doug Horne's *Inside the ARRB*, vol. 2, p. 647; they had the transcript and told Arlen Specter they did not. See also Mark Lane's *Rush to Judgment*, p. 53 for a source on the confiscated video tapes.

Dr. Perry archive: Arriving at the emergency room, placed a tube in the president's trachea to assist his breathing. There was a neck wound anteriorly, and a large wound to his head on the right posterior area.

Narrator: The day after the shooting and the Parkland press conference, Dr. Perry was seen by nurse Audrey Bell, who had been with him in the operating room.

Audrey Bell archive: Saturday morning when I got over there, Dr. Perry came up to the office. I said, you look awful. Did you get any sleep last night? He said, well, not too much. Between the calls from Bethesda that came in during the night. I said, what about? He said, Oh, whether that was an entrance wound or an exit wound in the throat. He said they were wanting me to change my mind.

> This issue is even more clear today, since it was ratified and expanded on by Perry himself in an interview he did with Martin Steadman. See

the online essay "The Ordeal of Malcolm Perry" by James DiEugenio at Kennedysandking.com.

Gary Aguilar: In his Warren Commission testimony, he basically retracted what he had said and they forced him to back down and sort of intimidated him on the witness stand. It was really quite embarrassing for me as a physician to see how someone else who was telling the truth was basically forced to recant his own opinion.

For instances of this, see Warren Commission, vol. 3, p. 375; vol. 6, pp. 12–14.

Don Miller: In 1975, Dr. Shires hired me on the faculty at the University of Washington in the cardiac surgery division. So I got to know Malcolm when I joined the faculty. We developed a professional relationship and we would operate together on complex cases. And I was particularly interested in Dr. Perry's position with the JFK assassination because he did the tracheotomy on him after he was shot. The problem is that Malcolm categorically refused to ever discuss the assassination. And he wouldn't answer my questions about that neck wound. And then one night, after we had operated together for many hours on a complex case, we were sitting in the surgeons' lounge alone drinking coffee. And I once again asked him about that neck wound. And this time he said it was an entrance wound, unquestionably an entrance wound. I took that admission as given in confidence. So it was sort of tacitly in confidence. And then when he testified in front of the House Select Committee on Assassinations a year later, he once again said that it was consistent with an exit wound, which, of course, was required if the single-bullet theory would hold water. One of the main reasons he changed his testimony and publicly agreed it was an exit wound is, a Secret Service agent put the pressure on him and that person was Elmer Moore. He apparently was also in charge of getting the doctors at Parkland, in addition to Dr. Perry, to change their testimony and agree that there was no big hole in the back of Kennedy's head and that the bullet wound in the neck was an exit wound. In 1970, Elmer Moore was the head of the Secret Service office in Seattle and a graduate student named Jim Gochenaur became friends with him and he admitted to Gochenaur that he regretted putting pressure and threatening Dr. Perry.

Dr. Perry was interviewed by the HSCA while working with Miller at the University of Washington. See HSCA hearings, vol. 7, specifically p. 306.

Jim Gochenaur: So I asked him directly. I said, Mr. Moore, did you pressure Dr. Perry? He stopped for a minute. He says, well, I was ordered to do that. He expanded on it and he said that Inspector Kelly had ordered him to talk to Perry and convince him that it could be either an exit or an entry wound—not an entry wound. And I thought it was pretty interesting that he would admit to something that's pretty close to a felony.

The ARRB opened up the subject of Elmer Moore. For a concise summary of the new record, see *The JFK Assassination: The Evidence Today*, pp. 166–69, which includes references to Jim Gochenaur and the Church Committee.

Narrator: Charles Crenshaw, a third-year resident, was in the emergency room at Parkland that day. He too, later said in public that he felt the wounds in Kennedy originated from the front.

There was evidence in the Warren Commission of Crenshaw's presence in the ER room, see Dr. Lawrence Altman's *New York Times* articles of May 20 and 26, 1992.

Gary Aguilar: Charles Crenshaw wrote a book, *Conspiracy of Silence*, in the wake of the film *JFK*, saying, look, I was at Parkland Hospital. I saw Kennedy, and was involved in the treatment. And Kennedy's wounds were not consistent with a shot from above and behind because he had a defect involving the right rear of his head.

Charles Crenshaw archive: I looked at the wound again. I wanted to know and remember this the rest of my life. And the rest of my life, I will always know he was shot from the front.

Crenshaw was interviewed on the ABC program *20/20* on April 3, 1992.

Narrator: Arlen Specter was a Yale Law School graduate working in the Philadelphia District Attorney's office when he was asked to serve on the Warren Commission. They placed Specter in charge of medical evidence, and when he questioned Humes and Boswell before the commission, they said two shots hit the president, one in the neck and one low in the rear skull, entirely supporting the Commission's final conclusions.

Humes's testimony on this point is in Warren Commission, vol. 2, p. 351. Boswell was in the room for Humes's testimony and told Specter he agreed with him on every point (Warren Commission, vol. 2, p. 377).

Narrator: However, when interviewed by the Assassination Records Review Board, Humes and Boswell admitted to meeting with Specter eight to ten times in advance of their testimony. And it is important to note that the wound drawings presented in the Warren Report were created in the days before that testimony and were not based on the autopsy photos. Instead, Harold Rydberg, the twenty-three-year-old head of the Medical Illustration Department at Bethesda, was given verbal instructions by Humes and Boswell who said: We'll tell you what to draw.

Humes's testimony about the Rydberg drawings is in commission vol. 2, pp. 349–50. The testimony about their meetings with Specter before they testified is in Humes' ARRB deposition, February 13, 1996, pp. 227–28 and Boswell's ARRB deposition, February 26, 1997, p. 207. For a summary of the Rydberg drawings affair, see Jim DiEugenio, *The JFK Assassination*, pp. 143–44.

Gary Aguilar: The Warren Commission heard testimony from a number of witnesses, including Parkland doctors, by the way, and including a Secret Service agent, Clint Hill, that the right rear quad of the head was missing.

Hill describes this wound in Warren Commission, vol. 2, p. 141. Dr. Kemp Clark described it in a similar manner in vol. 6, p. 20, as did Dr. Robert McClelland in vol. 6, p. 33, and Dr. Charles "Jim" Carrico, in vol. 3, p. 361.

Narrator: Hill was the only Secret Service agent to run to the presidential limousine during the shooting. He later said that there was blood and brain tissue hurtling back over the trunk of the car. And as he approached the president, he saw a large wound in the rear of the skull, which he could see through with no brain there.

At age eighty-six, Hill said the same thing about seeing no brain in the rear of Kennedy's skull as he ran into the car. See the story in *The Sun* online, November 22, 2018. See also the beginning of chapter 14 of Hill's book *Five Days in November*.

Doug Horne: The two FBI agents at the autopsy, Frank O'Neill and James Sibert, they reported what they heard during the autopsy, what they heard the pathologists say—specifically, Dr. Humes. They were interviewed by Arlen Specter in early 1964, and he proceeded to write very unfavorable comments about them in a summary memo for the record. We know with confidence why he didn't like what they had to say because they were providing evidence that the single-bullet theory could not be true.

Specter interviewed Sibert and O'Neill without swearing them in. He then wrote a memo to Chief Counsel J. Lee Rankin dated March 12, 1964 misrepresenting what they said to him. In that memo he said that Sibert made no notes and O'Neill took few notes at the autopsy, Sibert denied this was the case in his ARRB sworn interview of September 11, 1997, p. 137. (Specter's memo is at the History Matters website; it is MD 154 in their ARRB Master Set of Medical Exhibits.)

Narrator: This was as far as the investigation would go. Neither Sibert nor O'Neill were asked to testify for the Warren Commission, and their notes became classified. In 1997, their depositions were taken by the Assassination Records Review Board.

Doug Horne: Both Sibert and O'Neil were shown the photographs of the back of JFK's head, the autopsy photographs that are the most controversial. And they both said that they didn't see anything like that at the autopsy. O'Neill had said "it looks like it's been doctored. I don't mean the photos been doctored, it looks like the head has been put back together, you know, by embalmers and then photographed." That was what he said under oath. Sibert did not remember drawing a diagram of the wound for the House committee, so he drew a new one for the Review Board. And it's one of our most important wound diagrams. And it shows what could only be an exit defect in the right rear of the skull.

See O'Neill's ARRB interview, pp. 158 and 161–62. Sibert talks about the wound on page 66 and then traces it on p. 72 of his interview.

Narrator: In 1979, the House Select Committee report stated that the twenty-six people present at the autopsy in Bethesda all disagreed with the Parkland doctor's description of Kennedy's head wounds.

This quote appears in vol. 7, p. 37 of the appendixes to the report.

Oliver Stone: When you went through the declassified affidavits that the House Select Committee prepared, what did you find about the alleged differences between the Parkland and Bethesda witnesses on this issue?

David Mantik: Not only were we allowed to see their statements, but we were allowed to see the sketches where they had drawn the big hole on the back of the head. And this was totally opposite of what the House Select Committee had told us.

Gary Aguilar: When the Assassination Records Review Board came along, out come those witness statements, out come the diagrams. And lo and behold, it turns out that the witnesses at the autopsy all agreed with the doctors at Dallas that that defect involved the rear of the head. And the summary statement basically misrepresented that truth. They basically lied about what was there.

Aguilar assembled the chart about the rear skull wound largely from declassified HSCA documents. It shows more than forty witnesses from both Parkland and Bethesda agreeing about this posterior baseball-size head wound.

Narrator: To make this even worse, if one looks at the official back of the head photo, there appears to be nothing missing. But there likely was something. This was a piece of bone that did not arrive in Washington until after the autopsy was over. And if it came from the back of Kennedy's skull, it created even more problems for that picture.

David Mantik: The Harper fragment was a piece of fresh skull bone that was found in Dealey Plaza, not on the day of the assassination, but later by Billy Harper.

Billy Harper clip: And reached down and picked it up. And at that time knew that I had something that most likely was significant.

Gary Aguilar: It was found in a position where the FBI said that was in an area to the left of where Jack Kennedy was when he was assassinated. It was then taken in by this medical student in to his professors. And they looked at it and they said it looked like it was occipital bone, which is in back here.

Narrator: It measured approximately three by two inches and therefore would have fit neatly into the rear skull wound as visualized by Dr. McClelland. This bone was given to the FBI on the 25th, after the autopsy report had been written by Dr. Humes. The FBI gave it to Kennedy's physician, Admiral Burkley, at which point it disappears. All we have today are the pictures taken of it in Dallas. This bit of evidence raises the question that if the rear of the skull was mostly filled in by pieces from the limousine, then where in the back of the skull did the Harper fragment fit?

For discussions of the Harper Fragment see, HSCA vol. 7, p. 24; Jim Douglass, *JFK. and the Unspeakable*, pp. 282–83; the most complete review is in David Mantik's e-book, *John F. Kennedy's Head Wounds*, Sections 4–7. In the book, Mantik states that the FBI took X-rays and photos of the Harper fragment went it came to Washington from Dallas (p. 50 and p. 92). In the film Aguilar says it was found to the rear of JFK, but there is a debate about this so we corrected it in the transcript.

Narrator: At age thirty-four, Congressman John F. Kennedy realized that if he was going to challenge for a seat in the Senate, he needed to broaden his knowledge of foreign affairs. So he decided, in 1951, to take a seven-week journey to the Middle East and Asia, accompanied by his sister Patricia and his brother Robert. During their stop in Vietnam, Kennedy planned to meet with Edmund Gullion. Gullion was a career diplomat who had once helped Kennedy write a foreign policy speech. Kennedy and his brother made it a point to seek him out, meeting at a rooftop restaurant in Saigon.

This journey is described in Richard Mahoney's book *JFK: Ordeal in Africa*, pp 12–15; the meeting with Gullion is on p. 108.

Richard Mahoney: And it was one of the most important experiences in his prepresidential career. A war was going on—France versus the Viet Minh. 80 percent of their military material was coming from the United States.

America's ascending aid to France's war effort in Vietnam is reviewed in the Gravel edition of the Pentagon Papers, vol. 1, chapter 2. There it is listed as 78 percent of the French effort in 1954. The 1951 meeting with Guillon in Saigon was described by Robert Kennedy as having "a very, very major" impact on JFK's thinking (Mahoney, p. 12).

Narrator: And because of this, Kennedy wanted to see what the status of this brutal, colonial war really was.

Philip Muehlenbeck: When he met with the French generals, that's when he formed the impression that the war was going well, because that was what the French generals were telling him. His opinion started to change when he met Edmund Gullion. He had told Kennedy that the French were actually losing the war and that the war was unwinnable.

The meeting with Gullion and its impact is also described in Thurston Clarke's *JFK's Last Hundred Days*, pp. 54–55.

Philip Muehlenbeck: In fact, he said that if the US were to replace the French, that the US would also lose the war.

Lisa Pease: Because Gullion made JFK understand that nothing short of independence would ever win in Vietnam. And if independence had to come at the hands of the Communists, they would go with the Communists rather than stay a colony of any independent force.

An online summary of this episode was written by retired professor James Norwood: "Edmund Gullion, JFK and the Shaping of a Foreign Policy in Vietnam" at Kennedysandking.com.

Narrator: Gullion's warning that America was backing an imminent French defeat caused Kennedy to begin a six-year crusade to formulate an alternative foreign policy, one opposed to the confrontational with-us-or-against-us policy advocated by President Harry Truman. Truman had broken away from his predecessor Franklin Roosevelt's policy of cooperation with the USSR, creating a worldwide Cold War face-off, later amplified by Dwight Eisenhower and his Secretary of State, John Foster Dulles.

For a good volume on the FDR vision, see Elizabeth Borgwardt's *A New Deal for the World*. For Roosevelt's anti-colonialism in Africa, see Donald Wright's "That Hell-hole of Yours" in *American Heritage*,

October, 1995. For his view of Asian colonialism, see "FDR and the Colonial Question" by Lloyd Garner in *FDR's World,* pp 123–44. Anthony Eden deplored what had happened to Roosevelt's attempt at a postwar Grand Alliance. He said this to Robert Sherwood for his book *Roosevelt and Hopkins,* but refused to let it be printed there.

Oliver Stone: Can you describe the 1953 letter that JFK sent to Dulles about Indochina?

Richard Mahoney: He sent a letter to John Foster Dulles, who was then Secretary of State, asking him forty-seven questions about American support for France in Vietnam. One of those questions was "What specific evidence is there, Mr. Secretary, that France is winning the war?"

The letter is dated May 7, 1953 (Mahoney, p. 15).

Narrator: Foster Dulles's eventual answer to this letter was codenamed Operation Vulture. Vice President Richard Nixon was the main lobbyist for the air operation in Congress. Planned as a massive air armada, it featured scores of bombers and fighter planes designed to save the French position at what would become the location of the fatal siege of Dien Bien Phu in the spring of 1954. Vulture included the possibility of dropping two or three atomic bombs.

For a book-length treatment of the siege of Dien Bien Phu and the last year of the French war, see *Operation Vulture* by John Prados.

Aaron Good: The US leadership—John Foster Dulles in particular—took the initiative to offer the French the use of the nuclear weapons. And even the French themselves said this is going too far for us. This is going too far and we can't be a party to this.

This exchange was recounted by French Minister Georges Bidault (Prados, p. 208).

Narrator: Kennedy spoke on the Senate floor in strong opposition to Vulture.

JFK voice actor: No amount of American military assistance in Indochina can conquer an enemy which is everywhere and at the same time nowhere—an enemy of the people which has the sympathy and covert support of the people.

As Mahoney notes, Richard Nixon led the lobbying effort for direct intervention in Vietnam to save Dien Bien Phu. The siege extended from March to May, Kennedy's speech was on April 6 (Mahoney, p. 16).

Narrator: When Eisenhower could not get the British to sign on to the project, he rejected it. And as Ambassador Gullion predicted, France lost its colonial war in Indochina.

Secretary of State John Foster Dulles's failure to get London to sign on to Vulture is reviewed in Prados, chapter 8.

Narrator: Kennedy gave his support to the liberal presidential candidate Adlai Stevenson and began giving speeches confronting the shared Cold War orthodoxies of both parties.

John F. Kennedy speech: The determination of people to control their national destinies. In my opinion, the tragic failure of both Republican and Democratic administrations to comprehend the nature of this revolution has reaped a bitter harvest today. And it is by rights and by necessity a major foreign policy campaign issue that has nothing to do with anti-communism.

See Mahoney for the speech and the reaction from the candidate's headquarters (p. 18).

Narrator: Even for the liberal Stevenson, that was too much. His office wired Kennedy and specifically requested that he make no more foreign policy statements in any way associated with the campaign. The next year, in

1957, Kennedy found the perfect opportunity to assault Foster Dulles, Nixon, and Eisenhower and to establish an alternative American foreign policy.

Richard Mahoney: Algeria became the last stand for France in its imperium. There was about a million two hundred thousand French citizens who were resident in North Africa generally, but in Algeria specifically, called Pied-Noirs. And they were completely behind the war effort and they were threatening French politicians. And what had happened in the French officer corps that was very, very critical and very dangerous was that after the defeat in Vietnam, a secret organization called the OAS, the Organization de la Secrete, threatened the government in Paris that if there was any withdrawal or any negotiations with the Algerian nationalists, that that government would be overthrown.

The OAS terrorist role in French politics is described in the book *Target de Gaulle* by Pierre Demaret. In 2018, President Emmanuel Macron admitted to a secret council within the government that approved abductions and murders during the war (November 21, 2018, *New Statesman* article by Andrew Hussey).

Narrator: The Algeria conflict, fought guerrilla-style, devolved into terror, torture, and atrocities on both sides. France escalated the war—a point-counterpoint of terror act followed by retaliation.

Oliver Stone: Can you tell us how did support in Algeria differ from Vietnam?

Richard Mahoney: In Algeria, it was support in a political sense. We supplied them through NATO with some amount of weaponry and aircraft, but not to the extent that we had in Vietnam. It was a war that was so violent and so lethal that the Americans stood aside. They supported France, but they didn't want to be involved.

Kennedy mentioned this NATO support in his July 2, 1957, speech. Allen Nevins briefly described the horrors of the war in his compilation of

Kennedy's speeches, *The Strategy of Peace* (see pp. 62ff for the speech and p. 67 for Nevins's description).

Narrator: It was against this backdrop that Kennedy chose to express his differences with the monster that Dulles and Eisenhower had created, one now staggering out of control. He attacked both Washington and Paris for not seeing in Algeria a reprise of the 1954 French collapse in Vietnam.

JFK archive clip: I am introducing a resolution which I believe outlines the best hope for peace for the settlement in Algeria, to achieve a solution which will recognize the independent personality of Algeria and establish the basis for a settlement interdependent with France and the neighboring nations.

Robert Rakove: Very few people, none with his prominence, had been willing to say what he said, which was to challenge a kind of default Eurocentrism in American foreign policy, to challenge the kind of "Europe First" outlook, especially toward conflicts in the colonial world. And Kennedy could even say, look, this isn't even doing France any favors.

Robert F. Kennedy Jr.: And that speech earned him the vitriol, not only of Republicans like Nelson Rockefeller, Barry Goldwater, Ronald Reagan, etc., but also Democrats like Adlai Stevenson. Because they saw that colonial empire as the only thing that was holding the European economy together. And Europe was the bulwark against communism. We had to support their colonial aspirations and ambitions in Africa. My uncle said, "No, we shouldn't be doing that. That is going to, in the long run, weaken us. And in any event, it's against every American ideal. We should be supporting democracy wherever it pops up in the world."

Stevenson called the speech "terrible." Dean Acheson, another Democrat, also criticized Kennedy over the speech (Mahoney, p. 20).

Richard Mahoney: Well, Joe Kennedy, his father, who had a very significant role in his son's career at all times, took him aside and surprisingly said to him, one day people are going to see that you really knew what you were talking about. And in fact, that's exactly what happened. The fourth republic fell. De Gaulle came in and he immediately initiated talks with the Algerian nationalists.

For Joseph Kennedy's comments to his son, see Mahoney, p. 21.

Narrator: In the archipelago nation of Indonesia, President Sukarno had fought a long battle for independence from the Dutch colonists. A self-styled nationalist, he balanced the country's communist party, the PKI, with his military, attempting to create what he termed "guided democracy." Partly as a reaction to the CIA-backed overthrow of democratic governments in Guatemala and Iran, Sukarno and other Third World leaders arranged a conference in Bandung, Indonesia, in 1955, beginning what became known as the Non-Aligned Movement.

Oliver Stone: And how did Kennedy's approach to the Non-Aligned Movement differ from Dulles's?

Lisa Pease: John Foster Dulles had said that the policy of neutrality was immoral. John Foster Dulles and Allen Dulles came from a Christian background and they felt, you know, what they had to say was good enough for the rest of the world, that they knew more than the president. There were things they didn't tell Eisenhower that they were doing under his administration.

For Dulles's reaction to the Non-Aligned Movement, see Robert Rakove, *Kennedy, Johnson, and the Nonaligned World*, pp. 8–9.

Narrator: In 1958, Indonesian military dissidents rebelled against Sukarno and at Eisenhower's direction, the CIA initiated plans to assist them in overthrowing their president.

Bradley Simpson: The United States under, under John Foster Dulles and his brother Allen Dulles, who was the head of the CIA, saw support for the rebellion as a means of weakening Sukarno, potentially breaking up the archipelago and weakening the Indonesian Communist Party. And so for more than a year the United States carried out what up to that point was the largest and most destructive covert operation of the Asian Cold War, in which thousands of US troops were involved in which millions of dollars in weapons and supplies were given to the regional rebellions and in which thousands of people were killed.

For a concise summary of this attempt to overthrow Sukarno, see the late William Blum's *The CIA: A Forgotten History* (pp. 108–113). For a book-length treatment, see *Subversion as Foreign Policy* by Audrey and George McT. Kahin.

Narrator: A CIA pilot, Alan Pope, was shot down during the operation, exposing US involvement, and the coup attempt failed.

For the Pope downing, see Blum, p. 112.

Robert Rakove: Kennedy's looking at the broad scope of American history, American foreign policy was fundamentally neutral. World War I was the great exception, until, of course, the Second World War. He saw nothing wrong with it. He could also draw from the experiences he'd had traveling in the Middle East in the early 1950s. He could draw from the example of Ireland during the Second World War, which had achieved a kind of difficult and controversial neutrality.

Narrator: Kennedy's interest in self-determination for the Third World led him to become chairman of the US Senate African Affairs Subcommittee in 1958.

See, Philip Muehlenbeck, *Betting on the Africans*, p. 36.

Robert F. Kennedy Jr.: We had a delegation from Kenya come to our house on the Cape. And the head of that delegation was a man named Tom Mboya, who was a great labor leader in Africa. He came from a tribe called the Luo tribe, which is one of the smaller tribes in Kenya. Around 1959, the British said to Kenya, "We're going to leave, we'll give you five years to figure out how to rule this country." And Mboya looked around and said, "There's not a single black child in this country who has a college degree." So he wrote letters to every college in America. And he got a hundred of them, including Harvard, to commit to giving a scholarship to one Kenyan child. And he would choose the smartest kids in the country. My uncle was so impressed by him that he wrote him a $100,000 check to bring these kids over.

Robert F. Kennedy Jr. In 2004 the Democratic convention was in Boston and I was asked to speak on the environment. Right after I spoke, it was a young first-term, first-year Democratic senator from Illinois who nobody had ever heard of, who gave a speech that blew the roof off the convention.

Barack Obama speech: The hope of a millworker's son who dares to defy the odds; the hope of a skinny kid with a funny name who believes that America has a place for him too (cheers).

Robert F. Kennedy Jr. When I asked him about his life, I knew nothing about him. And he said that his father was Kenyan. And I said, "Oh, have you ever heard of Tom Mboya?" And he said to me, "Tom Mboya is the reason I'm in this country" because his father was the first kid brought over on the airlift.

This episode is discussed by Muelhenbeck (pp. 39–40). Obama's father was brought over on the 1959 airlift; Kennedy helped finance the second one in 1960 (*Washington Post* article by Michael Dobbs, March 30, 2008).

Narrator: Kennedy was now the man to see for visiting African dignitaries. During the 1960 campaign against Richard Nixon, JFK mentioned Africa nearly five hundred times. The night of the election, the Algerian rebels listened by radio from their hillside camps, hoping their American friend would win the seesaw battle. It came as a shock to many, including Eisenhower and Nixon, when Kennedy won a narrow victory.

For Kennedy's out-front posture on Africa, see Muehlenebeck, p. 39. For his repeated mentions of Africa, see Muehlenbeck, p. 37. For the attention of Algerian rebels, see Mahoney, p. 33.

NARRATOR: The JFK case was such a mass of confusion that the Warren Commission version of the firing sequence differed from both the FBI's and the CIA's. Although it never specified the order of the shots, the Warren Report had one bullet going through Kennedy and Governor Connally. Another missing the car, hitting a bystander on Commerce Street, James Tague. And the final shot hitting Kennedy in the head.

The FBI concluded that all three bullets had struck inside the car—two hitting Kennedy and one hitting Connally.

The CIA analysis said that the first shot did not come from the sixth-floor window. And further, that two shooters were involved. Their photographic analysis, based on the Zapruder film, was closely held. Records showing that it only went to director John McCone. Like the FBI analysis, the Warren Commission either never received it, or chose to ignore it.

This triangular dispute, which is not well known to the public, is described by Gerald McKnight in his book *Breach of Trust* (pp. 4–7, pp. 151–52). Also see the ARRB interview of CIA photo analyst Homer McMahon, July 14, 1997.

David Mantik: The Warren Commission put itself in a straitjacket. They could not possibly allow more than three shots because four shots or more would have clearly indicated conspiracy and they were not going there.

Cyril Wecht: When Oswald, under the Warren Commission's conclusion, had the best opportunity, it's a lineup, and as the cars approached on Houston Street, then getting closer and closer and there you are, Mr. Oswald, it's coming right at you. But you wait until the cars turn and they're going down Elm Street on a diagonal downward. And the vision is partially blocked by foliage on the trees. And that's when you shoot. So somehow the first shot, which he should have been better prepared for, he missed. And then the second shot is the one that ultimately they said was the hero of the single-bullet theory that went into Kennedy's back and produced the seven wounds in him and Connally. And then the third shot, hit, according to them, Kennedy in the head.

The Warren Report did not pinpoint which shots hit Kennedy (pp. 110–17). In those pages, the Commission arranges various scenarios as to which shot missed: first, second, third. Dr. Wecht is reciting a sequence which is as likely or more than another three-shot scenario.

Cyril Wecht: As they began to reflect upon this into March, April of 1964, they were faced with a seemingly impossible physical incongruity. Because they had a problem with a chronology of the Zapruder film, which showed that Connally is hit about 1.5 seconds after Kennedy is hit. Well, the problem was the best marksman they could find, it takes 2.3 seconds from shot to shot for this piece of junk, the most inferior weapon of the genre, the Mannlicher- Carcano, now 2.3 seconds versus 1.5 seconds. Arlen Specter, junior legal counsel later to become district attorney and then US senator from Pennsylvania, he is the one that gave birth to the single-bullet theory.

The FBI firing experiments are noted by Donald B. Thomas in his book *Hear No Evil* (p. 135). The timing problem with the Zapruder film is described by Josiah Thompson in *Six Seconds in Dallas* (p. 9). See also *The Assassination Chronicles* by Edward Epstein (p. 45, pp. 124–26). Epstein writes that both Specter and Norman Redlich, a senior counsel, determined the report had to say one bullet hit both Kennedy and Connally (ibid., p. 155).

Cyril Wecht: Aha! What if one bullet made all seven wounds? What if one bullet went into Kennedy's back and came out his neck and then went into Connally's back through his chest, out the front of his chest, into the back of his right wrist, out the front of his right wrist and into his left thigh? And that is the single-bullet theory, which Mark Lane, I think, was the first one to dub as "the magic-bullet theory."

Chapter 4 of Lane's book *Rush to Judgment* bears the title, "The Magic Bullet."

David Mantik: CE 399 was the magic bullet and all government investigations so far have treated that bullet as absolutely foundational to this case, never doubted that it was involved in the case, and never really looked at the provenance of the bullet.

Narrator: The other problem is the lack of damage to the bullet after going through two men, smashing two bones, and making seven wounds. Dr. Joseph Dolce was a much-honored battlefield surgeon during World War II. He worked for the Warren Commission.

Dolce clip: And so they gave us the original rifle, the Mannlicher-Carcano, plus a hundred bullets, 6.5 millimeters. And we went and we shot at cadaver wrists. And in every instance, the front or the tip of the bullet was smashed. Under no circumstances do I feel that this bullet could hit the wrist and still not be deformed.

Narrator: Dolce came to believe that two bullets had struck Connally. Since Arlen Specter prescreened the medical witnesses for the commission, Dolce's name is not in the Warren Report, and his testimony not in the volumes.

For Dolce's view on the two bullets striking Connally, see McKnight, pp. 186–87.

Narrator: In September of 1978, the House Select Committee on Assassinations tried again to link CE 399 to the case through the work of Dr. Vincent Guinn, and a test called neutron activation analysis, which attempted to show that all fragments and CE 399 came from only two bullets.

David Mantik: Robert Blakey, who was in charge of the investigation for the House, claimed that their work with neutron activation analysis was the linchpin of the case against Oswald.

Guinn testified last on Friday, September 8, 1978, the first week of HSCA open hearings. It was announced that his work was independently verified, by who was not revealed. See Donald Thomas, *Hear No*

Evil (p. 481). The results of his tests were leaked in advance, see *The Assassinations*, edited by James DiEugenio and Lisa Pease, p. 77.

Narrator: Partly because of the renewed interest in the JFK case, this test came under severe criticism.

Gary Aguilar: People who had deep experience in neutron activation analysis at Lawrence Livermore Laboratory, re-looked at that and said that those fragments that they came out might not have even come from Mannlicher-Carcano bullets, and they could have come from any one of five bullets, not the two. So that was that has been completely debunked. So much so that neutron activation analysis, which the FBI used to use in prosecutions, was given up more than ten years ago. They don't do that anymore because they know that it's junk science.

For examinations of why this kind of testing will not be used again, see William Tobin's study in the forensic journal *The Champion* of July 2004, pp. 12–22. See also the article by Erik Randich and Patrick Grant in *Journal of Forensic Sciences*, July 2006, pp. 717–28.

Narrator: Without this test, there is no proof that CE 399 and the fragments in Governor Connally's wrist are from the same bullet. And even Connally refused to accept the single- bullet theory.

Oliver Stone: Did the Warren Commission do experiments with the alleged Oswald rifle on skulls?

Gary Aguilar: They did human skull experiments in 1964 at Aberdeen Proving Ground. They filled human skulls with human-equivalent material and they were testified to under oath by Larry Sturdivan at the House Select Committee, he says, "As you can see, every skull, all ten of them moved away from the rifle."

Michael Chesser: The trajectory from the sixth floor of the Texas School Book Depository—Z312 or Z313—the trajectory would have resulted in a blowout through the face, and this was confirmed even by the government's own data.

> For the skulls moving forward in the direction of the bullet, see HSCA vol. 1, p. 404. For the photographs depicting a blown out front of the face, see Warren Commission, vol. 17, Commission Exhibits 861 and 862.

Narrator: And photos from the autopsy clearly show Kennedy's face to be intact. And the Warren Commission was aware of something else that was wrong with their evidence.

Archival NBC clip: "All kinds of ballistic tests show that the bullets, in fact, came from that rifle. That was his rifle. You took a picture of him with it. His palm prints and fingerprints were all over the School Book Depository." "No, no, no. You have been misinformed. The ballistics test did not prove anything at all."

Archive clip: This is the weapon that was used, a rather well-worn military rifle.

Narrator: Is this really true, or is it a myth that has been allowed to assume the status of accepted fact since few have challenged it?

Oliver Stone: Is the rifle in evidence today the same rifle the Commission said Oswald ordered through the mail?

Brian Edwards: The rifle that Lee Oswald allegedly ordered under an alias of Alex Hidell was obtained through Klein's Sporting Goods store in Chicago as a mail order. Got it out of *American Rifleman* magazine. He wrote on the coupon he wanted a thirty-six-inch model, Mannlicher-Carcano, 6.5 mm for $19.95. Robert Frazier was one of the examiners, he was a firearms expert for the FBI, and he testified that he did measure it and the measurement was 40.2 inches in length from barrel to stock. There's a 4.2-inch difference in the one he ordered versus what they found in the Book Depository.

The Commission avoided this issue of differing rifle lengths. But the *American Rifleman* ad which they said was sent in by A. J. Hidell described a thirty-six-inch model rifle. The coupon is in Warren Commission, vol. 17, p. 635. For the differing length of the rifle found in the Depository, see Warren Report, p. 553.

Narrator: Klein's may have indeed delivered a different Mannlicher-Carcano model to Oswald, but there are other anomalies to this story. The model that Oswald ordered showed these strap attachment points on the bottom of the barrel and stock.

Brian Edwards: In the photograph is Lieutenant Carl Day with the Dallas Police Department bringing a rifle out of the Book Depository. One of the straps at the back of the gun is on the left side of the stock embedded in the stock. That's clearly not the rifle that was ordered, or at least appears in the Klein's Sporting Goods store.

Narrator: The straps shown in the so-called backyard photos are on the bottom and not on the side of the stock.

Brian Edwards: Marina Oswald took backyard photographs of Lee Oswald holding a rifle and a pistol on his hip. And in that first photograph that she took three of, Commission Exhibit 133A and 133B, show a ring on the ring finger of the right hand. [On] 133C, the ring appears on the left hand. In effect, the Dallas Police show Lee Oswald one of the pictures while he was still in custody. He said, that's my face, but I don't remember ever having that picture taken of me.

See *New York Times*, November 21, 1997, "Interrogator's Notes say Oswald Denied Assassination Role."

Narrator: There is also the question of how Oswald received the rifle.

Brian Edwards : If the rifle was sent from Klein's to the post office box rented under the name Lee Harvey Oswald, using the alias of A. J. Hidell on the coupon, it would have been sent back immediately because Oswald's name was the only one on the post office box. He was the only one authorized to receive mail. Marina didn't have, her name wasn't even on there. So that rifle was addressed to a person who didn't have the authority to have any mail received at that box. It should have been sent back to Klein's.

> For the postal regulation which defines the issue of mail only being deliverable to the person assigned the post office box, see letter of May 3, 1966, from Ralph Rea, director of the post office Special Services Branch to Stewart Galanor in his book *Cover-Up* (Document 37). The FBI concluded there was no other name assigned to the Dallas Box at this time besides Oswald's (Warren Commission, vol. 25, Commission Exhibit 2585, p. 4).

Narrator: But after all of these questions are asked, the underlying mystery remains: why would anyone use a rifle in an assassination knowing there was a paper trail that would lead back to them?

Oliver Stone: Was there a palm print found on the rifle?

Brian Edwards: The foremost fingerprint expert the FBI had, Sebastian Latona, took that rifle and attempted to lift prints off of the rifle, the stock and or the barrel. He testified to the Warren Commission that he found no usable prints anywhere on that rifle, on the metal or the stock. But yet, Lieutenant Day in Dallas, before the rifle went to Washington, said he found a partial palm print on the trigger guard on left side and a partial print underneath the stock on the barrel. But Sebastian Latona said there was no evidence of a lift had even been attempted.

Oliver Stone: No partials at all?

Brian Edwards: Nothing that he could use in court. There has to be eight points of identification. He found nothing that would match that.

The trigger guard prints were described as fragmentary by Latona. (Warren Commission, vol. 4, p. 24). Henry Hurt described them as vague. (*Reasonable Doubt,* p. 106). Unlike what Edwards describes, they ended up as fingerprints. For an early analysis of the palm print on the barrel, see Sylvia Meagher in *Accessories After the Fact,* pp. 120–27. It was further questioned by Henry Hurt in *Reasonable Doubt* in 1985 (see pp. 107–09). Later, in 1993, and again in 2003, PBS' *Frontline* tried to revive the trigger guard print by neutralizing Latona in their special, "Who Was Lee Harvey Oswald?" They ignored the facts that Latona said he analyzed Dallas Police photos, examined the rifle with a magnifying glass, broke down the rifle into pieces, processed the entire weapon, and used every kind of lighting possible. And he still could not produce prints of value (Warren Commission, vol. 4, pp. 20–23). *Frontline* went further and said they found a lost set of fingerprints. After two experts failed to find these were Oswald's, the late Vincent Scalice said on the telecast that they were his. As Pat Speer has pointed out, there are two serious problems with the long-forgotten fingerprint. First the "set" is not a set, it was actually two photos, and they were not new. And Scalice had them when he worked for the HSCA, as did the FBI, and they were not found to be identifiable (see Speer's article at his website "Unsmoking the Gun" and also HSCA Folder M-3, pp. 5–5 at the Mary Ferrell Foundation website).

Tom Alyea archive clip: I was able to enter this building, along with the Secret Service, and shoot exclusive footage of the finding of the assassin's gun and dusting for fingerprints.

Debra Conway: Tom Alyea was the first reporter that made it up to the sixth floor. I would say that he was a friend to the Dallas Police because he worked as a photographer on many crime scenes and he probably knew most of these officers that were there. They found the shells that were ejected from the rifle and they found what looked like someone's lunch.

Brian Edwards: Alyea described the location of these three shell casings, were almost in a line, facing the same direction within four or five inches of the front of the building. When you eject them from a rifle, they're not going to land like that. They're gonna be everywhere. Captain [Will] Fritz was brought over and he picked up these three shell casings and held them out in his hand, flat. And Alyea took motion picture film of it.

Narrator: This was before Dallas police photographer Robert Studebaker took pictures of the shells on the floor. So clearly that was a staged photo. The X's indicate where Tom Alyea recalls the original placement. The Warren Commission never interviewed Tom Alyea and they never questioned if the crime scene had been altered.

> For Alyea's observations on the crime scene see Michael Benson, "Who's Who in the JFK Assassination," p. 12, and also Allan Eaglesham's website, *The Sniper's Nest: Incarnations and Implications*. According to Alyea, the Dallas Police rearranged the boxes at the window also. For more evidence that the shells were arranged close together see *Cover-Up* by J. Gary Shaw with Larry Ray Harris, p. 70; Deputy Sheriff Luke Mooney admitted this to the late Mary Ferrell in December 1975, see page 80, footnote 32.

Oliver Stone: How important is chain of custody in a legal proceeding?

Brian Edwards: Chain of custody basically refers to the integrity of evidence. If I pick up a piece of evidence and I transfer it to somebody else for holding or processing, my name is the first name on this list. The second person who touches this and takes possession of it is next. And if you don't do that, there's no way to prove that the evidence you collected on day one is the same one you get on day twenty-five when you go to court.

Oliver Stone: Can you walk us through the magic bullet's chain of custody from the Parkland employees to the Secret Service to the FBI?

David Mantik: Well, the magic bullet was supposedly found on a stretcher at Parkland Hospital and it went through several hands before it got to the Secret Service. Richard Johnson was the first Secret Service agent to handle it, and he carried it back to Washington, DC. When he got back to Washington, DC, he gave it to the chief of the Secret Service, who was James Rowley. And at the White House, James Rowley gave it to Elmer Lee Todd and Todd then took it to the FBI lab and gave it to Robert Frazier. We have interesting information produced by John Hunt, a private citizen who went to the archives on four or five occasions to track down the story about the magic bullet and what he found was truly astounding.

The best early chronicle of the chain of custody of CE 399, the magic bullet, is in Ray Marcus's pamphlet, *The Bastard Bullet*.

Debra Conway: He practically moved into the National Archives in Washington, DC. They allowed him to set up a desk with a computer and his own scanner. And he also did something different. He didn't interview policemen and FBI people, and he wasn't swayed by their excuses. He went straight to: this is what you told and you signed your name.

Narrator: Working with FBI and Warren Commission documents, John Hunt asked the most basic question: Was CE 399 in evidence the same bullet that was found on the stretcher?

David Mantik: At 7:30 at night, this is the day of the assassination, November 22, 1963, a bullet appears in the record and it's signed for by Robert Frazier, who is the main investigator at the FBI lab. And it's not just one document. There are multiple documents that indicate that Frazier signed for a bullet at 7:30 that night. Now, here's where things get interesting. Elmer Lee Todd received the bullet at the White House from chief of the Secret Service James Rowley. And Todd documents very clearly in writing that he got this bullet at 8:50 p.m. How is that possible? How can Robert Frazier receive the bullet in the lab at 7:30 from Elmer Lee Todd when Todd didn't get the bullet until 8:50?

Debra Conway: You would think that they would have handled it, you know, like it would've been gold going to the bank. There it is in the record. Someone is lying about when they got the bullet.

David Mantik: It gets worse, though. Todd initialed that bullet. The one that he got at 8:50, and everyone else who touched the bullet after that initialed it too, including Robert Frazier. I went to the archives to look at this bullet. And specifically what we want to know is do we see Todd's initials on this bullet? He said he initialed the bullet. It is not there. Todd's initials are not on the magic bullet.

The late John Hunt's two watershed essays on CE 399 are at the *JFK Lancer* website: "Phantom Identification of the Magic Bullet" and "The Mystery of the 7:30 Bullet."

Gary Aguilar: I was very interested in finding out what the review board would show us about this. So we began scouring their evidence and we found out something very interesting. We found out that the Warren Report had from the FBI a report saying that the guys that found the bullet later identified that as the bullet they'd seen. The internal record didn't show that at all. The internal record said this bullet didn't look like that bullet at all. But the FBI reported to the Warren Commission that it did—it lied. We then talked to the FBI agent that was supposed to have carried that bullet around. His name was Bardwell Odum. I got Bardwell Odum on the phone. I sent him the documents that said that he had done this. He said, "I never had that bullet. I never showed any bullet to anyone. If I'd had the bullet, there'd be a 302. I would have filed a report, particularly in that era, everybody was very uptight about getting everything right." So we scoured for 302 reports. His name appears nowhere in the record. This is just something that the FBI invented.

The essay by Aguilar and Josiah Thompson on Bardwell Odum and CE 399 is at the *History Matters* website. It is titled "The Magic Bullet: Even More Magical Than We Knew."

David Mantik: In 1966, Josiah Thompson, who authored *Six Seconds in Dallas*, interviewed O. P. Wright, who was head of maintenance at Parkland Hospital and who had handled the bullet. He showed him a photograph of the magic bullet, which has a rounded tip. And O. P. Wright said, "No, it wasn't like that."

Gary Aguilar: Wright, who worked as a policeman, he knew bullets, and he said, "No, no, the bullet that we found at Parkland had a pointed tip." And he just pulled one out of his drawer that had a pointed tip and showed it. And it looks nothing like 399.

> This exchange between Thompson and Wright is written about and illustrated with photos in Thompson's *Six Seconds in Dallas*, p. 175. Thompson also shows that, in all probability, CE 399 was not even found on Connally's stretcher (pp. 154–66).

David Mantik: It's conceivable that some mysterious bullet showed up from who knows where, Todd did not initial it, and it ended up in the FBI lab as the magic bullet. But then we have the second bullet that arrives at 8:50. Is this possibly the pointed bullet that was seen by O. P. Wright in Dallas and that then disappeared? We don't have any idea where it is today. That scenario would fit the known facts.

Gary Aguilar: So it appears that a different bullet was found on that stretcher than 399. 399 shows up after it's been to the FBI lab. And one can only surmise that somewhere in the FBI they realized they had to close the loop on Oswald's guilt. And so they just switched it out, because none of the four people, either the guys at Parkland or the two Secret Service agents could identify the bullet. The guy who is supposed to have gotten confirmation that they did identify the bullet said he never did it. And the record supports that. So there is there's good reason to be very suspicious about the magic bullet.

Henry Lee: The chain of custody doesn't start in the laboratory, it starts at the crime scene. Each piece of evidence should be photographed, documented, and preserved properly. From the scene, evidence is collected, sent to the laboratory. We have to keep the chain of custody when they enter the lab. Who examined? Who did the closer analysis, and each step have to maintain and until submit to the court. If this chain broke, then my evidence become inadmissible.

> The ballistics evidence is even more dubious than the above. For as Henry Hurt notes, the FBI found no copper on the curb where James Tague was hit (Hurt, p. 136). Considering the ammunition allegedly used by Oswald was encased in copper, this is hard to fathom. Further, reporter Jeff Meek has found FBI lab notes showing that no copper was found on JFK's necktie or the front neckband of his shirt. But copper was found around the back wound. Meek writes that this indicates the throat wound was a separate shot (*Hot Springs Village Voice,* January 4, 2022).

Narrator: Sunday, November 24th, 1963, Lee Harvey Oswald has been in detention for two days after he was caught in a movie theater just an hour after the assassination. He is being questioned for long hours, but there is no stenographer present and the police say there is no tape recorder in the room.

> There was no stenographic record and no tape recording made during the approximately twelve hours that Oswald was in detention and then charged for murder (see Warren Report, p. 180). There were summary reports made by Captain Fritz, two FBI agents, Secret Service Inspector Thomas Kelley and postal inspector Harry Holmes (see Appendix XI in the Warren Report). The longest of these was by Fritz, at about twelve pages. (Secret Service agent Forrest Sorrells had about a half page of Oswald notes in his Ruby notebook. See Warren Commission, vol. 21, p. 543.) In 1995, FBI agent James Hosty produced some notes he previously said he destroyed for his book *Assignment Oswald*. In 1997, the Review Board discovered several pages of handwritten notes made by Fritz (see "Oswald Interrogation Notes Released," *Greensboro News and Record*, November 20, 1997).

Oswald newsreel: I would like some legal representation. These police officers have not allowed me to have any.

Narrator: He has confessed to nothing. He has, in fact, denied any guilt to his only audience, the press and spectators in the hallways. Lee Harvey Oswald, while he was alive, in the strongest terms, denied he committed the crime.

Oswald newsreel: "Did you kill the president?" "No, I have not been charged with that. In fact, nobody has said that to me yet. First thing I heard about was when the newspaper reporters in the hall asked me that question."

Narrator: It would be hard to say that he shot Kennedy in some cause as a politically inspired shooter would proclaim.

Oswald: I'm just a patsy.

Narrator: He is about to be transferred to the county jail. The FBI has called the Dallas police on both Saturday and Sunday, warning them of threats to kill the alleged assassin of President Kennedy. The police have decided to proceed with the transfer anyway. As you watch, listen for the two car horns. One as Oswald emerges and the other the moment before Jack Ruby fires.

> For the warnings, see report by NPR correspondent Jessica Taylor of October 26, 2017.

Narrator: It was the shocking live murder of Lee Harvey Oswald that terminated the Dallas Police as investigators. J. Edgar Hoover wrote a memo to the newly sworn-in President Johnson that evening, saying, "The thing I am concerned about is having something issued so we can convince the public that Oswald is the real assassin." The day before, he had told Johnson that "the case, as it stands now, isn't strong enough to be able to get a conviction." The next day, Deputy Attorney General Nicholas Katzenbach wrote a memo to the White House saying the public must be satisfied that Oswald did not have confederates who were still at large, and that the evidence was such that he would have been convicted at trial. "We need something to head off public speculation or congressional hearings of the wrong sort." With those two memos, the FBI became the main investigatory arm in the JFK case. There was never any serious discussion that independent investigators were needed. The idea in Washington now became to contain the crime to Oswald. Therefore, cutting off any connections to a wider Russia-Cuba-communist conspiracy which could provoke the threat of atomic war.

Hoover's memo to LBJ is written about by reporter Alex Johnson in an NBC news report of October 26, 2017. The tape and transcript of Hoover saying that the case against Oswald is not that strong is at history-matters.com titled "LBJ-Hoover 11–22–63." The memorandum by Katzenbach is at the *Mary Ferrell Foundation* website, labeled simply "Katzenbach Memo."

Narrator: The day after he was murdered, the *New York Times* pronounced Oswald as the killer of President Kennedy.

Narrator: The Warren Commission concluded that Ruby shot Oswald acting alone. It was not premeditated or planned, and Ruby had no help entering the building.

The issue about Ruby's acting spontaneously with no help is described in the Warren Report (pp. 21–22, p. 219, pp. 354–57). The HSCA raised questions about this verdict and decided that, unlike the Warren Report, Ruby probably did not shoot Oswald by coming down the Main Street ramp (see HSCA, vol. 9, pp. 132–46). The HSCA also concluded that the Commission's polygraph examination of Ruby was filled with procedural and technical errors to the point it was so flawed as to be forensically worthless (vol. 8, pp. 199–221). For another examination of Ruby's polygraph test, see Don Thomas's *See No Evil* (pp. 537–57).

Jack Ruby archive: The people who have so much to gain, and had such an ulterior motive, have put me in the position I'm in, will never let the true facts come aboveboard to the world.

Narrator: Two months after winning his appeal and being granted a new trial outside of Dallas, Jack Ruby was found riddled with cancer in his prison cell. He was placed in the hospital, and one month before his new trial was to begin, he died. The Warren Commission never exposed Ruby's connections to the Mafia, the FBI, or with gunrunning and gambling figures in Miami and Cuba.

> See article by Brian Wice in *Houston Chronicle* of September 28, 2018, for the legal status of Ruby's case at the time of his death. Attorney Phil Burleson was the man most responsible for the successful appeal of Ruby's case. (See *New York Times*, June 1, 1995, obituary, "Phil Burleson, 61, Jack Ruby's Lawyer.") The HSCA examined Ruby's organized crime connections in vol. 9. This included people like gunrunner Robert McKeown, Dallas mob figure Joe Civello, local restauranteur Joe Campisi, and gambler Lewis McWillie, who worked for Santo Trafficante and whom Ruby visited in Cuba. The HSCA also stated that it is likely Ruby visited with Trafficante in Cuba. (See HSCA Final Report, pp. 151–54.) The Committee also did an analysis of Ruby's phone calls to various underworld figures in 1963, which the Commission did not. (vol. 9, pp. 188–204). See also "The Secret Life of Jack Ruby" by William Scott Malone in *New Times*, January 23, 1978. Ruby's status as an FBI informant was revealed and then publicized by the Church Committee (Henry Hurt, *Reasonable Doubt*, p. 177).

Brian Edwards: On other parts of the case that the government put against Lee Oswald. Obviously, he was dead. He had no chance to have cross-examined witnesses. He had no lawyer appointed. Mark Lane, an attorney out of New York, tried to get legal representation for Lee Oswald. In fact, went to the commission and asked can I represent Lee Oswald and they denied it. Because again this is, this is not a typical court hearing.

> Lane's request to represent Oswald and the refusal by Chief Counsel J. Lee Rankin is contained in Warren Commission, vol. 24, Commission Exhibit 2033.

Robert Tanenbaum archive clip: I can tell you from my experience trying several hundred cases to verdict, and being responsible for thousands of cases as the head of criminal courts and running the homicide bureau, that I don't believe there's any courtroom in America where Oswald would have been convicted on the evidence that was presented before the Warren Commission.

JFK: Destiny Betrayed

Chapter 3

Narrator: The one physician present at both Parkland Hospital and the Bethesda morgue was George Burkley, Kennedy's personal doctor. Like Knudsen, he was a Navy officer and as a rear admiral, he ranked above him. Burkley signed the autopsy descriptive sheet with a bullet in the back at the level of T-3, and he also signed Kennedy's death certificate, which also placed that wound in the back. That death certificate is not in the Warren Commission volumes, and the descriptive sheet in the commission volumes does not have Burkley's signature. Arlen Specter did not depose George Burkley, but Burkley went further than that.

Archive clip: Dr. Burkley told me a simple matter of a bullet right through the head.

Narrator: Dr. Burkley did an interview with the JFK Library in 1967 and was asked this question:

Archive audio clip: "Do you agree with the Warren Report on the number of bullets that entered the president's body?" "I would not care to be quoted on that."

Narrator: In 1977, through his lawyer, he wrote a letter to Richard Sprague, chief counsel of the House Select Committee on Assassinations. He said he had information indicating that others besides Oswald must have participated in the assassination. He was willing to talk about it at this time. Sprague, who had made clear his intention to fully investigate the CIA's involvement, was forced out two weeks later. Dr. Burkley submitted a written statement to the House Select Committee, but there is no official record of him being deposed as a witness.

Doug Horne: In 1982, he told JFK researcher Henry Hurt that, "I know there was more than one gunman." And when Henry Hurt tried to recontact Burkley for more details, Burkley cut him off at the knees. "I don't want to talk about it anymore." The very next year, Burkley talked to Michael Kurtz, another JFK researcher, [and] told him that he knew there was a conspiracy to kill the president and that he recalled an exit wound in the back of President Kennedy's head. Now, that's a very significant statement, that the only doctor we know of who was present at both Parkland for treatment and at Bethesda during the autopsy, told Michael Kurtz in 1983 that Kennedy had an exit wound in the back of his head. When Kurtz tried to recontact Burkley for more details, Burkley cut him off at the knees: "I don't want to talk about this anymore." Dr. Burkley was deceased by the time the review board was impaneled. So then Jeremy decided, well, we can ask the executor of his estate, his daughter, to sign a waiver so that we could go to the law firm that Mr. Illig used to work for, because he was deceased also, and see if there were any records in the file of Mr. Illig that would reveal what it was he wanted to tell the HSCA in detail. And she said she would do that. And then Jeremy called her on the phone, she had completely changed her mind and adamantly refused to sign it and terminated the phone call.

For the material on Burkley and his comments, see Henry Hurt, *Reasonable Doubt*, pp. 48,49; Horne, *Inside the ARRB* vol. 3, pp. 927–28; and the essays "The Missing Physician" at the Mary Ferrell Foundation website as well as Milicent Cranor's "Kennedy Assassination: Evidence Seen by JFK's Doctor Suppressed," at *WhoWhatWhy*, October 17, 2017.

Don Miller: When I was a teenager, Dr. Burkley and his family, four children and my father and our family and four children shared a duplex, lived together at the Newport Naval Hospital. He had a son, George, who was my age, sixteen, and we became buddies. I looked him up again in 2012 and I asked him about what his dad had told him and his siblings about his role in the Kennedy case. And the only thing that he would say was that he couldn't understand why the Warren Commission never asked him to testify. Dr. Burkley knew perfectly well why he wasn't asked to testify before the Warren Commission. The reason he didn't say anything to his children was that he didn't want them to know that he was intimately involved in the cover-up. Dr. Burkley's death certificate makes the single-bullet theory bogus. And the way the Warren Commission dealt with it was, they didn't publish the death certificate.

Oliver Stone: If the ARRB had been a criminal investigation, would you have granted Burkley immunity for his testimony?

Doug Horne: We should have re-deposed Humes and Boswell after giving them immunity. And if Burkley, had still been around, he would have been another candidate because he was at the center of the photographic cover-up. By the way, George Burkley was a rear admiral. He was promoted to vice admiral by Lyndon Johnson. So he promoted Burkley to the highest possible rank, kept him on as military physician, and the last person to walk out of the White House with Lyndon Johnson the day he left office was George Burkley.

Archive audio clip: Using the most precise medical terminology. OK, let's say it was on the right rear. And he lifted up the flap and you could see the hole and there was brain and spinal fluid dripping down out of it. Then I noticed it was dripping down into a bucket.

Narrator: In addition to this large avulsion of wound in the rear of the skull, seven personnel at Parkland Hospital saw cerebellum at the bottom of the skull.

Cyril Wecht: The brain consists of two large cerebral hemispheres. And then lower down, posteriorly are two hemispheres—the cerebellum. They differ in coloration. They differ in the topographical markings.

Oliver Stone: So seven doctors at Parkland Hospital claim to have seen cerebellum.

> The testimony is by Charles Baxter (Warren Commission, vol. 6, p. 41); Charles "Jim" Carrico (Warren Commission, vol. 6, p. 6); Kemp Clark (Warren Commission, vol. 6, p. 26, Warren Commission, vol. 17, p. 10); Marion Jenkins (Warren Commission, vol. 6, p. 46, and Commission Exhibit 391); Robert McClelland (Warren Commission, vol. 6, p. 33); Malcom Perry (HSCA Vol. 7, p. 302); and Paul Peters (ARRB interview of 8-27-98). Clark was a neurosurgeon, therefore his testimony carries great weight. As Milicent Cranor has pointed out, the cerebellum is not mentioned in the main autopsy report, nor was it discussed by the pathologists before the Warren Commission.

Michael Chesser: In 1963, it was one of the top trauma centers in the country, and it's still one of the top trauma centers. Dr. Robert McClelland said he saw a clump of the cerebellum, a large clump, fall out of the skull onto the emergency room bed. Then we have Dr. Kemp Clark. He went into detail with the Warren Commission about the result of all this loss of cerebellar tissue if President Kennedy had survived the wound. So there was no doubt that there was loss of cerebellar tissue.

NARRATOR: This reliable eyewitness testimony indicates that the wound in Kennedy's rear skull extended quite low. And also there was severe damage to that sector of the brain. Yet in the autopsy report written at Bethesda by James Humes, there is no mention of the cerebellum and he did not testify about it to the Warren Commission.

Cyril Wecht: So these guys, good old Texan respected doctors, and they've seen hundreds and thousands of brains, especially the neurosurgeon, saw cerebellum having been damaged, significantly displaced in the occipital area. The doctors who did the autopsy, read the autopsy report from Humes and Boswell. The cerebellum is intact. Who do you believe—do you believe these Texas doctors? Or do you believe the two career naval pathologists working under military control? Who do you believe as to whether or not the cerebellum was damaged?

Wecht here is discussing the supplementary autopsy report which was done later and has a handwritten date on it of December 6, 1963.

Narrator: There were many witnesses at Parkland and Bethesda who, in addition to seeing damaged cerebellum, also testified to seeing a severely damaged brain.

Michael Chesser: At Parkland, we have witnesses. One doctor, Walter Midgett, saw brain matter spray all over the interior of the limousine.

In an interview Midgett did with researcher Wallace Milam, on February 8, 1993, he said that brain was all over the back of the car. Nurse Diana Bowron noted Midgett's presence at the car in Warren Commission, vol. 6, p. 136, as did Nurse Bertha Lozano, vol. 21, p. 213.

Narrator: Interestingly, the Secret Service washed out parts of the limo before shipping it to Washington, thus removing blood, brain, and tissue evidence from the crime scene.

There is a photo depicting this, including a pail of water adjacent to the car. It was included in the documentary *Inside the Target Car.* The Secret Service agent who probably got the pail and did some wiping was Sam Kinney (See Commission Document 80, p. 1).

Gary Aguilar: Anybody who's seen the Zapruder film can see Kennedy's head explodes and debris flies all over the place. Jackie Kennedy climbed out onto the trunk of the limousine, picked up a chunk of the president's brain, had it with her, took it and gave it to one of the doctors at Parkland Hospital.

Dr. Marion Jenkins described the transfer from Jackie Kennedy to himself in the *Miami Herald* of October 20, 1988, p. 22A.

Michael Chesser: And then we have Dr. McClelland talking about the large clump of the cerebellum that fell out onto the emergency room.

McClelland's testimony is in Warren Commission, vol. 6, p. 43.

Gary Aguilar: And when you look at the autopsy photographs of the brain, which I've seen the originals of, you can just see that the brain is disrupted. But very little of the tissue is missing. Then we look at the autopsy report of the brain and what they call the supplemental brain examination. The brain in evidence that's weighed there weighs fifteen hundred grams.

The supplementary autopsy report is Commission Exhibit 391 and is included in the Warren Report beginning on page 544.

Michael Chesser: Fifteen hundred grams is an above average weight for an adult male brain. There was one report of eight thousand autopsies and the average weight of an adult male brain was thirteen hundred thirty-six grams, so they are saying that President Kennedy's brain was well above the average weight.

This was in a Dutch study published in June 1994 in the academic journal, *Der Pathologe*, and is available online.

Gary Aguilar: Where did all that brain tissue disappear to that flies around Dealey Plaza that Jackie has in her hand, that everybody's picking off of their clothes?

Doug Horne: An FBI agent, Frank O'Neill, told the Review Board that over half of the mass of the brain was missing. He saw the brain removed at the autopsy. A lot of the mass missing was in the back. That's what mortician Tom Robinson said.

O'Neill deposition of September 12, 1997, for the ARRB, pp. 116–17. Robinson's information is in a summary of his interview for the ARRB on June 21, 1996.

Michael Chesser: So it's impossible for the actual weight of President Kennedy's brain to be fifteen hundred grams. This is just one more reason that this cannot be President Kennedy's brain in the photographs we have stored at the Archives.

Oliver Stone: What's the purpose of sectioning a brain and how is it done?

Cyril Wecht: When a brain is to be examined in detail, you don't do it in the fresh state. Fresh brain has the consistency of a well-done soft-boiled egg. I don't mean to be crude, but this is the best metaphor I can think of. You fix it in formalin and in two weeks, the consistency becomes that of a hard-boiled egg. And now think of slicing a hard-boiled egg. They say—and look at the Warren Commission report, look at the autopsy report—it says serial sections, parallel sections of the brain are not made in order to preserve the specimen. Preserve the specimen? For whom? For Jacqueline Kennedy's mantelpiece? For the president's grandchildren? For a museum? Preserve it for whom?

This preservation issue appears in the Supplementary Autopsy Report Commission Exhibit 391 in the Warren Report, p. 544.

Michael Chesser: Without sectioning the brain, there was no way for them to properly trace the trajectory of the wounds.

Doug Horne: The review board had a consultant—a renowned forensic pathologist. He looked at the brain photographs and he said, this is a very well-fixed brain. It's all gray. It's not pink at all. It's been fixed for two or three weeks in formaldehyde. It's been fixed at least two weeks, maybe as long as three weeks. I looked at Jeremy Gunn and he looked at me and the hair stood up on the back of my neck, because I knew that JFK's brain was examined less than three days after he was killed.

Gary Aguilar: One can only imagine that they wanted the damage to the brain to be consistent with the hypothesis that Oswald had done the shooting. So if you had a defect going all the way to the back of the head, like so many witnesses testified to it, it might raise questions about whether that huge defect could have been caused by a single shot to the head, as Oswald is supposed to have done.

Michael Chesser: There are two photographs of the brain at the archives. I viewed those in 2015. The brain looked to me to be distorted. My first thought was that the brain had been sitting in a jar of formaldehyde for a long time. At a teaching hospital there was no shortage of brains. Autopsies were very frequent. Frequently the brain was saved for teaching medical students so it would not have been difficult to find a brain, a replacement for these photographs.

Gary Aguilar: Dr. Humes destroyed his original autopsy notes. Now, Dr. Humes, the chief autopsy pathologist, and what we all know as doctors—notes taken while you're doing something are much, much more important and are likely to be closer to the truth than anything you write later. And he admitted that he destroyed autopsy notes.

Cyril Wecht: You destroyed your original notes in a medical legal autopsy? And remember, that night Oswald is still alive. You're going to be asked, doctor, at some point in time under oath to give sworn testimony, "Why did you destroy those notes? Doctor, doesn't a pathologist keep his notes?"

> Horne was in the room during this testimony and his review of this issue is in vol. I, p. 95 of *Inside the ARRB.*

Gary Aguilar: And he said, well, I just destroyed my own autopsy notes because they were splattered with the president's blood. And I didn't want them to become objects of morbid curiosity. The third doctor, Dr. Finck, who was there, also wrote some notes and complained bitterly about the fact that his notes disappeared, too.

Doug Horne: He was so upset because he had to go home and reconstruct all his notes from memory.

> The ARRB found out about this through an affidavit submitted by Dr. Leonard Saslaw, a friend of Finck's, dated May 15, 1996.

Narrator: Today, after almost sixty years, due to an incomplete and questionable autopsy, no one can say for sure what happened. A riddle, like the Sphinx.

Narrator: The complete set of autopsy and brain examination photographs are housed at the National Archives, but are only available to congressional researchers and those experts authorized by the Kennedy family.

Oliver Stone: Who was the autopsy photographer?

Doug Horne: John Stringer. He was a Navy civilian. He was widely respected. He had written a textbook on medical photography for the Navy. So he was the photographer of record. He photographed the autopsy itself and also photographed the president's brain three days later.

David Mantik: So the brain autopsy or autopsies, there were probably two such events, occurred later and were not done on November 22nd. John Stringer reports that he was present at the brain autopsy, which apparently occurred on the Monday after, which would have been November 25th.

> In his book *Inside the ARRB*, Horne presents his case for a brain examination on November 25. In the form of a chart, he uses five witnesses and nine pieces of evidence (vol. 3, p. 791). The ARRB discovered evidence that there may have been an unrecorded brain dissection. This was then kept out of the official record.

Doug Horne: We were very careful to question Mr. Stringer at the very beginning of his deposition about all the photographs he took and ask him what kind of film he used for black and white. What kind of film he used for color. Jeremy Gunn showed Stringer the color positive transparencies of the brain. And Stringer immediately noted: Well, these aren't Kodak. These might be ANSCO also, he said, I don't see the name of the manufacturer on here, but these might be ANSCO, he says, but these don't have the right notches in the corner. So Jeremy Gunn said, "Did you use this film with these notches in it when you shot the brain?" He says, "Not as far as I know." Half of the brain photos are taken of a brain from above. Superior views. Which is what Stringer said he shot of the complete organ. But the other half of the brain photos in the archives are taken of the bottom. They're called basilar views. And he said, "Did you take basilar views?" Stringer said, "No, not as far as I know."

Stringer's deposition was on July 16, 1996; the points about him denouncing that he took the extant pictures of the brain are on pages 219–26.

Gary Aguilar: He testified to, as did two of the autopsy pathologists, that they took photographs of Jack Kennedy's head by peeling back the scalp to demonstrate the entrance wound in the back of the skull, both from the inside of the skull and the outside of the skull. There are no such photographs in the file.

For Humes's testimony on this, see Warren Commission, vol. 2, p. 352. For Pierre Finck's, see his HSCA interview of March 11, 1978, pp 89–91. Before the ARRB, the official autopsy photographer, John Stringer, and his assistant, Floyd Riebe, agreed this had been done. For Stringer, see ARRB interview of July 16, 1996, p. 71, for Riebe, see ARRB interview of May 12, 1997, p. 39.

Doug Horne: What we have here is evidence that impugns the authenticity of the brain photographs in the National Archives. If there was a trial today, these brain photographs would not be admissible as evidence.

The Legal Information Institute of Cornell Law School, for example, states that a witness has to identify the photo or film "as a correct representation of a scene with which he is familiar." He then adopts the picture as part of his testimony (Rule 1002, Requirement of the Original).

Narrator: Doesn't this all lead to the question, if Stringer did not take these photographs, then who did?

Narrator: Robert Knudsen was one of the most fascinating stories that the Review Board encountered. Knudsen was a Navy photographer who was detailed to the White House in 1958. If you read his obituaries in the *New York Times* and *Washington Post*, you will see that he is credited with photographing Kennedy's autopsy, except officially he was not.

See "Robert Knudsen, 61, Dies," *Washington Post*, January 29, 1989 and "Robert Knudsen Dies: Photographer was 61," *New York Times*, January 31, 1989.

Doug Horne: Robert Knudsen was not interviewed by the Warren Commission. So they finally found Robert Knudsen in 1978. And to its credit, the House Select Committee did a deposition of him. To their discredit, they never published it, they buried it for fifty years and it got released in 1993. And I know why they buried it. Because everything he told them about autopsy photography contradicted what they thought they knew.

Oliver Stone: What did Knudsen tell them?

Doug Horne: So he says Burkley had me develop these black-and-white negatives on Saturday, November 23rd, and that's when I saw photographs of probes in the body. Well, they didn't like that, they really didn't know whether to believe him or not, because there are no pictures of probes in the body in the official collection. But he was sure that he developed those negatives and saw them.

Knudsen mentioned the probes in the body and a close-up shot of a cavity in Kennedy's head in his HSCA interview of August 11, 1978 (pp. 21–22). He later said this cavity was in the right rear of the head (p. 37). These photos do not exist today.

David Mantik: He has never said he took photographs of the brain, but he implies that he was very busy taking photographs of the body. In fact, his wife was interviewed later by the Assassination Records Review Board. He told her that the photographs had been burned deliberately by the Secret Service and that one photograph in particular, presumably the back of the head, had been severely altered. Gloria Knudsen so disturbed by this after his death in 1989 that she actually contacted some of his colleagues there in the Navy, and they assured her that this was what he had told them, too. In fact, he had told them that he had seen photographs of the back of JFK's head that showed a large wound low in the back of the head.

The ARRB interviewed surviving family members of the deceased Robert Knudsen on May 10, 1996. Horne wrote a memo on this three days later. The matters mentioned by Mantik above, plus Horne's comments about the probes in the body, are in this memo. The information about other military associates confirming what her husband said to Gloria is in a phone memorandum by Horne of a call to Gloria Knudsen on October 8, 1996.

Doug Horne: Stringer's still the autopsy photographer of record. I think they both took pictures. And I personally think that many of John Stringer's pictures never made it into the official collection. And a lot of the ones we're looking at are Robert Knudsen's pictures.

David Mantik: Saundra Spencer worked at the Anacostia Facility, the Naval Photographic Center, which is quite separate from the Bethesda lab. And that weekend she received film from both James Fox and the Secret Service and from Robert Knudsen.

Knudsen acknowledged that he delivered film to the Anacostia lab in his HSCA interview of August 11, 1978 (pp. 5–6). These were given to him by George Burkley. In this deposition, Knudsen mentions Sandy Spencer working at the Anacostia lab (p. 14).

Doug Horne: The photographs that Saundra Spencer developed, which never made it into the official record, the only evidence we have of them is her testimony. Saundra Spencer was visibly upset when she looked at the official autopsy photographs. She started to cry.

Oliver Stone: In front of the review board.

Doug Horne: Yes, she started to cry in front of Jeremy and I and the person from the archives. Because she said, "I developed pictures of him and his family for almost three years, and he never looked like this." And she said, "He did not look this bad in the photographs I developed on Sunday." She said he looks terrible in these photographs. He's all beat up. There's blood everywhere, that open body cavity. She said there were no open body cavities. He was very cleaned up. It was very respectful. And in one of the photographs she developed, there was a brain, an intact brain sitting next to the body, the nude body of the president. Strange, first of all, that it's intact because we know from FBI Agent Frank O'Neill that the brain was more than half missing when they removed it from the cranium.

In Spencer's deposition of June 5, 1997 (pp. 44–56), she looked at the extant autopsy photos and denied they were the same as the ones she saw on the grounds that Horne describes above. One of the photos she saw was of full body length (p. 36). She also saw a photo of a wound in the back of Kennedy's head which was about an inch or two in diameter (p. 37). The brain she saw in 1963 next to the body was undamaged (p. 59).

David Mantik: Jeremy Gunn once made a comment. He said it's as if the autopsy materials were designed to hide what was really happening as opposed to what they should usually do. They're supposed to reveal the full extent of things.

This comment by Chief Counsel Gunn was made to Doug Horne in conversation and Horne verified it in an email communication on August 26, 2020.

Doug Horne: On November 1st, 1966, the National Archives and an official from the Department of Justice met with Humes, Boswell, photographer John Stringer, and the radiologist [John] Ebersole. And they looked at the autopsy photographs for the first time and they created a catalog, an inventory simply saying: this is what this picture describes. During this discussion, the DOJ witness, Mr. Belcher, who was an attorney, noted they were discussing missing photographs. Jeremy Gunn, my boss, the general counsel, did ask why these people signed an inventory which they knew not to be true. And Stringer said, "Well, some people do object, but they don't last very long."

The taking of this inventory is described by Horne in *Inside the ARRB,* vol. 1, pp. 146–47; a summary of the inventory of the photos is on pp 151–52; the quote by Stringer is on p. 213.

Narrator: An inventory of autopsy materials submitted in 1965 to the National Archives listed microscopic tissue slides, and a stainless steel container containing gross material—presumably the brain.

Cyril Wecht: In August of '72, I'm there at the National Archives and I'm looking, I have the executive agreement of April '65 and I have the inventory of October '66—a year and a half later. Aha! In addition to some X-rays and some photos that are missing, there's a large metal box that obviously contained the brain, listed in '65, no longer listed in '66. Goodbye brain.

Gary Aguilar: And the tissue slides that they'd taken have disappeared from evidence. And people say, well, what difference do the tissue slides make? I'll tell you what evidence they make—when you do a little biopsy of that tissue around there, you can tell whether the bullet entered there or exited there by whether you find dust particles from the lead.

The controversy over the chain of possession of these exhibits is thoroughly examined in HSCA vol. 7, pp. 24–31.

Cyril Wecht: You don't have the brain. This is the heart, no pun intended, of the defendant's case. Mr. Prosecutor, you don't have the brain. You're out of here. And as we sit and talk here today, all these years later, that brain remains missing.

Narrator: After the film *JFK* was released, several doctors went to the National Archives to view the X-rays of Kennedy's skull. They saw details in these X-rays which presented yet another problem for the Warren Report's claim that Kennedy was only shot from the rear.

David Mantik: Well, the government investigations did claim that there was no evidence of a shot from the front. But they didn't tell us a few things that were very important, which we have learned only in recent years. We have seen tiny metal fragments right at the forehead.

Dr. Michael Chesser: When you look at the X-rays that are stored at the archives now, on the lateral X-ray there is a fragment trail. It actually expands from front to back, and there are dozens of very tiny dustlike fragment particles up in this location.

David Mantik: Now why is that important? Well, what we know is that the larger bullet fragments travel farther, whereas the smaller ones tend to stay near the entry site. That's what we see on these X-rays. In other words, we can reasonably interpret these as being consistent with a frontal bullet, but being radically inconsistent with a posterior bullet.

Gary Aguilar: And that's not evidence you can erase. You can't make that disappear, but that's incontrovertible evidence of a shot from the right front by a non-jacketed bullet.

Michael Chesser reviewed this X-ray issue in his article "The JFK Autopsy Evidence" in the January 2020 issue of *garrison* magazine, pp. 89–91. The general phenomenon is in the US Army Medical Department's Office of Medical History publication, in chapter 3, pp. 227–29, available online. This issue is also analyzed in a letter by Gary Aguilar and Cyril Wecht to the Association of Firearm and Tool Examiners' *AFTE Journal*, vol. 48 no. 2, pp. 77–79.

Narrator: This new X-ray evidence, combined with the review board's declassification of forty witnesses who saw a hole in the back of Kennedy's head constitutes powerful evidence of a shot from the front.

Narrator: Because three shells were found on the sixth floor of the Texas School Book Depository, the Warren Commission was limited to only three shots. But one of the problems with CE 399 as Joseph Dolce said was its nearly pristine condition. Especially when compared with bullets the commission tested.

Joseph Dolce archive clip: No, it could not have caused all the wounds. Because our experiments showed beyond any doubt that merely shooting the wrist deformed the bullet drastically.

Narrator: As it turns out, there was an extra bullet. And it was misshapen. After the assassination, the motorcade raced to Parkland Hospital, where the emergency room doctors tried to save the president's life. After he was pronounced dead, Kennedy's personal physician, George Burkley, got in contact with his assistant, James Young, in the White House and told him to prepare for the autopsy.

Randolph Robertson: It was James Young who ordered Chiefs [Thomas] Mills and [William] Martinell, their assistants, to go to the White House and retrieve what they knew were skull fragments in the limousine at that time.

Narrator: The presidential limousine, while en route to Washington, was inspected and a three-inch triangular piece of bone was discovered on the floor near the rear jump seat. During the autopsy, Young sent his two assistants to meet the limo when it arrived at the White House garage.

Randolph Robertson: And they brought back an additional envelope with the bullet with the bent tip. He described the bullet, brass-colored, about five millimeters in diameter.

Narrator: As part of a Naval oral history project, Jan Herman, who had interviewed Dr. Young on this subject, got in touch with Thomas Mills, one of the two men who had gone to the limo to retrieve the skull fragments.

Randolph Robertson: Jan Herman called up Mills, and Mills says, "Hey, you remember Dr. Young calling you asking about this bent bullet?" He said, "Yeah, I remember that and him calling me." And he remembered it. He says, "Can you shed any light on it?" And he says, "I would rather not talk about that."

Oliver Stone: And what happened to this bullet?

Randolph Robertson: It went from Mills and Martinell to Young to Humes, it disappears. That evening there may have been as little as four people who saw that bullet before it disappeared.

> The best summary of this discovery is by Milicent Cranor in her article at *Who. What. Why.* That October 6, 2017, essay is "Navy Doctor: Bullet Found in JFK's Limousine and Never Reported." It consists of an interview with Robertson and references to his key sources.

Narrator: The reports of this extra bullet substantiate some researchers' claim that there was a fourth shot hitting the limo at Zapruder frame 328.

Randolph Robertson: The bullet itself is important, but what's more important is when it struck and where it came from. And previously at 313, when the bullet went forward through JFK's head, a small fragment had cracked the windshield from the inner surface. Later at the final shot was at 328 was when it struck. Both times there were flares of reflected light as the glass was deformed from the impacts of one of a fragment and two of a whole bullet. And these two events occurred in point nine seconds. So therefore, they couldn't have been shot from the same rifle.

Narrator: The Warren Commission's contention is that only three shots were fired and that one of them had missed its target completely. So how does one account for the extensive damage to the limousine?

> The missed shot which ricocheted up and hit James Tague is discussed in the Warren Report on page 116. A critical analysis of the Commission's Tague shot is in Henry Hurt, *Reasonable Doubt* (pp. 130–38).

David Mantik: There is a lot of damage in the car. The chrome strip, which went around the windshield, was dented from the inside, which suggests a projectile from the rear. Six witnesses reported a through-and-through hole in the windshield.

> The six witnesses are medical student Evalea Glanges, policemen Stavis Ellis, and H. R. Freeman, Ford employee George Whitaker, reporter Richard Dudman, and Secret Service agent Charles Taylor. These were collected by the late attorney Doug Weldon and he discussed the issue in various videos the reader can see on YouTube.

Narrator: After the Secret Service tried to scrub down the interior at Parkland Hospital, the presidential limo was then flown to Washington. The interior was completely cleaned up within thirty-six hours and the windshield was replaced within forty-eight to seventy-two hours. The car was then shipped first to the Ford factory in Michigan, and then to Cincinnati, where it was extensively rebuilt by a car restoration company.

> Commission Document 80 is a memo from Chief James Rowley of the Secret Service to J. Lee Rankin. On page four, it says this cleanup was requested to begin on Saturday afternoon, and officially began on Sunday. But Doug Weldon unearthed evidence from an internal Ford Motor Company memorandum that it actually began on Saturday. Weldon concludes that there are also two differing dates as to when the windshield was replaced: the Ford memorandum says it was the 25th, CD 80 says it was the 26th.

Narrator: At the trial of New Orleans businessman Clay Shaw, autopsy doctor Pierre Finck shockingly revealed that the wound in Kennedy's back was not dissected because an Army general ordered them not to. The failure to perform that standard practice led to a long trail of folly and error in assessing and locating this wound. Did the bullet perforate the body? Did it connect with the neck wound? Or was it perhaps made by a piece of shrapnel from the pavement in Dealey Plaza, creating a shallow wound with no exit?

Finck was examined by assistant district attorney Alvin Oser about this key issue on February 24, 1969, see trial transcript pp. 115–18. When asked by Oser who told him not to dissect the back wound he said he did not recall. But previously, on pp 48–49, Finck stated that an Army general was running the autopsy. He then added that the doctors had "to coordinate the operation according to directions."

Don Miller: The face sheet for the autopsy where it shows the front and back silhouette of the body, where you mark scars and bullet wounds and things . . . The face sheet showed the bullet wound in the back at the level of thoracic vertebra T-3—which is five and a half to six inches below—exactly where Dr. Burkley had it in the death certificate.

Narrator: That location coincided with what the two FBI agents wrote in their report. Both Sibert and O'Neill disagreed with the Warren Report's depiction of both the rear skull wound and the back wound when the review board showed them the pictures in 1997. This is what Sibert had to say about the drawings commissioned by Arlen Specter: "What a liar. I feel he got his orders from above and how far above, I don't know. They got that single-bullet theory by moving that back wound up to the base of the neck."

Sibert's quotes on the credibility of the single-bullet theory are in the 2005 edition of William Matson Law's oral history book *In the Eye of History*, pp. 187, 195, 219; O'Neill's comments on the location of the back wound are on pp. 159–60, his comment on the head wound is on page 163; Sibert's quote about Specter's personal credibility is in the foreword on page XV.

Narrator: The single-bullet theory evolved over time and began with a problem the doctors had at the autopsy with finding an exit point for the back wound, and ending when Arlen Specter decided the bullet needed to hit two victims.

Cyril Wecht: Darrell Tomlinson, a maintenance man at Parkland Hospital passing by the ER, found the stretchers blocking the way, bent down, moved the stretcher and there was a bullet. Keep in mind, it really is a magic bullet because on the night of the autopsy, Friday, November 22nd, 1963, Humes and Boswell, these two military pathologists, and they missed a bullet hole in the front of the president's neck the night of the autopsy. They saw a tracheostomy. Indeed, there was a tracheostomy. The doctors at Parkland Hospital earlier that day had determined that the bullet had fortuitously ripped through the trachea. So they enlarged that bullet hole. Let me finish on Friday night. What to do? Hey, we've got a bullet hole. The president's back, which they examined with the finger, then with an instrument, then took X-rays and took out the lungs. No bullet. God, I wish I were there to see them sweating and have their underwear staining and well, just like you say, a work of fiction. A call came in from the FBI in Dallas to the FBI in DC. A bullet was found! Now we know, when the president lay on the stretcher, supine position and pressure was applied to his chest for cardiopulmonary resuscitation. That pressure applied anteriorly forced the bullet which had gone deeply into the tissues, back out through—like a tunnel in and out, a car in reverse. Bullets don't work that way, when a bullet goes in. It produces damage. The bullet becomes encased. Bullets don't go in and out like that. But that was their conclusion. It wasn't until the next morning when Humes decided, hey, maybe we oughta talk with the surgeons at Parkland Hospital. And now they learned for the first time that there was a tracheostomy superimposed upon a bullet wound. So now as of Saturday, November 23rd, that magic bullet is from the front of the clothing. The bullet going through six, seven inches of soft tissue comes out, sees the starched white collar, gets frightened to death, plops into the front of his clothing. And that's where the bullet came from. Found by Tomlinson at the hospital. Four or five months later, under Arlen Specter's single-bullet theory, that bullet has been rejuvenated, it's been revitalized. That bullet has now gone through Kennedy, through Connally, piercing the lung, destroying four inches of the right fifth rib, exiting from the front of his chest, going into the back of the wrist, shattering the distal and the radius—and in a six-foot-four guy like Connally, that's a big, heavy bone—comminuted fracture, exits from the front of the wrist, goes into the left thigh. And now as of April of 1964, the stretcher bullet Commission Exhibit 399, the hero of the Warren Commission report, is now from Connally's left thigh. Whatever you want, whatever you need. This bullet happily and readily obliges you. It is indeed a magic bullet.

The sequence of events about the discovery of CE 399 is chronicled in Henry Hurt's *Reasonable Doubt*, pp. 69–70. Humes and Boswell confirmed the probing described by Wecht for Josiah Thompson in 1966 (ibid., p. 39). The call with the FBI in described by Hurt also (p. 40). The solution of the bullet dropping out through external cardiac massage is in HSCA vol. 7, p. 17, and the Warren Report, p. 88. The Commission's explication of the single-bullet theory is in the Warren Report (pp. 95–109). For the discarded concept that the bullet fell into Kennedy's gurney, see Warren Commission, vol. 2, p. 368.

Narrator: And in order to make the facts fit the theory of one bullet doing all this damage, the Warren Commission needed to raise the wound in the back so that it would align with the alleged exit wound in the front of Kennedy's neck. Commissioner Gerald Ford did this simply via the stroke of a pen, changing the description in their report from back to back of the neck.

Cyril Wecht: As I recall, they said about Gerald Ford that he could not chew gum and walk at the same time. Now, all of a sudden, he becomes a forensic pathologist and a photographer and a criminalist and an expert, and he knows where the bullet hole was and he moved it up.

See "Ford Made Key Change in Kennedy Death Report," *New York Times*, July 3, 1997.

Narrator: But then in 1979, the House Select Committee moved it lower in the back because they had pictures from the autopsy. But then so did the

Warren Commission. It is conceivable that at the time the Warren Commission thought no one would ever see the autopsy photos. When the Review Board declassified the notation showing what Ford had done, the former commissioner replied it had nothing to do with a conspiracy theory. He was only trying to be more precise. This is directly contradicted by a conversation Ford had with French president Valery Giscard d'Estaing. According to d'Estaing, Ford told him the assassination was not the work of one person. "It was something set up. We were sure it was set up. But we were not able to discover by whom."

The Warren Report says this wound was on the back of the neck (p. 87).

The HSCA said it was in the back (vol. 7, p. 80). The Warren Commission, contrary to popular belief, did have the autopsy materials (Executive Session transcript of January 21, 1964, p. 3). Those pictures clearly denote the wound is in the back. For the Ford discussion with d'Estaing, see *Le Parisien* magazine, November 21, 2013.

Narrator: In the 1960 campaign, Kennedy had been advised by former Air Force Secretary Stuart Symington that military intelligence stated that the Russians had a significant advantage in long-range atomic missiles. He used the issue against Richard Nixon, even after he was informed that it was inaccurate. When he got into office, he was told by Defense Secretary Robert McNamara that this was not only false, but America had a huge advantage. This led to a meeting in the summer of 1961. It included Kennedy, CIA Director Allen Dulles, and chairman of the Joint Chiefs of Staff Lyman Lemnitzer. In 1993, the first official document describing the meeting was declassified. Dulles and Lemnitzer were advising Kennedy about the potential effects of a first-strike nuclear attack on the USSR, which would occur in the fall of 1963, a time when they predicted America would have its optimum advantage over Russian counterstrike capabilities. The advisers wanted to press that advantage to its ultimate nightmarish end.

The Symington misinformation is in an interview with Secretary of Defense Robert McNamara at the National Security Archives website entitled *Sputnik*, Episode 8. Kennedy was briefed on the subject of Russian ICBM missiles by Allen Dulles on July 3, 1960. It is not clear if the matter was clarified to him at that time (Letter from Dulles to Eisenhower, August 3, 1960). The first-strike meeting was first revealed in the *American Prospect* of December 19, 2001, by James K. Galbraith.

***Dr. Strangelove* clip:** "You're talking about mass murder, general, not war." "Mr. President, I'm not saying we wouldn't get our hair messed, but I do say no more than ten to twenty million killed tops, depending on the breaks." "I will not go down in history as the greatest mass murderer since Adolf Hitler." "Perhaps it might be better, Mr. President, if you were more concerned with the American people than with your image in the history books."

James Galbraith: The importance of that meeting was that it showed that the strategic planners did, in fact, think of the military force that we were deploying at the time as a first-strike force and not a second-strike retaliatory force. And the fact that this was the case was what I think tied Kennedy, Johnson, and McNamara together over this entire period, that they simply had to keep those missiles in their silos. I called up Walt Rostow, who was a close friend and colleague by that time at the University of Texas. I said, "Walt, I'm writing an article on a meeting of the National Security Council that took place on the 20th of July, 1961." And he looked at me without any further word, he said, "You mean the one where they wanted to blow up the world?"

Narrator: After the meeting, Kennedy said to his Secretary of State, Dean Rusk, "And we call ourselves the human race."

The meeting was described by LBJ's military adviser, Howard Burris, in a memo to him of July 20, 1961. Roswell Gilpatric said Kennedy walked out of the meeting after asking a few questions (JFK Library interview, August 12, 1970). The Rusk comment is in his book *As I Saw It*, pp. 246–47.

Narrator: After his inauguration, Kennedy sent his aide, Arthur Schlesinger, on a tour of Latin America to come up with a plan to alter the Yankee gringo image of the United States in the region and also neutralize the appeal of communism. Kennedy organized a huge conference in Punta Del Este, Uruguay, inviting representatives from Latin America to propose projects and to establish the Alliance for Progress.

> The tour of Latin America is described by Schlesinger in his book *A Thousand Days* (pp. 175–85). Schlesinger details the Punta del Este Conference in that book (pp. 761–65).

John F. Kennedy speech: For no real progress is possible unless the benefits of increased prosperity are shared by the people themselves.

Robert F. Kennedy Jr.: They tried to create a program that would tie US aid not to military control and authoritarian support of US corporations, but rather to initiatives that would democratize the country and that would raise the poor out of poverty.

> The ideas about the alliance were formed by people like Schlesinger, Richard Goodwin, and Adolf Berle as a way to counter the extremes of fascism and communism in Latin America (Schlesinger, pp. 192–93).

Narrator: One of the least-acknowledged aspects of Kennedy's foreign policy was his perspective regarding the Middle East. As part of an effort to bring balance to the region, Kennedy had concentrated on forging a relationship with Gamal Abdel Nasser of Egypt.

Philip Muehlenbeck: Kennedy's overall policy towards the Middle East had a few pillars. One was to take a more evenhanded approach towards Israel on the Palestine issue than previous US presidents had. A second issue was to support what he viewed as the progressive nationalists in places like Egypt, embodied by Nasser, and in Syria, as opposed to what Kennedy referred to as "relics of the past," monarchies in places like Saudi Arabia or Jordan. Nasser was one of the foreign leaders that Kennedy had the most personal correspondence with. They sent over a dozen letters between each other. In those letters, Kennedy would disclose to Nasser some things that he was going to do in advance, like weapons sales to Israel. So Nasser really appreciated his communication.

Robert Rakove: Kennedy discerned that Nasser actually had qualities that made him an appealing ally for the United States, that he actually could, through the right inducements, forge a partnership with Washington. It wouldn't be close, but if the United States was generous in its support of Egyptian development, Nasser might, as his ambassador promised, keep the Arab-Israeli conflict in the icebox. That was the phrase.

> Kennedy's attempt to reverse Dulles's policy toward Nasser is described by Muehlenbeck in *Betting on the Africans* (pp. 124–32).

Narrator: The United Nations had abandoned their plan to repatriate Palestinian refugees. Kennedy took it up as a cause with Israel. This would have allowed the refugees a choice of staying where they were, moving elsewhere, or relocating back to Israel, all at the UN's expense.

> The Joseph Johnson UN solution had been turned down in a cable from David Ben-Gurion to Dean Rusk on January 24, 1963. Kennedy was trying to revive it in May 1963 (State Dept. cable from Tel Aviv to Dean Rusk, May 16, 1963).

Narrator: The other problem Kennedy faced with Israel was the construction of the atomic reactor at Dimona. JFK was strongly against any proliferation of nuclear weaponry. He had been assured by Prime Minister David Ben-Gurion that Dimona was designed for peaceful uses of atomic energy. In spring of '63, Kennedy demanded full inspections by the US of the Dimona reactor and threatened to place American aid for Israel in limbo if no agreement was reached. And at the time of his assassination, negotiations were in process for biannual inspections.

Author Roger Mattson has noted that no president before or since was more opposed to nuclear proliferation than Kennedy. (See *Stealing the Bomb*, pp. 38–40, 256.) Kennedy's letters to David Ben-Gurion expressing his demands about Dimona were dated May 10 and June 15, 1963. He clearly implied American funding for Israel would be placed in jeopardy if Tel Aviv did not comply. When Ben-Gurion stepped down, Kennedy continued this dialogue with his successor, Levi Eshkol. (See memorandum from McGeorge Bundy to Kennedy, August 23, 1963).

Narrator: The existence of communism so close to American shores kept Cuba on Kennedy's plate. And in late '61, he authorized covert efforts under the name Operation Mongoose. General Edward Lansdale ran the day-to-day operations of the project, but Robert Kennedy was above him to ensure it would not spin out of control as the Bay of Pigs had. The idea was to keep pressure on Castro so he would not export communism further into Latin America and endanger the Alliance for Progress.

Mongoose is summarized by David Talbot in his book *Brothers* (pp. 95–100).

OLIVER STONE: And despite later accusations of Kennedy's complicity in assassination plots, there is no known document that's emerged from the Mongoose files showing that he knew of any such attempts. This seems to be a remnant of the Eisenhower plan.

See Foreign Relations of the United States, 1961–63, vol. 10. The CIA's Inspector General Report, declassified by the ARRB, states there was no presidential approval for these plots to kill Castro (pp. 132–34).

Doug Horne: General Lansdale requests of the Joint Staff in February of '62. He requests that they come up with pretexts for a US invasion of Cuba.

Narrator: The following month, the Joint Chiefs of Staff presented a plan to Kennedy called Operation Northwoods, whereby the CIA would secretly perform terrorist acts in the US and blame them on Castro to justify bombings and an invasion of Cuba. The president declined the recommendation.

John Newman: And it takes only a few days before it's "mano e mano," a face-to-face showdown between President Kennedy and General Lemnitzer. Lemnitzer says, "We got a pretext. We can do this." Kennedy rebukes him.

Doug Horne: Pretexts were outrageous. Fake an attack by Cubans against the Guantanamo Bay sentries. Sink a US ship in Guantanamo Bay and blame it on Cuba. The one that scares me the most was very sophisticated. Take an airliner and fly it as a drone over Cuba without any people in it with a tape recording that would play, "We're under attack, we're under attack by Cuban aircraft! Oh, my God, they're gonna kill us!" Blow up the airplane, blow up this huge drone, and use that to start a war.

John Newman: Within a matter of weeks, Lemnitzer says, "Well, to hell with the pretext. To hell with it, let's just invade anyway." And you see all these plans being sent to McNamara and to Kennedy from Lemnitzer that basically say we gotta go in, just do, never mind and who cares. There's no pretext. There's no rationale. We just, we want to do it. President Kennedy has to fire Lemnitzer.

Doug Horne: So the Northwoods plan was our big coup, our big find in the way of military records. They're universally recognized today for their importance. And it's one of those releases that the Review Board members, the board members themselves were justifiably proud of that came out of the JFK Records Act.

> The Northwoods documents are at the Mary Ferrell Foundation website with a number of accompanying essays. Kennedy's problems with Lemnitzer over Cuba are described in chapter 15 of John Newman's *Into the Storm.*

Narrator: Throughout 1961, Kennedy rejected a total of nine attempts by his military advisers to send American ground troops into Vietnam, and both General Douglas MacArthur and French President Charles de Gaulle strongly agreed with him about not doing so.

The best chronicle of these attempts and Kennedy's noncompliance is in Gordon Goldstein's *Lessons in Disaster* (pp. 52–58). For MacArthur's advice, see Goldstein (p. 235). For de Gaulle's input, see *Johnny We Hardly Knew Ye* by David Powers and Kenneth O'Donnell (p. 13).

John Newman: The issue of what to do in Cuba and the issue of what to do in Vietnam were inextricably intertwined because you can't do all these things at once. We don't have enough soldiers. We don't have enough forces to do them. And it's not just Cuba and Vietnam. It's Cuba and Berlin and Laos and Vietnam. So Kennedy was most concerned actually about Berlin and was unwilling to put troops in Cuba because he would not be able to react if Khrushchev did something on Berlin. And Kennedy understood that, the Chairman of the Joint Chiefs of Staff understood that. Now, with that as the context, when it comes to Vietnam, Kennedy tells Lyman Lemnitzer, "Look, if we're not going to go into Cuba, what the hell are we going to go into Vietnam for?"

Kennedy's dialogue with Lemnitzer is in John Newman's *JFK and Vietnam*, 2017 edition, pp. 139–40.

Narrator: Near the end of his first year in office, Kennedy received a report from Walt Rostow and General Maxwell Taylor, his foreign policy and military advisers, that called for increased training of South Vietnamese troops, increased bombings of the north, and the use of US combat troops.

James Galbraith: At meetings later in November, I believe the 15th of November, the National Security Council meeting where this was thrashed out, Robert Kennedy was very explicit in saying, no, we're not sending combat troops. And it was clear from that point forward that this was the red line that John F. Kennedy would not cross.

There is a brief memorandum of this meeting by Colonel Howard Burris in the book *Virtual JFK* edited by James Blight (pp. 281–83). On

Robert Kennedy's comments, see David Kaiser, *American Tragedy*, p. 113.

Narrator: A third influence on Kennedy's reluctance to commit American ground troops was his ambassador to India, John Kenneth Galbraith.

James Galbraith: My father went to see Walt Rostow. He went in to talk to him. Rostow gestured on his desk to the pile of papers. The report, the Rostow-Taylor report, was plainly visible. My father asked to see it. Walt said, in effect, that his security classification wasn't sufficiently high. My father did not think that Walt Rostow's security classification was higher than his. And at a given moment, the phone rang. Walt turned to answer the phone, and Dad picked up the report and walked out of the office and read it. So from that point forward, he had an inside track on what was being, at that time, very closely held recommendation for a very strong combat intervention in Vietnam. And of course, he proceeded to counter it as best he could with direct advice to the president.

Galbraith's invisible hand in this meeting was described by his biographer Richard Parker in his article "Galbraith and Vietnam" (*The Nation*, March 14, 2005).

John Newman: It isn't until later in that month where the Vietnam decision is finally arrived at which is in NSAM 111 where Kennedy says no combat troops, but we'll increase the advisers. And that was his signal decision in the Kennedy presidency without respect to the withdrawal, but never to cross that line.

NSAM 111 is in *Virtual JFK*, pp. 284–86.

Narrator: In October of '62, U-2 surveillance flights detected Soviet nuclear missiles in Cuba—90 miles off the US coast. To this day, scholars debate Khrushchev's motivation. Was it because he feared a US invasion of Cuba? Was it because of American missiles in Turkey? Was it, as Kennedy believed, a negotiating tool over Berlin? Despite pressure from his military advisers, Kennedy chose the least provocative alternative.

> For the discovery of the Russian missiles in Cuba, see *The Kennedy Tapes*, edited by Ernest May and Philip Zelikow (pp. 45–46).

John F. Kennedy speech: I have directed that the following initial steps be taken immediately: first, to halt this offensive buildup a strict quarantine on all offensive military equipment under shipment to Cuba is being initiated.

Narrator: Kennedy's military advisers, led by Air Force General Curtis LeMay, considered his refusal to attack as pure folly—the equivalent of surrender.

Curtis LeMay audio: This is almost as bad as the appeasement at Munich—

Narrator: —a reference to Prime Minister Neville Chamberlain of Great Britain, and the appeasement of the Nazis in 1938 which eventually led to World War II.

> LeMay's comments were made on October 19 at Kennedy's only meeting with the Joint Chiefs during the crisis. The comments about Chamberlain are in May and Zelikow (p. 178).

Narrator: As the crisis progressed into its second week, a U-2 plane was shot down and Kennedy's civilian advisers began to side with LeMay, who wanted Kennedy to bomb the missile silos and invade the island. They did not know that the Cubans had short-range tactical nuclear missiles in place.

> The debate over retaliation for the U-2 shootdown is in May and Zelikow (pp. 571–73). At a January 9, 1992, conference in Havana, Soviet General Anatoly Gribkov revealed that, in addition to 162 medium- and long-range missiles already assembled before the blockade, there were two types of tactical missiles on the island, one with a range of ninety miles, and the other of thirty miles.

Narrator: Kennedy had his brother meet with Soviet ambassador Anatoly Dobrynin. According to the Soviets, Robert Kennedy warned that his brother was uncertain he could control the military much longer and that a deal could be struck along the lines Khrushchev had suggested—a no-invasion pledge and a withdrawal of American missiles from Turkey.

The negotiating cables between Kennedy and Khrushchev are contained in *The Armageddon Letters* by James Blight and Janet Lang (pp. 96–112), and RFK's visit with Dobrynin is described there as well (pp. 108–09). Dobrynin writes about Bobby Kennedy's warning about uncontrollable generals in his telegram to Khrushchev of October 27, 1962.

Narrator: Most Americans felt elated over the end of the crisis, but the Joint Chiefs of Staff and LeMay felt they had been defeated by the Soviets and denied the opportunity to topple Castro. Kennedy looked at it differently. He said, "If we followed the Pentagon's advice, nobody would be around to tell the generals they were wrong."

This quote is in *JFK's Last Hundred Days* by Thurston Clarke (pp. 97–98).

David Talbot: The main, I think, goal of the Kennedy administration is how to—working around the State Department, working around the CIA, working around the Pentagon—how can the Kennedy White House pursue its own policy of peace with the rest of the world? With Castro in Cuba, with Khrushchev in Moscow and so on, and avoid the horrendous mistakes of the past that almost got us into nuclear war.

Narrator: In the midst of these debates, Kennedy sent Galbraith to Saigon to write a report that would differ in its recommendations from what Taylor and Rostow had given to him.

James Galbraith: Kennedy knew what he wanted and he knew what my father would deliver, which he did, which is a very detailed and skeptical report about the efficiency of the South Vietnamese government, about the capacity of any military force to prevail in the security situation that existed in South Vietnam at that time.

Galbraith's visit to Saigon, his skeptical views of the conflict and his letters to Kennedy are described in Parker's article.

Narrator: Kennedy told Galbraith to deliver his report to Defense Secretary McNamara. And he, in turn, gave instructions to begin the withdrawal to General Harkins, the commanding general of all forces in Vietnam. The Pentagon dragged its feet on formulating plans, and McNamara called for a meeting in May of 1963. One of the most important finds of the Review Board are the notes from this meeting.

For Galbraith giving his report to McNamara, see Kaiser (pp. 131–34). For McNamara's giving the withdrawal order to General Harkins, commander in Vietnam, again see Kaiser (p. 159).

Doug Horne: McNamara says, "It's not fast enough. I want you to accelerate it." He says, "I want to pull out a thousand men in December, by the end of the year. And I want you to pull out complete units, not just individuals," because it didn't want to be an accounting exercise of pulling out, delaying other individuals coming in and saying, we pulled out a thousand men. He wanted units to come out, full units.

The declassified documents from this May 1963 meeting were the basis for the *New York Times* story of December 23, 1997, "Kennedy Had a Plan for Early Exit in Vietnam." They are also at the Mary Ferrell Foundation website under the rubric "Kennedy and Vietnam".

Narrator: After the withdrawal plan was approved, Kennedy sent Secretary of Defense McNamara and General Taylor to Saigon in September of '63. He planned on using their report as the basis to formally order the withdrawal to begin. Kennedy controlled the report since it was actually being written under the supervision of Bobby Kennedy. But still, men like Under Secretary of State William Sullivan and Taylor tried to remove the recommendation for withdrawal. Kennedy insisted that it stay in.

See the 2017 edition of Newman's *JFK and Vietnam* for Bobby Kennedy's role in the composition of the report (pp. 407–08) and Taylor's tinkering with the report (pp. 443–46). For Sullivan's, see *Vietnam: The Early Decisions* edited by Lloyd C. Gardner and Ted Gittinger (p. 165).

John Newman: Then Kennedy takes that, secretly, three days later, actually issues the order himself at the secret level. It doesn't become an NSAM, yet. It should. But once it leaks out into the newspapers, his opponents find out what he's done. Then it's in the newspapers. And McGeorge Bundy says to Kennedy, "Hey, look, you know, if they're talking about it in the newspapers, we might as well put it on paper." And they put it and it was NSAM 263. And that's how it was actually written and why. Well, here's one of the things McNamara said in the secret debrief. He said, "We had agreed, the president and I, that we had trained them, we had given them everything we could. And if they couldn't win, too bad we had to get out even if they were going to be defeated." So he and Kennedy, McNamara and Kennedy, had decided that they were willing to pull out of Vietnam in a losing scenario. That's very important.

NSAM 263 is in *Virtual JFK* (p. 302). Jim Douglass describes how Kennedy overrode the NSC and then had it announced to the press which forced it to be recorded as an NSAM (pp. 187–88). For the McNamara debriefs, see Gardner and Gittinger (pp. 165–67).

Oliver Stone: Can you tell us about the Air Force One tapes and General Curtis LeMay?

Doug Horne: On the new version of the Air Force One tapes, the Clifton tapes, it's revealed that Colonel Dorman, General LeMay's aide, was desperately trying to contact LeMay on the radio. A logbook was recovered by the ARRB from the Air Force Command Post at Andrews. And it was given to us by a civil servant named Chuck Holmes. And this logbook records in-flight conversations between a command post at Andrews and Air Force One as it's flying from Texas back to Washington. So this logbook shows that General LeMay at the time the assassination was in Canada. This is really interesting, because his official biographer says he was hunting in Michigan. But we know that's not true. He was in Toronto for reasons unknown, without his aide, Colonel Dorman, who went with him everywhere. This logbook reveals that he was ordered by Secretary Zucker to land at Andrews Air Force Base. Because all the federal officials were going to meet the president's body at Andrews Air Force Base. A transmission was made from LeMay's plane back to this command post. And it says: "General LeMay will not go to Andrews. General LeMay will go to DCA National Airport." According to this log, his plane lands at National Airport, DCA, at about 5:15 p.m., well before the autopsy started.

This material by Horne on the logbook, LeMay's true location, and his concealing his landing is from *Inside the ARRB* (vol. 2, pp. 478–82).

Narrator: Very few people in the Pentagon had a worse relationship with Kennedy than Curtis LeMay. During the missile crisis, he opposed Kennedy's solution of a blockade. When Kennedy left the room after this conference, LeMay openly ridiculed him. LeMay was strongly against the test ban treaty Kennedy was working on and signed in 1963. He wanted to escalate the Vietnam War with both naval and airpower by carrying the war north. He advocated bombing North Vietnam back to the Stone Age if need be, and was willing to use atomic weapons if the Chinese intervened.

LeMay's disagreements with Kennedy over the missile crisis are captured verbatim in the book *The Kennedy Tapes* where the authors transcribe the president's meeting with the Joint Chiefs during the crisis (Ernest May and Philip Zelikow, pp. 174–88). For LeMay's opposition to the Partial Test Ban Treaty, see *Kennedy* by Ted Sorenson (p. 832). For his comments on air war with Vietnam, see *LeMay on Vietnam* edited by Kenneth Williams (pp. 20–21).

Doug Horne: There were a lot of people at the Bethesda morgue. The latest count by all the researchers that I know of is about thirty-three people. There was a gallery of bleachers. Apparently all three rows were filled with people. Both Dr. Humes has complained after the fact and Tom Robinson, the mortician from Gawler's Funeral Home. They both equated it to a three-ring circus.

Although Sibert and O'Neill had a list of the people there, Sibert admitted they did not get everyone (see William Matson Law, *In The Eye of History* p. 188). For Robinson's description of the atmosphere at the autopsy, see his ARRB interview of June 21, 1996, p. 3.

Gary Aguilar: But these three autopsy pathologists who are not really credentialed to do that kind of an autopsy were given a body told here's the body, he was shot from behind, he fell forward, which they wrote in their autopsy report. Figure out how the wounds fit the known circumstances of the shooting. But what this really speaks to is the fact that the autopsy was not in the control of the surgeons that were charged at doing it. It was in the control of people who were there who were telling them what they could do and what they couldn't do.

The description of Kennedy being hit from behind and falling forward is in the opening section of the autopsy report titled "Clinical Summary." This was false since Kennedy's body went violently backward. For a summary of how damaging Pierre Finck's testimony at the Shaw trial was, see *Destiny Betrayed*, second edition by James DiEugenio, pp. 299–306. When Finck testified that Humes felt so constricted he turned around and asked, "Who is in charge here?" the Justice Department sent Thornton Boswell to New Orleans to discredit him. Ultimately, he did not testify.

Doug Horne: Paul O'Connor was a Navy corpsman helping the pathologists. He told me this in 1999. He told others this in 1992. He's told several people that Dr. Humes during the autopsy complained that somebody was smoking a cigar, tell him to put the damn thing out. So O'Connor went over to the gallery, the three rows of bleachers, and there was General LeMay sitting in his uniform with a big fat cigar in his hand, and LeMay looked at him after he asked him to put it out and promptly blew smoke in his face. Did LeMay go to the autopsy to gloat over the death of his nemesis?

O'Connor's encounter with LeMay is noted in *Inside the ARRB*, vol. 2 (pp. 487–88).

JFK: Destiny Betrayed

Chapter 4

Archive clip of Richard Schweiker during Church Committee:
This report documents the failure of the US intelligence establishment in their investigation of President Kennedy's assassination and their cover-up to the Warren Commission.

Narrator: During the 1975 Church Committee investigation of US intelligence activities, Committee member Richard Schweiker, in an interview at the time, remarked about Oswald that "everywhere you looked with him, there are fingerprints of intelligence."

This quote appears in many places including Henry Hurt's *Reasonable Doubt*, p. 192.

Narrator: Those fingerprints extended back to 1959 when Oswald defected to the Soviet Union. State Department intelligence officer Otto Otepka had noted the marked increase in the number of Americans defecting to Russia at the time. He also noted that some of them came from the military. He therefore suspected that some of these men were fake defectors. They had been assigned by the CIA to garner intelligence behind the Iron Curtain. He sent a letter to the CIA asking which ones were real and which were their agents. Oswald was one of the names on Otepka's list. Otepka's request was forwarded to James Angleton, chief of counterintelligence. He instructed that there be no research done on Oswald, but Otepka continued to work on the Oswald case.

For how Otepka's request was handled at CIA, see John Newman, *Oswald and the CIA*, pp. 170–72. Although the Commission knew about Otepka, there is no evidence that the Warren Commission interviewed him (Letter from J. Lee Rankin to Abram Chayes at the State Department , January 8, 1964). But the HSCA, through Robert Genzman and Harold Leap, did do a brief interview with him on May 11, 1978. For a book-length treatment of Otepka and his security problems, see William J. Gill's *The Ordeal of Otto Otepka*.

Lisa Pease: The only thing of significance was that he was really interested in Lee Harvey Oswald before the assassination, and he actually had a study of these defectors in his safe. Well, things got worse. His office was not only bugged, they planted people in his office to spy on him. They started putting confidential documents in his burn bag and then trying to blame him and saying he's burning confidential documents. The guy's gone, you know, wacko.

Narrator: And as a result, he was formally removed from the State Department on November 5, 1963, just seventeen days before the assassination. You will not see Otepka's name in the Warren Report, and he was not called as a witness before that body. In fact, James Angleton, the man who had access to all the Oswald files at the CIA, coordinated the agency's response to the Warren Commission's requests.

Richard Helms had Angleton replace John Whitten as the coordinator of all information going to the Warren Commission on Oswald (Gerald McKnight, *Breach of Trust*, p. 88).

Oliver Stone: Can you describe the setting up of the Oswald file at the CIA?

John Newman: It could be opened after a few documents arrived at the CIA from other intelligence agencies and that would be enough to trigger the opening of a 201 file. Sometimes they call it a personality file. And another thing that could trigger the opening of a 201 file would be an American citizen defecting to a communist bloc country. Well the interesting thing is Oswald met both of those criteria within nine days of his defection. And they didn't open a 201 file on him for thirteen or fourteen months. Immediately after the defection, Oswald's threat to commit an act of espionage, which his words were "something special about my Marine Corps experience"—which could only be the U-2, which is a program he'd worked on, a very secret CIA program—that threat caused him to be put on the mail intercept program and not opening a 201 at the same time. Which is a very, very unusual combination and can only be explained by Oswald being part of a very covert, very sensitive ongoing operation, which was the hunt for a mole. In the history of the KGB and the CIA, their wars are not actually shooting each other so much as trying to penetrate each other. And so we call them moles, or penetrations. And so it was an ongoing war—very, very, complicated. But that's what the mole hunters were doing for Angleton is looking for KGB moles inside of the CIA. So, 351164 was the file in the security office that was opened up right after his defection. And that was shared only with Angleton's mole hunting office, but not with any of the other components of the CIA.

The issue of the late opening of Oswald's 201 file is reviewed in John Newman's *Oswald and the CIA,* pp. 47–50 and 53–56; he discusses the mole hunt on pp. 87–89. Newman has updated the latter subject in his online essay "The Molehunt and LHO's Defection" at jfkjmn.com.

John Newman: The CIA and the FBI knew what the KGB would figure out very quickly was because of his assignment in Atsugi, Japan, where he tracked the supersecret U-2s at the time. So once you establish the lure, the place where you trap the animal isn't in the Moscow embassy, it's back at Langley where they thought the mole was. You want the KGB to contact their mole to ask questions. The moment that the mole asks a question, it's over. He or she is exposed. This program, which did not work, years later was put in front of probably our most celebrated and capable counterintelligence officer in the history of the Central Intelligence Agency. His name was

"Pete" Tennent Bagley. He began searching for the mole, he was the key person leading it for years with Angleton. Well, after he was retired, he attended a meeting of former CIA officers down in the Carolinas. And a British researcher happened to be down there, his name is Malcolm Blunt, and they met and got along well. And fortunately for history, a couple of years before Pete Bagley died, Malcolm sat down with him one day and showed him all those first documents that had come into the CIA on Oswald from the State Department and the Navy components at the embassy. And Pete Bagley looks at Malcolm and he says, "Was he witting?" And Malcolm didn't really know how to respond. And so Bagley raised his voice and insisted, "He had to be witting! He had to be witting!" That was a telling, seminal moment in the history of CIA/KGB spy wars, in the history of Lee Harvey Oswald. His early use by the CIA was just a very, very important one because finally, after all these years, a very senior CIA officer had just told Malcolm and us that Lee Harvey Oswald was a witting false defector when he went to Moscow.

This conversation is described in Newman's *Countdown to Darkness* (pp. 29–30).

Narrator: There was another unusual event that took place at the time of Oswald's defection—the source of his income changed.

Doug Horne: Oswald's last quarter of earnings in the United States before he defected to the Soviet Union should have been paid by the United States Marine Corps. And they weren't. Because we asked to see his Marine Corps earnings records that the Marine Corps deposited with the Social Security Administration. They did not pay him any money the last quarter he was in the United States before his defection. No income from the Marine Corps, which he should have had.

This information was from the ARRB liaison at the SSA.

Narrator: Could this all be coincidence, or was Otto Otepka correct in suspecting Oswald was not a legitimate defector? And is this why Angleton told his secretary to withhold information from Otepka?

Jeff Morley: The line that the CIA fed the Warren Commission, that we didn't really know anything about this guy. We now know that that was complete nonsense. Oswald was a figure of intense interest for four years before the assassination. And a dozen senior CIA officers were very well acquainted with him. Everything he did, where he went, what his politics were, his family life. I mean, remember, they were reading his mother's mail. That's how closely they were watching him, right up until Kennedy was killed. And then Kennedy was killed, Oswald's arrested, and they say, well we know nothing about this man.

Narrator: In fact, ARRB records show that James Angleton and the CIA were receiving reports on Oswald up until one week before the assassination.

See Jefferson Morley's biography of Angleton, *The Ghost*, p. 140.

Narrator: The Warren Commission pushed the idea that Oswald was a staunch communist, citing evidence of his distributing pro-Castro leaflets in New Orleans and by his supposed defection to Russia in 1959. But records show that Oswald was working with fiercely anti-communist elements. And not surprisingly, many of these groups were known, and in some cases supported, by the US government.

Narrator: In the spring of 1963, Oswald moved from Dallas back to his hometown of New Orleans, where he began associating with men who, it would be revealed, had clear connections with these government efforts.

Narrator: One of these men, David Ferrie, had been with Oswald in the Civil Air Patrol back in 1955, and was known as an extreme anti-communist. He was also a trainer and a pilot for the CIA in its secret war against Cuba. Oswald was involved in these Cuban exile training activities with Ferrie.

The relationship of David Ferrie in the CAP with Oswald, and Ferrie's anti- Castro activities are dealt with in William Davy's *Let Justice Be Done*, pp 3–10, 25–33; information about Oswald being at the training camp is on p. 30; that information is also noted in Dick Russell's book *The Man Who Knew Too Much* (p. 329). Ferrie's activities are sketched in *Deadly Secrets* by Warren Hinckle and William Turner (pp. 232–33). Ferrie's life and career is also written about in HSCA, vol. 10 (pp. 105–114).

Narrator: Another person Oswald was seen with in New Orleans in 1963 was Guy Banister. Banister was an extreme right-winger who was close to the FBI, the CIA, and the American Nazi Party. Banister gave Oswald his own office at 544 Camp Street. Oswald now began to use his office to print up and stamp pro-Castro literature, much of it associated with the Fair Play for Cuba Committee centered in New York. Against their advice, he began a chapter of the FPCC in New Orleans, of which he was the only member.

Banister and his relations with Oswald are written about by Hinckle and Turner in *Deadly Secrets*, 229–36; the relationship with Oswald is also detailed in Davy's *Let Justice be Done*, pp. 37–43; James DiEugenio, *Destiny Betrayed*, second edition, pp. 110–14; see also HSCA, vol. 10, pp. 123–32.

John Newman: The Fair Play for Cuba Committee was created in April of 1960, at exactly the same time that President Eisenhower ordered the creation of a program to overthrow Castro. Very interesting, the coincidence of those two events. Oswald had another job working with Guy Banister to develop adverse information on political leftists or communists or communist sympathizers. He did this at universities like Tulane. So all this stuff in New Orleans that he's doing that includes FPCC propaganda and other things, are done very publicly on television, on the radio, in the streets of New Orleans to develop this profile, to establish his bona fides as a hot-headed pro-Castro supporter. At some point, the FBI, I think probably after the assassination, decided they wanted to disconnect Oswald from the FBI. And of course, Banister, who's associated with the FBI would have to be disconnected as well. The problem with that, many of those handbills had the 544 Camp Street address on them. There was a message from New Orleans to the bureau written by a special agent Maynor, who actually mentioned pamphlets that had the 544 Camp Street address on it. And before that message was sent, it was scratched out.

The creation of the FPCC is from *Oswald and the CIA*, p. 95; the Maynor incident is from the same source (p. 310). See also Paul Bleau's two-part online series *Exposing the FPCC* at Kennedysandking.com.

Narrator: After the assassination, when the FBI questioned Banister—a former FBI agent himself—they did not ask him about Oswald.

See HSCA, vol. 10, p. 126.

Narrator: One of the places Oswald leafleted in front of was Clay Shaw's International Trade Mart. Shaw, who was arrested by New Orleans DA Jim Garrison on charges he was part of the conspiracy to kill President Kennedy, always denied he was associated with the CIA.

Archive clip: "You have never yourself had any CIA connection?" "None whatsoever." "Any association with the organization? "No, none."

Narrator: The Review Board has shown these denials to be false. Shaw was both a highly valued contract agent and had a covert security clearance for a project code-named QKENCHANT.

For the new information on Shaw, see Davy, p. 195 and Joan Mellen, *Our Man In Haiti*, pp. 54–55.

Narrator: New Orleans attorney Dean Andrews had worked with Oswald in May of '63 in an attempt to upgrade his military discharge from its undesirable status. After the assassination, a man calling himself Clay Bertrand phoned Andrews and asked him to consider going to Dallas to defend Oswald. Under oath, Clay Shaw denied that he was Clay Bertrand. And Andrews claimed that because of the medication he was on, he had only imagined the phone call. But today, because of the work of the Assassination Records Review

Board, we now have evidence and twelve people who confirm that Shaw used this name as an alias. Andrews later admitted that Shaw was Bertrand to author Harold Weisberg, but made him promise not to reveal this until after Andrews's death.

> Andrews's relationship with Oswald is described in Warren Commission, vol. 11, pp. 326–331; his relationship with Bertrand follows on pp. 332–37. During his trial, on February 27, 1969, Shaw denied using the name Bertrand (trial transcript, p. 23); for Andrews's alleged sedation, see WC Vol XI, p. 332–33; for declassified files on Shaw as Bertrand, see Davy, *Let Justice be Done*, pp. 190–94, also James DiEugenio, *Destiny Betrayed,* Second Edition, pp. 387–88; Ed Tatro learned that that the alias was well known in the French Quarter; the revelation by Andrews to Weisberg is in the unpublished Weisberg manuscript *Mailer's Tale,* chapter 5, p. 11.

Narrator: Evidence of another aspect of Oswald's time in New Orleans is supported by Robert Tanenbaum, the deputy chief counsel of the House Select Committee, and others who have seen film of Oswald, David Ferrie, and CIA director of Cuban Operations at anti-Castro training camps. David Phillips was a propaganda specialist and his tactics to neutralize the Fair Play for Cuba Committee included infiltration, surveillance, and recruitment of other agent provocateurs.

> For Tanenbaum's observation of the three men, see Davy, *Let Justice be Done*, p. 30. Phillips's and the CIA's operations against the FPCC are mentioned in *Oswald and the CIA*, p. 95, pp. 238–42, p. 301.

Narrator: David Phillips also created an anti-Castro Cuban exile group. The Student Revolutionary Directorate, or DRE, was based in Miami, and had a chapter in New Orleans led by Carlos Bringuier. Records released by the ARRB show the CIA was funding this group and helped plan activities, including the attack on a Cuban hotel which housed Soviet advisers.

For Phillips's role in forming the DRE, and the attack on the hotel, see Gerald McKnight, *Breach of Trust*, pp. 314–15. See also Howard Hunt's HSCA deposition of December 3, 1978, p. 77.

Jeff Morley: AMSPELL was the CIA's code name for the Cuban Student Directorate. The name doesn't appear in the final report of the Warren Commission. They certainly did not know that the group was receiving $51,000 a month from the CIA in 1963, and they didn't know that the group was being run from Miami by George Joannides, a psychological warfare officer who reported directly to Dick Helms. The DRE published the first JFK conspiracy theory saying that Oswald and Castro were the presumed assassins and that publication was paid for by the CIA under the auspices of George Joannides. The Joannides story tells us that Dick Helms's handpicked man in Miami was controlling the group that had the most to do with Oswald before and after the assassination.

Much of Morley's important information was published by the *Miami New Times* in a story titled "Revelation 19.63" on April 12, 2001.

I found out Joannides's identity many years later and I went to Bob Blakey, the head of the HSCA investigation, and I said, "Bob, did you ever know this guy Joannides?" And he said, "Yeah, you know, we dealt with him a lot, he was the liaison." And I said, "Did you know what he was doing in 1963?" And he said, "He wasn't doing anything in 1963, we had an agreement with the CIA that nobody who was operational at the time of the assassination would be involved in the investigation." And I said, "Bob, think again. Joannides was running those Cubans who were in touch with Oswald. He was running the Cubans who were blaming Castro for the assassination. And then he came along and he stonewalled you." The reason why they brought Joannides in to do it was to hide the connection to Oswald.

For Robert Blakey's view of this issue see his essay "The HSCA and the CIA: The view from the Top" at the Assassination Archives Research Center website. See also *New York Times*, October 16, 2009, "CIA is Still Cagey about Oswald Mystery" by Scott Shane.

Jeff Morley: He was definitely shocked because he saw just how clever they had been. They had gone right to the heart of his investigation and figured out how to paralyze it.

Dan Hardway (reading statement by Robert Blakey): "I no longer trust anything that the Agency has told us in regard to the assassination. It lied to the Warren Commission. It lied to the ARRB. It lied to the HSCA. In admitting that Joannides was employed in a covert capacity as liaison to the HSCA, it has admitted that it violated its charter and ran a domestic covert operation aimed at subverting the HSCA and its investigation."

Jeff Morley: On the night of the assassination, the spokesman for the DRE in Miami got on the phone and started telling reporters, "We know all about the guy who killed the president."

Jeff Morley: And they talked to ten or fifteen reporters that night. So they shaped the story. The CIA's propaganda assets shaped the story from the first hours after Kennedy was dead.

> This is described in Gerald McKnight, *Breach of Trust*, pp 349–50, also in Morley's *Miami New Times* article.

Narrator: Even the Assassination Records Review Board had trouble getting documents from government agencies. In late 1992, a month after the Records Act was passed, the Secret Service began its compliance plan, but by January of 1995, it had begun destroying important documents.

John Tunheim: And they destroyed a group of records which involve threats to President Kennedy in the fall of 1963. They have what are called threat sheets. And there were many threats made to President Kennedy's life during the year in 1963. They fought us on release of those records, they even enlisted Vice President Gore's wife to help them because she had a very legitimate concern for mental health records. And the idea was that this might disclose the names of people who had mental health problems. In the end, when we required agencies to disclose, to swear under oath that they had located all assassination records and had turned everything over to us, the Secret Service refused to sign the document under oath. I think that was telling.

Thomas Samoluk: The destruction of records is actually referenced in the Assassination Records Review Board Final Report. Very, very disappointing. They were records that related to trips that President Kennedy had taken in the fall of 1963 prior to him going to Dallas.

> The issue is concisely reviewed in the ARRB Final Report, p. 149; Doug Horne describes this dispute in more detail in *Inside the ARRB* vol. 5, pp. 1451–58.

John Newman: In the FBI, a stop or flash was placed on Oswald's files, which meant that no one could ask for a document in those files or no one could even add a document to those files without going through the FBI's espionage division. And that lasted for four years. It was essentially a blinking red light on Oswald's files at FBI. On 8 October 1963, an FBI agent whose name was Marvin Gheesling took that status off of Oswald's files. He dropped the flag on Oswald's files. What that action did was to lower Oswald's threat profile at the FBI just weeks before the Kennedy assassination, and what that would mean is it was no reason to put Oswald's name on the Security Index. One thing about the Security Index is when you have a presidential motorcade going through a particular route, anybody who's on that index has to be removed from where they are. They cannot be on the parade route. That action at the FBI, didn't happen in isolation. The same thing happened at CIA at exactly the same time. And of course, it exposes the president to a dangerous situation that he shouldn't have been.

> These circumstances at FBI and CIA are reviewed by Newman in his essay in *The Assassinations*, "Oswald, the CIA and Mexico City," edited by James DiEugenio and Lisa Pease, on pp. 222–23.

Narrator: Few people knew that there'd been at least two prior plots to kill President Kennedy in 1963. One was in Chicago on November 2nd. The second was in Tampa on November 18th.

Oliver Stone: Kennedy ended up not going to Chicago. Tell us about that plot.

Paul Bleau: An informant on October 31, an informant named Lee, who could have been Lee Harvey Oswald, gave a warning to the FBI stating that four Cubans were headed to Chicago to shoot Kennedy. The following day, a landlady reported to the Chicago police that she had rented a room to four people that had rifles with telescopic sights and a sketch of the motorcade. The FBI passed that on to the Secret Service. And the Secret Service botched the surveillance of these four individuals. Two of them escaped, but they actually picked up two of the snipers and they detained them. They were stonewalled by the snipers. They didn't get any information out of them. While this was going on, there was another threat coming in from another alternate patsy named Thomas Arthur Vallee, who was making open and loud threats that he would assassinate Kennedy. They only picked him up when Kennedy canceled his trip on November 2nd at 10:00 in the morning. One day before the trip, the Diem brothers had been assassinated. And that was the stated reason for the cancellation of the trip to Chicago.

Paul Bleau: What you found in Vallee and the whole Chicago plot is so many similarities to what eventually happened in Dallas that it can't be considered coincidental. Vallee, if we compare him to Oswald is an ex-Marine. He had been posted like Oswald in the Far East on a station that was linked to the CIA because there were U-2 surveillance planes on it. It was easy to portray him as disgruntled, anti-Kennedy, a loner, armed. He had another intelligence link that he shared with Oswald in that he trained Cuban exiles for combat, which was a CIA responsibility. And Oswald, we know, at least offered to do that, he most likely did train Cuban exiles, but we know he tried to. Oswald, as we know, was moved from New Orleans to Dallas in October to be there just at the right time for the motorcade. And he's placed in a tall building where he gets a job and he's adjacent to the perfect kill zone. Now, if we look at what happened to Vallee, he's moved like a pawn in August from Long Island to Chicago to be in there in time for the motorcade. And where does he get a job? In a tall building adjacent to the motorcade with a perfect view of a kill zone. It would have forced Kennedy's motorcade to do a sharp turn, slow down and be in a point where you could have that perfect triangulation of fire.

The Chicago plot is discussed in Jim Douglass's *JFK and the Unspeakable*, pp. 202–207 and 213–18; see also Edwin Black's "The Plot to Kill JFK in Chicago: November 2, 1963" in the *Chicago Independent*, November 1975, available online; and Abraham Bolden's e-book *The Echo from Dealey Plaza*, pp. 54–55.

Oliver Stone: And what about the trip to Florida?

Paul Bleau: On November 18th, Kennedy was scheduled to do a twenty-seven mile-long motorcade in Tampa. The Secret Service was very nervous about the Floridian Hotel where the motorcade would have gone by. It would have forced a sharp turn. Nobody fired away at him. But in this case, the alternate patsy would have been a Gilberto Policarpo Lopez. He was a Cuban exile. He attended Fair Play for Cuba Committee meetings. One day after the assassination on November 23rd, he makes his way to Mexico City. The Fair Play for Cuba Committee loaned him money for his travel, and he ends up being the lone passenger on an airplane to Cuba. The CIA, they found out about the Fair Play for Cuba Committee, the weird trip to Mexico City, the fact that he was a known passenger on a plane to Cuba. And they didn't pass on the information to the Warren Commission. So when the HSCA found out about this lead that wasn't pursued, even they called it "egregious".

Lopez is discussed in Larry Hancock's *Someone Would Have Talked* (pp. 14–15); Henry Hurt, *Reasonable Doubt*, pp. 420–21; House Select Committee Final Report, pp. 118–21. For the protection of Kennedy in Tampa, see Vince Palamara's website. A valuable source for both these plots is Vince Palamara's eponymous web site vincepalamara.com

Oliver Stone: And what do you think was the relevance of it?

Paul Bleau: Well, if he had been assassinated in Tampa, Lopez, he would have been the potential patsy. If they had to admit to a front shot because

Oswald was behind, there were rumors that he had assisted Oswald in the assassination in Dallas.

Oliver Stone: Had anyone, anyone, tried to speak to the Warren Commission about these incidents?

Paul Bleau: Abraham Bolden was the first black Secret Service agent assigned to the White House detail and he was handpicked by Kennedy. He was in Chicago when this plot went down. So he was there when the Secret Service was briefed about the four snipers and he witnessed how much the security was lax for Chicago. And he also witnessed after the assassination the steps that were taken to keep the Chicago plot completely secret. No paper trail, compartmentalized, agents ordered to keep silent about it. This information did not make its way to Secret Service agents that were protecting Kennedy for future motorcades, including Dallas.

> The information about Bolden trying to call the Warren Commission is in Jim Douglass's book *JFK and the Unspeakable*, p. 215. For the secrecy about the agent reports, see also Douglass, p. 214.

Narrator: Secret Service agent Elmer Moore was aware of Agent Bolden and the Chicago plot.

Jim Gochenaur: I met with Elmer three times face-to-face. Several phone calls, very short. One very long one. I first asked him, "Did you ever interview Thomas Arthur Vallee?" And he said, "Oh, Washington wouldn't let me see the files on that." I said, "Oh, well, what about a man, a Secret Service agent by the name of Abraham Bolden?" His demeanor completely changed. He stood up from his chair. He pulled out his revolver and he put it on the table, right in front of me. He leaned over the table and he says, "Jim, tell me right now, who are you working for?" I said, "I'm an independent researcher." He told me in a very loud voice, and with a very stern look on his face, "That goddamned lying nigger. We finally got 'em." I said, "You got him?" He said, "No, Kelly and the chief got 'em." I think that Moore and the rest of his crew were scared speechless that Bolden knew something.

Paul Bleau: Abraham Bolden was one person who did try to say what he knew to the Warren Commission, but they blocked him. He was blocked from talking and eventually railroaded into some phony crime and put into jail for a number of years.

> For the unfair treatment of Bolden, see Douglass, *JFK and the Unspeakable*, p. 215.

Jim Gochenaur: Moore leaned back in his big comfortable leather chair and he said, "Who killed Jack Kennedy?" Then he said, "Well, I'll tell you who didn't. With 100 percent certainty. It wasn't the Russians." And my head is starting to swim, I wanted to break in right at that point. But then he said, "I'll tell you why—JFK was the Russians' boy. He was giving away everything he could. That man, for all intents and purposes, dare I say it? Jim, I will say it, JFK was a traitor."

> The ARRB declassified a wealth of material on Elmer Moore. Prior to 1994 there had been very little written about him. For a synopsis, which includes work by Gary Aguilar and Pat Speer, see *The JFK Assassination: The Evidence Today* by James DiEugenio, pp. 166–69. Moore eventually became Earl Warren's personal escort on the Commission.

Narrator: The ghost of John Kennedy would turn over in his grave at these cruel words. But the truth is, the competing narrative of his life and death, as told us by Allen Dulles and his ilk— of a leftist assassin killing a president with three shots from a sixth-floor window—has won the day … and continues as the official story. … But the ghost will not be appeased.

1961

Narrator: After the Bay of Pigs debacle, JFK began to use his brother Bobby as a foreign policy adviser. Bobby was influential in the decision to fire Allen Dulles. He then figured as an important adviser during the Berlin confrontation, on Vietnam in both 1961 and '63, and during the Missile Crisis.

RFK's role in the aftermath of the Bay of Pigs is described by Arthur Schlesinger in *Robert Kennedy and His Times* (pp. 474–79). For the Berlin Crisis and RFK's role in it, see John Newman's *Into the Storm*, chapter 5.

Oliver Stone: After the Cuban Missile Crisis, wasn't President Kennedy attempting a back channel with Russia and Cuba and your father was aware of it?

Robert F. Kennedy Jr.: Jack had an intense interest in Cuban history and all the history of Latin America. And he believed that Castro had a point. In fact he sent a message to Castro that he read and admired Castro's declaration at the Sierra Maestra about the liberation of Cuba and the right of the Cuban people to exercise sovereignty over their nation, over their island. The message that he sent through Lisa Howard and Attwood was a message that: We don't care if you're communists. We don't care if you're Marxists. We don't care what kind of government you experiment with. The only thing we care about is you don't make your island a platform for Soviet aggression in the hemisphere. And that you stop your campaign against the Alliance for Progress nations, against the social democrats, Betancourt in Venezuela, Lleras Camargo in Colombia, people who really were trying to democratize their country and develop fair systems for the poor.

For the Kennedy/Castro back channel, see Schlesinger, *Robert Kennedy and His Times*, pp. 573–81.

Robert F. Kennedy Jr.: By '62, President Kennedy was actively engaged with Khrushchev and they had a secret exchange of twenty-six letters with each other. And they were operating through back channels, because both of them found themselves in identical positions; surrounded by war hawks, surrounded by a bellicose intelligence military establishment and all of them viewing all-out thermonuclear war, not only as inevitable, but in some cases desirable. The first of those letters was smuggled by Khrushchev through a KGB spy named Georgi Bolshakov. Georgi was a friend of my parents. My uncle wrote the first of his from Cape Cod and he talked about how his children and their cousins, which meant us, were playing in the yard and that these two leaders had no right to bring the world to a crisis that would destroy children like us who had no political involvement. And the millions of other people around the world who would be destroyed. And that it would be their failure and their sin if they allowed that to happen. And they proceeded along a course that ended up with them really talking very seriously about complete demobilization. And Khrushchev's career was ended by that as well.

The beginning of this correspondence is described by James Douglass in *JFK and the Unspeakable*, p. 23.

JFK speech clip: "Among the many traits the peoples of our two countries have in common, none is stronger than our mutual abhorrence of war. Almost unique among the major world powers, we have never been at war with each other."

Lisa Pease: Norman Cousins, who was then the editor of *The Saturday Review*, had gotten a meeting with Khrushchev. And so Norman Cousins goes to Kennedy and he said, "Let's talk about antinuclear plans. Let's see if we can, you know, go for some sort of form of disarmament." He's like, "What can I say as to your level of commitment?" And Kennedy's like, "I'm 100 percent committed to disarming our nukes." And that was very difficult because, again, there are hard-liners on both sides. And so they ended up with the Limited Test Ban Treaty where they banned all above ground testing. But that's what came of that meeting, in that conversation. But when he came back, he also said, "Khrushchev's going to need a real sign from you that you're really committed to this."

Cousins described his role in the exchange, which included Pope John XXIV, in his book *The Improbable Triumvirate*. For Cousin's role in Kennedy's American University speech, see Douglass, pp. 346–47. For his direct communications with Khrushchev, see the film *JFK: A President Betrayed*.

David Talbot: And of course, this became very eloquently real in June of 1963, when Kennedy gives the famous "peace speech," as it came to be known, at American University.

John F. Kennedy speech: I realize the pursuit of peace is not as dramatic as the pursuit of war. And every graduate of this school, every thoughtful citizen who despairs of war and wishes to bring peace should begin by looking inward, by examining his own attitude towards the possibilities of peace, towards the Soviet Union, towards the course of the Cold War, and towards freedom and peace here at home. First, examine our attitude towards peace itself. Too many of us think it is impossible, too many think it is unreal. But that is a dangerous, defeatist belief. It leads to the conclusion that war is inevitable. That mankind is doomed. That we are gripped by forces we cannot control.

Martin Luther King Jr.: I think Mr. Kennedy has done some significant things in civil rights, and I would include the attorney general. I think that both of these men are men of genuine good will. And I think there is a necessity now to seize the urgency of the moment.

Narrator: Although we've focused primarily on foreign policy, we cannot overlook Kennedy's battles in the South with Governor Ross Barnett of Mississippi and, in that June of '63, with Governor George Wallace of Alabama. In both showdowns, using federal troops, the Kennedy administration won admission of black students to the last public colleges in the South. George Wallace made it clear that this fight was not over.

> The confrontation with Barnett over admitting James Meredith is covered in Irving Bernstein's *Promises Kept* (pp. 75–84). For the confrontation with Wallace, see also Bernstein (pp. 97–101). Robert Drew made a documentary on the Wallace-Kennedy conflict called *Crisis.*

That night, Kennedy addressed the nation in what many consider the finest presidential speech on civil rights since Abraham Lincoln.

Archive clip: Kennedy's civil rights speech

Narrator: By the fall of 1963, Kennedy had made many enemies. He was working on an American withdrawal from Vietnam, an upcoming state visit to Indonesia in '64, an independent, unified democracy in the Congo. Through Nasser, a balanced policy in the Middle East. Normalization of relations with Cuba. And détente with Russia—even going so far as to offer them a joint mission to the moon. But on November 22nd, another face of America asserted itself.

Newsreel: Several thousand enthusiastic Texans are on hand to give the president and Mrs. Kennedy a warm welcome.

Narrator: On that day the world changed.

CONSEQUENCES

Narrator: Lyndon Johnson did not have the understanding of Third World countries, nor did he have the anti-colonial sympathies that President Kennedy had. Therefore, numerous changes in foreign policy took place within a very short period of time after the assassination.

Richard Mahoney: President Johnson did a 180-degree turn in terms of Congo policy. The US, which under Kennedy was a champion of African nationalism and the lead peacekeeper in the Congo, becomes the agent of white reactionary nationalism and imperialism led by the Belgians and the South Africans, and of all things, the anti-Castro Cubans.

> The Simba Rebellion and how it provoked Johnson's reversal of Kennedy's policy is described in Jonathan Kwitny's *Endless Enemies* (pp. 79–84).

Narrator: The CIA now began to furnish planes and Cuban exile pilots to fly sorties to stamp out the rebellion. According to one pilot, the CIA manned the embassy and brought members of a secret operation from the Bay of Pigs codenamed Operation 40.

The pilot who furnished this information was the late Carl McNabb who was interviewed by Jim DiEugenio and Lisa Pease in 1996 and '97 while he was living in San Luis Obispo.

Richard Mahoney: All of whom mount this operation to return a reactionary government to power under Joseph Mobutu and to bring Moïse Tshombe, who was the secessionist leader of Katanga back in as prime minister. And it was as if the United States had never really had this deep association with African nationalism under President Kennedy.

This turn in policy is also described in Richard Mahoney's *JFK: Ordeal in Africa* (pp. 230–31).

Narrator: Joseph Mobutu became the front man for imperial forces, profiting in the billions from the riches of the Congo. The Congo never recovered from the assassination of Lumumba, and today, despite its natural resources, it is considered a failed state where 80 percent of the population live in abject poverty.

For an estimate of the pinnacle of Mobutu's wealth, see the Associated Press report by George Gedda of May 14, 1997. That report also notes that, at the time of Mobutu's death, Congo was one of the world's poorest nations. For poverty estimates today, see "Facts about Poverty in the Democratic Republic of the Congo" on the Borgen Project website.

Narrator: Like Foster Dulles, Johnson now favored Saudi Arabia over Egypt and greatly favored Israel in the Middle East. The fairness and evenhandedness Kennedy was building was lost.

For the growing divide between Nasser and Washington, see Robert Rakove, *Kennedy, Johnson, and the Nonaligned World*, pp. 158–63; for the favoritism of King Faisal of Saudi Arabia over Nasser, see Rakove, p. 200 and Robert Dreyfuss, *Devil's Game*, p.. 131, p. 144.

Narraror: In 1968, when Johnson learned Israel had acquired atomic weapons, he made the decision to order CIA director Richard Helms not to tell the Pentagon or the State Department. In 1973, while Egyptian tanks were crossing the Sinai during the Yom Kippur War, Commander Moshe Dayan proposed the use of nuclear weapons. Kennedy's goals of peace through alliances with moderates and a solution for the Palestinian refugee problem were abandoned.

There are two books on the subject of how Israel acquired highly enriched uranium from the US: Roger Mattson's *Stealing the Atom Bomb* and *Divert!* by Grant Smith. For the Helms meeting with LBJ, see Mattson, p. 98. For Dayan's atomic push in the 1973 war, see *The Times of Israel,* October 3, 2013, story by Mitch Ginsburg.

Narrator: In Latin America, JFK's Alliance for Progress, a program promoting economic development, suffered as well under Johnson. In 1964, Johnson said you could take all the gold in Fort Knox and it would just go down the drain in Latin America unless the private investor could have some confidence that he could make his investment and it would not be confiscated. Johnson's private investment idea broke with Kennedy's policy, which was to make most of the loans out of the United States Treasury, thereby charging little or no interest. Under Johnson's leadership, the future allotments for '67 to '69 were reduced and much of it was shifted to military programs. By 1973, it was eliminated.

The quote by Johnson is in John Dumbrell's *President Lyndon Johnson and Soviet Communism*, p. 135. For the immediate changes under Johnson, see *Inevitable Revolutions* by Walter LaFeber, pp. 156–58.

Narrator: Under Secretary of State George Ball referred to the island archipelago of Indonesia as the true breaking point in Asia—more important to the United States than Vietnam.

This quote is in a phone call from Ball to National Security Advisor McGeorge Bundy on March 15, 1965. It is Document 117 of Foreign Relations of the United States (FRUS), vol. 26.

Oliver Stone: What were some of Kennedy's plans for Indonesia after 1964?

Lisa Pease: Three days before Kennedy was killed, he signed an $11 million aid package that included not just military weapons—because that's something they hadn't been willing to provide before Kennedy and Kennedy knew, look, if we don't give them the weapons, they are just gonna go get them from the Soviets. So he did agree to that. But Kennedy wanted to emphasize roads, infrastructure, education, you know, money for food, money to help levee places and create rice paddies. Kennedy wanted to help Indonesia become self-sufficient.

The eleven million was part of Kennedy's larger aid plan (Greg Poulgrain, *JFK vs. Allen Dulles*, pp. 196–99). Johnson's alteration to this aid package is dealt with in Roger Hilsman's memoir of his days in the State Department, *To Move a Nation* (pp. 407–9).

Bradley Simpson: President Johnson had a visceral dislike of Sukarno that led him to conclude that he didn't want to spend any political capital attempting to appeal to a leader that he viewed as a regional bully. So Sukarno bitterly criticized the US war in Vietnam. [He] signaled that he was going to pursue a radical, anti-colonial foreign policy that the Johnson administration saw as a direct threat to American interests and something that had to be stopped. The US State Department signaled to the Indonesian army that overthrowing Sukarno and killing lots and lots of communists would produce a political payoff.

This turn in attitude and policy is described not just by Hilsman and Simpson in his *Economists with Guns*, p. 126, but also by Poulgrain, pp. 202–5 and Vincent Goossen in his online University of Amsterdam dissertation, *A Far Greater Prize than Vietnam*, pp. 90, 97, 99. The communications with the Indonesian army were done though the

US embassy in Jakarta beginning in March 1964 and are in FRUS, vol. 26, pp. 33, 40. 76.

Narrator: September 30th, 1965. Following rumors of a suspected military coup against Sukarno, leftist officers tried to bring the disloyal generals to trial. Their plan quickly descended into chaos, and General Suharto took control. The Indonesian army, with CIA support, blamed the killing of the generals on the Communist Party. General Suharto then used this as a pretext to turn the army on the communists and eventually neutralized President Sukarno, taking his place as president.

See chapter 7 of Poulgrain for a depiction of the events of that evening and the next morning. Two recent studies based on newly discovered information reveal the immediate and direct role of General Suharto and the Indonesian army in the 1965 massacres: Geoffrey Robinson's *The Killing Season* and Jessica Melvin's *The Army and the Indonesian Genocide* (Margaret Scott, *New York Review of Books*, "Uncovering Indonesia's Act of Killing," October 20, 2017).

Lisa Pease: Five hundred thousand at least were killed. People that were identified as communists, whether they were or not, whether they even knew what communism was or not. If their name was on a list, they were killed.

The estimates of how many were killed range from three hundred thousand to a million (Poulgrain, p. 208).

Bradley Simpson: And this is the most consequential legacy of President Kennedy's assassination, the coming to power of a president who not only didn't care about Indonesia, but who surrounded himself with officials who had a stake in a far more confrontational approach towards Indonesia that ultimately resulted in a spasm of mass killing in which nearly half a million unarmed civilians were killed by the Indonesian army.

The US had a more direct role than has been revealed in the overthrow. For many years, the stipulation had been that the State Department and CIA had only submitted lists of names to be rounded up and imprisoned (see *New York Times*, July 12, 1990, article by Michael Wines). With later declassifications and work by Simpson, we now know that the CIA supplied small arms, communications equipment, and medicines to Suharto's forces. Goossen, p. 133, and FRUS, vol. 26, p. 165. The best explication of what really occurred in Indonesia on September 30, 1965, is outlined in Poulgrain's book, pp. 221–48.

Narrator: Regarding Vietnam, a review of the declassified record shows that Kennedy continuously pushed back against the Pentagon by refusing every request to commit combat troops there. This conflict is reflected in a National Security Action Memorandum—NSAM 273. Drafted in the days before his death, in its final form it allowed for direct American involvement in Vietnam.

Gordon Goldstein chronicles these refusals in his book *Lessons in Disaster*, pp. 52–55.

John Newman: McGeorge Bundy, who's the national security adviser, puts together a memo based upon the truth about the war, which is it's going terribly. And he does it in a way to try and make sure that Kennedy would be able to go along with it. So the way he writes the first draft of 273 is to say, look, we need to intensify the war effort against the communists. But the way we're gonna do it is to increase South Vietnamese forces. There's not a word about American forces or Americanizing the war.

Narrator: In fact, after much maneuvering, Kennedy, Bundy, and Secretary of Defense McNamara had already settled on a plan to withdraw one thousand US troops by 1963, with the goal of having South Vietnam responsible for its own combat operations.

This discussion of NSAM 263 between JFK, McNamara, and Bundy is in transcript form in *Virtual JFK* edited by James Blight (pp. 296–98). The National Security Action Memorandum is on p. 302.

John Newman: While Kennedy's body is still in the casket in the rotunda over on the Capitol building is when Johnson changes NSAM 273 to a new version. It's Sunday and McGeorge Bundy has to take the old version around town and show it to Rusk and show it to all the principals and get their input. And when it comes to the key paragraph, paragraph seven, which talks about how we're going to intensify the war, all of a sudden, the restrictions that McGeorge Bundy had put on that, instead of changing a few words, there's two big hash marks through that paragraph and it's completely rewritten. And I asked Bundy in an interview, I said, "Who told you to do that?" He said, "Johnson did."

The two versions of NSAM 273 are online at the Mary Ferrell Foundation website under the rubric "Kennedy-Johnson transition in Vietnam."

Narrator: In the Review Board's declassifications, there is evidence that Johnson was fully aware of Kennedy's Vietnam withdrawal plans, disagreed with them, and worked on Robert McNamara to make him renounce them.

LBJ clip: I always thought it was foolish for you to make any statements about withdrawing. I thought it was bad psychologically. But you and the president thought otherwise and I just sat silent.

The above is from a phone call of February 20, 1964. The book *Virtual JFK* contains a documentary section, including this call and others, between LBJ and McNamara which demonstrate how Johnson turned his defense secretary around on Vietnam. This issue is also touched on in Gordon Goldstein's *Lessons in Disaster*, pp. 105–6.

James Galbraith: McNamara came into this decision to withdraw US forces, and in my view, he implemented it faithfully until the time that Kennedy was killed.

As Jim Douglass writes in *JFK and the Unspeakable*, the two men who implemented Kennedy's withdrawal plan were John Kenneth

Galbraith and McNamara (pp. 119–26). See also *Virtual JFK*, edited by James Blight, p. 129.

Narrator: These changes allowed the US to unilaterally engage in combat in Vietnam, rather than simply supporting and advising South Vietnamese troops, which led to serious consequences.

John Newman: And within days, we're talking about sending out the DESO-TO missions, these naval excursions along the coastline of North Vietnam. That ends up with the *Maddox* and the so-called Tonkin Gulf attacks and then the resolution in Congress opening the door to intervention in Vietnam.

Newman argues in the 2017 edition of *JFK and Vietnam* that it was Johnson's alterations to NSAM 273 that allowed direct American involvement in the war (pp. 447–458). Edwin Moise dates the start of these joint OPLAN34A CIA/Pentagon operations against the North from December 15, 1963 (*Tonkin Gulf and the Escalation of the Vietnam War*, pp. 5–7). David Kaiser also discusses this issue and writes that the Pentagon realized that if the US struck into North Vietnam this would cause retaliation and therefore give Johnson the excuse to begin bombing (*American Tragedy*, pp. 293–94).

Robert McNamara clip: In retaliation for this unprovoked attack on the high seas, our forces have struck the bases used by the North Vietnamese patrol craft.

John Newman: But the new news there is it wasn't Johnson who figured out, you know, the day after Kennedy was shot that he needed to change this NSAM. He just rubber-stamped what Taylor had been doing covertly ever since NSAM 263.

For General Taylor's tinkering with NSAM 263, see the 2017 edition of *JFK and Vietnam*, pp. 443–46.

Narrator: And, as declassified memos have revealed, by autumn of 1964, during his campaign against Barry Goldwater, Johnson had already decided that he was going to escalate the Vietnam War. In fact, the directive that would become the Tonkin Gulf Resolution had been written before the Tonkin Gulf incident itself.

> The drafting of the Tonkin Gulf Resolution was begun in May and revised in June 1964 (see Moise, p. 27). Johnson's escalation of the war is dealt with in chapter 5 of Blight's *Virtual JFK.*

LBJ clip: We are not about to send American boys nine to ten thousand miles away from home to do what Asian boys ought to be doing for themselves.

Narrator: On August 7th, three months before the election, Johnson had already planned for an extensive air war. It was to begin after his inauguration.

> August 7, 1964, was when the Tonkin Gulf Resolution passed Congress. But Johnson had already made the decision to go to war in Indochina months before (see Moise, pp. 26–27; Goldstein, pp 108–16; Fredrik Logevall, *Choosing War*, p. 129). As Logevall writes, the *New York Times* reported that by March 21st, all thoughts of withdrawal had been rejected.

LBJ clip: We intend to convince the communists that we cannot be defeated by force of arms or by superior powers.

JFK speech clip: And no nation in the history of battle ever suffered more than the Soviet Union in the Second World War. At least 20 million lost their lives. Countless millions of homes and families were burned or sacked. A third of the nation's territory, including two thirds of its industrial base, was turned into a wasteland. A loss equivalent to the destruction of this country east of Chicago.

Narrator: After his brother's death, Robert Kennedy knew that relations with the Soviet Union hung in the balance.

Robert F. Kennedy Jr.: On November 29th, which is one week after the assassination, my father had a meeting with Bill Walton, who was a friend of the family and was on, it was a cultural trip to the Soviet Union. And he asked Walton to convey a message through Georgi Bolshakov to Premier Khrushchev, saying that our family knew that the Soviets were not involved in the assassination, that it was a right-wing plot from our own country.

David Talbot: In other words, the CIA, or forces aligned with the CIA. They said they also believed that Bobby Kennedy intended to run for office, and that eventually he would get back to the White House. And when he did, he planned to resume his brother's policies of détente and peace with the Soviet Union. But they had to bide their time and wait for that political opportunity. This is a stunning message to be delivering to Bolshakov, because, of course, Bolshakov is going to take this right to the Kremlin.

Narrator: When Khrushchev paid his respects to President Kennedy at the American Embassy, he was reportedly holding back tears. Castro got the news of Kennedy's death while discussing détente with the French journalist Jean Daniel. He then exclaimed, "This is bad news. Everything is now going to change." Like Bobby Kennedy, neither man believed the conclusions of the Warren Report.

> The Walton mission is described in *One Hell of a Gamble* by Tim Naftali and Aleksandr Fursenko, pp. 344–46, and also in David Talbot's *Brothers*, pp. 25–34. For Khrushchev's weeping over JFK's death, and his lack of belief in the Warren Report, see William Taubman's *Khrushchev: The Man and his Era*, p. 604. Castro's reaction was recorded by French journalist Jean Daniel, who was with him at the time, in "When Castro Heard the News," *The New Republic*, December 7, 1963. Castro's speech doubting Oswald's guilt is in the Warren Commission, vol. 26, Commission Exhibit 2954.

Lisa Pease: When news came of Kennedy's death, all over the planet, people were mourning and crying and going to embassies. In Latin America, where people just lit candles because they didn't even have electrical power. But they wanted to honor his killing. In the Yucatán Peninsula, peasants cleared an area and planted a peace garden.

Worldwide reactions by continent are captured in the article "The Shot Felt 'Round the World" at the Association for Diplomatic Studies website. See also Rakove, p. xvii and Muehlenbeck, pp. 226–31.

Philip Muehlenbeck: Nasser learned of Kennedy's death in the middle of the night. He got up, dressed, went down to his office, and then realized there's nothing I can do about this. According to his son, Nasser went into a great state of depression after Kennedy's death. Relations with Egypt gradually deteriorated and they increasingly shifted their allegiance towards the Soviet Union as well.

Muehlenbeck, p. 228.

Robert Rakove: A mass was held in the leading Catholic church in Cairo, which has a capacity of six hundred. They somehow fit four thousand people into that church. Algeria, which had a special feeling for Kennedy, declared a state of mourning for a week. Flags were flown at half-mast. The US ambassador to Egypt said that he thought the Egyptians had seen in Kennedy the best of what they saw in Americans, that Kennedy had represented a kind of ideal of America to ordinary Egyptians.

For the Cairo mass, and Algeria's mourning, see *Support Any Friend* by Warren Bass, pp. 241–42, for the Egypt reaction see Muehlenbeck, pp. 228, 231.

Robert F. Kennedy Jr.: They poll historians, they poll the American people and say who are the most popular presidents. One metric that you can use to objectively at least judge their foreign policy is how many boulevards are named after that president in foreign countries, how many hospitals, how many colleges, how many schools, how many statues are standing of that president in capitals all over the world? And in that sense, President Kennedy beats every other president hands down.

Narrator: That feeling is not held only abroad. Many people at home felt that after Kennedy's death, a period of depression and cynicism overtook the country and that America was somehow changed forever. Our overwhelming disbelief in the Warren Commission's findings contributed to increased skepticism of all our foundational beliefs about government.

For polling results on this issue see Larry Sabato's *The Kennedy Half Century,* p. 416; 91 percent of the respondents said JFK's murder changed the nation "a great deal."

David Talbot: I think there's a direct thread between the events of 1963 and the kind of horror show that America is having to endure right now. And I think once you kill a president in broad daylight on the streets of an American city, and everyone knows that powerful forces did it, and it can never be solved, that crime, that sends a signal, not only to the American people, but to the American media, to American future leaders. And if America really wants a democratic society, then we should get to the bottom of this traumatic crime that continues to reverberate throughout American history.

Narrator: The Assassination Records Review Board made many startling discoveries in the four years of its existence.

Narrator: In October of 2017, in compliance with the JFK Records Act twenty-five-year deadline, President Trump said unless he was in receipt of further information, he would not block declassification of the last of the files. Six months later, he postponed releasing the last batch, which the Review Board had previously delayed from 1998. This means that fifty-six years later, the US government is still maintaining secrets about the JFK case. Can a democracy survive if it does not know its deepest secrets about the darkest days of its past?

For the delay, see Ian Shapia's *Chicago Tribune* story of April 26, 2018.

Oliver Stone: Do you think there was any connection between your father's assassination and your uncle's?

Robert F. Kennedy Jr.: I don't think anybody has connected all the dots. There are dots there. There are dots that look like certainly that are, that we should be investigating. And my father's death has never been investigated properly.

There are several good books on the Robert Kennedy assassination. The most recent, and perhaps the most comprehensive, is Lisa Pease's *A Lie Too Big to Fail.*

RFK clip: Because I think we can do better. And I think we can do better around the rest of the world. I'm not going to be satisfied until that war is over and American soldiers are brought back here.

JFK peace speech clip: I have therefore chosen this time and place to discuss a topic on which ignorance too often abounds and the truth too rarely perceived, and that is the most important topic on Earth: peace. What kind of a peace do I mean and what kind of a peace do we seek? Not a Pax Americana, enforced on the world by American weapons of war. Not the peace of the grave or the security of the slave. I am talking about genuine peace, the kind of peace that makes life on earth worth living, is the kind that enables men and nations to grow and to hope and build a better life for their children. Not merely peace for Americans, but peace for all men and women. Not merely peace in our time, but peace in all time.

Afterword
by James DiEugenio

The time was August 20, 2019. The scene was Oliver Stone's office in West Los Angeles. Oliver talked to each interview subject before they went before the camera.

Cyril Wecht: How many interviews did you schedule?

Oliver Stone: About thirty.

Cyril Wecht (Looking surprised): Thirty?

It took three years to write, produce, and edit both versions of *JFK Revisited.* One of the main reasons it took so long was the simple fact that probably no JFK documentary ever did as many on-camera interviews as this one did. And if not for some unfortunate extenuating circumstances, the number would have been even higher.

As the reader can see from viewing *JFK Revisited* and reading the annotated transcripts of both versions, the film is bifurcated into two general evidentiary sections. The first deals with the forensics of the assassination of President Kennedy. The second section deals with Kennedy's developing foreign policy ideas, his attempt to enact them as president, and their reversal after his murder. This second section is dealt with in more aspects and at greater length in the four-hour version, *Destiny Betrayed*.

Concerning the forensics, as the screenwriter, I decided to focus on what I thought were three pillars of evidence which, by any objective person's account, appear to be quite solid. One of my standards was: Could an attorney present this in court? If so, could it survive cross-examination by the prosecution and be made credible to a jury?

The first pillar was CE 399. At the start we must differentiate CE 399 from the single-bullet theory. They are not the same. The single-bullet theory is a trajectory hypothesis dreamed up by the late Arlen Specter for the Warren Commission. It was created by necessity from the paucity of shells found at the alleged crime scene: the sixth floor of the Texas School Book Depository. The Commission concluded that one bullet completely missed Kennedy's limousine. Another bullet struck the rear of Kennedy's skull, its head and tail landing on the floor of the front seat. Consequently, the Commission was left with one bullet to do all the bodily damage to Kennedy and Governor John Connally. Therefore, Specter created what he called the single- bullet theory: one bullet transiting two people, breaking through skin seven times, and smashing two bones in Connally.

Warren Commission defenders have done everything under the sun to try and make Specter's seven-wound trajectory work. This necessitated the construction of several Rube Goldberg contraptions which, upon analysis, are rendered rather humorous. This includes the work of Thomas Canning for the House Select Committee on Assassinations. (For a critique of Canning, see *Hear No Evil* by Don Thomas, pp. 421–50.) This effort reached the realm of low camp with what Dale Myers did on ABC for the 2003 program *Beyond Conspiracy*. Myers's cartoon has been taken apart by Pat Speer, Bob Harris, Larry Schnapf, and John Orr.

What we did in *JFK Revisited* was to focus the question as such: If there was a magic bullet, what bullet was it? Because it sure as heck was not Commission Exhibit 399. Our intent was to show that CE 399 was not fired in Dealey Plaza that day and would likely never be admitted into a court of law. If it *were* admitted, it would be rendered worthless—actually worse than that—upon examination. As the reader can see, we did this through multiple lines of evidence. One was Dr. Joseph Dolce, who actually worked for the Commission. He states that the idea that a Mannlicher-Carcano bullet could do all this one supposedly did and lose only *2.4 grains* of its mass is simply not possible. He also states that he could not duplicate that feat in his Commission experiments. (For more on Dolce, see Gerald McKnight's, *Breach of Trust*, pp. 185–89.)

This is one plane of evidence impeaching CE 399.

The second plane involves the legal doctrine of chain of custody. In the film we have two professionals discuss this topic: Brian Edwards and Dr. Henry Lee. Brian was a veteran police investigator who testified at many trials and today teaches criminal justice. Lee was a police captain in Taiwan for five years. He was later Commissioner of Public Safety in Connecticut for two years. In those functions he supervised many criminal investigations. He is without question one of the foremost criminalists in America.

With these two men explaining the importance of the issue, the film demonstrates just how indefensible the chain of custody for CE 399 is. There is no other way to say this, and we prove it in the film: it was so bad that the FBI lied about it. In more than one way. The exposure of the charade of agent Bardwell Odum interviewing O. P. Wright and Darrell Tomlinson, the first two people to handle the bullet, owes to the investigation by Gary Aguilar and Josiah Thompson. Which owes much to the ARRB. (See *The Assassinations*, edited by James DiEugenio and Lisa Pease, pp. 282–86.)

But it's worse than that. Because the work of the late John Hunt shows that the FBI lied about Elmer Lee Todd's initials being on CE 399 and also the time it arrived at FBI headquarters that evening (James DiEugenio, *The JFK Assassination: The Evidence Today*, pp. 248–50).

We could have gone even further in our impeachment of this exhibit. As Josiah Thompson and Don Thomas both showed in their respective volumes, the Commission could not prove that CE 399 was found on John Connally's stretcher. Which is where it would have had to have been discovered for Specter's invention to work. In all probability, the stretcher Tomlinson picked the bullet up from belonged to a young boy named Ronnie Fuller (see Thomas, pp. 392–99; Thompson *Six Seconds in Dallas*, pp. 154–65). It is clear through Arlen Specter's interview of Tomlinson that he understood this problem. Specter's whole line of questioning with the man would not have been allowed in court since it was a textbook example of a lawyer leading a witness (Warren Commission, vol. 6, pp. 128–34).

Thompson gave an important speech at the 2003 Duquesne University JFK Assassination Conference. He revealed that, in a 1993 interview, O. P. Wright's widow—who also worked at Parkland Hospital—said that more than one nurse had approached her in the twenty-four hours after the assassination because they also found bullets on gurneys.

In reality, Commission Exhibit 399 was always an example of a cat chasing its tail. The question that should have been asked by everyone involved—the FBI, the Commission, the Dallas Police—was this: Who planted this bullet? This leads to my second pillar.

In 2011, author Barry Ernest first published his fine book about witness Victoria Adams and her relationship with attorney David Belin during the proceedings of the Warren Commission. In *The Girl on the Stairs*, Barry also brought in Victoria's corroborating witnesses: Sandy Styles and Dorothy Garner. The long-suppressed document showing Garner's agreement with their testimony—a document the Commission had—was made available due to the ARRB. Barry's book showed, through these three witnesses, that Oswald had a strong alibi for where he was at the time of the shooting. In all probability, he was not on the sixth floor when the Commission needed him to be there.

The question of whether or not the pictures in the National Archives represent Kennedy's brain was only made possible due to the ARRB. It is difficult to comprehend, but it took thirty years for the evidence undermining those pictures to surface. But once it did, it exploded on the scene. As ARRB analyst Doug Horne states in the film, because of John Stringer's testimony before that body, the extant photos in the Archives would not be allowed in a court of law. Stringer disagreed with the depiction of the brain photos on five different and substantive grounds (Douglas Horne, *Inside the ARRB*, p. 810). We also point out the fact that the official weight of Kennedy's brain is above what the average weight should be. This is highly suspect considering all the damage done to Kennedy's skull when he was hit at Zapruder film frame 313 (Horne, p. 797).

I personally felt that these three pieces of evidence would be enough to acquit Oswald. Especially since the first and the third strongly indicate that there is fraud in the evidentiary record. The second suggests witness manipulation and the concealment of exculpatory evidence. These grounds would be more than enough for an attorney to request a dismissal of charges. But we did bring in other areas that I also thought could be introduced at trial:

- The pressure brought to bear on Dr. Malcolm Perry to change his story about the origin of Kennedy's throat wound
- Reporter Tom Alyea's observation that the positioning of the shells found at the crime scene had been altered
- The serious questions about whether or not Lee Oswald actually ordered the rifle in evidence
- FBI expert Sebastian Latona's testimony that he found no prints of value on that rifle when he examined it in Washington
- The fact that the HSCA had falsified its report and had buried evidence that Kennedy had a baseball-sized hole in the rear of his skull
- A neurologist's testimony that the particle trail in Kennedy's skull betrays a front-to-back trajectory
- The likely probability that it was Robert Knudsen who took a different set of autopsy pictures of JFK
- The testimony of Saundra Spencer who told the ARRB that she saw a set of pictures different than those in the Archives
- The evidence that there were two prior plots to kill Kennedy in November, one in Chicago and one in Tampa
- The fact that the FBI tried to conceal the relationship between the alleged Marxist Oswald and the right-wing fanatic Guy Banister
- The fact that the CIA lied to the HSCA about their liaison George Joannides and what he was really doing in the summer of 1963

Almost all of these had been known in the critical community for a while. But even though many TV documentaries had been broadcast after the ARRB closed shop in 1998, virtually none of this information had been relayed to the public. Make no mistake; that is the way the networks want it. For instance, at a dinner during a two day JFK mock trial in Houston in 2017, attorney Larry Schnapf interviewed Alec Baldwin. He asked him why a liberal like Rachel Maddow would support the Warren Commission. Baldwin said he could explain that since he had a show on MSNBC in 2013 and had planned a program for the fiftieth anniversary of the Kennedy case . He even lined up his guests. The episode was canceled. He was told by a senior producer that NBC policy was to support the Warren Commission. About a month later his show was taken off the air. Also at that fiftieth anniversary, former TV producer John Barbour got in contact with Tom Brokaw since he knew Brokaw was producing a program on the JFK case. He told the newsman he would like five minutes on his program to talk about what he knew about Jim Garrison since he had done a long interview with the district attorney. Brokaw told him, "No Garrison, John."

With that unofficial but very real embargo in place, it fell to Oliver Stone, producer Rob Wilson, and myself to put together a program. If we had not, it is doubtful the public would have ever learned about the discoveries of the Review Board. They would have existed in an historical vacuum, in an alternative universe. Considering the impact President Kennedy's assassination had on America and the world, that would have been like continuing a national amnesia bloc of Jungian dimensions. Why that would have been the case is explained by the other part of the film, where we explore who John F. Kennedy really was, and how his ideas on foreign policy were formed and enacted. This writer feels that the establishment's cover-up about this has been even more rigorous and systematic than the one about the circumstances of his assassination.

The 1991 film *JFK* relied on the work of the late Fletcher Prouty and former military intelligence analyst John Newman for one of the film's theses. Namely that Kennedy was withdrawing from Vietnam at the time of his assassination, and this was reversed by Lyndon Johnson within days of him taking office. As we show in the film, there is even more evidence to prove this today. Newman presents it in the film while James Galbraith describes his father's role in advising Kennedy on his planned withdrawal.

But due to new work by other scholars—who are in the long version of *JFK Revisited*—we present evidence that Kennedy's reformist foreign policy had a wider reach than Vietnam. His ideas impacted Indonesia, the Middle East, Latin America, and Africa, as well as American relations with Cuba and the Soviet Union. After the assassination, those policies all reverted back to what they were under President Eisenhower. The fact that this quite visible shift happened relatively quickly after JFK's death indicates that his murder constituted a coup d'état. In the *Destiny Betrayed* version of the film, we suggest that two possible suspects in the coup were former CIA Director Allen Dulles and Air Force Chief of Staff General Curtis LeMay.

JFK Revisited is the first film to broadcast to a worldwide market the things we have learned about this epochal event from the Review Board. In fact, after the film debuted at the Cannes Film Festival last summer, the distributor collected the European reviews, which were quite positive. The long version of the film sold in Australia and created strong media reaction: three national news atories and an appearance by the writer on a national morning program. Both versions played the Rome Film Festival in theaters about a mile from each other. The Sky network picked up the long version in the United Kingdom.

But predictably, when Showtime distributed the film in the United States, the MSM had to chime in. One of the most ridiculous counters to the film is a mythology used by, for example, Tim Wiener in *Rolling Stone*. Borrowing from author Max Holland, Tim said that Jim Garrison got his ideas about a JFK conspiracy from an Italian newspaper and its revelations about Clay Shaw's employment by a mysterious business entity in Rome. This nonsense ignores the facts that Garrison had been investigating Shaw since December of 1966, three months before the Italian story appeared (William Davy, *Let Justice Be Done*, pp. 63–64). Garrison also knew about the alleged Marxist Oswald at the wildly rightwing Guy Banister's office at 544 Camp Street, and the DA had already read about Oswald taking a Russian language test in the service (Jim Garrison, *On the Trial of the Assassins*, p. 22, p. 24). By February 24, 1967 Garrison suspected Clay Shaw was Clay Bertrand, the man who had called a New Orleans lawyer to go to Dallas to defend Oswald (Davy, p. 120). In addition, he was well aware of Oswald's relationship with David Ferrie, who knew both Banister and Shaw. Based on all this, and more, Garrison arrested Shaw before the story in Italy was published. So much for Tim Wiener.

JFK Revisited: Through the Looking Glass was first shown at the Cannes Film Festival in July 2021. When all is said and done, it will have created news stories and bulletins, formed controversies, and been seen by an ever widening worldwide audience for the duration of almost one year. No prior

JFK documetary has ever had the global impact this film has had. We are grateful to Showtime for allowing the film to reveal so much about one of the darkest days in the second half of the twentieth century. We should not continue to live in darkness. It's a shame that America had to wait so long to learn these unpleasant but important truths.

Preface to the Interview Excerpts

In 2013, writer James DiEugenio made a speech at a conference held at Duquesne University. Producer Rob Wilson and director Oliver Stone were at this event. The speech was about President Kennedy's foreign policy. He prefaced that presentation by saying that he was going to speak on the subject without talking about Vietnam and Cuba, which was the inverse of 90 percent of all books dealing with the Kennedy assassination. The point of the speech was to counter two popular paradigms about Kennedy. The first was that Cuba and Vietnam were special cases that all but consumed Kennedy's three years in the White House. The second aim of the speech was the idea that Kennedy's foreign policy was radically changed after the Missile Crisis. I argued that Kennedy's reformist ideas extended as far back as 1951, and culminated in his famous Algeria speech in 1957 before a near empty senate.

A few years later, publisher Tony Lyons of Skyhorse Publishing called Oliver Stone and asked him to write an introduction to my book *Reclaiming Parkland.* (That book was later retitled *The JFK Assassination: The Evidence Today*.) Stone asked the author to come to his office to discuss main topics to be addressed. Rob Wilson was there, and somehow the 2013 speech came up. Wilson had seen that speech, but Stone had not. DiEugenio added, "Oh, it brought down the house." Which it had: there was about a twenty-five-second standing ovation that followed. A few weeks later, Rob

Wilson called DiEugenio and told him to come down to the office and bring that particular PowerPoint presentation. At this point, Stone committed to the project.

The script was bifurcated into two parts: one dealing with Kennedy, and one on the forensic aspects of his murder. The latter centered on the work of the Assassination Records Review Board. Producer Wilson told DiEugenio to make a list of all the people he would need to fulfill the working draft of the screenplay. There was no limit placed on the number of interview subjects. When the production—which went to five cities—was all over, the film had about forty-eight hours of interviews to fit into the shape of the screenplay. In truth, *JFK Revisited* could have been a six-hour series for the simple matter that no JFK documentary had ever assembled such a stellar cast of interview subjects from such a wide variety of disciplines. Or to put it another way: until now, there has never been such a lineup of talent and knowledge about Kennedy or his murder ever put together in one film. And there will likely never be another. Where will one find people like James Galbraith, Henry Lee, and Jefferson Morley in one documentary? With filmmakers like three-time Oscar winner Stone, three-time Oscar-winning cinematographer Bob Richardson, a distinguished three-man editing team, and narration by Oscar winner Whoopi Goldberg and Emmy winner Donald Sutherland.

As I said, *JFK Revisited* could have been a six-hour film; that is how much interesting and important material was gathered in the interview process. This included things that were not in the script, since the author was not aware of them when he wrote it. One example being David Mantik holding CE 399 in his hand at the National Archives and not seeing Elmer Lee Todd's initials on the bullet.

Generally speaking, what follows is material that was not included in either version of the film, the two-hour cut, called *Through the Looking Glass*, or the four-hour version, *Destiny Betrayed*. In certain interviews where some information needed to be addressed again—as with Donald Miller, Debra Conway, and Randy Robertson—it is repeated here.

Interview Excerpts

Jefferson Morley

Jefferson Morley, is a veteran journalist and author of *Our Man in Mexico: Winston Scott and the Hidden History of the CIA* and *The Ghost: The Secret Life of CIA Spymaster James Jesus Angleton*.

Oliver Stone: Well, speaking about Oswald here, how did the incident on Canal Street with Carlos Bringuier of the DRE begin?

Jeff Morley: So in the spring of 1963 Oswald started communicating with the Fair Play for Cuba Committee in New York. And he said I want to form a chapter. And the Fair Play for Cuba Committee, a pro–Cuban Revolution group that was popular on college campuses discouraged him and said, you know, it's not safe in a Southern conservative city like that, you need to get together with like-minded people, please don't do this. Oswald ignored all of that, which is one sign that he was a provocateur and not a true believer. Because he disobeyed what the FPCC wanted him to do. So that summer he began handing out pamphlets for the Fair Play for Cuba Committee which he had ordered. And some of them he stamped 544 Camp Street which was an office in downtown New Orleans, actually near where the CIA's offices were, right across the street in fact. There was also the home of the Cuban Revolutionary Council which was the leading anti-Castro group. Why would a pro-Castro activist put his headquarters in the same headquarters as the leading anti-Castro group in the country? Because he was a provocateur most likely.

Stone: So the fight seemed like a manufactured event?

Morley: That's what the people on the scene said. And it was. And what's interesting about the fight is that here's this guy who had no real connection with the Fair Play for Cuba Committee, which had discouraged him from going public. He goes public and the two organizations in New Orleans that give him publicity are instruments of the CIA: the Cuban Student Directorate was paid by the CIA $50,000 a month through the leaders in Miami. They maintained the network of delegations in the United States and in Latin America. That was a CIA group and the Information Council of the Americas, which also publicized Oswald's group, was also in league with the CIA and helping them, you know, for example lure Castro's sister into defecting. So the publicity of Oswald's pro-Castro activism was entirely generated by CIA front groups.

Stone: And at the fight, Oswald was arrested. He didn't even throw a punch. He's the one was arrested. The other guy threw a punch.

Morley: Well, four guys were taken in for disturbing the peace. Oswald was the only one who was convicted. They let the Cubans go. And Oswald got the fine.

Stone: Did the Warren Commission ever discover the relationship between the CIA and the Student Revolutionary Directorate?

Morley: No, they did not. … They certainly did not know that the group was being run from Miami by George Joannides, a psychological warfare officer who reported directly to Dick Helms.

Stone: And it was called?

Morley: AMSPELL was the code name, the CIA's code name for the Cuban Student Directorate.

Stone: But after the assassination, didn't Bringuier blame Castro, just to bring it full circle?

Morley: Yes, Carlos Bringuier and the DRE did seek to blame the assassination on Oswald instantaneously. The DRE published the first JFK conspiracy theory saying that Oswald and Castro were the presumed assassins and that publication was paid for by the CIA under the auspices of George Joannides.

Stone: Almost the same day, on the same day, or day after the assassination?

Morley: On the night of the assassination, Carlos Bringueir was the DRE delegate in New Orleans and Jose Antonio Lanusa, the spokesmen for the DRE in Miami, got on the phone and started telling reporters, "We know all about the guy who killed the president." And they talked to ten or fifteen reporters that night. So they shaped the story. The CIA's propaganda assets shaped the story from the first hours after Kennedy was dead.

Stone: Who is the CIA case officer who consulted in 1977 with the House Select Committee?

Morley: The self-same George Joannides.

Stone: But the HSCA is not even aware of his status back in '63 I'm told.

Morley: The HSCA knew nothing about this. Joannides was assigned to work with them and was very difficult and made things very difficult for them.

Stone: Just out of curiosity, how did Chief Counsel Robert Blakey react when he learned about Joannides's hidden relationship to this case?

Morley: I remember talking to Bob Blakey when I told him the news that Joannides had been involved in the events of 1963 and he was really shocked. And I think that it changed his mind about the case. Before that, he had given out statements that the CIA had cooperated with his investigation. You know, he stopped talking that way after he learned the Joannides story.

(Editor's note: near the end of the interview, Stone questions Morley about his Freedom of Information Act lawsuit for more information on Joannides, which went on for sixteen years.)

Stone: And on one of those appeals, didn't Brett Kavanaugh vote against you?

Morley: Brett Kavanaugh was the guy who killed the case. Three times we took the case to the DC appellate court, and three times the appellate court said that the District Court Judge Richard Leon had decided the case wrongly by refusing to pay my legal fees. Three times we won at the appellate court level. The fourth time we came up was in March of 2018. And Brett Kavanaugh presided over the hearing . . . In July, that appellate court, the three judges handed down their decision and it was two to one against me. Brett Kavanaugh cast the deciding vote saying he CIA's behavior was reasonable.

Stone: So now that he's appointed to the Supreme Court, that shoots down other cases involving the CIA, or anything of this nature.

Morley: Yeah, I mean, my case was the last case that Brett Kavanaugh decided before he went to the Supreme Court. He sent in the decision at 9:00 in the morning, and that afternoon Trump appointed him to the Supreme Court. Now think about it: was Brett Kavanaugh going to rule against the CIA on a JFK assassination issue on the day he was up for the Supreme Court? There was no chance, ever. The fix was in. You know, he was never going to rule in my favor, given his political position. So, the judicial system as the instrument of finding the truth, it was completely corrupted at that point.

Aaron Good, PhD

Aaron Good, PhD is the author of the book *American Exception* and editor of the Patreon series American Exception.

Aaron Good: Henry Luce was overtly saying ... it was implicit when he writes things like there's a lot of money that's going to be made in Asia. And if we don't do this right, we're going to miss out on billions of dollars.... And this was his big disagreement that Kennedy was dealing with was what form should decolonization take? Should it be neocolonial or should it result in real independence for the rest of the world, the formerly colonized world?

Jim DiEugenio: Describe what sociologist C. Wright Mills meant when he had this marvelous phrase, which he termed "crackpot realism," and how it was ingrained in both political parties?

Good: Crackpot realism was C. Wright Mills's term to describe the worldview and cosmology that the power elite were able to foist on the rest of society. … And if you didn't accept that worldview, you just didn't have the chance to rise in these hierarchies. And so everybody has to accept the fundamental principles that comprise crackpot realism, this worldview where capitalism is depicted as a utopian ideal and pursuit, and any dissent from that was very questionable and dubious. And it's bigger than just the conservative Republic[an] Party. It transcends both parties. … The creation of the national security state and the military-industrial complex is done largely by Democrats. Harry Truman was a Democrat.

DiEugenio: At his meeting with Edmund Gullion in 1951, how did Kennedy begin to break out of this kind of crackpot realism that had been advocated by the national security state?

Good: He met him a couple of years before, but he went to meet him in Indochina to see how the war was going. And he got a very sort of uncensored view of things from Edmund Gullion, who viewed the French situation as totally hopeless. And according to Robert Kennedy, these conversations, they had a big effect on Kennedy's thinking. And after that, he returns to the United States. And he says that the US cannot be on the wrong side of these nationalist struggles. That it really was all about nationalism; the French were on the wrong side of history, we needed to get on the right side of history by backing Vietnamese independence. And even if we're going to fight communist insurgents who are the nationalists in Vietnam, we need to make sure that the French are promising not to hold on to their empire. That the assistance that we offer the French and the Vietnamese to fight communism is conditioned upon Vietnamese independence at the end of the conflict.

DiEugenio: And I guess the one way to really give you an example of crackpot realism was Operation Vulture, right?

Good: In 1954 the French go deep into Indochina and they are there at Dien Bien Phu and they are being attacked on all sides by Ho Chi Minh's forces. ... And there are people who are arguing, John Foster Dulles among them, it would be the time to break out the nuclear bombs. ... Kennedy was completely against this. He said how is this policy of massive nuclear retaliation going to work in the age of guerilla warfare? And for a number of reasons Operation Vulture is called off. But the fact that is was so close, that it was considered, and it was almost executed, shows how powerful this crackpot realism is.

DiEugenio: Describe what happened as an example of the reaction Kennedy had to the meeting with Gullion, to a speech he made in 1954.

Good: The French are pinned at Dien Bien Phu and its looking very hopeless. Gullion is briefing Kennedy on these matters. And he gives him a whole lot of information and updates to use in a speech that he gives in the spring of 1954. And Kennedy reiterates his main points, that nationalism is what's at stake here. ... The result of this is a very critical speech on a pillar of Eisenhower's foreign policy. The very next day, Eisenhower gives his famous Domino Theory speech. ... And another reason to think that it may have been inspired by Kennedy's speech is what happens to Edmund Gullion, who was one of the experts working on Vietnam for the US at that time. He gets taken off of the Indochina desk. And he's not a party to the talks in Geneva that take place after that.

DiEugenio: Most people who study this would say that Kennedy's hallmark was the 1957 speech in the Senate on the subject of another civil war in order to maintain the colony of Algeria off the north coast of Africa.

Good: Kennedy sees in Algeria the same thing that happened in Indochina. … So he gives this speech in the Senate about Algeria and how doomed the French policy was. And he takes a lot of flack for it from the Republicans and lots of Democrats, the paragons of crackpot realism like Dean Acheson. But even some of the establishment liberals like Adlai Stevenson thought that Kennedy had gone too far in making this speech.

Kennedy's concept of nationalism was an affront to the idea of imperial hegemony that was laid out by people like Henry Luce, Paul Nitze, and Dean Acheson. Kennedy was a nationalist himself. … He believed he was pursuing America's national interest by creating a cooperative international environment without colonial exploitation.

Barry Ernest

Barry Ernest is a journalist and the author of *The Girl on the Stairs*.

Barry Ernest: David Belin, in an early internal memo, stated that one of the objectives of his area of investigation was to determine precisely when Vicki Adams went down the stairs, something that he obviously did not do.

Oliver Stone: So when you caught up with her, she was a scared woman.

Ernest: Yes, she had been interviewed many times and realized something was wrong because no one was believing her—the Dallas Police, the Warren Commission—and that scared her quite a bit. Especially the night that the Dallas Police showed up on her apartment doorstep. This would have been in 1964. She was new to that apartment. The apartment was not in her name. It was in her roommate's name. She had at that point never even given a forwarding address to her boss or post office. But the Dallas Police showed up that night saying that they needed to interview Vicki again and when she asked why, she was told that there had been a fire at Dallas Police headquarters. But that scared her that they were able to find her as they did. And that's why she tended to go underground with it from that point on.

Stone: Wasn't there also an issue because when the Dallas Police followed her, at that time, hadn't the FBI and the Warren Commission taken over the case? Was the Dallas Police authorized to do that?

Ernest: That's correct. When they interviewed her in February of 1964, the Dallas Police were no longer involved in the investigation. … And in that Dallas Police interview, that was the first time she mentioned seeing Billy Lovelady and William Shelley on the first floor, a comment that was repeated then two months later in her Warren Commission testimony. But in all the years I knew Vicki, she continually told me that she never made that statement to the Dallas Police or the Warren Commission. And she actually felt those words had been inserted into her testimony to specifically make her appear wrong.

In light of that, I went to the National Archives searching for her original testimony. I wanted to see if she actually said she saw Shelley and Lovelady on the first floor. I didn't want the paper transcript of her testimony, which could have been subject to alteration. I wanted the original stenographer's tape that was made by the court reporter, the only other person in the room when David Belin interviewed Vicki Adams. And I knew the National Archives had those tapes. In fact, they had the tapes of all 552 witnesses who had been deposed by the Commission. But when I asked about Vicki's tape, I was told that the tape was missing. They couldn't find it. And later I learned that that tape had been destroyed by the Warren Commission for no apparent reason.

Stone: So we have Sandra Styles, who we'll get to, and we have Vicki, and she named three people who can corroborate her and the Commission had an affidavit from one of them. Who are the three people?

Ernest: The three people were Elsie Dorman, who was a coworker, happened to be filming the motorcade from the fourth floor window. Sandra Styles, a coworker, and Dorothy Garner, who was Vicki's immediate supervisor and had stood at the window with Vicki. … There were four women total including Vicki Adams. … Not a one of them was called as a Commission witness. And the interesting thing about that is, Sandra Styles was a very important witness. She wasn't even mentioned in the Warren Report.

Stone: And Lovelady, did he say anything, or did Shelley say anything about seeing her?

Ernest: They interviewed both men and they asked William Shelley for example: Did you see Vicki Adams that day? He basically said: Not on the first floor, I saw her on the fourth floor later that afternoon. … Billy Lovelady, if you read his testimony, it has sparks of collusion about whether or not he did see Vicki Adams on the first floor. But the bottom line, what he said was: he saw a girl, but he didn't know who it was.

Stone: But the way you're describing it, then how come Sandra Styles has not become a major missing witness here?

Ernest: That's the question. Sandra Styles was interviewed by the FBI just like every other employee. But she was never called to become a Commission witness. When I interviewed her, she corroborated everything Vicki had said. She came down the stairs with Vicki, she didn't see or hear anyone on the stairs, and she didn't see Shelley or Lovelady on the first floor. But she didn't recognize the significance of what she had done in relation to Vicki's trek down the stairs. And this was no doubt the intention of the Warren Commission, because not much was being written about her.

Stone: Did the Warren Commission say that Styles ran down the stairs with her?

Ernest: No. The Warren Commission in its report did not even mentions Sandra Styles's name.

Stone: Not even on the fourth floor?

Ernest: Not even on the fourth floor ... It's only by way of Vicki's testimony that you find out that Sandra Styles exists.

Stone: Why'd they pick out Vicki Adams and not Sandra Styles?

Ernest: Well, because discrediting one woman was easy to do, but discrediting a corroborating witness, that may have been a little tougher.

Stone: Did the House Select Committee ever call in Victoria or Sandra to testify?

Ernest: The short answer to that is no. When the Committee was formed in 1976, I wrote several letters to them suggesting that they look into Vicki Adams's story a bit more and I never received a reply. But later, when I was going through documents in the National Archives, I did find that the Committee had an interest in Vicki Adams and specifically their interest was focused on when she came down from the fourth floor.

Professor Bradley Simpson

Bradley Simpson is a professor of history at the University of Connecticut and the author of *Economists with Guns*.

Oliver Stone: I just asked you about the neutrality movement in the 1950s, the Third World. Can you talk about that a bit?

Bradley Simpson: Sukarno was one of the leaders of what became known as the Non-Aligned Movement, which was an informal grouping of post-colonial states which were seeking to find a sort of third way in the Cold War between the United States and the Soviet Union. This was at a time when both the US, and after 1956, the Soviet Union, were providing military and economic and technical assistance to postcolonial states in the hope of inducing them to side with either Washington or Moscow in the Cold War. A variety of US officials sought to figure out ways of co-opting the dangers of what John Foster Dulles, the secretary of state, at the time during the Eisenhower administration, called the plague of nonalignment. Many US officials saw the Cold War as a moral struggle in which countries such as Indonesia could not pretend to be neutral.

Stone: Can you talk about that meeting In Bandung?

Simpson: In 1955, the first Afro-Asian meeting was held with representatives from about two dozen postcolonial states. They issued what became known as the Bandung Declaration, a sort of neutrality in the Cold War that went further in calling for postcolonial states demanding human rights, self-determination, noninterference on the part of the great powers. Basically calling for a third force in international politics that would be neither East nor West, neither pro-Soviet nor pro-Washington but would pursue the interests of postcolonial states and not the interests of the great powers. Those interests being genuine independence, and economic development.

Stone: Describe for us briefly if you can the 1950s atmosphere and the attempt to remove Sukarno in 1958?

Simpson: Beginning in 1955, US officials began to worry about the growing power and popularity of the Indonesian Communist Party, which at the time was one of the largest Communist parties in the world outside of the Soviet Bloc, and one of the three largest parties in Indonesia. The Communist Party did very well in regional elections and that suggested that it would emerge as the largest party in Indonesia if its power was unchecked. So beginning in 1957, US officials began working with dissident colonels and others who were upset and opposed to Sukarno and opposed to the centralization of power in Jakarta. They began sponsoring a series of regional rebellions known as the Permesta rebellions in which they tried to set up an alternative government and secede parts of Indonesia from Java and set up a competing government. … And so for more than a year the United States carried out what up to that point was the largest and most destructive covert operation of the Asian Cold War in which thousands of US troops were involved, in which millions of dollars in weapons and supplies were given to the regional rebellions and in which thousands of people were killed. A CIA pilot was carrying out a bombing run and was captured after his plane crashed following an air run in which he dropped dynamite sticks on a church and killed dozens of civilians. Alan Pope was captured. … It was later revealed that Alan Pope has in fact been working for the CIA. The revelation of the US support for these regional rebellions really helped to radicalize Sukarno and to convince many Indonesians that the United States was working to overthrow Sukarno, which was in fact the Eisenhower administration's goal. … So that by 1960, when President Kennedy comes into office, Indonesia is one of the few countries in the world where both the United States and the Soviet Union are providing both military and economic assistance, making it a valuable prize in the Cold War. And in the minds of many American officials, the most important country in Southeast Asia, far surpassing the strategic value of Vietnam.

Stone: Can you then take us through Kennedy's approach to Indonesia when he came into office in '61 up to '63?

Simpson: John F. Kennedy, when he arrived in Washington, brought with him a set of experiences which inclined him to be far more sympathetic to the ambitions and aims of nationalist leaders in the Third World. … He had criticized French colonial rule in Algeria and was widely viewed as someone much more empathetic to the aims of neutralist leaders and colonial leaders such as Sukarno.

Kennedy invited Sukarno to Washington, DC, he increased economic and military assistance, and more generally tried to encourage Indonesia to modernize as was the social, scientific idea at the time along lines that were compatible with Western interests. This was especially important because Indonesia was also the largest producer of oil in Southeast Asia and many US rubber and petroleum companies were heavily invested in there. And so Indonesia was not just a source of strategic importance for the United States but it was also a country with lots of American investments.

The first meeting that Kennedy and Sukarno held in the spring of 1962, after this meeting the United States extended significant economic and military assistance to Indonesia. The most important example of Kennedy's willingness to accommodate Sukarno came in 1962, when Sukarno launched a campaign to try and recover the territory of West New Guinea, which was a part of the former Dutch East Indies West. The Netherlands had kept a hold of it after Indonesia independence in 1949. And most Indonesians, including Sukarno, had long considered this to be an integral part of the Indonesian nation. After Sukarno threatened war with Netherlands, the Kennedy administration helped to broker negotiations through the United Nations, in which the Dutch agreed to turn over West New Guinea to Indonesia. … And for Indonesia, this was the most hopeful sign that the United States was indeed recognizing Indonesia's political importance in the region and was willing to accommodate Sukarno's anti-colonial ambitions in order to help restore the territorial integrity of Indonesia.

Stone: Then Kennedy was assassinated in November of '63. What is Sukarno's reaction and what is the change in policy?

Simpson: In the fall of 1963, relations between the US and Indonesia are starting to become more rocky. Predominantly because the government of Britain had decided to form the country of Malaysia out of the remnants of its former Southeast Asian colonies and Indonesia decided to oppose the formation of Malaysia. … But the Kennedy administration was committed to continuing to negotiate with Indonesia and to appeal to Sukarno and the personal relationship which he felt he had established with President Kennedy.

Kennedy's assassination led to the political marginalization of a number of officials who had helped to spearhead his accommodationist policy towards Indonesia.

Stone: So when Sukarno made his "Year of Living Dangerously" speech in 1964, did he understand what was in store for him?

Simpson: Over the course of 1964, relations between the US and Indonesia began to dramatically deteriorate. ...The Johnson administration was deeply opposed to Sukarno's policy of confrontation with Malaysia. ... In the fall of 1964, Sukarno gave a speech on Indonesia's National Day titled "The Year of Living Dangerously" in which he foreshadowed a year of confrontation with the forces of what he called neo-colonialism and imperialism. ... Sukarno bitterly criticized the war in Vietnam. He tilted more in the direction of China and away from the Soviet Union. ... And so the US and Great Britain put in place a program of covert action in which they sought to encourage Indonesian military conflicts to overthrow Sukarno and to engage in a military conflict with the Indonesian Communist Party.

Stone: Well besides providing lists for those to be eliminated your book describes other ways in which the CIA helped overthrow Sukarno once the coup began in 1965.

Simpson: In the lead-up to the events of September 30, 1965, in which a small number of Indonesian Communist Party officials and military allies kidnapped and killed six Indonesian generals, the Indonesian army launched sort of a countercoup in which it sought to exterminate the Indonesian Communist Party and overthrow Sukarno. Now, US covert operations for the past year had been geared towards precisely this end. Although American officials were surprised at the actual events of September 30th, they were determined to take advantage of this opportunity to encourage the military of Indonesia to annihilate the Indonesian Communist party. And so they extended various kinds of assistance to try and signal to the Indonesian army that the US desired that it engage in a campaign of mass murder against the Indonesia Communist Party. ... US officials provided small arms that were ferried to Indonesia covertly through Thailand, and through other countries where the CIA was operating. The US State Department provided tens of thousands of dollars to paramilitary organizations that had been set up by the Indonesian army to carry out mass killings in different parts of the Archipelago. It provided medicine, it provided communications equipment. And most importantly, they signaled to the Indonesian army that overthrowing Sukarno and killing lots and lots of communists would produce a political payoff in the form of resumption of US economic and military assistance and US support for whatever regime emerged in the aftermath of the overthrow.

Stone: And your book does I believe say that we were not only helping, we were monitoring army transmissions through the NSA. Including orders on who to kill. That's through the National Security agency. That's pretty significant.

Simpson: Yes. So as the killings got underway in early October 1965, the Johnson administration decided that the most urgent need of the Indonesian army was for communications equipment which the US provided. And this equipment enabled the army to more effectively coordinate its military campaign against the Indonesian communist party, but also enabled the US to monitor and listen in on secret army communications and to monitor the progress of the killings as they were being carried out.

Stone: What are the best estimates today for how many were killed in the overthrow?

Simpson: Between October of 1965 and March of 1966, scholars estimate that upwards of half a million Indonesians were murdered directly by the army or by militias that were organized by Islamic groups.

Stone: Was there any attempt by the US to either halt or curtail the massacres?

Simpson: I have read every document produced by the US government between October 1965 and March of 1966. Upwards of fifty thousand declassified pages of US documents. I have yet to come across a single episode of any US official criticizing the campaign of mass murder carried out by the Indonesia army. In fact, many US officials were gleeful in reporting on the dramatic change in circumstances in Indonesia and saw this as a great victory for the US in the Cold War.

Stone: I've read that McGeorge Bundy said that he was surprised at the time that the Vietnam operation was perceived as more important than the Indonesian operation. He felt that the Indonesian operation was a supreme victory in Southeast Asia and was enough to satisfy our ambitions.

Simpson: Yes. Many officials considered Indonesia to be more important than Vietnam. They called it at times the super domino of Southeast Asia. And the extermination of the Indonesian Communist Party in many ways eliminated the rationale for US intervention in Vietnam.... And so we can ask what might have happened had President Kennedy lived. Had the US still pursued more cordial relations with Indonesia. Had the Johnson administration not enacted this campaign of covert operations that was geared toward provoking precisely the kind of bloodbath that erupted in the fall of 1965. Indonesians, who would have to live with the military dictator Suharto for the next thirty-two years, doubtless wonder the same thing.

Brian Edwards

Brain Edwards was a member of the Lawrence, Kansas Police Department for twenty-two years. He is an instructor in Criminal Justice at Washburn University and the co-author of the book *Beyond the Fence Line*.

First Interview, Georgetown, September 11, 2019

Oliver Stone: Here we have a strange story, where Oswald is under questioning for hours and yet we have no tape of what he says.

Brian Edwards: I confronted Jim Leavelle many, many years ago in front of eight hundred people. And I asked him point-blank, why didn't you take notes of what this guy was saying? And you know what he told me? It wouldn't have changed the outcome of the case. This is the day before Oswald was shot. They're still building the case.

Stone: Jim Leavelle, the cop who was alongside him when he was shot?

Edwards: Yeah, the one in the white hat and the white suit. He just passed away last week. But you know, these guys are building a case and he says I didn't kill anybody, I didn't shoot anybody.

Stone: How do you justify a lack of a record?

Edwards: I can't. I can't justify that. It's unheard of.

Stone: You didn't mention there was a postmaster general.

Edwards: There was a Dallas postmaster Harry Holmes who was an FBI informant. He was, he would have been given information about subversive groups and communists and supporters of left wing and right-wing causes for the FBI for years. He was invited into the Dallas Police headquarters interrogation room to interview Oswald. Oswald is charged with a murder. Why would a postal inspector have any business being in there? He doesn't.

Stone: Well maybe because he knew about left-wing groups so therefore he would have known something about Oswald. Well, let's go back to chain of custody again....no defense for Oswald.

Edwards: Obviously he was dead. He had no chance to cross-examine witnesses. He had no lawyer appointed. Mark Lane, an attorney out of New York, tried to get legal representation for Lee Oswald ... and they denied it...

Stone: In your years of study and considering your past experience, was the Warren Commission a true fact-finding body?

Edwards: The Warren Commission ... was a whitewash. Nobody in the history of any legal proceeding would ever accept their findings. J. Edgar Hoover was asked by the Warren Commission: Why do you think Lee Oswald didn't shoot President Kennedy when he was coming down Houston Street? And Hoover obviously had never been to Dealey Plaza and never seen this picture. He said, well the trees blocked his view. There's no trees on Houston Street.

Stone: You were a sniper, would you have had any success with those shots?

Edwards: I was. And I make sure the first shot is the best. I don't have any other choice. The first shot has to hit the target.

Stone: So could you have fired three shots, do you think?

Edwards: I couldn't have. Every time you operate it, you have to take your eye away, you have to look through the scope....

Stone: You have to reacquire the target.

Edwards: Yes, and remember you've got a moving target, inside a moving vehicle, moving away from you downhill. ... And from high to low is the most difficult shot. ... No matter how many times you practice from high to low, the first shot is always going to be high. Every time.

Second Interview, Los Angeles, January 6, 2020

James DiEugenio: Why don't you give us a sketch of your past career in law enforcement?

Brian Edwards: My career started in 1978 and I was a police officer in Kansas and then in 1981, I joined the Lawrence, Kansas, Police Department and served twenty-two years there. I was a member of the assault team, I was a countersniper. I taught in the police academy, firearms instructor and a range master and senior crime scene photographer. I have a master's degree in criminal justice and I have sixteen hours towards a PhD in administration of justice.

DiEugenio: And you've been a witness in criminal cases about how many times?

Edwards: I would conservatively estimate probably one hundred times, both in civil and criminal cases.

DiEugenio: So you're very familiar with court procedure?

Edwards: Yes.

DiEugenio: Describe the difference between the rifle the Warren Commission took into evidence versus the rifle that Oswald ordered.

Edwards: The rifle that was ordered through Klein's Sporting Goods store in Chicago appeared in *American Rifleman* magazine, February issue of 1963. It advertised a thirty-six-inch, 6.5 Italian carbine, which is a smaller, shorter version of a longer-barreled rifle. Classification of one is called a short rifle, which is the 40.2 inch, the carbine is the thirty-six inch, that's considered a carbine. The rifle that is in evidence, secured by the Dallas Police Department was measured at 40.2 inches. … The rifle that Lt. Day brings out of the

Texas School Book Depository on the afternoon of the 22nd of November has left side mounted sling, sling swivel. And you can clearly see that there were several photographs taken of that. That, to me, just is clear evidence that that's not the same rifle that was ordered. The rifle that was ordered had bottom mounted sling attachments. The rifle that was brought out of the Book Depository had left side, left side stock rifle and sling attachments.

DiEugenio: Now on the left side stock side attachments you're talking about. Wouldn't those have to be screwed into the wood?

Edwards: Yes. The stock of the left side at the rear had the sling attachment embedded into the stock, actually physically embedded into the wood. So that's not what was ordered. In other words, the classification of the rifle is different, the length is different, the swivels are different. It's pretty common sense to examine that just by the photographs that those are not the same weapons.

DiEugenio: In your opinion, in addition to being so familiar with firearms, you've done a lot of studying on this case. Do you think the Warren Commission's David Belin didn't know the difference?

Edwards: No, absolutely not. They had to have known. They had the coupon that was used to order the rifle. The bottom-mounted slings are in that picture. And if you read the testimony that David Belin extracted from one of the executives of Klein's Sporting Goods, they avoided that. He avoided the subject.

DiEugenio: How long did the Warren Commission say that it took the coupon and money order allegedly sent by Oswald to be mailed, picked up, delivered to Klein's and placed in their bank account?

Edwards: The coupon issue getting from Texas to Chicago was less than twenty-four hours. That was before PayPal.

(Editor's Note: Not only was it before PayPal, but it was before zip codes, high-speed sorters, widespread computer technology and sensors. Dallas was about one thousand miles from Chicago. When the film producers conducted an experiment, they had Debra Conway mail a letter from the Evray Street Post Office in Dallas to Michael LeFlem, a writer who was living in Chicago about one mile from where Klein's used to be located. That letter took six days to arrive, five days subtracting Sunday. And this was without the step Klein's used for sorting incoming funds by in and out of state and by denomination: checks, money orders, and cash. And also the final step of taking it over to the bank for deposit.)

DiEugenio: Who was Sebastian Latona, and why is he important to the JFK case?

Edwards: Sebastian Latona was the FBI's top fingerprint expert.

DiEugenio: In 1993, PBS did a special on Lee Harvey Oswald and they said that there was another print, a fingerprint, on the trigger guard that was bypassed by the FBI. But the Dallas Police actually had photographs of that and they said that Latona didn't have those photographs and didn't do any work on it. Is that accurate?

Edwards: No, that's not correct. According to his testimony to the Warren Commission, Latona had photographs sent to him from the Dallas Police, photographs of that entire trigger guard of the rifle. When they said he didn't have pictures or didn't examine any photographs, that's not true.

DiEugenio: And he did his own photographs also?

Edwards: Yes. He had an FBI photographer come in and assist with taking the pictures. And still found no usable prints.

DiEugenio: Did the Warren Commission ignore the chain of custody problems with the evidence and could that have ever been allowed to happen in a trial?

Edwards: The Warren Commission ignored just about every protocol of chain of custody of all the physical evidence in this case. They ignored it because they had their assumption, they had their guy and it had to fit the scenario that they came up with. But those chains of evidence are standard protocol, legal protocol for going to court.

Oliver Stone: How do we know that the rifle he ordered—supposedly thirty-six inches—how do we know he received a thirty-six-inch rifle?

Edwards: We don't know that he received a thirty-six-inch rifle or a forty-five-inch rifle or any rifle. Nobody at the post office ever testified or gave a statement that yes, I delivered a stick in this guy's box to say, hey, you've got a package that's longer than our mailbox, you need to come to the counter and get that. Nobody ever did that.

Stone: Although…

Edwards: Although he had an alias of A. J. Hidell, he could have shown that and got the rifle.

DiEugenio: But in that case he would have had to talk to somebody at the counter. He would have had to prove that he was both people and then somebody would have had to gone in the back and picked up a five-foot carton and brought it out and given it to him. Something like that would have gone up to a supervisor.

Edwards: That would have been difficult to forget. Very difficult.

Cyril Wecht MD, JD

Cyril Wecht is one of the most famous and accomplished forensic pathologists in America. He has been a prominent critic of the Warren Commission since 1965. His latest book on the JFK case is *The JFK Assassination Dissected,* coauthored with journalist Dawna Kaufmann.

Oliver Stone: And I gather, why was sectioning of the brain so important to this autopsy?

Cyril Wecht: In 1968, there was the Ramsey Clark panel. One of them was my chief where I had trained, Dr. Russell Fisher from the Baltimore Chief Medical Examiner's Office.... They never mentioned that the brain was missing. And indeed they come out, these top-notch people, and corroborated the Warren Commission in 1968. It wasn't until 1972 when I was finally admitted to examine, the first nongovernment forensic pathologist to get into the National Archives. And that's a story in itself, how long it took for me to get in, and what was necessary to gain this permission. But it wasn't until then that I made the discovery. Of course, all kinds of people knew this, it wasn't you know like Columbus discovered America. ... So I discovered the missing brain.

Page One story, August 27, 1972. Look it up Fred Graham, top investigative reporter for the *New York Times*: "President's Brain Missing." And as we sit and talk here today, all these year later, that brain remains missing.

But think of the cover-up from '63. And then with that Ramsey Clark Panel in '68 and other people who should have come to know. It wasn't until I was there in '72 looking as this cockamamie phony executive agreement that they had come up with saying that Jacqueline Kennedy was the owner of all the materials. ... She was the owner. Well, the last person in the world I think to have ever wanted to see any of that would have been Jackie Kennedy. But in April of 1965 they came up with this totally absurd, completely illegal, absolutely new, executive agreement, so that there could be what we call a "constructive transfer." She never had physical possession of this stuff, but on paper she transferred it back to the United States.

But let me just jump a year and a half later, in October '66. Now they go back and two of the people involved in the original autopsy and a couple of others, do a detailed description of what is present. And so now, in August of '72, I'm there at the National Archives. I'm there at the National Archives and I'm looking. I have the Executive Agreement of April 1965. And I have the inventory of October '66, a year and a half later. In addition to some X-rays and some photos that are missing, there's a large metal box that obviously contained the brain listed in '65. No longer listed in '66. And nobody said a word about it until I had that opportunity to discover it.

Stone: So when the Review Board came into existence, they discovered that James Humes, the lead autopsist, what he did with his notes and the first draft? What did he do?

Wecht: Humes did something that would undoubtedly lead to a murder case being thrown out, I do believe. If I went as a coroner … and I said that I had destroyed them. … This is something else that people have to be reminded about—how this conspiracy continues to play out, not a step is missed. To make sure that things are not left in place that can open the door.

Stone: Who arranged for the illustrations drawn by Harold Rydberg?

(Editor's note: Rydberg was the illustrator who was told by Drs. Humes and Boswell to draw the two wounds in Kennedy. But the doctors came to the meeting with no pictures or X-rays, only their memories.)

Wecht: But they instructed Rydberg to illustrate this and the illustration that they have shown has the president's head bent down and a bullet hole back up and coming down at an angle which is totally erroneous. That is not at all the way the president's head was situated when he was shot. … Quite different from Boswell's face sheet. So you see, from the very beginning, you have this inconsistency. … But I think there is too much to simply attribute to incompetence. …They certainly know basic anatomy. They were pathologists.

(Editor's note: the face sheet prepared by Dr. Boswell shows the back wound to be about six inches down from the shirt collar. Well into the back area. Quite different from the Rydberg drawing, which shows the wound in base of the neck. Yet Boswell was instrumental in the preparation of both.)

Stone: Did the Commission know the true orientation of Kennedy's head before the fatal shot?

Wecht: I do not believe that the Warren Commission knew the real orientation. They did not have a forensic pathologist on the Commission, and I don't know of any who were consultants at that time. It wasn't until 1968, when they brought in the panel of doctors, Russell Fisher and a neuropathologist and others, they said that the bullet hole was actually … four inches higher. So how can you be four inches off? I have said talking to schoolchildren and to other audiences, if you took just a kid, a ten-year-old kid and you gave him a ruler and you gave him a skull and you put an X in one place, and you said: "Jimmy or Susie, would you measure this for me?" Would Jimmy or Susie be four inches off? We're not talking about four millimeters. We're talking four inches. How is that possible?

Stone: There were also tissue slides missing?

Wecht: There were some microscopic tissue slides missing too. And by the way, tissue slides are important when you're looking at gunshot wounds to try to differentiate entrance from exit: looking for carbonation, pigment deposits and so on. So some of the slides are missing also.

Stone: By what means did the House Select Committee connect CE 399 to the assassination?

Wecht: Neutron Activation Analysis came into play, as I recall, some time in the seventies or so. And it was deemed to be very, very specific, as in this case whether some of the fragments found in Governor Connally, found in the car, came from Commission Exhibit 399, the magic bullet. And the Neutron Activation Analysis, as it was used in those days, set forth the conclusion that yes they did. … Not only that kind of ammunition, but that particular bullet, that 6.5 millimeter, copper-jacketed lead-core bullet—that's where those fragments came from.

Well, it was ultimately then shown in further studies by top-notch people … that neutron activation analysis was not specific like that. Indeed it came to the point that the FBI announced that they were no longer accepting Neutron Activation Analysis.

(Editor's Note: the precise term for the use of the NAA test for bullets is Comparative Bullet Lead Analysis.)

Stone: You've described a shot, another shot, next to the fatal head wound, coming right after it or coming around the same time.

Wecht: I think the president is hit at 312/13, and the other shot comes in about 327/28, referring to the frames of the Zapruder film. So you're talking about five-sixths of a second. And I think that explains the movement of the president in the car, too. I do not believe that that movement would be consistent with a shot fired from the rear. The Warren Commission defenders and sycophants, they came up with the "jet effect" and neuromuscular reaction, leading to decerebrate or decorticate reactions.

(Editor's note: These terms describe certain abnormal anatomical postures the doctor will now describe.)

Wecht: But decerebrate and decorticate do not fit. You don't see the features—an arched back? A protruding chest? And with decerebrate, the arms then out and flexed in, and decorticate, the arms extended outward. Neither of those are shown with Kennedy's position in the car. You see him in limp fashion falling backwards. ... That shot from the right front is what caused him to move backward. Blood, brain tissue from the skull came backward. A motorcycle policeman riding behind and to the rear was sure, for several seconds that he had been shot. ... That's the way everything moved. That was the directionality of that shot: from the right front side.

Dr. David Mantik

Dr. David Mantik is a radiation oncologist and has a PhD in physics. His web site is called *The Mantik View*. He is the author of the ebook *John F. Kennedy's Head Wounds*.

James DiEugenio: You read X-rays for a living. How long have you been doing this?

David Mantik: It's almost forty years now that I've been in this field.

DiEugenio: And then how long were you a professor of physics?

Mantik: I was on the faculty at Michigan for three years.

DiEugenio: Did the Warren Report ever bring up the dispute between how O. P. Wright described the bullet vs the copper-jacketed bullet we have in evidence today?

Mantik: In 1966, Josiah Thompson who authored *Six Seconds in Dallas*, interviewed O. P. Wright, who was head of maintenance at Parkland Hospital and who handled the bullet. He was the second person at Parkland to handle it. And Josiah asked O. P. Wright about the bullet, in particular he showed him a photograph of the magic bullet, which has a rounded tip. And O. P. Wright said, "No it wasn't like that." He opened his desk drawer and pulled out a more pointed-tipped bullet and he said, it was more like this. And Thompson published that image in *Six Seconds in Dallas*. But no, this never came to the attention of the Warren Commission because this was 1966. Two years afterwards.

(Editor's Note: There was no deposition done by the Commission with Wright.)

DiEugenio: Now, didn't Thompson also bring into question about the stretcher the bullet was actually found on?

Mantik: Where the magic bullet was found is an excellent question. Darrell Tomlinson was the first person at Parkland to find it. ... So he was carefully quizzed by the Warren Commission about whose stretcher this was. Of course, what the Warren Commission would like to hear is that it was preferably Connally's, because he was the last one wounded by the magic bullet. But Tomlinson refused to buckle under their pressure and he said I am not going to tell you something that I can't live with. So even Tomlinson refused to identify the bullet as being from Connally's stretcher even when he was pressured to do so. So there's always been a question of whose stretcher this was and whose bullet this was, how did it get there?

DiEugenio: Doesn't the death certificate, and didn't the FBI report, also locate this wound lower in the back than where the Warren Commission places it?

Mantik: The official death certificate signed by Admiral Burkley, JFK's personal physician, locates the entrance to the back wound at T3. That's the third thoracic vertebrae. But I personally spoke to John Ebersole, the radiologist. Ebersole wasn't merely a diagnostic radiologist. Like me, he was a radiation oncologist, which means that he really needed to pay attention to external landmarks, like the scapula for example. So you have to know the correlation between the external and internal anatomy. So when Ebersole tells me what level this was at, I need to pay attention. And he said it was probably closer to T4. So, if that's true, then the magic bullet is a total loss. It's impossible.

DiEugenio: What would you estimate that as being, for the layman, in inches below the collar.

Mantik: It would be at least four or five inches.

DiEugenio: You've done a lot of work on this trajectory of the so-called neck wound that was supposed to have gone through JFK, exited the front of his throat. Explain to us how even on its own terms it is simply not sustainable.

Mantik: When I first got involved in this case, I was aware of previous work that had been done on this back wound, in particular by professor of pathology, John Nichols. Now, in 1963, we did not have CT scans. So I realized that what we should do is look at a CT scan of a somewhat similar patient to JFK in order to determine whether the trajectory was even reasonable in a cross-sectional view. I was easily able to obtain such a cross section from one of my patients, and lo and behold it wouldn't work. Either you run into the lung and the lung should be punctured, but we know that did not happen from the pathologists. Or the bullet runs into the cervical vertebrae which are actually quite wide at that site. It's unavoidable that they would strike the vertebral bodies and cause a serious fracture. But we know from the X-rays that that did not happen either.

DiEugenio: Now isn't Harold Rydberg's drawing of the fatal head shot also off?

Mantik: Rydberg dew the sketch without any access to photographs. But we have access to the Zapruder film and we can compare the orientation of JFK's head in Rydberg's sketch, which is tilted very far forward, to the image in Zapruder frame 312 which is presumably when the headshot occurred and they are very different from each other. They do not match.

DiEugenio: How did this false presentation of what Rydberg illustrated, versus what was actually in the Zapruder film at about frame 312, how did this go ahead and create this review of the original autopsy called the Ramsey Clark panel?

Mantik: In 1967, an investigation was started in New Orleans into the case again. This made national media, it caught the public eye, and raised a lot of questions about conspiracy in the JFK assassination. To help quell this, the Clark panel was set up under the direction of Attorney General Ramsey Clark. He convened four specialists to reexamine the autopsy materials. And they discovered something totally new. On the front-to-back X-ray of JFK's skull, they saw something that no one had ever seen before. Inside the right eye socket on this frontal X-ray, they saw a 6.5 mm almost round, whitish or transparent object that looked like the cross section of a bullet. Now at the autopsy in 1963, multiple X-rays were taken of JFK's skull looking for objects just like that. There is nothing in the autopsy report about any such object. But there it was as clear as day on the frontal X-ray. Of course the Clark Panel paid serious attention to that and as a result they totally changed the entry site for the skull wound. The Warren Commission had placed the entry site in the low back of the head, near the external occipital protuberance. But the Clark Panel raised it about four inches in order to be more consistent with this newly found, supposedly metal, object. The size of 6.5 mm is ironic in a way isn't it, because the supposed weapon that Oswald used was 6.5 mm caliber.

DiEugenio: In your opinion, since you've been studying this case for decades on end, which version of the autopsy report is in existence today?

Mantik: Doug Horne has looked very closely at the sequence of autopsy reports and he makes a very compelling case in chapter 11 of his book *Inside the ARRB*. The first one was burned that Sunday morning by Dr. Humes and no one has ever seen that one since. The second one is listed in paragraph 9 of the list of materials given to the National Archives. That autopsy report never showed up anywhere. Its disappeared. What we have therefore is probably the third version of the autopsy report.

DiEugenio: You say that the original autopsy report was burned on Sunday.

Mantik: Yes. James Humes burned his first version of the autopsy report on Sunday. And that was the same day that Oswald was shot.

DiEugenio: How many volumes of evidence did the House Select Committee publish in 1979?

Mantik: The House Select Committee published its primary report, but it was supplemented by twelve additional volumes.

DiEugenio: Now, the raw data that it was based upon was classified and would have stayed classified until 2029. In that raw data … how did they deal with the gaping avulsive wound in the rear of Kennedy's skull that so many doctors at Parkland saw?

Mantik: They sealed many of the witness reports. These were not available to the public and were not supposed to be released to the public until 2029. The House Select Committee basically tried to assure us that everything was kosher and that there was no big wound in the back of the head and that the witnesses agreed with that. So, after Oliver Stone's movie *JFK* came out, we finally got the JFK Act and we were allowed to see the witness statements. Not only were we allowed to see their statements but we were allowed to see the sketches where they had drawn the big hole on the back of the head. And this was totally opposite of what the House Select Committee had told us. It was actually a lie. Virtually every witness who was asked drew a large occipital hole consistent with what the Parkland doctors had been telling us all along.

DiEugenio: Now, did the House Select Committee say that one of the reasons that they thought that all of the autopsy materials [were] genuine was because there was no evidence of a shot from the front?

Mantik: Well, the government investigators did claim that there was no evidence of a shot from the front. But they didn't tell us a few things that were very important. On the lateral X-rays in particular, the findings of Michael Chesser and myself are quite remarkable. We have seen tiny metal fragments right at the forehead on these lateral X-rays and Chesser in particular has seen a small hole in the skull at that site consistent with the passage of a bullet through the forehead. None of the government investigations have ever told us about these things.

Further, most of the bullet fragments that we see on the lateral skull X-rays are in the anterior half of the skull. These are for the most part very, very tiny. Many of them only one millimeter or so in size. Now why is that important? Well what we know is that the larger bullet fragments travel further, whereas the smaller ones tend to stay at the entry site. That's what we see on these X-rays. In other words, we can reasonably interpret these as being consistent with a frontal bullet. But being radically inconsistent with a posterior bullet.

DiEugenio: Isn't there a dispute between John Stringer and a man named Robert Knudsen who also says he took autopsy photographs?

Mantik: Knudsen was a White House photographer who was absent from home for two or three days that weekend. And his claim was that he was directly involved in taking autopsy photographs. In fact, his wife was interviewed by the ARRB and she tells amazing stories that she heard from Robert. He told her that the photographs had been deliberately burned by the Secret Service and that one photograph in particular, presumably the back of the head, had been severely altered. Gloria Knudsen was so disturbed by this after his death in 1989, she contacted some of his colleagues there in the Navy and they assured her that this was what he had told them too.

DiEugenio: Was Knudsen interviewed by the Warren Commission?

Mantik: Knudsen was not interviewed by the Warren Commission. And since he died in 1989, he could not be interviewed in the 1990s by the ARRB either.

DiEugenio: Saundra Spencer told the ARRB that she had developed pictures delivered to her by Knudsen. Is that correct?

Mantik: Spencer worked at the Anacostia facility, a Naval photographic center, which was quite separate from the Secret Service; and from Knudsen, who was the Navy photographer at the White House. And she describes the images that she saw. In particular she saw a small hole in the back of JFK's head which she described as maybe two, two and a half centimeters in size. That's interesting because that's smaller than most of what the witnesses at Parkland and Bethesda recalled. It is as if some alteration has occurred in the back of the head.

DiEugenio: What you're saying is that what Knudsen saw and what Spencer saw takes us all the way back to the drawing directed by Dr. McClelland at Parkland Hospital. What he saw.

Mantik: Robert McClelland was in the emergency room standing at the back of JFK when he was being ministered to there. McClelland … was very clear about what he saw. He said that he had been standing there for a significant period of time, not just a minute or two. But ten, fifteen minutes. And while he was standing there at the back of JFK's head, he could look in through the skull and see cerebellum which is low on the back of the head. That's much more consistent with the Warren Commission wound and not at all consistent with the House Select Committee which raised it four inches.

DiEugenio: Did the Warren Commission or the House Select Committee ever interview Saundra Spencer?

Mantik: The Warren Commission did not interview Spencer. The House Select Committee did not interview her either. Her name only came up for the ARRB.

DiEugenio: What was the Harper fragment?

Mantik: The Harper fragment was a piece of fresh skull bone that was found in Dealey Plaza. Not on the day of the assassination, but later by Billy Harper. Harper showed this bone fragment to his uncle Jack Harper, who was a pathologist at Methodist Hospital in Dallas. Altogether three different pathologists saw this Harper fragment and they all agreed that it was from the occipital area. In the early 1990s, we did a radio interview with one of these three pathologists, Gerard Noteboom. He said he stood by his statement. He said it was occipital. He also said that he remembered seeing a lead type stain on one edge of one corner … which suggested to him that a bullet had entered at that site.

The Harper fragment is the center of a lot of controversy because it so radically disagrees with the HSCA which basically said the occipital area was intact. And we have the official photograph of the back of the head which shows virtually no blood, no trauma on the back of the head. The hair looks as if it was just washed. People who support the government position necessarily have to claim that the Harper fragment did not come from the occipital.

DiEugenio: What's your analysis of all this?

Mantik: My view is that it came from the right rear of the head and that is consistent with the Parkland doctors and also consistent with the Bethesda witnesses.

DiEugenio: Did the House Select Committee authenticate the X-rays?

Mantik: They used Gerald McDonnell from Los Angeles. He made a nice list of things that he looked for on the X-rays, and he claims that none of these odd events happened. But in my own work, I have shown that at least three of those four things are in fact compatible with X-ray alteration. One of the things he missed was the fact that emulsion is missing under a T-shaped inscription on the lateral X-ray. It's like somebody took their fingernail and wiped off the emulsion. So you can see a figure T on the X-ray there. So I looked closely while I was at the Archives to see if the emulsion was scraped off at that site. Well it's not. How is that possible? The only way that can happen is if somebody made a copy of the original X-ray. That way that T-shaped area would show up on the copy. But the emulsion would still be there on the copy. So the answer is that the so-called authentication by the House Select Committee on Assassinations was far less than ideal.

David Talbot

David Talbot is the author of *Brothers* and *The Devil's Chessboard* and the founder of *Salon*.

James DiEugenio: Did the CIA manipulate President Kennedy into approving the Bay of Pigs operation?

David Talbot: When President Kennedy came into office, he knew the Bay of Pigs operation was already planned, had been planned under the Eisenhower administration. But he was very reluctant to go ahead with it. He was actually forced into doing it by the CIA and his national security advisers. They said it would be a slam dunk. And so Kennedy was very reluctantly persuaded to go ahead with the mission. Now Allen Dulles was head of the CIA and he knew in advance that this couldn't possibly be a slam dunk. And the fourteen hundred or so Cuban exiles were not capable of pulling off such a mission as toppling Castro in Havana. He knew that at some point they would get bogged down on the beaches and that their success required massive intervention by the US military. He wasn't telling this to Kennedy though, he was telling Kennedy that this motley brigade of Cuban exiles could pull it off. But he knew that at some point when their mission was in critical danger, Kennedy would be forced to send in the Marines, the Air Force, and so on. So, in effect, he was sandbagging President Kennedy.

DiEugenio: Didn't the CIA keep a very crucial document away from Kennedy which admitted this had to be a joint CIA-Pentagon operation?

Talbot: The CIA knew well in advance that this couldn't be done by the Cuban exile brigade alone. They'd studied it quite exhaustively. Even back in November of 1960, before Kennedy took office, there was a meeting of the Cuban task force within the CIA and they came to the conclusion that this could only be a success … if the Marines and the Air Force, the full might of the US military came in. So they knew this in advance. In fact, the CIA staffing on the Bay of Pigs mission was a joke. Later, Lyman Kirkpatrick, who is the Inspector General of the CIA … thought that the staff people the CIA had selected to man the operation were some of the lowest-rung people in the organization. So this, in every way, was set up to fail, to force Kennedy's hand at the crucial moment to send in the Marines.

Allen Dulles, years later, in fact, confessed that the mission was bound to fail as planned by the CIA without US military support. He confessed this while preparing an article for *Harper's* magazine with the young editor Willie Morris. They spent quite a bit of time together walking around Georgetown where Dulles lived. And Dulles explained his side of the story. Dulles was still, years later—after President Kennedy's assassination—very angry and bitter about this forced resignation. In talking about Kennedy, he said, "That little Kennedy, he thought he was a god!"

DiEugenio: How was the manipulation and subterfuge discovered by the president?

Talbot: Well, President Kennedy figured out, and Bobby Kennedy, of course, who was JFK's right-hand man. Right away, they called for a presidential commission chaired by Maxwell Taylor. He was kind of a maverick within the Pentagon. And also there were some Kennedy loyalists within the CIA. One of them was Lyman Kirkpatrick, who is the Inspector General. It was his job to look into things that had gone wrong. And he began to study the Bay of Pigs right away.

DiEugenio: Now, as a result of this investigation, what does Kennedy do?

Talbot: He does move to decapitate the top of the CIA. He lets it be known that Allen Dulles, his legendary director, his days are numbered. As well as his two top advisers, Richard Bissell, who is also very involved with the Bay of Pigs, and General Cabell, who is the right-hand man to Dulles. He forces them out before the end of the year. He also lets it be known that he's going to start cleaning house … the agency is going to be downsized. He wants for instance, CIA station chiefs around the world to answer to the ambassadors rather than act on their own. He trusts his close aide, historian Arthur Schlesinger, he gives him the job of basically rethinking the CIA. And he comes up with a plan for how to do that. He even wants to rename the CIA, because he thinks the CIA brand is so contaminated.

DiEugenio: By the summer of 1961, would it be accurate to say that Dulles had misinformed Kennedy about the Bay of Pigs, had not told him about the death of Patrice Lumumba, and had actually sided with the French generals to try and overthrow de Gaulle over the dispute for independence in Algeria?

Talbot: In the same month, in April of 1961, he was also being lied to about a coup in France, a military coup that was aimed at overthrowing President Charles de Gaulle, one of our strongest allies. They'd never really liked each other, de Gaulle and Dulles. He was stubbornly nationalist and Dulles and the hard-liners in the US were suspicious of him. He also wanted terribly to wind down the bloody colonial war in Algeria. A war of independence that young Senator Kennedy had said that Algeria, like many countries in the Third World, should be allowed to pursue independence. De Gaulle understood, even though he was more conservative than JFK, that this war was bleeding French resources and it was unwinnable and had to be brought to a conclusion.

But in doing that, he antagonized his own military hard-liners, including the military generals who are fighting this bloody and terrible war in Algeria with great bloodshed on both sides. And so they vowed to resist. And the talk in the press, it was openly discussed in the French press, was the plotters would only be so bold against the French government because they were getting CIA support. Because Allen Dulles in particular was giving them a signal that he was on their side. So there's an uproar in Washington. The French ambassador speaks to the White House. JFK assures the French ambassador, "I have nothing to do with this. I stand in full support of President de Gaulle."

DiEugenio: Do you think the letter to the ambassadors may have been caused by the fact that Dulles never told Kennedy that Lumumba had been killed?

Talbot: Patrice Lumumba, he understood, was a rising, very charismatic force for change within Africa. And, in some ways, the hopes of the entire African continent for throwing off their colonial masters and determining their own national affairs resided in this one man, Patrice Lumumba, which had been ruled for decades by a horrible colonial regime under Belgian control. Finally, Patrice Lumumba is elected and is trying to throw off the yoke of history, and people like JFK and progressives in the United States are supporting this. The CIA is adamantly opposed to Patrice Lumumba. So there are people on the ground, CIA people, who are conspiring against Lumumba. And he is finally put under house arrest. There is a military coup underway in Congo. He runs for his life at one point. And he is very close to freedom, to a province that remains loyal to him, when he's captured. The CIA knows this as Kennedy is being prepared to be inaugurated in January 1961. And so what happens? Larry Devlin is the CIA man in the Congo. He makes sure Lumumba is delivered to his enemies, his worst enemies, who horribly torture and murder him. But do they inform the new president of what happens to Lumumba? No. It takes weeks for Kennedy to find out the truth about Lumumba's fate. Who finally tells him? He's informed by his UN Ambassador Adlai Stevenson. And there's a famous photo of Kennedy taken at the moment, the very moment when he hears that terrible news from Stevenson. His face crumples, he's holding his head, he's grimacing in anguish. I feel that in some way, this look of anguish on Kennedy's face, hearing about the assassination of Patrice Lumumba—a man who he had invested so much hope in for the future of Africa—when he heard this, I think he knew on some level about the dark powers that he himself was up against.

DiEugenio: Would you say that this dispute between Allen Dulles and Kennedy is really about different paths, different choices, different decisions about American foreign policy in the Third World?

Talbot: In many ways they represented two totally different ways of looking at America's role in the world. Kennedy was really set on leading the country out of the Cold War. Not only that, but he knew that America couldn't play a dominant role in the world, telling other countries what to do, and robbing their resources. The world had to be more of a multipolar configuration. Not Allen Dulles's view. He thought Kennedy was an appeaser, he was weak, and that he wanted to be loved. In fact, Dulles gave a speech shortly before Kennedy's assassination and he said this was the problem with the current administration—it wants to be loved by the rest of the world. Whereas the US should aspire to be feared and respected.

This becomes eloquently real in June of 1963, when Kennedy gives the famous peace speech, as it came to be known at American University in Washington. And here, he actually puts into words the kind of language that Premier Khrushchev in Moscow had himself used in writing to Kennedy, you know, "Russians are human beings." And this is what Kennedy says picking up on this theme: "that we all have children, that we're all human, we all breathe the same air and we all want our children to live in peace." This is a remarkable thing for any president to say at the time, but particularly at the height of the Cold War—that we can empathize with our so-called enemy.

DiEugenio: Was Allen Dulles really fired?

Talbot: In reality, Allen Dulles recovers very quickly. He retreats to his home in Georgetown and he begins basically to set up a government in exile there. The top people at CIA do not regard John McCone, the new CIA director, really as their boss. So people like Richard Helms, James Angleton still feel they're part of the Allen Dulles circle. They go to his home frequently or at the Metropolitan Club. Dulles is not only seeing his old CIA lieutenants, but generals, admirals, the national security network. He begins to operate a government in exile that is opposed to Kennedy policy and is creating opposition to the Kennedy administration.

DiEugenio: In your many years of research, was the Warren Commission a true fact-finding committee?

Talbot: The Warren Commission was meant to cover things up, not to get to the bottom of the truth. It was meant to let the country move on, to not disturb people, to not go after the powerful forces that were obviously behind the crime. And the point was to "lay the dust" to cover things up. John McCloy, who was a member of the commission, used that term "lay the dust." So it was never a true investigative committee. It was meant to reassure people so America could go back to sleep. Not to wake up America to this terrible new reality.

DiEugenio: Wasn't Allen Dulles the most active member of the Commission because he was the one who didn't have a job?

Talbot: Dulles was, in many ways, the most active member of the Commission. He was retired, supposedly. He didn't have a day job. He could devote virtually all his energy to the job. And so he comes from day one with reading material for the others to show that, according to this book, you know presidents are usually killed by lone gunmen. Like you know Abraham Lincoln. Of course the Lincoln plot was much more vast than John Wilkes Booth. In other words, he was trying to determine where the Commission was going from the very beginning, from day one. And, of course he was the former director of the CIA. So other Commission members deferred to him on matters of investigation. They thought he was the authority. So he had great influence over the proceedings of the Warren Commission. In fact, many people have said that it should have been called the Dulles Commission.

Dr. Gary Aguilar

Dr. Gary Aguilar is an opthalmologist and college instructor at UC San Francisco.

First Interview, Los Angeles, August 19, 2019

Oliver Stone: What happened to Malcolm Perry as a result of the November 22, 1963, press conference?

Gary Aguilar: Dr. Perry performed the tracheotomy to help Kennedy breathe, and at a press conference right after the failed resuscitation efforts in Dallas, he was asked, "Where was the bullet?" And he said it looked like the bullet was coming at him. He had an entrance wound in the throat, and he said it three times.

Well, that caused a huge problem. Because apparently, later on that night, one of the nurses there said that during the night Perry got a lot of phone calls saying: no, you can't say that. That's not what happened. And he was put under a lot of pressure. In his Warren Commission testimony, he basically retracted what he had said. When you look at the transcript, the news reports were exactly right. He had said three times that the bullet had appeared to be coming at him. And they basically forced him to back down and sort of intimidated him on the witness stand.

Stone: Didn't Charles Crenshaw also disagree with the Warren Commission version of all the shots from the rear?

Aguilar: Charles Crenshaw was a surgeon at Parkland and he wrote a book called *Conspiracy of Silence*. It was published initially in the latter part of 1992 in reaction to the film *JFK*. He was saying that "I was there. Kennedy had a wound in the back portion of his head that does not fit the scenario of being shot from behind." He was immediately reviled in the press and then the *Journal of the American Medical Association* (*JAMA*), starting in May of 1992, went after him with a vengeance. And they interviewed other Parkland doctors. And they had them saying, "Well Dr. Crenshaw is, you know, not telling you the truth. That's not what happened. In fact, Dr. Crenshaw wasn't even there."

It turns out that had anyone at the *Journal of the American Medical Association* bothered to look at the index of the Warren Report, they would have found that Crenshaw's name was mentioned five times. And more important, two or three of the doctors who were interviewed in *JAMA* saying that he wasn't there, testified under oath in 1964, that he was there. Lawrence Altman of the *New York Times* wrote in an article that *JAMA*'s research was "less than thorough" because they had missed that entirely. Dr. Crenshaw ultimately sued the *Journal of the American Medical Association* and the American Medical Association settled in an out-of-court settlement for almost a quarter-million dollars.

Stone: When they had the Garrison trial, why did the defense call Pierre Finck to testify in New Orleans?

Aguilar: The prosecution of Clay Shaw brought in an expert, John Nichols, who was a certified pathologist from Kansas, a professor actually. And he looked at the evidence, at the Zapruder film, and he testified under oath that it looked to him like Kennedy had been shot in the right front because he was driven back to the left. That caused some serious problems because Oswald was supposed to have shot from behind. So they brought in Dr. Pierre Finck and Finck came in to refute Dr. Nichols. Finck then caused a lot of problems on his own, because Finck testified that while he was sitting there, he heard Dr. Humes, who was the chief pathologist, saying, "Who's in charge here?" And an Army general in the morgue said, "I am." And Dr. Finck was asked: was this Army general a doctor? And he says, "No, he wasn't"

And he also said that he was ordered not to dissect the back wound. If you read the transcript, he bobbed and weaved. He was asked the question eight times. Finally, the judge forced him to answer, he says: I did not dissect the back wound because I was ordered not to. Finck's now releasing all sorts of very damaging information about the way the autopsy—that the doctors weren't in control of the autopsy. So they then contacted Dr Boswell, who'd also been part of the team, and they flew him down. He read the transcripts to go in there and refute Dr. Finck. Boswell was never brought in and probably for good reason. And that is that Dr. Finck had been Dr. Boswell's expert.

Dr. Finck did admit afterward in a memo to his superior that he was denied Jack Kennedy's clothing during the autopsy. When you look at a body, knowing where the bullets went in is obviously what you have to determine on the body. But knowing how the clothes sit against them is very important. When you're doing an autopsy and you are denied the clothes, you're not in control of that autopsy. There would have been no legitimate reason not to have the clothing. Looking at the clothing would have been quite simple, and they had the clothing available.

Stone: How did the HSCA, the House Select Committee on Assassinations, deal with this information about the avulsive wound in the back of the head?

Aguilar: They said that all the witnesses at the autopsy, they all agreed to those autopsy photographs. But they suppressed the witness statements themselves. When the ARRB came along, and out comes those witness statements, out comes the diagrams. And lo and behold, it turns out that the witnesses at the autopsy all agreed with the doctors at Dallas: that the defect involved the rear of the head. They basically lied about what was there.

There was a conference in the early nineties, and two of the principals Dr. [Michael] Baden, who was the chief forensic pathologist was there. Dr. Cyril Wecht was there. Robert Blakey was there and one of the people who conducted these interviews was sitting on the podium with me, Mr. Andy Purdy. I showed the statement where the House Select Committee on Assassinations says that all the autopsy witnesses refuted it and the Parkland doctors were wrong because all the autopsy witnesses at Bethesda agreed with that, with the photographs. I then showed their diagrams, I showed their testimony. And I said, "This basically was a lie." And then I asked Mr. Blakey and he denied having written that section. Andy Purdy denied that section. But more importantly, on the podium with me was Dr. Michael Baden and Dr. Wecht. I said Dr. Baden, Dr. Wecht, this is important medical information. Did either of you ever see these witness statements or these diagrams. Neither had seen them. So not only had the HSCA lied about what their own witnesses told them, they didn't share this very relevant medical information with their own medical consultants. Huge scandal, I think.

Stone: Let's go to the second autopsy, the famous Clark panel, Ramsey Clark. How much of a revision was it to the original?

Aguilar: So the Clark Panel came together and they brought in four experts to look at this stuff. The original autopsy report says that the bullet entered Jack Kennedy's head low, in the back of the head. Well, the Clark Panel then looked and said no, they missed the in shoot and the bullet entered actually ten centimeters higher, up here in a different bone. That's a whopping error.

They also said that, whereas the autopsy doctors said there was a trail of bullet fragments from this low entry point—and there isn't one, I've seen the original autopsy photographs myself—they said that the trail of fragments went in this higher location, from here forward. But, in fact, the fragment trail doesn't go to either of these locations. It's much higher than that in the skull.

But all three of the autopsy doctors insisted, "No it was low." And there's good reason to believe it was low. And the reason is that there's one document that survives from the autopsy and it's what we call Boswell's face sheet. There are Kennedy's bloodstains on that sheet. Boswell drew a diagram and on that diagram it says seventeen missing. And he was asked under oath, what does that mean? He said, Well, when we got the body, the defect in the skull was seventeen centimeters, or seventeen centimeters of skull missing. If you measure one centimeter back, you're way back here at the back of the skull, way back down here. And we have that on the basis of the original autopsy doctor saying that.

This would be very difficult to explain as a shot from a single bullet striking the back of the skull like that.

Stone: But this is potentially another bullet?

Aguilar: I think there's strong evidence that there's another bullet that struck in the back of the head. There's X-ray evidence, probably the strongest of all. Because when a jacketed bullet, which is Oswald's type of ammunition, jacketed bullets, when they hit bones, they don't immediately fragment into tiny little fragments. They just scatter a few bullet fragments across the skull. And in fact, that's what happened when they did skull duplications shooting tests in 1964. They shot Mannlicher-Carcano bullets into skulls filled with brain-equivalent material and you can see some small fragments scattered across the skull. That is not what you see in Kennedy's autopsy photographs. There are a couple of fragments, but there are also a cloud of tiny little fragments in the right front part of his head. And those tiny fragments don't come from jacketed bullets. They come from non-jacketed bullets or soft-nosed bullets. And the reason they are up there in this area and the reason I would say that proves a shot from the right front is that when a non-jacketed bullet hits a skull it immediately breaks into tiny little pieces. And those little pieces don't go very far. The larger pieces have the momentum to drive through tissues. Small pieces are stopped very quickly. We know they are tiny little fragments up there that are inconsistent with Oswald's ammunition.

Stone: You're saying that he was, Mr. Kennedy, was shot from both the front and back?

Aguilar: I would submit that he was shot from the right front, as well as from the back.

Stone: Did the media note the Ramsey Clark Panel changes?

Aguilar: No. The media, as it typically does, basically heralded the Ramsey Clark findings as basically having endorsed the official conclusions of the autopsy.

Stone: I just want to repeat one thing. The autopsy report from, I guess the Warren Commission, the original from Bethesda begins with the statement three shots were fired and Kennedy fell forward.

Aguilar: The autopsy report says three shots were fired and Kennedy fell forward. In the original handwritten one, it says three shots were fired and Kennedy fell forward to the floor of the limousine. They cut that in the printed version. But what that did was reflect the fact that the doctors that did the autopsy were under the impression that Kennedy got shot in the head and they were told he was shot from behind. They didn't see it but they were told that. They wrote that in their autopsy report—and then he fell forward. We all know from the Zapruder film that he actually went backwards. But these three autopsy pathologists ... were given a body, told here's the body: he was shot from behind, he fell forward, which they wrote in their autopsy report. Figure out how the wounds fit the known circumstances of the shooting.

Stone: Was there a shot after Zapruder film frame 313?

Aguilar: I think the first shot hit him from the right front, drove him back; the second shot after frame 327 hit him in the back of the head and drove him forward. The main explanation for why Kennedy went backward was that he had this "neuromuscular reaction" that's supposed to throw you back. There are two options … they are called neuro decorticate and decerebrate. The key feature is that the legs extend. Kennedy's legs don't extend. They don't extend at all. It couldn't have been neuromuscular reaction. Shortly after that, point seven seconds later, he's recoiling forward when neuromuscular reaction should have had him still recoiling backwards. It was the impact of the bullet that moved him backward.

Stone: What about the mess that was in the limousine—all the fragments and the spray there?

Aguilar: Brain material and that sort of thing—there was a lot of brain material. And this goes into a very, very central question in the case. Anybody that has seen the Zapruder film and could see Kennedy's head explode and debris flies all over the place. Jackie Kennedy climbed out onto the trunk of the limousine, picked up a chunk of the president's brain, had it with her, took it and gave it to one of the doctors at Parkland Hospital. And then there was everyone splattered with the brain. Then we looked at the autopsy report of the brain and what they called a supplemental brain examination. The brain in evidence that weighed 1,500 grams. Now a normal brain weighs 1,350–1,400 grams. A full complete brain weighing 1,500 grams is not common. And yet the brain in evidence is supposed to weigh 1,500 grams. That's one of the reasons we don't think that the brain that they have in evidence is actually Jack Kennedy's brain.

Second Interview, Los Angeles, January 6, 2020

James DiEugenio: Can you describe the rather odd way that the Warren Commission Report and the Warren Commission volumes were issued in the fall of 1964?

Gary Aguilar: There was a *New York Times* edition of the Warren Report. And there were two introductory essays in there. Harrison Salisbury said that no question remains unresolved as of the events of November 22, 1963. And Anthony Lewis said that the Warren Commission had released all the documents that it had assembled as evidence, redacting only a few names. So here you have the *New York Times* assuring the public that all the documents have been released and no question remains unresolved. In the absence of having seen any of the twenty-six volumes of supplementary evidence. The *New York Times* as you know, whether it's the Gulf of Tonkin incident, whether it's the rush to war in Iraq with the imminent threat of weapons of mass destruction, it has always followed the government's lead on this.

I wrote Anthony Lewis a couple of times asking him how he got the information. Because it turns out that when the ARRB came along to declassify documents, there were still three thousand pages of Warren Commission documents still held in secret after a thirty-year history of their having been releasing documents all along the way. So it was clearly untrue that the Warren Commission had released all the documents. In fact, we now know that a lot of evidence has been suppressed or destroyed. I wrote Anthony Lewis and asked him: Did you just make this up out of whole cloth, or did somebody tell you this? I wrote him twice. He never answered. I'm sure that Anthony Lewis didn't make that up. I'm sure somebody on the Warren Commission told him that, and it was untrue.

DiEugenio: The media was endorsing the Warren Commission Report two months before anyone, theoretically at least, could read the testimony and exhibits. Which are twenty-six volumes, about seventeen thousand pages. So how could you possibly make a judgment based on the report when almost all the footnotes are based on volumes you have not seen yet? But that's what they did, right?

Aguilar: That's precisely what they did. And more importantly, if you see the *New York Times* edition of the Warren Report, they admit that they were working with the Warren Commission. They were collaborating with the Warren Commission.

That pattern, established by the *New York Times*, has been followed clearly throughout. To the great shame of my organization, the American Medical Association by the *Journal of the American Medical Association*. They published some articles that were laughably absurd and were ultimately repudiated even by members of the mainstream media. They've been rarely referred to since then. And they were basically doing what the mainstream media has always done in this country. And that is tout the government's version of events.

DiEugenio: For the magic-bullet theory to be viable, that bullet had to have been found on John Connally's stretcher, right? Isn't there a question that it was actually found on Connally's stretcher?

Aguilar: Oh yes. The stretcher that it was supposed to have been found on was almost certainly not John Connally's stretcher. The witnesses who found the bullet on a stretcher said that also on that stretcher was a stethoscope, some rubber gloves, and physician's paraphernalia. Well, the guys who took care of John Connally said that there was blood on some sheets. They cleaned those sheets off, sent the elevator back down to the lobby where the stretcher was found. And there was nothing on Connally's stretcher when it got down there. The stretcher that had the gloves and the stethoscope and the physician's paraphernalia was the stretcher of a boy who had come in with a laceration who had been crying named Ronnie Fuller. It wasn't John Connally's.

DiEugenio: Who was Thomas Canning and what did he do for the House Select Committee on Assassinations?

Aguilar: Canning was really a rocket scientist. He'd worked at NASA on Apollo. Canning was an expert who was called by the HSCA to do trajectory work on the Kennedy assassination to determine whether the wounds would align with a shot from Oswald's position. So Canning came in and he concluded on the basis of his analysis that the wounds and the trajectory through Kennedy and Connally were such that they pointed to the southeast corner of the Texas School Book Depository, where Oswald was.

But when people began looking a little more closely at his work, they began realizing that even though he said that he had used the wound locations given to him by the forensics experts, he hadn't used them at all. He basically made them up. And rather than doing a trajectory analysis going from the School Book Depository through Jack Kennedy's throat and from his back through his throat, he back projected from where he placed the wounds on Kennedy's throat and where he placed the wound on Kennedy's back and projected backward. Well, that sort of trajectory analysis is just rubbish. There's no one who would stand by that. In fact, the forensics panel suggested he not do that. That it would be entirely invalid. I think one can take that analysis like so much scientific analysis in the Kennedy case and ignore it.

DiEugenio: Discussing another very controversial subject, how many witnesses are on the record as seeing the severely damaged brain of John F. Kennedy?

Aguilar: The question of John F. Kennedy's brain is an utterly fascinating one, and it's one of the things that I think is perhaps most important in the case. Dr. Humes said in a *JAMA* article—one thing that is probably true—he said that two-thirds of the right cerebrum, which is the major lobe of the brain, had been blown away. One of the autopsy photographers named Floyd Riebe said that half of the brain was missing. An FBI agent who was there said that, yeah, there was about half the brain was missing. And then, of course, you have the limousine occupants splattered with brain matter. You have the police to the left rear of the limousine ... hit with brain material. And you have brain material scattered on the trunk. So there's a lot of brain that is evidently missing. It's visible in the Zapruder film and testified to by people who are credible witnesses.

So what happens? There's a question about there having been two different autopsy examinations of the brain because it was done at a separate time. But the one that's in the official record is one that was done sometime later. There's a pen-and-ink diagram of it in the HSCA volumes. I've seen the original at the National Archives and you can see that there is some disruption of the right parietal lobe, but very little of its missing. But here's a brain that's supposed to have been blasted away and it weighs fifteen hundred grams. There's a very good reason to suppose that the brain we have in evidence is not Jack Kennedy's brain. How could it be when everyone we're talking about, two of the thee pathologists, an FBI agent, another doctor who was present at the autopsy, and other witnesses say that a substantial portion of the brain was blasted away.

DiEugenio: What would be the reason for substituting a different brain?

Aguilar: If they substituted a brain, one can only imagine that they wanted the damage to the brain to be consistent with the hypothesis that Oswald had done the shooting that killed him.

DiEugenio: When is the first official entry made into the record as to the weight of the brain? Because it was not entered that evening at Bethesda, was it?

Aguilar: The night of the autopsy there is a brief description of the brain that gives no detail and no brain weight is given for that. It was then apparently put in formalin. That makes the brain firm up a little bit so that now it's firmer, you can do sectioning to be able to track the bullet through the brain. That was not done.

DiEugenio: What was the reaction of John Stringer when he was shown the photographs of Kennedy's brain?

Aguilar: Stringer said he did not take the autopsy photographs of JFK's brain that are in the current record now. They're not the ones he took. He was there. He did take brain photographs, but the photographs that appear now are not on the film that he used then. … Stringer also said that there was some damage to the left side of the cerebellum. And the autopsy photographs just don't show that. … And again, that raises real questions about the brain that we have in evidence.

DiEugenio: The House Select Committee on Assassinations concluded that the autopsy photographs that we have are not altered in any way. Is that really accurate?

Aguilar: They said that they were unable to completely close the loop because they were unable to obtain the original camera that had been used to take the autopsy photographs. Well, when the ARRB came along, they released some documents and it turns out that is not precisely true. It turns out that they had tested the camera that was sent to them by the Navy, said to be the camera in use at Bethesda. And they tested the camera against the autopsy photographs. And they didn't match. So they wrote a letter back to the Secretary of the Navy saying: Well thank you very much for this camera, but it doesn't match. Would you please send the original one? The Secretary of the Navy wrote back saying: Look, this is the camera that was used. There is no other camera. This is it. So the camera sent to them to authenticate the autopsy images we have don't match. So that's a key point here. And what's happened to the camera? It has since disappeared.

DiEugenio: You're saying that was only made possible through the ARRB. We wouldn't have known it if there had been no ARRB.

Aguilar: Without the ARRB, we would have not have known that the magic bullet has no chain of custody. Without the ARRB, we would not have known that the autopsy camera failed a fundamental authentication test.

Dr. Michael Chesser

Dr. Michael Chesser is a practicing neurologist in Little Rock, Arkansas, who has written several essays on the JFK assassination.

James DiEugenio: At the time of the House Select Committee in 1976, there had been two divergent autopsies on the John F. Kennedy case. One that was recorded in the Warren Report, and then what they called the

Ramsey Clark Panel in 1968. So when the HSCA convened, which one of those two autopsies did they decide to abide by?

Michael Chesser: The Clark Panel actually reviewed the medical evidence. They didn't perform a second autopsy. The HSCA went with the Clark Panel report as far as the head wounds. The Clark Panel was formed in order to counter some of the criticism of the medical evidence in the Warren Commission. They had three pathologists and a radiologist on the panel.

DiEugenio: And how did they alter the original autopsy?

Chesser: The Commission placed the entry of a bullet fired from the sixth floor of the Texas School Book Depository low in the back of the head. Right next to what is called the external occipital protuberance. The Clark Panel and the HSCA moved this four inches up here, into the parietal bone. Four inches is quite a distance from the original location of the entry wound.

They did this for several reasons. They knew that an entry in the lower location would cause tremendous damage to the cerebellum. The brain photograph which is purported to be Kennedy's brain, the cerebellum is untouched. They also knew that the X-rays did not support an entry in that location. In the autopsy report of the Warren Commission, Commander Humes said that there was a fragment trail extending from the external occipital protuberance up to the exit location. But when you look at the X-rays, the fragment trail is all up at the top of the skull. So that didn't fit either.

DiEugenio: So there is no diagonal like that leads upward in the present X-rays.

Chesser: The X-rays at the archives do not show a fragment trail extending from low up to here. They show a fragment trail from the back of the parietal bone to the frontal bone. But the fragment trail doesn't fit the conclusions of the Clark Panel or the House Select Committee. For several reasons. I think the most important reason is that the tiniest fragments on that trail, and there are dozens of them, are very tiny or just inside the frontal bone. And the largest fragments are at the back of the skull. This goes against all forensic evidence that the tiniest fragments were not going to travel that far. So it's impossible for a shot here, in the back of the skull, to result in all of the tiniest bullet fragments in the frontal region.

DiEugenio: You're saying that the fact that there's all these dustlike particles in the front of the skull would indicate a point of entry from the front.

Chesser: Yes it does. It's very strong evidence.

DiEugenio: And you're also saying that because the larger fragments were in the back, that also would indicate a shot from the front.

Chesser: Yes. And the fracture pattern does seem to support the bullet entry low in the occiput.

DiEugenio: Since you are a neurologist, how many witnesses at Parkland and Bethesda describe a severely damaged brain?

Chesser: In reviewing the testimonies of the Warren Commission, and the House Select Committee, and also other sources, there were at least twenty witnesses at Parkland who saw a huge skull defect consistent with an exit wound in the back of the skull. Kemp Clark, who was chairman of neurosurgery at the time, was trained at Columbia Presbyterian in New York, which was the top neurologic center in the country at the time. Clark testified that there was an exit wound or large wound in the back of the skull. He termed it a tangential wound, which means that the bullet most likely struck at a glance.

DiEugenio: But doesn't he also talk about blasted and damaged cerebellum?

Chesser: He definitely said there was damaged cerebellum. And also loss of occipital lobe and parietal lobe. Dr. Marion Jenkins … he sat at the head of the table directly in front of the president's head during the resuscitation. And he again described a large defect in the back of the head. And he said there was cerebellum tissue protruding out of the skull.

DiEugenio: This blasted-out cerebellum would indicate just how low this wound in the back of the skull went. Because although the cerebellum is connected to the brain, it's actually below the brain. And doesn't it look different and isn't the texture different?

Chesser: The cerebellum is part of the brain. When you talk about the brain, you've got the cerebrum, the cerebral hemispheres, and the cerebellum sits basically on that, behind the brainstem. Very delicate appearing folia. It looks markedly different from the lobes of the brain. It's very distinctive, easy to recognize.

DiEugenio: So isn't it kind of impossible to believe that Kemp Clark, who was chief of neurosurgery, could be wrong about seeing that?

Chesser: I think so. Yes.

DiEugenio: One of the things I want to talk about is this whole problem that we have with the [medical illustrator] Harold Rydberg drawing. Which is the rendering of Kennedy's position in the car when he's hit at Zapruder frame 313.

Chesser: On the Rydberg illustration ... they markedly exaggerated the forward inflection. But it was not a true illustration.

DiEugenio: So this is one of the reasons you think that they raised his rear head wound back here to the cowlick area, up here?

Chesser: Yes. The trajectory from the sixth floor of the Texas School Book Depository at Z frame 312 or 313, would have resulted in the blow out through the face. And this was confirmed even by the government's own ballistic data.

DiEugenio: Didn't the Clark Panel discover a disc-shaped 6.5 millimeter spot on the X-rays in 1968 that none of the pathologists at Bethesda, or the FBI agents at Bethesda, who also looked at the X-rays that day, never noted?

Chesser: That's right. During the autopsy, there was quite a commotion because the radiologist and then the pathologists could not find a large fragment, or bullet, inside the skull or anywhere in the body. There was quite a bit of puzzlement about that. This bright object on the X-ray suddenly shows up between the Bethesda autopsy and the Clark Panel. I think it most likely occurred or was placed there shortly after the autopsy.

Dr. David Mantik has talked to radiologist John Ebersole. He interviewed him back in the nineties. And when he got to the point of asking him about this bright 6.5-millimeter object which, you know is the same diameter as a Mannlicher-Carcano bullet. When he got to that question, Ebersole stopped the interview and abruptly hung up.

DiEugenio: Is it credible that all three pathologists, and the radiologist and his assistant looking at the X-rays would have missed the 6.5-millimeter skull object in the rear of the skull that night at the autopsy?

Chesser: It's not credible.

DiEugenio: Now as you mentioned earlier… is it that the 6.5 millimeters just happens to be the caliber of the bullet that the Warren Commission says was used in the assassination?

Chesser: Yes. When you look at what is supposed to be the original X-rays at the archives, this has a very strange appearance. It's very dense at the top. And then it's not as dense at the bottom. There's a gradual increase in density from lower to upper. And the fragment is in the scalp. This is from the HSCA's radiologist's own words.

DiEugenio: Doesn't the official story say that the head and the tail of the fatal head shot were found in the front of the car?

Chesser: Yes.

DiEugenio: If the head and the tail were found in the front of the car, wouldn't the 6.5 millimeter object have to come from somewhere in the middle of the bullet?

Chesser: Yes, according to the official version, there was only one bullet that struck the skull of the president. And they are asking us to believe that that bullet that you see on the X-rays is from the midsection. And that is one of the most ludicrous things that we are asked to believe about the medical evidence.

DiEugenio: How could a bullet split into three parts upon impact and have the rear somehow go through the skull and leave the middle on the rear table of the skull?

Chesser: Well, the forensic specialists tell us that that does not happen.

DiEugenio: But it did in this case.

Chesser: Yes.

DiEugenio: Do you think that is credible?

Chesser: No.

DiEugenio: As a neurologist, you understand about what a forensic pathologist does to trace bullets in a skull. It's called sectioning. And what does that consist of?

Chesser: They basically take slices of the brain after it's been fixed with formalin. And they track the cavity where the bullet traveled through the brain and they can then, it helps them determine trajectory. And it's part of a thorough forensic examination of the brain after an injury like this.

DiEugenio: But would it also tell you how many bullets?

Chesser: Yes.

DiEugenio: Without that being done, without there being any sectioning of the brain, how can you determine with certainty what the trajectory of the bullet or bullets were through the skull?

Chesser: You couldn't do it. The autopsy examination of President Kennedy was not a standard autopsy, everyone agrees on that point. One of the main deficiencies of the autopsy was the lack of sectioning of the brain. After the brain is fixed, it's sectioned. Then through the microscope, the pathologists would look at the section and it really is vitally important to help them determine the trajectory of the bullets and in determining the number of the bullets. Without it, you know there is just a very incomplete autopsy. … Without sectioning of the brain there was no way for them to properly trace the trajectory of the wounds to the brain.

The president's brain was weighed and then examined a few days after the autopsy. It had been infused with formalin and was sitting in formalin for a few days. Most weights are taken after formalin fixation and fixation only adds about fifty-nine grams to the weight. But fifteen hundred grams, [Kennedys' brain weight] is above average for an adult male. There was one report of eight thousand autopsies and the average weight for an adult male brain was 1,336 grams.

Douglas Horne

Douglas Horne was the Military Records Analyst for the ARRB and he is the author of the five-part book series *Inside the Assassination Records Review Board.*

Oliver Stone: I gather [Pierre Finck] was a reluctant witness at the Garrison trial?

Douglas Horne: Dr. Finck was a reluctant witness at the Garrison trial, and he was a reluctant witness before the Review Board. But we finally located him and we did take his deposition. And many of his response were "I don't remember." Or "I can't answer that."

Stone: What about the other two pathologists, Dr. Humes and Dr. Boswell?

Horne: Humes and Boswell were a good exercise in how you should do depositions. Whereas in the past, they were an example of how you should not do them. Before the Warren Commission, Humes, Boswell, and Finck were in the room at the same time. So Dr. Humes testified before Arlen Specter, while Boswell and Finck were in the room. So they didn't have much to say except: Me, too. The House Select Committee had Humes and Boswell appear before them, the forensic panel, at the same time in 1977. That's not the right procedure. The Review Board took the depositions of Humes, Boswell, and Finck separately. And for the first time, their stories weren't the same. They did not come together at all. They were very different in many respects.

Particularly with regard to: Was there bone missing in the back of the skull? Dr. Humes told the Review Board under oath that there was no bone missing. It was badly fractured, but it was basically intact. Dr. Boswell said that's not true. All the bone was missing on the right side of the cranium, in the back of the head. It was all missing on the top, and part of it on right side. So how did we get Boswell to tell us that? He had made a sketch at the autopsy, on the back of the descriptive sheet he drew a sketch of the damage to the skull at the autopsy. He drew the top of the skull. And he drew a big circle with a dotted line and he wrote 10 x 17 centimeters missing. So we wanted to ask Boswell, your sketch only shows the top of the head, was there bone missing in the back of the head? And he said, "Yes there was." I brought out the skull model and we asked him to turn his two-dimensional sketch made at autopsy into a three-dimensional diagram on a skull model. And the area of missing bone was the top of the head, part of the right side, and the entire right rear of the cranium.

Stone: Wow, that's a big difference.

Horne: A big difference. And that skull model can be viewed by any American citizen today if they go to the archives and make an appointment and they can see the model themselves.

Boswell gave up other things to us also. If you look at the autopsy photographs, there was one called the right superior profile, which shows the president lying on his back. His head is in a head brace and you're looking at the president from this view. It's in color and you see a bright red gash in his forehead above the right eye. Bright red, V-shaped gash. And Dr. Boswell called that an "incised wound." That means he's saying an incision. And it's interesting that he would identify that as an incision, because number one, that's what it looks like. Number two, nobody in Dallas saw such an incision in the president's forehead.

Stone: What does that tell you?

Horne: Tells me there was an entrance wound right there, which other people saw in photographs. The photographs that did not make it into the official record. There was a small entrance wound .... removed with a scalpel before the autopsy started.

Stone: How would you remove it, the bullet hole?

Horne: With the scalpel.

Stone: How do you do that? Just dig it out?

Horne: Yes. And all you can see in the photograph—all I can see in the photograph—is a bright red triangle where the outer skin is removed. And right behind there is some disrupted bone sticking up. We asked Dr. Boswell during his deposition in 1996: Do you see the entrance wound in the back of the skull on any of the autopsy photographs? And he said: "No I don't." Which really was new information and leads one to trust the back of the head photos even less than one already did. So he doesn't even see the entrance wound that they described so carefully in the autopsy report. Yet the doctors have testified that they photographed the entrance wound, took extreme close-ups of the entrance wound in the bone from the outside of the cranium, from the inside of the cranium. None of those photos are in the collection. So the autopsy of John F. Kennedy is probably the evidentiary mess of the twentieth century. It's the worst thing imaginable.

Dr. Finck was raising hell about where's the entrance wound and where's the exit wound. He didn't see evidence of entrance or exit at the time. As a forensic pathologist that was very disturbing to him. How can I say what happened if I don't have evidence of entrance or exit? That's when the Secret Service brought in three fragments. And the doctors were able to fit the middle fragment into the back of the head and recreate the rest of the circumference of the entrance wound. They then photographed the entrance wound, close-ups from the outside and the inside. And those photographs are not in the record. They took great pains to illuminate the chest and photograph the interior of the chest. That's not in the collection.

Stone: And in 1966 did the Justice Department do an inventory about the autopsy photographs?

Horne: Yes, on November 1, 1966. The Department of Justice met with Drs. Humes, Boswell, photographer John Stringer, and radiologist John Ebersole. And during this discussion, the Department of Justice witness, Carl Belcher, who was an attorney, noted they were discussing missing photographs. Photographs that they remembered having been taken that they did not see in the collection. And he was so alarmed by this conversation that he conducted an investigation for more than a week. He couldn't get to the bottom of it. So they were thinking why did ten days go by between the time the inventory was made of what's in the collection and when it was signed. And the first draft was going to have cosigners, Mr. Belcher and the head of the Archives. If you look at the signed version, Belcher took his name off, the head of the Archives took his name off. And a statement was added to the draft: these are all the photographs that were taken and none are missing. Belcher basically called their bluff. He said: OK, you know, if you don't want to admit there's missing photographs, I'm going to make you sign to that. So they signed a statement, those four people—Humes, Boswell, Stringer, and Ebersole—that they knew was not true.

Stone: Were all the pictures there in 1966?

Horne: If you study all the testimony that's been given by anyone who was questioned by the Warren Commission or the House Select Committee or by the Review Board, there are at least eighteen views missing. There are also photographs taken that don't reflect what anyone saw. Most particularly the back of the head photographs. The photograph showing the back of JFK's head seemingly intact is something that no witness saw at Parkland or Bethesda.

There were men in suits [during the autopsy] telling the doctors to stop what you are doing, move on to the next procedure. And the two witnesses for this were Paul O'Connor and James Jenkins. They were the Navy corpsmen who were assisting the three pathologists during the autopsy. And they told this to the HSCA. So we learned all this in 1993. Dr. Burkley seems to have been in control of the developing of all the autopsy photographs that were taken at the autopsy. Burkley ordered the developing of all the autopsy pictures on Saturday, November 23rd, on Sunday November 24th. In 1965, the person [Robert Kennedy] wrote the memo to was George Burkley. So George Burkley went to the Executive Office Building, got the materials out of a Secret Service safe, and created an inventory of what he was turning over to Robert Kennedy. So he was the controlling agent it seems with what photographs were developed and I presume with what photographs made it into the official collection. Included in the photographs that are not in the collection that should be are photographs of probes in the body. Two people recall there were photographs taken of probes in the body. One of the people was Dr. [Robert] Karnei. Karnei was a thirty-three-year resident at Bethesda. ... The other person was Robert Knudsen, who is a Navy chief photographer's mate. He worked at the White House. Knudsen was told to develop autopsy film by Burkley on Saturday, November 23rd. And he developed a roll of black-and-white film which showed probes in the body. Those photographs are not in the collection.

If they [the Warren Commission] had published the autopsy photographs, I think the whole cover-up would have been unraveled right then. Because the Dallas doctors would have gone nuts. That's not what we saw. ...Those are not the wounds we saw at Parkland Hospital.

Stone: Was Burkley alive for the Review Board?

Horne: Dr. Burkley was deceased by the time the Review Board was impaneled. ... I think Burkley was ridden by a profound sense of guilt and shame over his role in a massive cover-up. And I think that from time to time he sought absolution through confession. And then as soon as he would start to tell what he knew he would have second thoughts.

Stone: The FBI contemporaneous report on the autopsy differs from the official report in what way?

Horne: The two FBI agents at the autopsy, Frank O'Neill and James Sibert, wrote a report based on their notes which they took at the autopsy. They wrote a report the day after the funeral on November 26. It's an FD 302, standard FBI report still used today. They did not inject any opinions or impressions of their own. It differs from the autopsy report in significant ways. The most significant way is that assured that the wound was in the upper back. That this bullet could not be found in the body and did not transit the body. There was no exit for that entrance wound. Dr. Humes had decided by this time that the bullet entered high in the back, low in the neck, whatever you want to call it. And it exited the throat.

But the FBI report says that the entrance wound has a steep downward trajectory of forty-five to sixty degrees. That is not in the autopsy report. By the way that is a lot steeper than the Book Depository window. In their report the pattern is clear. The president was hit by two shots. Shortly after they left the morgue at 11:00 ... Humes got on the phone and calls Dr. Perry in Dallas. We know this happened from John Ebersole who testified to that under oath to the HSCA. And we know it happened because that's what Dr. Perry said. Humes denied it. Perry told Humes that the president had a bullet wound in his throat. This is after the FBI agents had left the morgue. Or it would be in their report. Humes changed his two-hit conclusion to a three- hit conclusion. And the witness for that is the military aide to General Wehle, Lt. Richard Lipsey. He was in and out of the morgue during the autopsy and he recalled specifically to the House Select Committee that Humes made an official statement very late that night that there were three hits to the president. And he drew a diagram for the HSCA. Wound number one that Lipsey recalled hearing Humes describe was in the upper back and did not exit the body, and no bullet was found. Wound number two that Lipsey talked about entered very low in the skull at about the hairline, right where you see a white spot in the autopsy photos today. That bullet entered very low on the skull and came out the front of the throat.

This is nowhere in the autopsy report and nowhere in the FBI report either. And bullet number three hit the skull in the back and exited. The importance of this is that it shows the truth was malleable. This three-hit scenario is undoubtedly the content of the first draft of the autopsy report which Humes and Boswell reviewed on Saturday. They reviewed a typed draft together at Bethesda. And then Humes burned it in his fireplace on Sunday. I think I know why. The first written draft was reviewed on Saturday at Bethesda by Captain Canada. I'm sure he and others told Humes this is unacceptable. You can't have three bullets hitting President Kennedy. One bullet hit Connally and there's only three shell casings.

Stone: Doug, since you were there with the Review Board can we talk just for a. moment about the culture and the mentality of it—the atmosphere?

Horne: It was a great privilege of course. But man, it was challenging. It was strange. When I got to work there, I was warned by Chief Counsel Jeremy Gunn, who was my boss, that none of the five Board members believed that there was a conspiracy to kill JFK. Or that there was a cover-up. I said if they didn't even believe there was a cover-up, why are they trying to get records released? The Review Board was all about releasing records. He said they don't approve of secrecy and they believe openness in government is good and secrecy is bad and they want to get all the documents released that they can.

He said be careful about how you express your enthusiasm. He said if you walk around the office talking about a conspiracy, or even cover-up … he said it would not be healthy for your career. He was frustrated himself because we would take a deposition of a medical witness, one of the autopsy doctors or FBI agents or photographers, and many times he tried to brief the board members after the deposition. What did we learn. They had no patience with this. Not only did the Board members not attend any of our eleven medical depositions, not one of them attended any of the depositions. They had no interest in hearing Jeremy or even [executive director] David Marwell explain what had happened. They had no patience with somebody who questioned the evidence or who thought the evidence needed to be clarified.

So thank God that Congressman Louis Stokes met with the Board members at the time of their confirmation by the Senate. He told them that the HSCA had done a very bad job with the medical evidence. He was aware of that. He was honest enough to tell them and he encouraged them to do all they could to clarify the medical evidence, the conflicts in the evidence. I was told this by several members of the senior staff after I arrived. So it was for that reason, and I think that reason alone, that the Board members allowed Jeremy Gunn and I … to take depositions.

There was no master plan. It was one by one incremental piecemeal approval … at the end of it all they're eleven depositions. But we were not allowed to say what any of it meant. Which is why I ended up writing a book. Because I thought, who has the time to go and spend six months at the National Archives? It was kind of like navigating a ship through a minefield and trying not to hit a mine. There was considerable opposition on the staff to doing these medical depositions. About a third of the staff were Warren Commission supporters and thought we were muddying the record, didn't approve of what we were doing. About another third didn't have any interest in the assassination because the executive director, David Marwell, went out of his way to hire people who would not be a strong advocate one way or the other. I was one of the few people hired who already had an extensive reading knowledge of the assassination literature. And because I had read all the books at the time, of course I knew about a lot of the conflicts in the record, and I was very curious about them. And so was Jeremy. But we were lucky that we got done what we got done.

Stone: In addition to Judge Tunheim, that was Anna Nelson, she was a history professor.

Horne: Tunheim was the nominee of the American Bar Association. Nelson and Kermit Hall were two history professors nominated by the two historical societies. Bill Joyce was an archivist, and Henry Graff was a nominee of the White House. He was a history professor who wrote textbooks.

Stone: Tough atmosphere to work. I just want to get back real quickly and hit one more note on Sibert and O'Neill, the two FBI agents. They were interviewed by Arlen Specter ... in a preinterview, correct? And they apparently took good notes. But tell us what happened.

Horne: They were interviewed by Arlen Specter. Basically, he lied and said they did not take any notes at the autopsy. Presumably because he didn't like what they had to say. Because they were providing evidence that the single-bullet theory could not be true. So he never did take their depositions He never did interview them under oath before the Warren Commission. So we did. To my joy, they couldn't wait to be deposed. They felt they'd been slighted and so they were cooperative witnesses and they gave us a lot of valuable information.

Both Sibert and O'Neill were shown the photographs of the back of JFK's head. And they both said that they didn't see anything like that at the autopsy. O'Neill said I didn't see the back of the head look anything like this. He said it looks intact, it looks like it's been doctored. It looks like the head has been put back together, you know, by embalmers. And then photographed. Sibert said, I didn't see anything like this at the autopsy. He said this looks like a reconstruction by the embalmers. So they both impugned, disowned those photographs. And they were there for the entire autopsy.

Stone: I'm curious, how did they put the head back together? I mean the skull, how did they put that back together?

Horne: I don't know whether they were created by photographic alteration or by simply moving scalp around from the side of the head. Massively relocating scalp to cover up a big hole for five minutes so that pictures could be retaken. I honestly don't know which one of those it is. But I know the hair in those photographs doesn't look right in the middle of the image; the hair has been washed and cleaned and combed. Jeremy Gunn kept asking over and over, was the hair washed and cleaned and combed during the autopsy? Everybody said no.

But remember, the Review Board was not allowed to reinvestigate. So Jeremy Gunn never called on photographic experts to study the back-of-the-head photos. Because he knew that David Marwell would not have allowed it. The Board would not have allowed that.

The fix was in when the JFK Records Act was written. The Review Board was not allowed to reinvestigate. It was not allowed to come up with findings of fact or conclusions. Tax information, tax records could not be released. That's really unfortunate because I can tell you right now there's some tax records for Lee Harvey Oswald's earnings that are peculiar, that should be released. But they can't be released unless the Congress passed new legislation. There are earnings records of people who worked at the Book Depository that have interesting information in them that should be released. The IRS told me: We will release these documents on Oswald's earnings, or on the earnings of people at the Book Depository if a law is passed that allows us to do that.

Stone: What were some of the anomalies in the Oswald tax file?

Horne: If I told you they would come after me.

Stone: Go ahead. Fuck them, they're not gonna come.

Horne: You're ready for this. This is all new stuff. Oswald's last quarter of earnings in the United States before he defected to the Soviet Union should have been paid by the Marine Corps. And they weren't. Because we asked to see his Marine Corps earning records that the Marine Corps deposited with the Social Security Administration. They did not pay him any money. That has serious implications to me because of all the speculation that he was a fake defector. So if he was in training for that, somebody else was paying his salary. But I can tell you the Marine Corps wasn't. I asked the lady at the Social Security Administration who was dealing with me and our staff attorneys. … She was a tough customer and I said, is there any possibility that the Marine Corps could have made a mistake and not reported this, or your records could be wrong. She said: Listen honey, and took a drag on a cigarette, blew the smoke in my face, and said: We don't make mistakes like that.

The other information that the public should know about is that there is another record that's sequestered in the JFK collection. Just like Oswald's earning records. The other information is about employees at the Book Depository who were paid and the name Roy Truly, Oswald's supervisor, is not on the list of people who were paid. And I don't understand that. But I think it's kind of strange and it merits investigation. He's not listed as one of the official employees at the Book Depository so if he wasn't, who was he working for? That's my question. So those are two. Now I'm going to jail, OK.

Stone: OK, back to the head photos.

Horne: In opposition to those photographs are key wound diagrams that the Review Board had executed by witnesses. Nurse Audrey Bell from Parkland Hospital. She was in Trauma Room One for five minutes. She described the occipital wound to the back of the head and the top of the head intact, side of the head intact. The other witness from Parkland who made a drawing for us was Dr. Charles Crenshaw. He was in Trauma Room One. He drew an occipital parietal wound. The third wound diagram that I mentioned is very important, is FBI agent Sibert, right rear of the head. Mortician Tom Robinson of Gawler's Funeral Home who was at the autopsy in Bethesda drew for us on a page from an anatomy textbook. So it's clear you're looking at the occipital bone and the back of the head. And he drew a large hole smack in the middle of the back of the head.

Then the final witness that made a very important drawing was Saundra Spencer. … And the significant thing about her drawing was that it represented what was shown was the photograph she recalled after embalming was completed. That's a significant point that I cannot overemphasize. In other words, all of the autopsy photos in the official collection are before the embalming was done. She recalled a set of photos that showed the president very much cleaned up, no blood on the body, no open cavities, the chest wasn't open. The back of the head was largely intact, but there was a big blown-out chunk in the middle of the back of the heard, and she recalls that there were clearly taken after embalming. So this means that the intact-back-of-the-head autopsy photos are not honest. In some way they're misrepresenting reality and they're not to be trusted.

Stone: When the Board interviewed John Stringer, the official autopsy photographer, what was his reaction upon seeing the pictures of the brain?

Horne: He was very widely respected. He had written a textbook on medical photography. So he was the photographer of record. He photographed the autopsy itself and also photographed the president's brain. So we were very careful to question Mr. Stringer at the very beginning of his deposition about all the photographs he took and ask him what kind of film he used for black and white, what kind of film he used for color. What angles did you shoot, what views did you get. He said he shot black-and-white negatives on Kodak film in duplex film holders. The color were color positive transparencies taken on Kodak Ektachrome film, E3.

At the end of his deposition we showed him the brain photos in the collection. And the response we got from him was stunning. Stunning. We came to the brain photographs and we pulled out the black-and-white negatives. He suddenly became energized. He started looking at the black-and-white negatives in the collection. He said: Can I see some black-and-white negatives of the body? Which he took three days before [on the 22nd]. He said those negatives of the brain are not duplex film. He said they're numbered. A film pack is a roll of film that is not cut up until after it's developed and each frame is numbered. These are numbered and the film is very thin like you would expect from a film pack. This is not what I shot. And also in these black-and-white negatives there's no notch. Portrait panned film should have a notch in the corner that the photographer would feel in the dark as he's loading the duplex holder. He said there's no notches. He also said, these are not Kodak. These are Ansco; it's a different brand of film. He shot Kodak portrait pan. Jeremy Gunn said: "Did you take these pictures?" "Not as far as I know." And he started to get agitated.

So then we showed him the color positive transparencies of the brain. He said, I don't know what brand this is. He said these might be Ansco. But the notches in these color transparencies are not the notches you find in Ektachrome film. He said Ektachrome E3 film has certain type of notches on it. He said these notches are different. Jeremy Gunn said: 'Did you use this film with these notches on it when you shot the brain? And Stringer says: "Not as far as I know."

The first brain images that Jeremy actually showed Stringer were the basilar view, the bottom of the brain. And he asked Stringer, what type of view is this. Stringer said, basilar. And he said: Did you take basilar views and Stringer said not as far as I know.

So what John Stringer had done is give us courtroom evidence that these are photographs of someone else's brain. The brain photos in the Archives are not Kennedy's brain. And this is why the Associated Press and *Washington Post* both brought out articles about this finding of mine in 1998 on the day we released our office files to the National Archives. George Lardner of the *Washington Post* interviewed me. His article came out on November 10th. The Associated Press came out on November 9th. They both talked about this. The fact that there were two brain exams … is not only highly irregular. It's just nonsensical. Once you examine a brain and slice it up and do sections, there's nothing left to examine a second time. The fact that there are two brain exams is the best indication that we have of a cover-up. The fact that Stringer told us under oath that he did not take the brain photographs in the Archives is the proof of the pudding.

Stone: Did the Warren Commission ever interview Stringer?

Horne: The Warren Commission did not interview John Stringer.

Stone: Was Robert Knudsen deposed by the Warren Commission?

Horne: Robert Knudsen was not interviewed by the Warren Commission. The House Committee became aware of his name through a memo that the Secret Service had written about autopsy photography. They wrote a memo trying to explain when these photos were developed. His name was part of that paper trail. So they finally found Robert Knudsen. They took his deposition but they never published it. You can tell from the deposition that they were very skeptical of this man … because there are no pictures of probes in the body in the official collection. But he was sure that he developed those negatives and saw them. But Knudsen always told his family I photographed the autopsy. It was the hardest thing I ever did in my life. Jack Kennedy was my friend.

Knudsen was deceased. But we got his wife Gloria … and two of his grown children to come in and talk to us. They talked about how he had always said he photographed the autopsy… and he was gone for three days. They didn't see him for three days. He told a photography magazine in 1977 that he photographed the autopsy. … He probably took photographs later after the autopsy was over. He told his son four or five of the photographs were badly altered. And one of them was so bad that it looked like hair was literally drawn on the back of the head. But the import of his statement to his son was that he looked at them before an official body of some kind in 1988. He told them there was something wrong with these photographs and these are not the way they should look. They don't look like what I saw. We don't know what panel he appeared before but it was in 1988.

Stone: Briefly describe Saundra Spencer. I know you mentioned her before. Are the pictures she developed anywhere to be seen today?

Horne: No. Spencer was the first-class petty officer photographer in the Navy who developed color negatives of President Kennedy's postmortem images on color negatives. Those photographs are not in the record today. And she remembered the process, the C22 process. She said they were not color positive transparencies. The only photographs that Stringer said he took were color positive transparencies. Knudsen developed black-and-white negatives from a film pack that were numbered and Stringer didn't use a film pack either. … "Beat up" was the street talk that Vince Madonia and Spencer used to describe the impression they get when they look at the official autopsy photographs. The photographs that Spencer developed which never made it into the official record was a cleaned-up, respectful-looking President Kennedy with no body cavities, no blood … but still a hole in the back of the head.

Her testimony was so persuasive that Jeremy Gunn told me after her deposition that she was the most credible medical witness we deposed. Jeremy Gunn and I wanted very much to re-depose Humes and Boswell as we learned more and more.

Stone: And would you have investigated LeMay as a person of interest?

Horne: I think LeMay should have been investigated as a person of interest. Why would you disobey orders of civilian authority during a national crisis and not go to Andrews Air Force base? I don't know where it would have led, but it should have been investigated.

Stone: The irony of course is that since our film [Stone is referring to *JFK* from 1991], the Zapruder film was sold for some sixteen, or eighteen million dollars whatever it was. But the copyright which went to the Zapruder family went to the Sixth Floor Museum. Now tell us about the Sixth Floor Museum.

Horne: One of the debacles that we had during the Review Board's tenure ... was the business of the Zapruder film. We were pretty sure from the beginning that we were going to be doing a taking of the film. Taking the film by declaring it an assassination record and saying this is now government property, not private property.

So the Zapruder family had it in the Archives under courtesy storage. They were afraid we were going to take it as a taking, which of course we did. And so they tried to get it back from the Archives before we went in business and the Archives said, not so fast. This might be declared as [an] assassination record. ... The way it works under law is if you take something from someone, the US government has to give them just compensation. So the just compensation was handled by the Justice Department after the Review Board shut down. And I think they really blew it. Initially, the attorney for the LMH company for the Zapruder family said if you give us 18 million dollars we'll give you the film, all the film element, and you can keep the film and the copyright and we won't care anything about it.

And so for some reason, Justice rejected that. And decided on their own—this is where I start to smell something bad—decided on their own that the government wouldn't own the copyright. So eventually there was a three-man panel that decided how much the film was worth. And by a vote of two to one, there was a minority dissent ... they said it's worth sixteen and half million plus interest from some arbitrary date for this film.

The original is in the freezer now. And the Archives says we're never taking it out again. So to make things worse, the Zapruder family, after getting all this money, after this windfall profit, they decide to donate the copyright and the film elements—give them and the copyright to the Sixth Floor Museum, donate them. And they did that in writing December of 1999. So starting in January of 2000, it's the Sixth Floor Museum's right to approve or disapprove your request to publish the film. Even if you have—already have your own film copy of it. You have to negotiate with them, and they are charging an arm and a leg for licensing rights, and making it very difficult for some people to get licensing rights.

James Galbraith

James Galbraith is a professor at the School of Government, University of Texas. He is a prolific author and essayist, a regular contributor to *The American Prospect* and *The Nation*. He has written several essays on Kennedy's Vietnam withdrawal plan.

Oliver Stone: Can you describe the relationship between your father and John Kennedy prior to the 1960 election?

James Galbraith: My father first met the Kennedys on his way up to join the Harvard faculty in 1934. And when John F. Kennedy came there as an undergraduate, my father was his economics tutor at Winthrop House. So they had a relationship that spanned Kennedy's entire adult life.

Stone: He should have been Secretary of State. But from his position as Ambassador to India, how did your father attempt to directly influence policy towards Vietnam in November of 1961?

Galbraith: Well, my father's interest in Vietnam preceded the visit that he made to Saigon at Kennedy's instruction in November of 1961. He was strongly conscious of the complexity and difficulty of the Vietnamese situation. He shared Kennedy's skepticism that this should ever be a primary battleground in the Cold War. Kennedy had been there in the early 1950s, and had formed the view that it was not a winnable conflict. And my father shared that view. … He did go in 1961 at Kennedy's instruction. The instructions were given because of the visit immediately prior by General Taylor and Walt Rostow. My father was sent by Kennedy essentially to give a second opinion.

He admitted many times in the years following, he said Kennedy sent me to Vietnam because he knew I did not have an open mind. Kennedy knew what he wanted and he knew my father would deliver what he did. Which was a detailed and skeptical report about the efficiency of the South Vietnamese government. About the capacity of any military force to prevail in, certainly a foreign military force, an American one, to prevail in the security situation that existed in South Vietnam at that time. If the South Vietnamese government with an army of a quarter of a million people couldn't prevail against less than twenty thousand insurgents at that time, it was not a situation in which an outside force stood much chance of changing the outcome.

Kennedy was prepared to concede the arrival of a certain number of advisers. … In Kennedy's mind, he was drawing the line saying, "We will do some things but we will not put combat troops in."

Stone: And then he was in Washington in April?

Galbraith: Yes, in April of 1962 he was back in Washington. And at that point, Kennedy basically instructed him to prepare a memorandum that could be given to Robert McNamara, Secretary of Defense, to begin the process of planning for the full withdrawal of US forces that were in Vietnam at that time.

Stone: Was there a meeting about a first strike against Russia in the summer of 1961?

Galbraith: Yes there was. And this is work that I uncovered in the Kennedy Library. A memorandum to Vice President Johnson from his national security aide Howard Burris which described the presentation to the president of a plan for a preemptive nuclear strike on the Soviet Union with the date of that hypothetical strike set for the end of 1963. In other words, what would be the effects given the extent of the buildup that was going on, if our strike would be launched at that time.

Stone: At the end of 1963?

Galbraith: At the end of '63, that's correct. What I did, with a coauthor, was to prepare an article on the subject. And what we did was to look through all the memoir literature and we discovered that everyone mentioned the meeting. They mentioned it in oblique terms. But it became very clear that this was, in fact, a very important meeting. And in which Kennedy emerged from in a state of disgust, if you like, at the plan that he'd been presented. So this was a telling meeting about what the military planners, in fact thought the nuclear forces were for.

Stone: Who did you get confirmation on this from? Did you get it?

Galbraith: We based the article entirely on written sources. But we did go and talk to a number of people. My coauthor went to Washington and spoke—had lunch, in fact—with the author of the memorandum, Howard Burris, Lyndon Johnson's national security aide.

So Kennedy drew the line at combat troops. Johnson held that line for a certain period of time. Gave way on it in early 1965, but Johnson held the line at nuclear weapons.

Stone: Was the more influential adviser to Kennedy, would it have been McGeorge Bundy or Walt Rostow?

Galbraith: Bundy was certainly the closer adviser at that time. He was the national security advisor. Walt … Kennedy eventually moved him to Policy Planning in the State Department after a short period in the White House. But I have to say, on Vietnam, I'm convinced that the most important and influential adviser was, in fact, my father. Because he was the one, first of all, who had Kennedy's confidence for the longest period of time. Almost thirty years by that point. And he was the one whose views on Vietnam were in line with the president's own views.

Stone: By the way, may I ask you your father's reaction to Kennedy's death, the assassination? How old were you?

Galbraith: I remember it vividly. My father was in New York when the news came and he flew back to Washington and went directly to the White House. He told my mother it was the worst day of his life. And he proceeded to do what he could. He helped arrange for Mrs. Kennedy to have a place to stay, because he knew Johnson would be coming back immediately to the White House. And then he went to work and did a draft, which was not the draft ultimately used of President Johnson's opening speech to the joint session of congress.

Stone: May I ask you did he have a reaction to Robert Kennedy's death in 1968?

Galbraith: Again, an exceedingly painful episode. My father had been instrumental in persuading Eugene McCarthy to challenge Lyndon Johnson, and I remember being at the house in late 1967 when McCarthy basically made the decision he would run. Of course, when Bobby Kennedy got into the race, the Kennedy people were anxious to have my father join, which he declined to do. He felt an obligation to stay with McCarthy. But the night of the California primary, a call came in asking him if he would begin to organize the McCarthy people to come over to Bobby. And he agreed to do that. And an hour later or so, less than an hour later, Kennedy was shot.

Jim Gochenaur

Jim Gochenaur was a Church Committee witness. His appearance in *JFK Revisited* was the first time he appeared before a national audience to share his experience with Elmer Moore of the Secret Service.

James DiEugenio: You had a mild interest in the JFK case before you met with Elmer Moore?

James Gochenaur: Very mild. I was not a critic. I was not a formal critic on any level. I was consumed with my studies at the University of Washington in Seattle more than anything.

DiEugenio: Tell us how you came to meet Elmer Moore, the Secret Service agent, and how your relationship developed over time.

Gochenaur: On February 23, 1970, I was in the midst of trying to put together an art project, looking for a real clear resolution of the photo that Mary Moorman took of President Kennedy's assassination. I did not realize it was a Polaroid. So I thought: who might have some information on it? So I called the FBI in Seattle, the field office. The agent that talked with me said: "Well, we would not have anything to do with that. But I know the guy that handled photography for the investigation for the Secret Service. I'll put you through directly to him. Hold on."

And that's how I met Elmer Moore. He introduced himself. I introduced myself. I told him that I wanted to get that for an art project. And he said, "Well, you're out of luck. There's no guns hanging over the fence, Jim. Why are you a critic? Have you read the Warren Commission Report?" I said, "No. And I am not a critic. I just want to get a better picture." And he said, "Oh, well, let me tell you about the investigation." He went on, in a kind of bragging way, about his involvement. He claimed he was the lead investigator for the JFK investigation. He went on and on, and he said to me that the whole experience of being in that investigation led him to be a student of American political assassinations. The word *political* sort of resonated with me. I said: What do you mean by that? And he said well, from John Wilkes Booth to Lee Harvey Oswald, there is a succession of political assassinations.

I said, "Well, what do you consider political versus somebody that is a loner on it. Because Booth certainly wasn't a loner." He agreed with me. So we went through Booth. We got to McKinley and he says, "Hey, you know quite a bit about this stuff. Tell you what, why don't we get together sometime for lunch and talk about this stuff?" I said, "Great." Then he said,

"I'll tell you what. I am in the Warren Commission, Vol. 11, p. 230. And I was involved in guarding Chief Justice Warren. And we came to Dallas to interview Ruby. Why don't you jot down three good questions about that interview and call me in a few weeks?"

So that's how I initiated a conversation with the guy. He liked the idea that we were talking about things that he was interested in and I had some background on Booth. So it worked.

DiEugenio: Now, how many times did you meet with him one-on-one, in person?

Gochenaur: In person, three times. One extremely long telephone call. That first telephone call was almost two hours. The guy loved to talk.

DiEugenio: What did he tell you about his dealings with Malcolm Perry?

Gochenaur: I had been researching, almost at his insistence, other types of critics. I came across the idea that he was accused of pressuring Perry to change his testimony about the neck wound. And Moore explained to me what he did was, he pulled Perry aside when he and agent Roger Warner went to Parkland Hospital. They had a couple of copies of the autopsy report and they debriefed the doctors, according to Moore. He said he didn't bang his head against the wall. He was just persistent.

DiEugenio: Did he not reveal to you his political feelings about JFK?

Gochenaur: My nervous system was in full shock mode when he talked about that. He said, "He was giving away everything he could [to the Russians]." I said, well, then why wasn't he exposed? Moore asked me, "Who would do it? He had control of the media. His brother was the attorney general, and his father was an appeaser. Just like he was." I was taken aback. I mean the guy is telling me he's investigating a murder and he's got a bias already. Amazing.

DiEugenio: Now, did you discuss with him the plot to kill Kennedy in Chicago?

Gocheanaur: Moore … grabbed for my camera, a Pentax that was on the table. And he started dissembling it. And he says, "I'm not recording you. Are you recording me?" And I said, "No. Do you want to pat me down?" He said, "No, no, no. That's OK."

DiEugenio: So you got the impression that the Chicago plot was a very sensitive area with the Secret Service?

Gochenaur: I think that it was a very, very sensitive thing. I think Moore and the rest of his crew were scared speechless that Bolden knew something. I think they, they had to do something. So they brought him up on a bribery charge that, on its face, is not very strong. But they got him.

DiEugenio: In your conversations with Elmer Moore, did he ever show you an autopsy photograph?

Gochenaur: He did. Right after him disassembling my camera. He said, "Look, I got something to show you." He went from the table to a closet to his right and kneeled down. I didn't see it, but it sounded like he was working a safe combination. He pulled out a large black satchel. Very heavy. I said, "Can I help you with that?" He said, "No." He struggled. He got it on the table. He says, "Aw dang. What I wanted to show you first is on the bottom." He showed me a book from the Texas School Book Depository. The book was signed by Roy Truly. He said he got it from "Where Oswald was shooting from." It was a textbook. It was a grade school mathematics book.

And then he showed me—another shock—he showed me a color photograph, 8 x 10, of President Kennedy in autopsy I assume. It was different from Mr. Groden's pictures in that this side of the face, the right side of the face, the eye was swollen. And it was black and blue.

DiEugenio: I don't remember ever seeing an autopsy photo like that, that you described.

Gochenaur: I don't like to talk about it. I'll talk about it with you.

Oliver Stone: You never talked about it yet?

Gochenaur: No.

Stone: So what you're saying is Moore had an autopsy photo?

Gochenaur: He had a lot more than that. He had a stack of photographs that were that thick.

Stone: Did you see them?

Gochenaur: I tried. He slammed it down. I asked him if I could copy: "No."

DiEugenio: What year was this?

Gochenaur: May 7. Seven days in May.

DiEugenio: This is 1971, you said. All the autopsy photographs were supposed to be in the National Archives at this time. So obviously, Moore had bootleg photographs.

Gochenaur: And I can prove it. Our friend Arlen Specter said that Moore showed him an autopsy photograph way before that. Mr. Moore collected things.

DiEugenio: And you say that he took out this one autopsy photograph, and you had the distinct impression that it was on top of a series of photographs?

Gochenaur: It was the first one out of a folio of photographs, fairly thick. It was an 8 x 10 folio. But it was, you know a large—it wasn't a small folio. It was a thick folio.

I wonder if he really was supposed to have them. I'll tell you why. When Moore testified for the Church Committee, when they subpoenaed me, they had him the next day. And Mr. [Paul] Wallach, who was a counsel, asked him: "Did you bring your scrapbook?" And Moore said: "No. It's at home."

They were aware of the fact that I talked about the satchel when I gave them a summary. They asked me for a summary of my meetings with Elmer Moore. I wrote out a number of things and I gave it to Wallach when I came for the pre-deposition interview. And he asks a very weak, softball question. They didn't follow up on it.

DiEugenio: They should have confiscated it.

Gochenaur: I would think so. Yes.

Stone: Why didn't you grab the rest of the pictures and run out?

DiEugenio (laughing): He probably would have pulled his gun out again. When Moore was detailed to Earl Warren, Warren already had a bodyguard at that time, correct?

Gochenaur: Yes. In fact Elmer told me as we were sitting there, it was a very awkward situation because he already had a bodyguard. He said that he had known Earl Warren personally. Apparently, Moore was a detective before he went into the Secret Service. And so he knew Warren. So he was sort of implicating, the way I felt he was talking about it, that it was easy for them to ease him into being his bodyguard.

DiEugenio: But it sounds to me more like he was an aide-de-camp kind of a character, not a bodyguard. He already had a bodyguard.

Gochenaur: I agree with you. When I first came to the pre-deposition interview for the Church Committee, Paul Wallach asked me, he got right up in my face and he says: "Jim, you gotta help us get Elmer Moore. Did he tell you that he sat in on executive sessions?" I said, "No, he never told me that. But he did say he took documents and tapes to the White House." So they had an inkling of inappropriate law enforcement behavior.

I had the impression that he was, like a microphone. He was making sure that Warren stayed on script. The other thing is that I asked him, "Well, did you discuss the case with the Chief Justice?" He said, "Oh yeah. We talked about that all the time." That's totally out of whack.

DiEugenio: Did Moore admit to destroying evidence concerning Jack Ruby?

Gochenaur: He said that he visited Eva Grant's home a number of times. And one time he saw a picture that he wanted to take with him. He asked Eva if he could take the picture. She said yes. He took it to the Secret Service office. I assume he showed it to Inspector Kelly. Inspector Kelly says: "Enough is enough. I'll take it. Don't talk about it anywhere. Don't make any reports."

DiEugenio: What happened to the picture?

Gochenaur: No one knows. He said it was Ruby sitting with a group at a table, like a nightclub or a dinner arrangement of some sort. That's all he said.

DiEugenio: Didn't he tell you that he advised Ruby to stop talking about Oswald?

Gochenaur: Yes. Another amazing situation. I asked him a series of questions about Ruby and he would give one-word answers. Sometimes he expanded upon it. And he said that Ruby started to loosen up about the shooting of Oswald and Moore said: I had to shut him down. Because we didn't want to, you know preclude, you know premeditation. We didn't want to include it in the talk, the interview.

I was astounded because I have an uncle that was a detective … and I can't imagine a law enforcement officer not wanting to know the story and stopping somebody from talking.

DiEugenio: Why do you think he did that?

Gochenaur: Probably ordered to. Moore told me that he was on leave the weekend of the assassination. On Monday the 25th, I believe it was, he was ordered to Washington. So he didn't go to Dallas right away. He went to Washington. My theory is that he was debriefed: This is what you will do. This is what you've got to say. And he did say that he took an oath on the case.

DiEugenio: Did he describe what the oath was?

Gochenaur: No. He broke it apparently in talking with me.

DiEugenio: Didn't he once tell you that when he had the autopsy report, he went to Dealey Plaza and he couldn't figure out how you could match up the trajectories with the autopsy report?

Gochenaur: He wrote a report on December 11, 1963, that described that the true trajectories cannot be ascertained by the president's wounds. That the wounds couldn't tell you the trajectories. He mumbled: "Aww, the angles are all wrong. The angles are all wrong." He spent some time talking about his report. But didn't let me copy it. He studied the Zapruder film. He interviewed witnesses. And he said the conclusion is inconclusive.

DiEugenio: Let's shift to Carver Gayton. Describe who he was and how you met him.

Gochenaur: In December of 1970 … my wife answered an ad from a man by the name of Carver Gayton. He had a duplex for rent, fairly cheap near the university. Mr. Gayton told my wife that he demanded to meet people that wanted to rent from him in person. So on December 18, 1970, and Mr. Gayton was in the apartment when I got there. We introduced each other. I was telling him I was practice teaching … at Garfield High School. We talked in the kitchen for maybe about an hour … and he said "Well, I used to be an FBI agent." I said, "Where were you?" He said he was in Kansas City, his first assignment. You know, by the way he met Jim Hosty. He said, "You know who he was?" And I said, "Oh yeah. He was involved in the JFK investigation." He says that Hosty told him that Oswald was a paid informant. A PSI, but he wasn't informing.

So we became friends. He would take me to school every now and then because, he was, at that time, an administrator at the University of Washington. And every now and then, about three or four times, we went out to dinner with him and his wife, my ex-wife, and I. So I had a pretty good rapport with Carver. He told me that one of the reasons that he left the FBI was the rampant racism involved in it. He told me when he graduated from the FBI Academy, he was in line to shake hands with Director Hoover. And Hoover stopped the line at him and put on white gloves to shake hands with him.

DiEugenio: When Carver Gayton testified before the Church Committee, he told them that same story, did he not?

Gochenaur: Yes, he did. And when the House Committee talked to Carver, he completely denied it.

DiEugenio: Let's talk about your Church Committee meeting. You said you did a pre-deposition interview. Then you did a formal interview, correct?

Gochenaur: The pre-deposition was … with Paul Wallach and Dan Dwyer. They talked with me for about twenty minutes. They took my summary. And what happened is I got in the room and they introduced me to an Army major. To the other side was Senator Schweiker. Just after I took the oath, two naval officers came into the room and sat directly behind me. So I asked Wallach who these gentlemen were. So he went over and he whispered to them and he came back: Its OK. They're all right. He would not tell me who they were. The interview with Schweiker went on. At the end of the conversation, it seemed like it was about an hour and half maybe, the two naval guys left and they closed down the interview. To this day it is not available. My testimony does not exist. But I was there.

Stone: Did either agent Hosty or Moore—either one—express to you an opinion about whether Oswald shot the president?

Gochenaur: With Moore, the first series of questions I asked him after the shocking situation about the Russians and being a traitor, he said: "What's your theory on Oswald?" I said, "Well, I think Oswald was involved, but I think he had help." And Moore said, "Well I think you'd be surprised to know that I agree with you." I was stunned again. What happened next was he sort of said that the way he phrased it was, I still think Oswald did some shooting. He left it at that.

Stone: And Hosty?

Gochenaur: Carver Gayton didn't give me any indications that Hosty blamed Oswald or not. One of the things that came up in discussion was that Hosty thought that some of his reports were altered. Never made a comment about whether or not he thought Oswald was the shooter or not.

DiEugenio: Let's talk about the House Select Committee—did they contact you?

Gochenaur: Yes. In 1977 I got a phone call at my place of work. A man by the name of Gilbert said he was with the House Assassinations Committee. Wanted to know if I would have some time to be interviewed over the phone. I was nervous at that point because I was working for an executive search firm. And the CEO of that firm would occasionally—and you could see it in a lit-up light on a telephone—listen into your conversations, to criticize them, to offer critiques. And about five or ten minutes into it, I notice that my boss's light lit up. So I was under stress that I was talking with these guys without permission of my CEO, and that he was listening. But the House Committee people asked me a number of interesting questions. But they never followed up on what I was saying. They're just sort of like: that this or that happened and I would say yes. The questions were very puffy, softballish.

The entire interview was over the phone. I never signed an affidavit. No person met me face-to-face. I was not subpoenaed. I was just telephone interviewed. When I asked Gilbert from the House Committee, I said, "Well did you see my testimony in front of the Church Committee?" He says, "We didn't know you were involved in the Church Committee. You were subpoenaed?" I said, "Yes, January 5, 1976." They said, "Oh, we don't have any record of it." Then they started talking to me. So they didn't have any reference point.

My opinion is because there was such a military presence at the Church Committee; when I was sitting there in the lounge waiting for Wallach and Dwyer to come back and get me for testimony, I noticed that coming and going there were various Air Force officers, Navy officers. There was one Marine Corps guy going back and forth with paperwork and grabbing up. A military guy came and said, "We're ready to go." My thought is this: It might be in military files of some sort. It might not exist anymore.

DiEugenio: Were all those military guys there meant to intimidate you? Do you think that is why they were there?

Gochenaur: I believe they were.

DiEugenio: Thank you so much. And I'm glad you got it all out of you today.

John Newman

Newman is a professor of history at James Madison University. He is the author of several books on both the JFK case and his presidency, including *JFK and Vietnam*, *Oswald and the CIA*, and *Into the Storm*.

First Interview re: Vietnam, Georgetown, September 12, 2019

Oliver Stone: About the beginning. This is very close to the beginning with Mr. Eisenhower. When did President Eisenhower order the assassination of Patrice Lumumba in the Congo and how was that order implemented? And if you can, also talk about the whistleblower who is inside on this.

John Newman: The order was actually given in a National Security Council meeting, which is very unusual. You are not supposed to talk about killing people, especially a president, in an NSC meeting. That would be done through his emissary in a special group meeting. But Eisenhower got very impatient with Allen Dulles. He had told him to get rid of Lumumba. And it wasn't happening. So he got very frustrated in the middle of an NSC meeting and just blurted out an order to kill. Not to anyone in particular, but blurted out to everybody assembled there, to kill Lumumba. What happened was, everybody just didn't know what to do. They didn't react. They just kept on talking. But somebody had to actually take some notes and that was Robert Johnson. And he didn't know what to do. He was standing in. It wasn't his regular job.

Stone: Who was Robert Johnson?

Newman: He was actually taking notes. He was just a minor player who worked for the National Security Council Secretariat, a notetaker. But not the usual one. It was his first day on the job basically. And he hears this order from the president to kill Lumumba. And he didn't know what to do. So he went to his boss afterwards and he said, "What should we do about this?" And he was told: "Don't put it in. Delete it." And it stayed that way for years. And he had a sort of crisis of conscience and he approached the Church Committee. He said: You know, I just need to get this off my chest and it's been all these years. So he told them the story and in great detail, he was absolutely firm that he heard the order. The directness and the wording was something he could never forget.

Stone: And Johnson said that, the word "kill"?

Newman: He was very clear on that when he was interviewed by the Church Committee. There's a postscript to this story which involves the president's national security advisor, Gordon Gray. He was deposed by the Church Committee about the subject. Now in the deposition, he professes sort of, "I can't remember now." He got very wishy-washy. But in the interview prior to that deposition, he told the truth. And what happened to that prior interview years later, it disappeared or pages were missing. The truth he actually told the first time was suppressed. But we do have it. I ended up getting a copy of Gordon Gray's actual document. It's hard to find it now. But we do have it.

You asked me how it was implemented. There's a couple of stages to that. Initially you have [Sidney] Gottlieb going over there with some poison. That turns out to be too hard to get access into the building where he was actually living. So then comes QJ/WIN. And we can argue about who that is or isn't. But it's less important than what he did. His mission at this point was to get Lumumba out of that house, away from the encirclement of the UN … and get him on the run. And then to use the local resources, including a CIA helicopter to help people locate him, seize him, and take him to the province of Katanga where they hated him, and to murder him.

Stone: He was murdered by a firing squad, right?

Newman: Yes, and his bones were broken apart. He was burned and buried and unburied two or three times before it was over.

Stone: During the November of 1961 debates when Kennedy was president, they argued—they debated about Vietnam. There was a parallel debate about Cuba. Can you take us into that debate and what Kennedy's position was? Would you call it cantankerous debates?

Newman: Yeah. [Joint Chiefs of Staff Chairman Lyman] Lemnitzer thought Kennedy was an inexperienced young president who didn't know what he was doing. And when he got rebuffed by Kennedy … he became more and more insubordinate. ... That's just the beginning. The answer is "No" to Vietnam. The answer is "No" to Cuba. And he digs his heels in. But that's only the beginning of the story. What happens in 1962 is another story completely.

Stone: And he sends Galbraith, his ambassador to India and ex-professor from Harvard, he sends John Kenneth Galbraith to Saigon.

Newman: Yes. Who then asks him: What in the hell is this piece of real estate worth in the space age? I don't get it. And Kennedy understood that, and he said: You know what, I agree with you. And at that time, which is in the spring of 1962, Kennedy says: All right, let's get a plan to withdraw from Vietnam. We should have one.

Stone: Let's keep going from 1962 into 1963. Go ahead.

Newman: Berlin was settled, miraculously. Eventually they settled Laos. And they ended with Vietnam still on the table. And that's when they decided OK, let's start Mongoose, this new Cuban anti-Castro operation. A lot of lies were spawned about what was going on in the battlefield. But that calmed the Vietnam thing down while Cuba moved into center stage.

Now what people don't understand about Ed Lansdale—who the Kennedy brothers liked, and who brought him in as the operations officer for this Mongoose operation—he was a snake. People think of him as a CIA guy. But once Dulles was fired, there was nobody who liked him at CIA. He went over and worked in the Pentagon. When the part of the story in 1962 unfolds, he was working at a very high level under the Secretary of Defense, as the head of special Operations.

Stone: That's where Fletcher Prouty was.

Newman: Yeah, exactly. So Lansdale starts writing these tasks, and we're not even at the end of January 1962, when he inserts the false flag operation to kill our own people: sink our ships, attack Miami, all that stuff that was later known as Northwoods. Way back in January. Lansdale inserts it as a Mongoose thing because he is actually acting as a stalking horse for Lemnitzer, chairman of the Joint Chiefs.

He is siding with them … and going against the orders of President Kennedy. Who told him in no uncertain terms: We are not invading Cuba. And what does he do? He comes up with a plan for the invasion of Cuba, using a pretext. It takes the Kennedy brothers about six weeks to figure out what Lansdale is up to. And they kneecap him. They say: Get us some intelligence, but you're done.

And so what this does is force Lemnitzer into the open. He's not afraid of coming out in the open. By this point, he hates Kennedy. And you see all these plans being sent to McNamara and to Kennedy from Lemnitzer that basically say: We got to go in. There's no pretext. No rationale. We just, we want to do it. Lemnitzer knows that the axe is coming. On the first of October, just days before the Missile Crisis, that's when the Kennedys fire Lemnitzer. And makes the mistake of replacing him with somebody they liked, or thought they liked.

Stone: "They" being the Kennedy brothers.

Newman: Yes. What they didn't understand was that Maxwell Taylor was good friends with Lemnitzer. They worked together in the Eisenhower administration. We're moving into 1963 now. And by that point, because the Cuban thing has largely been settled, Kennedy is able to pay attention, much closer attention to this information coming out of Vietnam. And it's all false. He starts sending people out there. He starts asking for access to the raw cable traffic coming out of Saigon. And he figures out, around about December of 1962 or January of 1963, that … the war never got better. The Viet Cong never were cut down, they were only getting bigger and stronger. When he figured out this is the time he and McNamara decided to get out of Vietnam. So they set a timetable for getting out—maybe a few guys in 1964 during the election campaign and everybody out in 1965.

That timetable gets upset. Because in the spring of 1963, you had the Buddhist crisis and it knocks the political bottom out of Saigon. It causes Kennedy to accelerate the withdrawal plan. He's afraid if he doesn't get it going and getting out into concrete, he'll never get it started. So the trickle-down thing, which becomes the one-thousand-man withdrawal actually has to happen earlier. It has to happen in 1963 in order to get it started.

So he sends McNamara and Taylor to Vietnam and to have a look around. But it's a setup from the beginning. He wants to be told we can get out now. It's a judo move. You tell me we're winning the war in Vietnam, good. We can come home. They don't like that. Because now he's using the myth of success against them to get out. And so he actually steamrolls over everybody.

Stone: Who wrote the Taylor-McNamara report?

Newman: Actually, Victor Krulak did. If you can believe it. There was a guy, General Krulak, was a Marine and he was supposed to be on the trip list, but he wasn't. He was in Washington the whole time, round the clock, even working with RFK every day going over to the White House. And they had the report written before anybody went over there. The Under Secretary of State, William Sullivan, he challenged McNamara. He said, "What is this about a withdrawal plan. We can't get out of there. We've got to put more people in. If you guys do this, I'm submitting a dissenting report." And McNamara said, "We'll take it out." And Taylor says, "OK, you know, ditch that."

They come back to Washington. And Kennedy says, "Just a minute, guys." And he takes McNamara and Taylor into the next room, and they put the withdrawal plan back in the report. And that's how the report was actually written and structured and caused open warfare in the White House on the second of October when they found out that Kennedy had done this.

Stone: What's the fallout from NSAM 263?

Newman: It's an order to withdraw from Vietnam and prevent a war that everybody else wanted.

Stone: But wasn't that also regarded as a public relations stunt as I remember by his enemies?

Newman: Yeah, but it wasn't of course. And his enemies knew that, which is why they went public with NSAM 263 and he wanted it kept secret.

Stone: They wanted?

Newman: Yeah, yeah, absolutely. Because why would they do that? Because they don't want him to be able to get out of Vietnam in a winning scenario. They want to make him do it in a losing scenario. So they're going to actually confront everybody at Honolulu, just before the assassination with the truth about the war.

Stone: May I ask, how did the *New York Times* for example, and the *Washington Post* treat the announcement of NSAM 263?

Newman: It was big news. And it was leaked from the Pentagon. The people who were telling the story, they know where it's coming from. They know it didn't come from Kennedy.

It was big news, because when he was on television, in the media, he would always say we shouldn't withdraw. He would say: It's their war, they're the ones who have to win it and we can help them as advisers. Send our guys out there. But we shouldn't withdraw. He kept saying that. So this story about NSAM 263, which wasn't actually an NSAM yet, but the story that he was going to start pulling troops out, and everybody out, that was news.

Stone: Well, did the enemies have any effect?

Newman: It made Kennedy nervous. That's why he was afraid that he would look too optimistic. Because if people understood what was really going on: How would he justify things? He would have to face somebody in an election, Goldwater in an election in a losing scenario and still try and win, and he was afraid about that.

Stone: Keep going.

Newman: Two days before the president's murder is when this happened. McGeorge Bundy, who's the national security advisor, puts together a memo based upon the truth about the war, that its going terribly. And he does it in a way to try and make sure that Kennedy would be able to go along with it.

Stone: So Kennedy had not seen the draft?

Newman: He was in Texas. But Bundy, by crafting this thing in a way that he expected Kennedy to be alive, shows you that he was not in on a conspiracy. He actually expected Kennedy to be alive to read the thing. Bundy was actually for combat troops. Bundy was a loyal adviser and so he crafted a memo that didn't mention anything about US troops or even any US direct actions, covert or anything. And so that was changed under Johnson.

Kennedy's body is still in the casket in the rotunda over in the Capitol Building. While his body's over there is when Johnson changes NSAM 273 to a new version.

Stone: What day is that?

Newman: Three days afterwards. It is Sunday.

Stone: OK, so the funeral happens Monday. Then what?

Newman: Then you have the implementation of all the things that can be done because of the changes to NSAM 273. The real story that people don't know, that is new, this research I've done for the new edition of *JFK and Vietnam*, things I should have looked at, I didn't thirty years ago. After McNamara and Taylor returned with their report at the end of September, and the first days of October, General Taylor decided to change everything secretly. What he did is he led an effort to completely scuttle the one-thousand-man withdrawal. And Kennedy was very clear that he wanted combat troops coming out of there, the helicopter units and all those things.

He's also replacing it with the Americanization of the war. It's called OPLAN 34A. And without McNamara being told one bit about this. He's working with Admiral [Harry D.] Felt at CINCPAC [Commander in Chief Pacific Fleet Headquarters] in Honolulu. And he's working with General Harkins in Saigon. They're putting together this op plan which is the Americanization of the war, from small pinpricks all the way up to major operations against the north.

Stone: I know you had a relationship with Robert McNamara as he wrote *In Retrospect*. Can you talk about that?

Newman: When my dissertation was published as *JFK and Vietnam*, and your movie *JFK* came out, I had decided that I would show a particular chapter to McNamara, chapter 13, "Secrets in Saigon." Where he was being lied to. It upset him and he sent a message to me saying, "I'd never been lied to." And he didn't want to meet with me and that was the end of that for a while. Then, one day, I was still in the Army working Army intelligence, then one day the lady at the front said, "Hey Major Newman, there's some guy named McNamara on the phone." I picked it up and he said, "This is Bob McNamara. I'm ready to talk."

Stone: What year is this now?

Newman: This is months after your film came out. I get in my car, headed for the hotel in downtown Washington DC. He says, "Look, you know, I don't know what's in my oral histories or anything, but I have a policy of not talking on the war." And I push back, I said: "As a historian, I have a problem with that. Everybody else has. And you were with two presidents." And so we had an argument about that. And eventually he started to talk to me, lecture me.

He told me an example of where scholars are wrong. It's because they think we should have used all of our power in Vietnam in the sixties. He didn't know that I had three degrees in East Asian history. Eventually he understood that we agreed on something. So I called Sterling Lord who, at that time, was my agent. I said, "Sterling, I want to change my book." It was going to be [about] Kennedy in Cuba. And I said [change it] to McNamara and Vietnam. He said, "John, you shouldn't do that." I said, "Why not?" He said, "Because McNamara just called this morning and he wants to do his book."

Then we got along better and he began inviting me over to his office while he was working on *In Retrospect*. And I helped him work on that. And there's couple of things I'd like to share with you … that happened as I worked with him during that time. One day he looked at me as if he was looking through me, from a subliminal state of mind. And he just asked a question….So McNamara says, "When did I know?"

Stone: He says what?

Newman: When did I know. I figure out, he's asking me: When did I know the truth about the war? My response was, "I can't tell you when you figured it out, but I can tell you when you had the opportunity to know. It's about December of 1962, or January of 1963." He wasn't done. He was quiet and then he said, "Where am I in trouble?"

So I had to think about that one a little bit more. And then I thought about Honolulu. And the fact he didn't react to what they put on the table. So I said, "Well, maybe you ought to take a look at what you were doing out there in Honolulu with the generals on November 20, 1963."

Stone: What was his reaction?

Newman: There was no reaction. There was part of him that had been suppressed, or repressed.

Judge John Tunheim

Judge John Tunheim is the Chief Judge for the US District Court for the District of Minnesota. He was the chairman of the Assassination Records Review Board during its four-year tenure.

Oliver Stone: In 1978 there had been the House Select Committee on Assassinations?

John Tunheim: Right.

Stone: And so it'd been, it'd been a relatively quiet situation in the Kennedy murder.

Tunheim: Well it was quiet until the movie *JFK*. Which you know, I give great credit particularly to the trailer, when you explain to the public that a lot of the records underlying the assassination were still secret and were being hidden from the American people. Congress reacted appropriately and passed this law which gave independent authority to a separate federal agency to have control of the declassification of intelligence and enforcement records and congressional records for the first time ever. It hasn't been repeated but it was a very good way to release records quickly.

Stone: So this was unprecedented?

Tunheim: This was unprecedented. And it hasn't been repeated since. Congress allowed an independent board to determine what should be declassified. And that was the first time that had ever occurred. Normally, an agency decides when to declassify records pursuant to an executive prodder that's issued by each president. Some presidents are more forthcoming in getting the reviews of records and allowing them to be released. But for many reasons, the Kennedy assassination records had never really been reviewed and released.

Stone: What is the difference between the Freedom of Information Act and the ARRB?

Tunheim: Well, people who are interested in the Kennedy assassination had used the Freedom of Information Act, or attempted to use it for a long time. The Freedom of Information Act however exempts operations records of the

Central Intelligence Agency, and Congressional records are not subject to FOIA.

Congress, of course, held the records of the House Select Committee on Assassinations, and by House rules they were deemed sealed until 2029. A fifty-year period, which was too long for people to wait.

Stone: We mentioned that in the film at the end, and there was quite a bit of furor. And were there documents being held or redacted from the Warren Commission when you started?

Tunheim: Most of the Warren Commission records had been released by a series of orders issued by President Johnson. And the Review Board released all of those records.

Stone: And a lot of the CIA connections of Oswald? Am I correct?

Tunheim: Yes. Oswald's connections and records about him dated back to the 1950s when he had defected to the Soviet Union and was being traced for a time by the FBI, and followed of course by the CIA. And those records were really not released until the Review Board had a close look at this classified record.

Stone: And that included James Angleton, the counterintelligence chief of CIA, keeping the 201 file of Oswald, right?

Tunheim: Yes. Angleton you know took control of the CIA's investigation into the assassination and compiled a large series of records. Those records, when we tried to find them, some existed in various part of the Agency. Most were no longer maintained as a collection. I think it's pretty clear that Angleton destroyed records before he was summarily dismissed from the CIA.

Stone: This includes I gather a lot of information about Oswald in New Orleans?

Tunheim: It did. Oswald was of course in New Orleans in the summer of 1963. He was arrested. He was on the radio. He was sort of the self-appointed chair of the Fair Play for Cuba Committee, and he, a lot of connections in New Orleans at the time. The House Select Committee looked very closely at the New Orleans situation. The New Orleans aspect of this was really interesting because we held a public hearing in New Orleans. That public hearing led to the release of a lot of files. Files from [Jim] Garrison's investigation, all of the files of the Clay Shaw's defense attorney, Edward Wegmann, were turned over to us, and it was really a treasure trove of information that we were able to uncover in New Orleans that really was not part of the prior investigations. Including files brought to use by an investigator who had been fired by Harry Connick, the successor to Garrison. And he brought the files to Washington. Connick sued us over that. He wanted the grand jury records from the Garrison investigation to be returned to the state of Louisiana. And we won that battle in court. Although I had to stay away from New Orleans for a while.

Stone: You had a fight with Connick, Harry Connick? He's not my favorite guy.

Tunheim: He fought us hard on that. He was embarrassed because he testified that all records had been preserved, and turned over everything to use. When in fact he had ordered records to be destroyed. And they weren't destroyed. They were turned over to us and he wanted them back.

Stone: And it included some, also some medical records. Am I wrong?

Tunheim: Yes. You know, when we began our work at the National Archives, we found fading 1960s-era photographs from the autopsy. Many were missing. There were still about fifteen photographs that were there. The X-rays were there. We had them digitalized. So they were sharp and preserved for all time. And we looked very carefully at those records. We had experts look at them and tried to clear up the record as much as we could. We were not an investigatory body, but we did have subpoena power. We did have the ability to try to clarify the record.

We were strongly urged by Congressman Louis Stokes, who'd been on the House Select Committee on Assassinations to do our best to clarify the medical evidence in the case. And we did what we could, given the evidence that was still available in the 1990s.

Stone: We talked to Henry Lee and we asked him what, could he make a conclusion on the autopsy, and he said he could not based on the evidence, make any conclusion. Basically, I'm putting words in his mouth. But he characterizes the autopsy as a mess.

Tunheim: Well, it surely was a mess. We tried to clarify it by digitalized records. So the photographs were clear, the X-rays clear. We did depositions of the autopsy physicians. We interviewed many of the Parkland Hospital personnel. Just tried to clarify the record as best we could.

So it was quickly done, and then you know notes were destroyed. The first draft of the autopsy report was destroyed. This was not the way it should have been done. And what was interesting was it should have been done under existing law in Dallas. Because it was simply a state law murder case at the time. There was no federal jurisdiction over the murder of the president in 1963.

Stone: Did you also attempt to release the records of the Church Committee?

Tunheim: The Church Committee had a subcommittee that investigated the Kennedy assassination and whether there was any CIA involvement in it. The records of the Church Committee resided in 1994 at the Senate Select Committee on Intelligence and so we got all of those records and there were about five thousand records that had not been released. They were released by the Review Board and I think with minor, if any, redactions. So we found what we could from the Church Committee as well because they did look into the assassination.

Stone: Did they look into the assassination of foreign leaders, in the records that you saw?

Tunheim: They did. That was part of their review. Wasn't really part of our purview, however.

Stone: Can you describe your first meeting with the CIA and their representative Mr. McQuiston?

Tunheim: The CIA was a very interesting organization to work with. We had I guess a bit of a love/hate relationship with them. They had a lot of records. A lot of records that had not been released. And when we sat down at our first meeting, we explained the act and our responsibility and the response was well you can't release this information. It will impact intelligence gathering. My response to that was well you're going to have to tell us why and how it would impact intelligence gathering today. Otherwise, we're obligated to release these records. The reaction was, well you can't do that. And so finally, he turned to the CIA lawyer who was there, and he mouthed the words: "Can they do that?" And the lawyer nodded his head up and down.

In other words, we had control over these records. They disclosed why we shouldn't release records. The vast majority of time, we didn't agree and we released the records anyway. We understood that there were good points once in a while, but not really very often.

Stone: Did the Secret Service destroy records they knew you would be requesting from them?

Tunheim: The Secret Service was one of the most difficult agencies that we had to deal with. The fact was that they destroyed records without really an explanation for us after we were in existence. They also fought us vigorously on the threats that were made over the course of 1963. I'm not really sure what eventually happened. I think those records were eventually released. But the Secret Service appealed our decision to the president. And it was still pending at the time we finished our work.

Stone: Is it true that the declassification process continued after you closed your doors in 1998?

Tunheim: Well, it was supposed to continue. We have no real reports to verify that agencies are still declassifying records. We did redactions that had release dates attached to them. If we redacted a name, we put a release date. And I think all of the release dates had passed by 2008. We were trying to identify a time where someone was no longer in danger by release of their name. Now, agencies are still required under the law to turn over any new assassination files they found. That part I am not really sure how it has worked, to be honest with you.

Stone: Has the National Archives told you that they received anything?

Tunheim: In fact, we signed agreements with the agencies in which not only did they agree to follow the law and continue to send records to the National Archives. They promised in the agreements to do so. But there's never been any oversight of those agreements that I'm aware of.

Stone: So the final date for all documents to be declassified, was there one?

Tunheim: Was twenty-five years after the day the act was signed, which would have been October 26 of 2017. That was the date all remaining redactions were supposed to be released.

Stone: And that's the date we came to with President Donald Trump?

Tunheim: That's correct. And he was required under the law to certify if there were any records that were not going to be released, certify that there would be grave harm to the national security by releasing the records. But there were records that were not released. I for one cannot think of any reason why those records shouldn't be released.

Stone: But is this legal?

Tunheim: The information was intended to be released in 2017. Only under extreme circumstances was a president in 2017 supposed to continue to protect the records. And they didn't, as near as I can tell, they didn't provide that certification.

Stone: It's very disturbing that there must have been something that, it makes us all more suspicious.

Tunheim: My experience with the CIA was they didn't want any records released at all. And you know, if they had a choice, if they could go into the president and say, don't release these records and could get by with it, they would do it. And so I think that's probably the reason: just the idea that we don't want any records released.

Stone: Now you make a point about George H. W. Bush, his attitude toward the Review Board. Could you tell us about that?

Tunheim: President Bush opposed the bill which eventually became law which created the Assassination Records Review Board. He opposed it on constitutional grounds. Because he said Congress was improperly interfering with the president's right to control executive branch records. Some say he opposed it because he was a former Director of Central Intelligence. So he probably knew that there were records in there that probably shouldn't be released.

However it became an issue during the presidential campaign in 1992. With Governor Clinton strongly supporting the creation of the Review Board. And I think under pressure he signed the bill on October 26, 1992. A couple of weeks before the election. And then he did not make the appointments to the Review Board, which were required to be made in twenty days. He just ignored it. And so we got a late start, because President Clinton made the appointments in the following spring. And then it took a year for us to get security clearances, confirmation by the Senate, hiring staff, getting an appropriation. So it took much longer than anticipated to get started. Partly because President Bush moved very slowly.

Stone: You had a two-year mandate, and then you had to go for extensions twice?

Tunheim: We had a two-year mandate. Which obviously we could not fulfill because we really didn't get started for about a year and half. And so we got the extra year initially in our first appropriation; and then we went back and asked for one more year. So we got about three and a half years to do our work.

I think it was a mistake by Congress to make it a temporary agency. It was not our desire to run this agency for years and years and years. But I think given more time without the deadline, we could have got into additional records, reviewed them more thoroughly, and we would not have started losing our staff, who understandably wanted jobs when the Review Board ended.

Stone: So would you recommend this process be used in other cases?

Tunheim: The process that we followed, with a presumption of public disclosure ... and the agency was supposed to convince us by clear and convincing evidence, which is a high standard that the danger of release outweighed a public interest. And the public interest in the Kennedy assassination is as high as you can get. ... And so if you want to release records quickly about a significant event in America, this is the way to do it. ... We all know that trying to use FOIA to release records about important events that are classified just doesn't work very well.

Stone: You mentioned there was this declassification in 2017 where hundreds of documents labeled not believed relevant. Can you talk about that?

Tunheim: As we reached the end of our work, we realized we just did not have the staff or the time to go through word by word for word every single page of every record. There was so much information and we had to make a quick look and decide that we believed it not to be relevant. But we ordered all that material turned over to the National Archives. So it's there. I'm not sure how much of it they have released, but we just didn't have the time or the staff to go through everything word for word.

Stone: Do you remember the file on George Joannides?

Tunheim: Yes, a CIA agent. We were misled by the CIA about Joannides as was the House Select Committee on Assassinations. He had been assigned to be a liaison to the HSCA. It turned out that he had been involved in the Miami station … which made him a central character in a lot of the concern about what happened before the assassination especially with the anti-Castro group. And we didn't know that. We were simply told he was a liaison to the House Select Committee. So we were misled. We had his file in hand. But we decided that it was just a personnel file from the CIA. And they have been fighting release of that ever since. Which I think is terribly misguided because the information should have been released a long time ago.

Lisa Pease

Lisa Pease was the coeditor of *The Assassinations: Probe Magazine on JFK, MLK, RFK and Malcolm X*. She is the author of *A Lie Too Big to Fail: The Real History of the Assassination of Robert F. Kennedy*.

First Interview, Los Angeles, August 20, 2019

Oliver Stone: When JFK came into office, what was his approach to Indonesia?

Lisa Pease: His approach was a radical break from his predecessor. In an oral history interview that Sukarno gave after John Kennedy's death, he said words to the effect that what made Kennedy special is that he believed nonalignment was not amoral as it had been under John Foster Dulles. I thought that was an interesting way of putting it. You know Sukarno came to power fighting for Indonesian independence. He didn't want to be a subject of the United States. He didn't want to be a subject of Russia.

Stone: How did Kennedy find out about the CIA attempt to overthrow Sukarno in 1958?

Pease: I'm not sure when he first found out. But I do know that on February 14th in 1961, after Kennedy had been in office just a month, Dean Rusk sent him a memo about Sukarno and he said Sukarno was under the impression that we are trying to overthrow him. I'm sure if Kennedy read that he probably went and called the CIA, and said, "Well, are we trying to overthrow him?" Because Allen Dulles then prepared a top secret briefing for Kennedy and brought it to him and told him in sparse terms about the failed 1958 coup. Which was really kind of the Bay of Pigs before the Bay of Pigs. It was the CIA's biggest international failure to that point. And, by the way, no one was punished for that failure.

Stone: Do you know when Dulles told this to Kennedy?

Pease: Dulles briefed Kennedy in April of 1961.

Stone: Do you want to talk a little about Allen Pope, the CIA pilot?

Pease: In 1958, during the failed coup, Allen Pope, a CIA pilot who was working for Civil Air Transport, a CIA subsidiary, was shot down, claimed he was a mercenary. Had CIA papers on him so no one really believed it. But that was kept out of the media. That story was kind of whitewashed for the public. So after Kennedy is elected, but before he took office, all over the papers was the story of Allen Pope's wife who went to Sukarno and cried tears in front of him because he was known to be soft toward women who cried. And she tried to plead for her husband's release.

She was unsuccessful. Kennedy wanted that to be a condition of turning over West Papua to Indonesia. Now he sent Bobby Kennedy to Sukarno in 1961 in the fall to try and negotiate Pope's release. Bobby was firm and asked him many times: Now you told my brother there was a chance he would be released, you know Pope, and we want to make sure. Sukarno was very firm: I'm going to do what I'm going to do and you're not going to tell me what to do. After they had this go round a few times, Bobby understood that Sukarno had every intention of honoring his promise to John Kennedy to release Pope but he wanted to do it under his own terms. Pope has been tried and convicted of murder. He was given the death sentence. He wouldn't have lived much longer if the Kennedys hadn't gone and rescued him.

Stone: Did he give Dulles orders at that point to pull away and not seek to destabilize Indonesia?

Pease: That's why he invited him to the White House and gave him the red-carpet treatment. Which was a lot better than Eisenhower had given him when Sukarno came the previous year. When he visited Eisenhower, he was made to sit alone in a room by himself for an hour, as if he was just some waitress and brought his family. Kennedy really talked to him and especially really listened.

And as I read Sukarno's own words through the oral history interview just recently, it struck me how intelligent Sukarno was. And Kennedy was highly educated and erudite. And I'm sure they really connected with a shared worldview. Both really wanted independence for the nations of the world.

Stone: Sukarno got little support from Eisenhower in his attempt to get the Dutch to give West Irian to Indonesia?

Pease: Right and the area of West Irian is now called West Papua. And I want to use that term because the people there are still fighting for their independence. When Kennedy brokered the deal to get the Dutch to give up this region that I call West Papua, Sukarno did it. But Kennedy put in a caveat that there had to be an election in 1969 in which the people could then choose to remain under Indonesian rule or go their own way and have independence.

However, by 1969, Sukarno had been ousted in a CIA coup from 1965. And, of course, by 1969, not even Robert Kennedy was left to fight for the original agreement and observers on the ground thought the event at that time was rigged.

Stone: Well, how rich was West Papua? How rich was Indonesia in natural resources in this period?

Pease: Even before West Papua, Indonesia is remarkably rich in resources: oil, tin, rubber, materials needed in war. So it was a prized region originally. But West Papua was special. There was a mountain of gold. It had overt streaks of copper on the outside, but when they started digging into it, they found it was full of gold. And the discovery of the gold there had been made in 1932. But had been kept hush-hush. Allen Dulles was one of the very few people who had seen the original figures. After that, some dummied-up figures that made it look like there was much less gold there were released.

Stone: So Kennedy's plan never worked because West Papua stayed Dutch until?

Pease: It stayed Dutch until 1963. Then it was given to Indonesia. But the CIA knew they were going to overthrow Sukarno. In fact, there is a memo that surfaced in Pakistani files in December of 1964 that said, West Irian's about to fall into the Western lap like a rotten apple. There is going to be a fake coup staged. It will look like a communist coup. Then the army will come in and use that as an excuse to protect Sukarno. And basically put him under house arrest. Now that was December of 1964. That is exactly what happened in October of 1965.

Stone: And that was under Lyndon Johnson's administration?

Pease: Lyndon Johnson's administration.

Stone: After [Kennedy] was killed, Johnson takes over and by later the next year, the coup is being planned, is in progress for the overthrow of Sukarno?

Pease: That's right.

Stone: What was Sukarno's reaction when he learned of Kennedy's death?

Pease: He was devastated. He said to his biographer: I loved John Kennedy. He considered him his friend. He said: Why did they have to kill Kennedy?

Stone: Sukarno had been invited by Kennedy to go to the White House in roughly what time?

Pease: Sukarno came to visit Kennedy in April of 1961. But then Kennedy was going to be the first president to visit Indonesia. And that was set for the spring of 1964. Sukarno even built him a guesthouse on the palace grounds. That's how much he loved Kennedy.

Stone: Did Johnson cancel the trip?

Pease: Johnson sent Robert Kennedy instead. Sukarno liked Bobby. He respected Bobby. But it wasn't quite the same.

Second Interview, Los Angeles, January 7, 2020

James DiEugenio: In all of your research going back to 1993, you obviously came across the investigation of Frank Church in the mid-1970s. You want to describe to us how that started and what it entailed?

Lisa Pease: It was the Senate Select Committee to Study Governmental Intelligence Operations, this really long fancy name. Well, how did this come about? During Watergate, there were CIA burglars, you know, arrested at the scene. And some people in Congress wanted to know what the CIA was doing in a domestic tapping operation because that was illegal. And then that led to a 1974 article, on Christmas Eve. Seymour Hersh in the *New York Times* wrote this explosive expose: the CIA's been illegally taping and monitoring people in the United States, US citizens. And it was interesting to me because information like that rarely reached the public. So I was curious: Why did that reach the public?

It turned out there was an internecine war in the CIA at the time, where current director William Colby was trying to remove James Angleton, who had been the head of counterintelligence for twenty-five years. And part of the reason for the article was to expose what Angleton was doing as a wedge to get him out of the Agency. So that got exposed. And so then people who knew what the CIA had been up to said: well, we need a blue-ribbon panel. And that's what President Ford then did. He appointed a blue-ribbon commission with highly conservative people who were very friendly to the CIA. One of the press people said, "Well, why did you pick all these people who are obviously cover-up guys?"

And he said: Well, there are very sensitive things they might stumble upon. And they're like, "Like what?" He said: "Like assassinations." Ford immediately added: That's off the record. But since he said it after the fact, a couple of the reporters there said: No that was on the record when he said it. And the key point there again is this was about CIA domestic operations, not foreign operations. Now, what domestic assassination would Ford know more about than the assassination of President Kennedy? He was a member of the Warren Commission. It seems obvious to me that he was very worried that any investigation of CIA domestic activities might lead to the CIA's involvement in the JFK assassination. And for that reason, he wanted Ronald Reagan and Douglas Dillon, and people who are very faithful and loyal to the CIA and that part of the establishment.

This did not go unnoticed by Senator Frank Church and Congressman Otis Pike. Both the House and the Senate realized this would be a cover-up and that there were probably some serious things that needed real investigation. So they set up their own committees. The House committee came to be known as the Pike Committee, after Congressman Otis Pike and the

Senate Select Committee became known as the Church Committee, after Senator Frank Church. It was kind of the end of his political career and the end of Pike's career.

DiEugenio: Would you say that in historical terms, the Church Committee was very likely the most extensive examination of the crimes of the CIA and the FBI?

Pease: The Church Committee and the Pike Committee, it's really the only investigations the CIA has ever really had. The only in-depth one where their operations were analyzed and really looked at. Both Pike and Church came to the conclusion that the CIA was a rogue elephant operating independently of the president.

DiEugenio: One of the things that the Church Committee had access to … was the legendary CIA Inspector General report on the CIA-Mafia plots to kill Castro. This is the first time that it ever made it into any kind of media, these secret plots to kill Castro. Now you want to describe those a little bit and what the authors of the report concluded about presidential propriety?

Pease: In March of 1967, Drew Pearson and Jack Anderson broke a story about the fact that the CIA had been running these plots to kill Castro. He suggested at the end that maybe the plots had been turned by Castro back against Kennedy. And the timing of the story is interesting, because that's when Jim Garrison down in New Orleans was just getting deep into his investigation of the CIA's possible role in the assassination of President Kennedy.

LBJ calls them [the CIA] up and says, "What's this about?" This report was never meant to be released to the public. In fact, it wasn't released to the public until the JFK Act was passed in the wake of the film *JFK*. And when it comes right down to it, they realize at no point did they ever have presidential authority. At the end of the report, the question is, can CIA claim that they had executive authority for these plots? And they answer their own question: Not in this case.

DiEugenio: Who was Otto Otepka? And why is he important to the saga of Lee Harvey Oswald?

Pease: Otto Otepka was the top security officer at the State Department. And to that end, he kind of had to keep a tab on what our own secret agents were doing. And so he had heard about this group of defectors that had gone from the US to the Soviet Union. There was a list of about fifteen of them. So he was trying to figure out, are these ours, are these double agents? Who are these people? He was a careful man and he took his job very seriously. And so all of a sudden he finds himself being relegated to lesser tasks and kind of being moved aside. They tried to kind of gently ease him out of there. They tried all kinds of ways to get this guy out of there. I'm reading a book about his life going, what did he do that was so important or what did he find? And honestly, after reading it, the only thing of significance was that he was really interested in was Lee Harvey Oswald before the assassination.

He actually had a study of these defectors in his safe. Things got worse. And in his safe, they literally drilled a hole into his safe and put a little mirror in to see what was there. There was something in the safe that people were obsessed with. Well, what was in the safe but his study of defectors, including his unanswered questions about Lee Harvey Oswald. He has written the CIA in 1960 and said, what do you know about these guys? And one of those people was Oswald. So they needed to discredit him in advance and dislodge him in advance so that after the assassination, nothing he said would be believed. It was like a three-year campaign. They finally got him out of office like two or three weeks before the assassination. And he told Sarah McClendon, the lady who would always sit in the front row at the White House, he said he knew who had killed Kennedy. But he would say no more on the subject.

DiEugenio: Explain the meeting between the Kennedy brothers and State Department diplomat Edmund Gullion in 1951.

Pease: In 1951, JFK took two world trips. The first trip he took went through Europe. In the second half of the year, he went through the Middle East, Asia, stopping in Vietnam. There he ran into an old friend, Edmund

Gullion, who is working with the State Department. Gullion had a huge impression on him. Robert Kennedy said later it was a very, very significant impact that conversation had on him. Gullion made JFK understand that nothing short of independence would ever win in Vietnam. If the Americans would step in, it would be no different. And when he came back, he was 100 percent convinced the French war was never going to succeed. Their only chance of getting out gracefully was to help Vietnam achieve independence. Of course, that was ignored. He ended up being proven right. Going into Vietnam during his own administration, he sent advisers ... he took it seriously. But he also knew we could never win a war of attrition in Vietnam. And, had he lived, that war would have been much shorter.

During their conversation, Gullion made it very clear that should the US try to take over for the French in Vietnam, that the same fate would happen again. They would rather die before they would submit to any other foreign nation.

DiEugenio: How did Kennedy's attitude towards the Third World and foreign policy change after his meeting with Gullion in Saigon?

Pease: This is what people want: They wanted the right of self-determination. And this is what the previous president never offered them. So when Kennedy spoke up for Algeria in 1957 in the Senate, and gave a speech saying the French should get out of there and the Algerians deserved their independence and what a mess that is. Torturous, barbarous acts being committed on both sides. Kennedy viscerally understood that. One of the reasons he understood is he was Irish and the Irish [had] been a colony under the British for hundreds of years. Speaking to Gullion just brought it into focus for him in Vietnam.

DiEugenio: Did Allen Dulles secretly approve the attack on the Suez Canal by Israel, France, and England against Nasser?

Pease: In 1956, Nasser, who had been one of these independent, non-aligned, non-communists trying to bring independence. He needed funding for the Aswan Dam. He came to the United States, and the US made a deal to give him the money. But when he recognized the leader of China as Mao

Zedong, they withheld the funding. So Nasser nationalized the canal. The canal was important to the world economy because that's where all the oil from the Middle East was shipped through. So nationalizing that allowed him to have huge control over the oil market. That really frightened the world powers. And so the British, the French, and the Israelis concocted this kind of remarkable plan that Israel was to do an attack on the canal. And then the British and the French were going to come and put down the attack while really taking control. And they would say: We have to be here to ensure that the canal always stays open. From my own research, it appears that Allen Dulles and possibly his brother silently signaled the British that this plan was OK. They could get Eisenhower to back it. Because they thought once this was in play, Eisenhower would just support our allies. Eisenhower did the opposite. Eisenhower was really upset.

DiEugenio: Why did the book *The Ugly American* appeal so much to Kennedy?

Pease: The book was written to show how America looked from the outside. We would send in these … educated people abroad and station them at a foreign mission. And they had no sensitivity to the local culture. And so this book was kind of written to expose that ugly side of how America acts abroad. When Senator Kennedy read this, he thought it was so important that he bought copies for every senator and distributed it. Kennedy liked the book so much he paid for an ad in the *New York Times*. He's like, we have to understand what they want and we have to listen to them and talk to them.

DiEugenio: If you had to compare the Warren Commission inquiry into Mexico City and the House Select Committee inquiry into Mexico City, how would you characterize the difference?

Pease: When I was growing up, there was this show on TV, the *Columbo* series. And he would be dogged and he would follow people around, and he would ask questions until they pretty much wanted to kill him. That's how the Warren Commission should have been. And that's actually how the House Select Committee behaved. They were Lt. Columbo in Mexico

City. The Warren Commission was almost the opposite. They didn't want to know. They didn't want to go: OK we gotta go. We've got to go to Mexico City, but we don't want to ask a lot of questions. And it was basically as if you went up to a criminal and said, "Did you do it?" And the criminal says: No, and they're like: OK. That's good enough for me. That's basically how the Warren Commission investigated Mexico City.

They asked the CIA and FBI, the State Department ... some really basic questions. Got some really basic answers. And didn't follow up on any of the obvious leads there. There were three people in Mexico City who were saying the guy at the Cuban consulate who was supposedly Lee Harvey Oswald, trying to get to the Soviet Union through Cuba; they said well, that guy who was killed in Dallas on TV didn't look like the guy that we saw at the Embassy. The guy we saw was short and blond. This was not Oswald. This is what the HSCA uncovered through their dogged research. The Warren Commission didn't want to find that and they didn't.

DiEugenio: Was there ever a photograph produced by the CIA of Lee Harvey Oswald going into either the Russian or the Cuban consulate?

Pease: One of the most curious facts about the Mexico City episode with Oswald is that despite his having supposedly visited the Cuban and the Soviet embassies five different times, there are no photos of Oswald in Mexico. These embassies are heavily covered. It's not like they have just one camera and one cameraman. They are heavily covered, because as David Phillips called it, it was the spooks' mecca. Everybody is spying on everybody else in Mexico City. Yet we are to believe that Oswald just managed to elude the camera ten different times, coming and going five times? It makes no sense unless you believe those who say, gosh, the guy who did come was not Oswald.

DiEugenio: On the voice on the tape that was sent to Dallas right after the assassination, was that voice Lee Harvey Oswald's voice?

Pease: According to the records, the FBI listened to a tape of Oswald in Mexico City, and they didn't think that it matched the voice of the Lee

Harvey Oswald that they'd come to know. Interestingly, on the tapes, the guy spoke very good Spanish and broken Russian. And that's just the opposite of what Oswald was known to do. Oswald spent a couple of years in the Soviet Union. He spoke Russian well.

J. Edgar Hoover, head of the FBI, knew that was not Oswald in Mexico City. And he told President Johnson. At that point: Look, we've listened to the tape and it's not Oswald. We've looked at those photos that they say were Oswald, that turned out to be some mystery man. We know that's not Oswald. LBJ's whole point of view was kind of I don't care because I'm very afraid if it was a conspiracy that it might have been the Soviets and that could get us into World War III. So it's better to just pretend it was all the act of one man. … I understand that point of view at that time. But it wasn't a fact-finding mission. It was a fact-covering-up mission. And people need to understand it in that context for it to make any sense.

DiEugenio: Did Richard Helms try to convince President Kennedy to take action in Venezuela in November of 1963 thereby seeking to break up the Alliance for Progress?

Pease: Three days before Kennedy was killed in Dallas, Richard Helms goes to the Oval Office. He brings Bobby Kennedy with him. He'd gone without Bobby Kennedy first and hadn't convinced him. So the two of them end up in the Oval Office. Helms at that point is the CIA's Deputy Director of Plans, and he is very much interested in getting Kennedy to invade Cuba because Cuba's exporting the revolution to Venezuela. After the Missile Crisis, JFK said: I will never invade Cuba unless they try exporting their revolution to the rest of Latin America.

And so here is Richard Helms now trying to convince Kennedy that that's what is going on. He brings a rifle into the Oval Office. … Kennedy is not cowed. Helms is telling him, look we have this rifle here and we know it's Cuban, because it used to have this little Cuban number on it. And we found a very specific chemical that if we put that chemical on the rifle, the number would magically appear once, just long enough for us to photograph it. And then the number would disappear forever. How JFK didn't laugh at that point I do not know. But in any case, Helms was unable to convince

Kennedy that this weapon was really a Cuban weapon and the Cubans were exporting their revolution.

DiEugenio: What was James Angleton doing in advance of the Clay Shaw trial?

Pease: Angleton was not just investigating the people that Garrison was looking into. You could see why the CIA would want to stay one step ahead of him: Who's he interviewing and what do they know? But Angleton actually asked his staff to do background reports on the jurors. The only reason for that would be they were contemplating jury tampering.

DiEugenio: What was the reaction to Kennedy's Algeria speech?

Pease: Kennedy stood up in the senate and gave this speech advocating for Algerian independence and saying, we should stop funding our French allies in this terrible war. There were, I want to say, 130 editorials, in that ballpark. Of those two-thirds were completely negative: How dare he go against our president and speak out? What does he know about foreign policy? Kennedy actually started to get a little nervous. He called his Dad: Did I do the wrong thing? And [Joe Kennedy] said: You lucky mush. You don't know it yet and they don't know it yet, but you're 100 percent right. And in a year, everybody's going to be agreeing with you. And that's exactly what happened. And so Kennedy ended up looking prescient. In fact, about a year later, he got this first *Time* magazine cover. The story was headlined "Man Out Front."

DiEugenio: What was Kwame Nkrumah's reaction to Kennedy's death?

Pease: Nkrumah was the leader of Ghana. He had led his own country to independence. He had his tussles with Kennedy, but overall he liked him. Kennedy had been a supporter of his work for independence. Nkrumah had come up against the CIA numerous times in his dealings. So when Ambassador [William P.] Mahoney handed him a copy of the Warren Report he opened it, he pointed to Allen Dulles's name on the Warren Commission. He handed it back and said, "Whitewash."

DiEugenio: Can you describe some of the Third World's reaction to Kennedy's assassination?

Pease: Kennedy was beloved beyond any foreign leader probably has ever been beloved around the world. When news came of Kennedy's death, all over the planet, people were mourning, crying and going to embassies and lighting candles. In Latin America, they talked about a plaza where people just lit candles because they didn't even have electrical power. In France, even after we had those battles with them over Algeria, even de Gaulle said you'd think he was their leader the way they were mourning him. Even the Soviet Union, and that's the one that really shocked me. They were just so sad because they saw what could have been. That was the first real hope of peace between our countries.

And I want to add a little piece about [journalist] Pete Hamill. Hamill was in and out of Mexico a lot of times. And one time he had a flat tire on a road in the middle of nowhere. There was a little house nearby and a town further down the road. Mexico is not always the safest place: If I go to the house, am I going to be safe there? With some trepidation he approached the front door and knocked. As soon as the guy opened the door, Hamill looked behind him and there was a picture of the Virgin of Guadalupe, the other was President Kennedy. And he knew he would be safe there.

Dr. Henry Lee

Henry Lee was the commissioner of Public Safety for the State of Connecticut from 1998 to 2000. He is currently the distinguished chair professor in Forensic Science at the University of New Haven. He is a prolific author, a frequent expert trial witness, and has hosted his own show on truTV.

Oliver Stone: How many gunshot homicides have you worked on?

Henry Lee: In the early days I used to remember the number. But now I've been a forensic and criminal investigator for almost fifty-six years. Over a thousand.

Stone: What was your reaction when you heard about the murder of President Kennedy?

Lee: At that time I was a young captain in the Taiwan police department. I heard the news. Of course, at that time, I knew very little about US history, but I know he was the youngest president, very good president.

Stone: As a result of the JFK Records Act, it created the Assassination Records Review Board. I know they invited you to give them your opinion on the autopsy materials for the assassination.

Lee: Actually at the end of 1997, they contacted me. On January 22, 1998, I went to review this case.

Stone: And what was your opinion of the quality and the quantity of the work done in the JFK autopsy?

Lee: Autopsy protocol and autopsy procedure did not vary too much during those years. The autopsy is less than desired, the quality and quantity.

Stone: So is it reliable and complete?

Lee: The forensic scientist's view is we need a complete autopsy to do the reconstruction, to do the analysis. Whatever the autopsy report, the photographs I got, I didn't have enough material to do what I needed for the reconstruction of the shooting.

Stone: Would the medical examiner in New York City at that time, Dr. Milton Helpern, would he have been the right choice, a good choice?

Lee: Yes. Excellent choice. He probably, at that time, was the most famous medical examiner. Definitely, a good choice.

Stone: So it's important to dissect the track of a gunshot wound in this case?

Lee: It's very important. Not only dissecting the gunshot wound. We also have to shave the hair under the bullet entrance area so we can see more detail of the bullet hole.

Stone: If that is not done, is there any way to reconstruct it?

Lee: It's very, very difficult. You have those unknowns, because some of the issues we were never able to answer. Such as whether the bullet changed the direction. Because that's one of the major points of the argument. Somehow the trajectory in the JFK case apparently turned in a ninety-degree angle.

Stone: And that was the trajectory of which bullet?

Lee: That's on the head.

Stone: The kill shot.

Lee: Yeah, that's the fatal shot.

Stone: And that was what trajectory?

Lee: There's three shots. At least three shots were fired. According to the Warren Commission, one shot missed Kennedy. The second went in through the back shoulder and came out the front. The third shot, the most important shot, entered the back right side of the head, and came out the front right. So the bullet actually then turned that angle

Stone: How many degrees would you say?

Lee: That's approximately ninety degrees.

Stone: That much?

Lee: I wasn't there so I only can read the record.

Stone: And if a victim dies of a gunshot wound to the brain, and there is a trial, isn't it important to section the brain?

Lee: Sometimes, yes. Most of the time you have a forensic pathologist do a complete job, a thorough job. And he should dissect the brain.

Stone: Did you see any evidence that that was done in this case?

Lee: When I reviewed the record in 1998, one of the questions we raised was: Is the brain still available? Can we go back to reexamine the brain to actually determine the bullet trajectory? And the answer is they cannot find the evidence. ... As far as Kennedy's brain, I think it's important to look at the trajectory inside of the brain. We did not find those records, or the information.

Stone: You're aware of the differences between the Clark autopsy review in 1968 and the 1963 autopsy?

Lee: I understand from the record, the distance moved of four inches, which is kind of strange. I did not do it, so I really cannot make too much of a comment.

(Editor's Note: Stone is talking about the Clark Panel moving the rear skull wound up four inches from the original autopsy in 1963, from near the bottom of the skull to the cowlick area.)

Stone: When you were doing this, did you have access, did you ever look at the Zapruder film in any detail?

Lee: We tried to use this information. But again, you have to find the exact location of Zapruder. The angle of the camera. The speed of the film. At that moment I do not have that information.

Stone: What was your ultimate conclusion after looking at the records?

Lee: The ultimate conclusion is: I don't know. I have no idea. . . . With Commission Exhibit 567 and 569, we made a recommendation to do a trace analysis and a biological analysis. For those two pieces in the front seat of the limousine.

(Editor's Note: those two exhibits are allegedly the head and tail of the bullet that pierced Kennedy's skull and landed on the floor in the front of the car.)

Stone: At an evidentiary hearing—that is before the trial—if you had been a defense lawyer, would you have called one over CE 399?

Lee: Of course. You know, this 399—what happened? How did it get on a stretcher? Who collected it? It should have been photographed and documented before. Of course, nobody can say what happened with 399. And is that the bullet in fact that hit Kennedy, came out and hit Connally?

Stone: As a professional criminalist over your lifetime, how many cases would you say, "I don't know?"

Lee: I cannot give you a definitive number. At least 10 percent I cannot issue any opinion. Most of the cases I can issue a partial opinion.

Stone: But you can't in this case.

Lee: Yes. In this case, there are just too many unknown factors.

Paul Bleau

Paul Bleau is an instructor at St. Lawrence College in Quebec City. He has written many essays on the JFK case, including a long two-parter titled "Exposing the FPCC."

Oliver Stone: Describe please the prior plots around John F. Kennedy before Dallas and explain for us their importance.

Paul Bleau: Well, the complete failure by the Warren Commission to look into at least seven plots that failed during the last six months—

Stone: Seven?

Bleau: At least seven, seven that failed in the last six months of Kennedy's life, is a glaring example of how the Warren Commission investigation was inept. Because had they done so, they would have recognized the template, they would have been able to build an offender profile, and even round up suspects.

Stone: Well, what is the first plot?

Bleau: There was one in Nashville ... in May of 1963. Where Kennedy was waiting for a helicopter after a motorcade and he was approached by a gunman who had a gun hidden underneath a sack. And the Secret Service spotted the gunman and picked him up. What's key is there is no file on it.

Stone: No file on it?

Bleau: There's no file, there's nothing known about it.

Stone: Was it witnesses, was it seen?

Bleau: Oh yes. This was in Nashville. Governor [Frank] Clement talked about it to his son.

Stone: And the gunman was arrested?

Bleau: He was picked up but he was let go by the Secret Service. And there's no identification. Nobody knows anything about him. So the key for this one is the secrecy about it.

Stone: Well, how do you know?

Bleau: Because articles came out later that the son of the governor talked about what his father related to him.

Stone: Second plot?

Bleau: Second plot would be Los Angeles in June, when Kennedy actually attended the showing of *PT 109*. Which was a movie about his war heroics. The alternate patsy in this case would have been Vaughn Marlowe, and Vaughn Marlowe had many similarities to Oswald. He was ex-military and he headed a chapter of the Fair Play for Cuba Committee in Los Angeles. And he could be portrayed as anti-Kennedy.

Stone: Third plot?

Bleau: The third plot takes us to Chicago, and Chicago stands out as perhaps the clearest forerunner of what eventually happed in Dallas. This would have occurred on November 2nd in Chicago.

Stone: Two plots, but it doesn't make sense unless it's a separate—

Bleau: Well, what would be similar is, if you look at the similarities now with what happened in Dallas ... But what happened in Chicago is you had these snipers show up and Thomas Arthur Vallee was probably being set up as an alternate patsy, because when it comes to patsy credentials, he and Oswald were dead ringers.

Stone: And this plot was thwarted? Why was it thwarted? How was it thwarted?

Bleau: Because of the informants. The informants who spoke to the FBI, the Chicago Police. The informant named Lee, the landlady, and you know the fact that they eventually had to do something.

Stone: And the public found out in 1975?

Bleau: That's when Edwin Black wrote an article after nine months of excellent journalism on his part.

Stone: Is there any evidence that the Secret Service in the Dallas detail knew anything about the Chicago plot?

Bleau: There is no evidence.

Stone: Can you go over the Tampa thing?

Bleau: There was a threat there that a sniper would shoot him from a tall building. The Secret Service was apparently afraid of or nervous about the Floridian Hotel where the motorcade would have gone by. Which was, at the time, Tampa's tallest building. So finally, you know it got under control. Nobody fired away at him. But in this case, the alternative patsy would have been a Gilberto Pilicarpo Lopez. He, like Oswald, got into a seemingly pro-Castro fistfight, which Oswald had done in New Orleans.

Stone: If Chicago had gone, how would they have nailed Vallee then?

Bleau: He would have been right there in the building beside the plot. You know, he had made threats. He stuck out like a sore thumb because of all the noise he made beforehand. He would have been in Chicago's equivalent of the Texas School Book Depository.

Stone: Has Lopez ever said anything?

Bleau: He ended up going to Cuba. But there is a report that he's actually in Florida right now.

Stone: So he landed in Cuba?

Bleau: On November 23rd, he made his way to Mexico City. So he goes to Mexico City and he ends up being the lone passenger on an airplane to Cuba.

Stone: And Lopez came from the military at all?

Bleau: Lopez was a Cuban defector, a Cuban exile and not much more is known of him.

Stone: And there was no evidence that the Warren Commission knew any of it?

Bleau: There was no evidence that the Warren Commission knew any of it.

Stone: So in your study of this, the Fair Play for Cuba Committee comes up the most?

Bleau: Yeah, well, if you take these subjects, these nine subjects, if you include Oswald. You find that seven were ex-Marines. You find seven tried or did make weird trips to Mexico City in an attempt to get to Cuba. And seven were easy to link to the Fair Play for Cuba Committee. They were either members, they had documents, they attended meetings. The reason that sticks out like a sore thumb is that the Fair Play for Cuba Committee was infested with infiltrators and largely inactive.

Dr. Philip Muehlenbeck

Dr. Philip Muehlenbeck is an instructor at George Washington University. He is the author of the 2012 book *Betting on the Africans: John F. Kennedy's Courting of African Natioanalist Leaders*.

Oliver Stone: John Kennedy, as a congressman, went to Saigon in 1951. It was one of the most, I gather one of the most important trips of his life, in terms of his thinking on foreign policy. Can you describe that trip?

Philip Muehlenbeck: Kennedy, as a congressman, decided to make a trip to Southeast Asia. Kennedy went to the US Embassy in Saigon. He met Edmund Gullion, who was working there as a consular official. He had told Kennedy that the French were actually losing the war. That the war was unwinnable and that, in fact, he said that if the US were to replace the French in the war, the US would also lose the war.

Stone: He was thinking the US would come in?

Muehlenbeck: Yeah. And so for Kennedy, when Kennedy came back to the US he made a speech on the radio saying that the US supporting the French in this war is becoming more colonialist in the minds of people in the developing world. Kennedy's own father criticized John F. Kennedy for making this speech and these comments related to his trip to Southeast Asia.

Stone: Nineteen fifty-one was the heart of the Korean War, as well as the McCarthy period in Washington, very strongly anti-communist. So the French war must have been identified with the fight against communism, correct?

Muehlenbeck: Yes. You know it was not a popular decision or popular opinion to make for sure. But Gullion was very influential with Kennedy. Kennedy respected that opinion that Gullion had. To the point that when Kennedy later came back to the US, Gullion became one of his foreign policy advisers, before Kennedy became president. Kennedy later made Gullion his ambassador to Congo. And during the Kennedy administration, there was a crisis in the Congo which was one of, if not the hottest Cold War crisis during the Kennedy administration. So that kind of illustrates the faith that Kennedy had in Gullion and his ability to kind of identify with the nationalists in the developing world, and kind of be sympathetic to their position.

Stone: I'm half French, so I'm kind of curious. What was the French reaction to Kennedy at that time?

Muehlenbeck: To be honest, I don't know about the reaction to Kennedy at that time. I can tell you that after he made his Algeria speech, the French were, as you might imagine, very upset with Kennedy. As a matter of fact, they warned him not to visit France, that he might be assassinated were he to visit France after his speech on Algeria.

Stone: So, *The Ugly American* comes out, that book in 1958?

Muehlenbeck: *The Ugly American* was a novel which its publisher advertised as "the inside story of how we're losing the Cold War." It depicted fictional diplomats in a fictional Southeast Asian country who were kind of bumbling, culturally insensitive, couldn't speak the native language, and just didn't understand the situation on the ground. This really resonated with Kennedy. To him, it kind of illustrated the approach, what he thought was a bad approach of the Eisenhower-Dulles foreign policy towards the developing world.

Stone: That title *The Ugly American*, reverberates. I remember, I was young, but when I heard that title, it shook up America.

Muehlenbeck: He took out a full-page advertisement in the *New York Times* in support of it. He also bought a copy of the book to give every member of the senate. Later on, as president, he helped the movie based on the book to be produced when he kind of pulled some strings with the Thai government, which was initially unwilling to allow them to film the movie in Thailand.

Stone: But I remember that, it was very well publicized and controversial.

Muehlenbeck: Yes. So this is another instance of Kennedy kind of taking this view of the US is on the wrong course in the developing world. Not only in policy but even in the types of people we have on the ground in the embassies. When Kennedy later became president, he made an emphasis on instead of sending long-term State Department officials to the top positions in embassies in the developing world, he sent kind of area experts you could say, people who spoke the language, who were sympathetic to the nationalist cause, who had relationships with the leaders of those countries. And I think this made a big difference in US relations with many of the countries.

I think another influence on his mindset that counterinsurgency—like the Green Berets in Vietnam—was a better approach towards the developing world in places like Vietnam. This would be more effective than the more heavy-handed military interventions and military support.

Stone: When it comes to the Algeria speech in 1957, Mr. Kennedy became the so to speak unofficial ambassador to Africa?

Muehlenbeck: Kennedy gave a controversial speech in 1957 in Congress in support of the Algerian cause in its colonial war against the French. This made him kind of the man to see for African diplomats. He became kind of the unofficial US ambassador to Africa. He later became the Senate chairman of the African subcommittee.

There was so much opposition to Kennedy's Algeria speech, not only from the Republicans in the Eisenhower administration, but even from the Democratic Party. It made Kennedy the first major US politician to support a colonial cause publicly. I think that's important. So in France there was a lot of backlash. There were warnings that Kennedy shouldn't visit France, that he might get assassinated should he do so. I believe there was even a bomb threat, a fake bomb threat made against Kennedy's office. Perhaps from some French sympathizer. And so the Africans—not just Algerians and Arabs in the Middle East, but also sub-Saharan Africans—really respected Kennedy for his stand on Algeria.

I think there was even some skepticism that he was doing this kind of as a stunt to get his name in the national spotlight, maybe more than a sincere belief in the position. Although I don't believe that.

Stone: So this attitude must have shaken up not only the Middle East, Mr. Nasser in Egypt, but also Mr. [Jawaharlal] Nehru in India.

Muehlenbeck: When Kennedy met with Nehru, it was kind of a somewhat awkward meeting. They didn't have as much rapport as Kennedy was expecting. He thought their views would be more in line. But at one point, Nehru tries to give Kennedy a lecture on the evils of colonialism and Kennedy kind of cuts him off. He says, Look, I'm an Irishman. We know about colonialism. We've been under colonialism from the British for hundreds of years. … I don't need to be taught about the evils of colonialism.

Stone: We have the Algeria speech, and of course the Vietnam incident. When he was elected president, Kennedy must have been popular in places like Iran and Egypt?

Muehlenbeck: Well I think Kennedy's overall policy towards the Middle East had a few pillars. One was to take a more evenhanded approach towards Israel on the Palestine issue than previous presidents had. A second issue was to support what he viewed as the progressive nationalists in places like Egypt, embodied by Nasser, and in Syria, as opposed to what Kennedy referred to as "relics of the past"—the monarchies in places like Saudi Arabia and Jordan.

Stone: And Iran. What about Iran?

Muehlenbeck: In places like Iran and Saudi Arabia … he's trying to push both governments towards more progressive reforms with limited success. Probably more in Iran than in Saudi Arabia. But I would lump Iran with Saudi Arabia, governments that he didn't think were progressive and wanted to push toward reform.

Stone: Let's talk about Nasser for a minute and talk about the Muslim Brotherhood and Islamic fundamentalism. What is Kennedy's shift toward Nasser?

Muehlenbeck: Kennedy made a great effort to try to form relations with Nasser. He was one of the foreign leaders who he corresponded with the most. I think he thought that Eisenhower and Dulles had really screwed up the situation by rescinding funding from the Aswan Dam and turning their backs on Nasser because of his positions. Kennedy viewed those positions as more of a neutral not the positions of a Soviet stooge. The fact that Nasser had stood up to British and French imperialism at the Suez Canal made Nasser wildly popular throughout, not only the Middle East, but also sub-Saharan Africa. So for Kennedy to try to win the hearts and minds of the developing world, Nasser would be a good person to form relations with.

Another thing that Kennedy liked about Nasser is the fact that he was not religiously dogmatic. He wasn't a fundamentalist. He didn't have close connections with the Muslim Brotherhood. He also didn't have relations with the Communist Party of Egypt, despite Eisenhower and Dulles kind of labeling him a communist. Another thing Kennedy liked about Nasser was that he was a progressive. He was a nationalist. And Nasser was so popular in the Middle East. I mean young Arabs had pictures of him on their lunch canteens and their lunch boxes.

Stone: And what about Nasser's views on Yemen. Wasn't he for the independence of Yemen?

Muehlenbeck: Right. So similar to today. Yemen in the 1960s was a complicated situation with a civil war. You had two factions. One was kind of more fundamentalist, a monarchy what was supported by Saudi Arabia and Jordan and Great Britain. The other side was more nationalist, progressives and they're supported by Nasser. This is a complicated situation for Kennedy. Since all of his allies are supporting the side that he views as a relic of the past, not the future. Not the side the US should really be supporting. So Kennedy attempted to take a somewhat evenhanded approach towards the civil war. Wanting to, I think, support Nasser, but on the other hand not to burn bridges too much with traditional allies. For Kennedy, the Yemen war was a real complication in his relations with Nasser. Without it, it would've been much easier for him to have better relations with Nasser.

They never met though. And Kennedy met with a lot of leaders from the developing world, more than any US president. One of the reasons probably the main reason he never met with Nasser is because of the domestic backlash that may have arose from that. Particularly from the Jewish Americans and the Israeli Lobby. Although there are indications that Kennedy had said at least once that he would likely invite Nasser to the White House in his second term. But he wanted to get reelected before he invited Nasser. So I think that kind of illustrates the nature of the tightrope.

Stone: Did he have the same issue with Sukarno? Oh, Sukarno did come to the White House. But bottom line, I mean, US policy in that era under Dulles and Eisenhower was definitely pro-fundamentalist, was it not?

Muehlenbeck: I think there are two things going on. One is they are supporting the traditional religious monarchies of the Middle East, especially Saudi Arabia. They tried to build up King Saud as, you might say, "their man in the Middle East" through his religious authority, he's going to lead in the Middle East. The other element is a kind of if you're either with us or you're against us mindset. You are either pro-US or if you're not pro-US then you are automatically pro-Soviet. So they had no room for neutrality under the Eisenhower-Dulles administration. John Foster Dulles even said that neutrality is immoral in his view. So if a country like Egypt were to take neutralist positions in the Cold War, that was a total no-go for Eisenhower and Dulles.

Stone: So as it is today, the United States relationship with the Middle East is a mess.

Muehlenbeck: I think that's fair to say.

Stone: What was Nasser's reaction to Kennedy's death?

Muehlenbeck: When Nasser learned of Kennedy's death in the middle of the night, he got up, dressed, went down to his office. And then realized there's nothing I can do about this. According to his son, Nasser went into a great state of depression after Kennedy's death. I think that for Nasser, he realized that after Kennedy's death, his relations with the US were going to deteriorate. No longer would he have somebody in the White House who was going to take the time to write him letters to explain things like, "I'm about to sell weapons to Israel and here's why. But here's why we still want to have relations with you."

And so for Nasser it was a tough blow. After Kennedy's death, relations with Egypt gradually deteriorated and they increasingly shifted their allegiances towards the Soviet Union as well.

Stone: And what were some of the reactions to Kennedy's death in the Third World?

Muehlenbeck: It was dramatic. I might even argue that it was perhaps even more strongly felt in places like Africa than the United States. For example, the film of Kennedy's funeral was shown in Cairo five times. In places like Kenya and the Ivory Coast, tens of thousands of people came to memorial services in those countries. Soon, schools, streets were named in honor of Kennedy in the developing world. His image even graced currency in Guinea for a while. And postage stamps in other countries.

So in the developing world, there was this great feeling of loss. Not only because of how Kennedy was the first, they felt, the first US president who's showing interest in their countries, sympathy toward their part of the world, but the kind of future that was lost in his death.

Thomas Samoluk

Thomas Samoluk was the Deputy Director and press officer for the ARRB.

Oliver Stone: Why was the Review Board so unprecedented in American history?

Thomas Samoluk: The authority given to the Review Board had really not been seen before, so it was a difficult challenge but the law gave us a lot of authority.

Stone: In other words, the Freedom of Information Act … that was the only method by which an average person could see documents, right?

Samoluk: Right. So with regard to the assassination, in the aftermath of the movie *JFK*, there was such an outpouring of interest and some outrage that there records that were decades old, literally, that were not available to the American public. It really prompted Congress to act in an unprecedented way.

Stone: The Board had the power to declassify material?

Samoluk: That's right.

Stone: And no board like that has existed before?

Samoluk: Right. I mean the Board, much to the chagrin of the intelligence community, had the authority to tell them what records could be made public, and their only recourse was to appeal to the president.

Stone: Well, there was one flaw it seems to me in the original structure. You were not open-ended in time. Am I right?

Samoluk: You are right. My sense was, at the beginning, there was resistance and there was always a level of resistance during the course of the Review Board tenure. They adopted, the intelligence agencies kind of adopt that approach, that they will eventually go away. The Review Board won't last forever. We'll still be here. They'll be gone. To quote Muhammad Ali, [it] was a little bit of a rope-a-dope strategy, I believe.

Stone: And the Board went from 1994 to 1998?

Samoluk: September 30, 1998. The final report was literally handed to President Clinton in the Oval Office. We shot the lights out. And that was it.

Stone: What were your personal highlights?

Samoluk: When the Board came into existence, we heard about film and photographs that most likely were out there that had never been seen. One was a film taken by Dave Powers, an aide to President Kennedy. He had been traveling in the motorcade in Dallas in the Secret Service vehicle behind the presidential limousine. He had a movie camera with him, which was not unusual. When the president traveled, Dave Powers can be seen in other films nearby with his home movie camera. We had heard he was filming during the motorcade. Several people, experts in photography around the assassination, said you need to find the Dave Powers film, and we did.

Stone: What happened when you tried to get records of the Jim Garrison investigation out of the new DA's office in New Orleans, Harry Connick?

Samoluk: Harry Connick had succeeded Jim Garrison. There was no love lost between the two of them. We went to New Orleans to get whatever records there were in connection with the prosecution of Clay Shaw. We met with District Attorney Connick. He told us that many of the records connected with the prosecution of Clay Shaw had been pilfered by the Garrison team which had left office when Connick came in. He said something similar to that at a Review Board public hearing.

A former employee, an investigator who had worked for Connick, was watching on TV. He heard Harry Connick say that and said to himself, "That's not true." Because he had grand jury records that he had kept for over twenty years that District Attorney Connick had told him to destroy. He thought they were valuable historic records. So the investigator did not take them to the city incinerator. He took them home in the trunk of his car and kept them for twenty years. Until he saw Harry Connick say to the review board at our New Orleans public hearing that Garrison employees had stolen the records. He eventually gave them to a New Orleans TV reporter who sent the records to us in Washington. And that was the beginning of a huge fight with Harry Connick. A legal battle that led our counsel at the Department of Justice to tell us, those on the Review Board staff, we advise you not to go to Louisiana until this is resolved, because you may very well be arrested by Harry Connick.

Stone: And the result of the litigation?

Samoluk: The Review Board won. There were some records that, in addition to the grand jury records, which were physically in our possession as a result of the New Orleans reporter sending them to us. There were other records that did exist in Connick's office that he was refusing to send to us. But we won in court. So we ended up getting those records as well as being able to keep the grand jury records. All of which are now in the JFK Collection at the National Archives.

Stone: Do you know if Connick destroyed any records?

Samoluk: We don't know. The Clay Shaw records that were the subject of the conversation between Connick and the investigator were grand jury records that he said, "The case was over. Clay Shaw had been acquitted." He saw no value in them. Of course, the investigator disagreed and kept them in his private possession, until they ended up with us. As far as the other records, I'm not sure.

(Editor's Note: The investigator was former policeman Gary Raymond and the television reporter was Richard Angelico. It later turned out that Connick admitted to destroying some Garrison records.)

Stone: Did the Secret Service destroy records?

Samoluk: We learned the time that the Review Board was in business, that the Secret Service had destroyed records. They were records that related to trips that President Kennedy had taken in the fall of 1963 prior to him going to Dallas.

Stone: Would that mean Chicago?

Samoluk: I think that Chicago is very important in the assassination story. There were anti-Castro Cubans in Chicago that were very active. There was a government informant who heard people talking about assassinating JFK. Literally the day before JFK was killed. The investigation was sent to the Secret Service, who began to investigate. Then President Johnson created the Warren Commission, the FBI had the lead. The Secret Service turned their records over to the FBI. That lead was never pursued.

(Editor's Note: Samoluk is referring to informant Thomas Mosely. Mosley was selling machine guns to Cuban exile Homer Echevarria. Echeverria was part of the 30th November Group, associated with the DRE, who Oswald had interactions with that summer in New Orleans. He is correct that the FBI quickly dropped the lead.)

Stone: And what did the FBI do when you first tried to declassify their records?

Samoluk: I remember distinctly a meeting where we were viewed clearly as an aggravation to the FBI. Who was this Review Board? This supposed authority that they had? And I remember being in a meeting where there was a sampling of records that were being looked at and we were intending to declassify. And I remember one FBI official who had probably never looked at the actual text of the JFK Act before, started furiously flipping through the law, a copy of which was on the table. Red-faced, he's flipping through and he's saying, "Uh, uh, you can't declassify that record." And he found under section seven of the law, he said "personal privacy." This personal privacy was irrelevant to the records that were at issue.

Stone: And under the broad definition of records with the JFK Act, wasn't the Board also allowed to seek and declassify records dealing with Kennedy's foreign policy?
Samoluk: We're primarily taking about Cuba and Vietnam. Again, the Review Board was not reinvestigating the assassination. But we were tasked with adding to the record. And I think we pushed the envelope under the law. But in a very fruitful and positive way to make those records available to the American public.

Stone: And you did get the records of the SecDef meeting in Hawaii with McNamara requesting withdrawal orders from Vietnam as well as the schedules for that?

Samoluk: The records we uncovered related to Vietnam and Secretary of Defense McNamara have been viewed as key missing links into the story of Vietnam. And the same thing with some of the documents that we released relevant to Cuba.

Stone: And apparently in the Cuba matter, it led to the discovery of the Northwoods operation?

Samoluk: The Northwoods records are really, I have to say, bizarre … that what was being discussed in the military about creating situations that would make it look like Cuba had committed terrorist acts, had downed a US jetliner as a pretense to invade Cuba.

Stone: Did you go back to Congress to get a reauthorization for an extension?

Samoluk: Twice we went back to Capitol Hill, went to the appropriators and said that we need more time and we got it. What was going to be a two-year operation became a four-year operation. Could we have used more time? Absolutely. Was it politically possible? I don't think so. One of the deficiencies of the law has been shown that what has happened with certain records post Review Board. The National Archives doesn't have the authority … to push for some of those records.

People will continually just stretch it out until public interest wanes or they find some other excuse not to release. And it leads to cynicism among the American public. And who more than the American public has a right to see the records of what their government had done or not done?

Stone: Some of the documents are still being released. But not all the documents. And some are being released I'm told in redacted form. Including CIA and FBI documents. Are they breaking the law?

Samoluk: It is really frustrating what has happened. Because the law said that anything that was not released ... needed to be released under the law by October 26, 2017. Now there is a clause that says if the president certifies, under certain conditions, that the records would not be released. I don't think the process under the law was followed. The records have not been released in total, and I don't think any good reasons have been given.

(Editor's Note: Samoluk is correct here. President Trump did not specify reasons for not releasing the hidden records in 2017.)

Stone: Did you see any redactions when you were counsel?

Samoluk: I'll give you an example. The CIA might come to us and say there is the name of a CIA operative in this particular document. And if the document is released with the individual's name, who retired overseas, he will be killed if his name is known. Again, this is 1995–1996. And there were incidents where the Review Board respected that and said we will not release the record now. But it will be released twenty-five years from now or upon the death of the individual.

Dr. Robert Rakove

Robert Rakove is a professor of history at Stanford. He is the author of the book *Kennedy, Johnson, and the Nonaligned World* published in 2013.

Oliver Stone: Dr. Rakove, what was different about Mr. Kennedy and his relationship with the Middle East, especially with Gamal Abdel Nasser? What was different about what he did than what the previous administration, under John Foster Dulles and Dwight Eisenhower, had done?

Robert Rakove: Eisenhower and Dulles had edged onto a course of confrontation with Nasser. They'd all too often seen his nationalism as favoring the expansion of Soviet power in the Middle East. Most famously in 1956 after he opened relations with the People's Republic of China, they canceled a loan that Nasser depended upon for the Aswan High Dam. This set the Suez Crisis in motion as Nasser nationalized the Suez Canal.

Dulles saw neutralism/nonalignment as immoral. Kennedy did not. Kennedy thought it was a perfectly natural choice in a terrifying postcolonial Cold War world. And Kennedy looked at Nasser as someone who was reasonable, who was susceptible to dialogue, and who actually thought the right inducements and encouragements might avoid another Arab-Israeli war which would be cataclysmic for all involved.

Stone: Tell me about John Kennedy when he came into office in 1961?

Rakove: Kennedy came into office thinking that fundamentally the United States needs to take a new tack with nonaligned states, including Egypt, which was a country that few Americans held much regard for. Americans had tended to see Nasser as a dangerous nationalist with pro-Soviet tendencies, with an antagonism toward Israel. Kennedy discerned that Nasser actually could, through the right inducements, forge a partnership with Washington.

Kennedy discerned he was actually quite modern, quite rational, quite forward looking. Nasser wanted to pursue modernization of Egypt in a way that was actually relatively open toward Western investment in commerce. He had no truck with Islamists, he put them in prison. He saw religious fundamentalism as a step backward, as a step into the past. And it didn't help that his leading adversary within the Arab world, Saudi Arabia, was quite conservative and quite fundamentalist. He was actually also quite distrustful of communists, like Kennedy. He was someone who was young and very forward looking. They could kind of achieve a natural harmony together.

Stone: It's an interesting parallel to modern day in that there was a conflict over Yemen back then, with Egypt going up against Saudi Arabia. Can you tell me a bit about Yemen?

Rakove: Then as now Yemen was a sort of area of contestation between Arab powers, Middle Eastern powers. Back at the turn of the sixties, it emerged as the proxy, as a sort of proxy conflict between Saudi Arabia and Egypt. Whereas now it's Saudi Arabia versus Iran. Nasser felt that in a way he had been dragged into it. There was a moderate degree of Egyptian involvement with the Republicans in Yemen, not that much though. But he felt that his credibility was on the line. He also perceived himself to be alone in the Arab world. His adversaries, especially Saudi Arabia, thought here was a quagmire. Here was a place where they could pin him down and make him bleed.

Stone: So let's get to his 1957 Algeria speech. Kennedy is on the floor of the Senate. It was bracing and controversial.

Rakove: Very few people—none with his prominence—had been willing to say what he said. Which was to challenge a kind of Eurocentrism in American foreign policy. To challenge the kind of "Europe First" outlook especially toward conflicts in the colonial world. And it wasn't a popular stance in its time. John Foster Dulles irately suggested that he should have criticized communist misbehavior in Western Europe. Adlai Stevenson, the two-time Democratic nominee for the presidency, privately thought it was a grave mistake on Kennedy's part. He stood apart from much of the sentiment in his party. There were a few isolated voices that could join him on the issue. But very much it was an iconoclastic speech.

Stone: So how did Kennedy's *Foreign Affairs* journal article further outline his difference with Dulles and Eisenhower?

(Editor's Note: This refers to a long article that Kennedy wrote in that journal as a follow-up to his Algeria speech. It appeared in the October, 1957 issue and was titled "A Democrat Looks at Foreign Policy.")

Rakove: Kennedy said the Eisenhower administration has put too much emphasis on military strength. On lining up states and creating this trip wire of alliance throughout the Third World. We haven't actually pondered whether these states fit together well, whether their interest are shared either within their own ranks or with the United States. He also suggested the era in which the world can be divided into opposing camps is over. If it's not over, it is coming to an end soon. Decolonization is an ongoing fact. And on top of it all, there's a rise of medium powers in the world. Such as India, such as Egypt. They are not going to take direction from either side. He fundamentally challenged the key paradigms of US foreign policy in that article.

Stone: And also you could point to Franklin Roosevelt, who was a big influence on Kennedy?

Rakove: Roosevelt himself thought that imperialism and empire was outmoded and fundamentally destructive. And it was no basis for a postwar world. Kennedy got to view the situation farther along—Algeria, Indochina, and the British withdrawal from India. These were accomplished facts. And so the finish line, or at least where this process was leading to, this was much clearer. But still there were many rocky hurdles ahead.

And Kennedy was well-traveled. He visited Iran in 1951 in the middle of the oil crisis with Britain. He went to Indochina on that trip. He also visited Yugoslavia under [Josip Broz] Tito who had broken with [Joseph] Stalin. Tito had broken with Stalin. But Tito was also repressing Catholics, and Kennedy thought it was important to meet with this controversial but potentially supportive leader, that Tito could actually, through his defiance of the Warsaw Pact, become an asset to US security.

Stone: He met with Tito when?

Rakove: This was in 1951. Another difference he identified with Eisenhower was that he saw in Khrushchev, a flexible, creative, nondogmatic adversary. Khrushchev could travel the world and promise aid despite differences. . .. Kennedy said in his *Foreign Affairs* article: Next to this, the Eisenhower administration looks much more dogmatic, looks much more wooden.

Stone: And how did Kennedy feel toward India?

Rakove: Kennedy, like a number of Democrats, thought India was really the keystone in South Asia. That Nehru was a leader of immense unequaled stature to whom much of the world would listen. And that Indian democracy was critically important to democracy in the world. He thought India could offer an example of non-communist development. He thought the success of Indian modernization was pivotal to the waging of the Cold War in the Third World. And then, in 1962, when the Sino-Indian border conflict heated up, Kennedy rushed assistance to India. He rushed to show solidarity with the nonaligned state despite the fact that this made the Pakistanis quite upset.

Stone: Do you want to talk about using foreign policy with foreign aid?

Rakove: There's another area where Kennedy differed from his predecessors and successors. Kennedy was very wary of the image of the United States trying to seek leverage for its aid. And he had Aswan as this damning example. And what happened? The Soviets stepped in. They funded the dam instead. And Kennedy was always very wary of seeming to play that same card throughout his presidency. It didn't mean he thought aid could be given charitably, altruistically. He would attempt to advise recipients of the problems that he faced in getting his foreign aid bills passed. And Kennedy's last foreign aid bill in 1963 was basically pecked to death by the Senate.

However, Kennedy did not want to humiliate recipients. He thought that was bad business. Johnson, on the other hand, who followed him, he had this iron notion of reciprocity and it came from being a Senate Majority Leader before he was Vice-President….It was humiliating for recipients to have to jump through hoops in order to receive aid allotments. And worst of all, that compromised their fundamental legitimacy. If they were seen to kowtow, to sort of go cup in hand to Uncle Sam.

Stone: Didn't Kennedy send his old professor from Harvard to India as the ambassador?

Rakove: John Kenneth Galbraith is a great example of Kennedy's unconventional approach to diplomacy. Kennedy thought that Eisenhower had been sending too many patronage appointments overseas. It wasn't that Kennedy wanted to rely on career diplomats. He wanted to send people who were fitted to the position whether they came from the foreign service or not. And Galbraith had interesting ideas about development economics that Nehru found quite interesting.

Galbraith proved a very, I think, adroit advocate of development and a good ally for India within the US foreign service. There was quite a lot of skepticism toward India from the career people and Galbraith was willing to make India's case within the bureaucracy.

Stone: What was the reaction then in the Third World to Kennedy's death?

Rakove: There was grief, grief across the Third World. And I could offer examples that would literally fill the hour. Nehru got before the Indian Parliament and decried a great crime. He called it a crime against humanity. He said: A man has been struck down in the prime of youth and achievement, a man of ideals, vision, and courage, who sought to serve his own people, as well as the larger causes of the world. Algeria, which had a special feeling for Kennedy, declared a state of mourning for a week. Flags were flown at half-mast. The U.S. ambassador to Egypt, circling back to that case later, said that he thought the Egyptians had seen in Kennedy the best of what they saw in America. That Kennedy had represented a kind of ideal of America to ordinary Egyptians.

Stone: Did Secretary of State Dean Rusk make any attempt to continue, or did Lydon Johnson make any attempt to continue Kennedy's policy of engagement?

Rakove: There was a certain momentum behind engagement. And so it didn't expire. The machinery was still in place. Aid programs that Kennedy had approved that had been enacted and funded would continue in the Johnson years. But by early 1964, the diminished emphasis that the policy had was apparent. Leaders of the Third World wanted to meet Johnson…. But their requests to meet him were generally declined. Johnson didn't have the same kind of interpersonal interest that Kennedy had. He didn't necessarily want to meet with leaders from the Global South. And when he did, the meetings weren't conversations. They were cursory, they were peremptory. LBJ didn't have that same kind of interpersonal curiosity that Kennedy applied to this specific area.

That was one indicator. Johnson's willingness to use aid punitively to twist the arms of recipients to get their support of his war in Vietnam for example, or other policies. That was another indicator as well. And finally thirdly, was the Vietnam War, which nonaligned states, only after they lined up early in 1965 to try to offer mediation, in ways actually that North Vietnam and China didn't like. But by 1965, '66, they could conclude that Johnson didn't have the interest in their issues that Kennedy did.

He didn't understand that actually the politics of aid are complicated. That when a state is a recipient it feels a need to demonstrate its independence often in ways that can seem frustrating or aggravating for the United States. But when we give out foreign aid, we're not buying serfs. We're not buying supplicants. We're attempting to work with another government to advance a project that we both think is desirable. Is worth attaining. And Johnson wanted too much from recipients.

I think Kennedy's interest in the Third World was relatively unique…. The problems of decolonization, the problems of development in the Global South … he found these issues compelling. He found these issues interesting and he made time and space to understand them and to engage in serious sustained dialogue with the leaders of the Third World.

Professor Richard Mahoney

Richard Mahoney is a professor at the School of Public and International Affairs at North Carolina State University. His father, William Mahoney, the ambassador to Ghana under Kennedy, was part of the inspiration for his milestone book on Kennedy's foreign policy, *JFK: Ordeal in Africa.*

Oliver Stone: you wrote a book in 1983, *JFK: Ordeal in Africa*, which I think was quite a groundbreaking history. What was the situation that France found itself in in Algeria?

Richard Mahoney: They had five hundred thousand troops and they were committing atrocities, summary executions, mass torture. And so Kennedy was responding to that.

Stone: What was the difference between the French colonial war in Indochina and the one in Algeria?

Mahoney: The big difference was that the French military was going to overthrow the civilian democratic government if it didn't go along with the war effort in Algeria.

Stone: And what was Kennedy's intent then in making his 1957 Algeria speech?

Mahoney: He did some research. He had fixated on this issue. He had his wife translate some books that were written in French about the war. So John F. Kennedy got up on the Senate floor on July 1, 1957, and said, very simply, whether France likes it or not, has our support or not, sooner or later, one by one, all of its overseas possessions are going to become independent. So we need to face facts. And we should call for Algerian independence. We should establish relationships with Algerian nationalists—who were thought to be terrorists and murderers—and we should cease to support France.

Stone: What was the reaction to this speech?

Mahoney: The reaction was just explosive. He was denounced by Democrats and Republicans. The Eisenhower administration said, you know, this guy's irresponsible, he's dangerous. The reaction in France, which was on the verge of civil war, was incredibly negative. And *Time* said, "One American has unified France finally against himself: John F. Kennedy."

Stone: Did anybody help him or ally with him?

Mahoney: Very few people did. Adlai Stevenson denounced the speech. Most liberals, except for Chester Bowles, who was governor of Connecticut at that time, he supported the speech. But most everybody on both sides of the aisle said it was dangerous, it was irresponsible. France was a vital NATO ally and he was associating himself with Algerian terrorists.

Stone: Do you want to talk about Alistair Cooke?

Mahoney: Yes. Cooke was a Brit who wrote a bimonthly column in the *Saturday Evening Post*. Alistair Cooke said, you know, this guy has gotten enormous attention. His name is John F. Kennedy, he's gotten enormous attention from taking the stand and if he's right about the power of nationalism, about the primacy of having the US back these independent nationalist movements, he's going to get great credit for that.

Stone: Did they know this speech was coming?

Mahoney: No. The Kennedy staff held it tightly because they anticipated that the reaction would be, you know, negative.

Stone: Almost immediately after taking office, how did President Kennedy alter Eisenhower's Congo policy?

Mahoney: In the second week of December 1960, about a month after he was elected president, he was in Palm Beach. He got a call from [U. N. Secretary] Dag Hammarskjöld. The subject of the call was the fate of Patrice Lumumba. Lumumba was the first Congolese prime minister, a very charismatic, popular figure. Who had been overthrown by the Belgians with the help of the Central Intelligence Agency. Hammarskjöld was appealing to Kennedy to basically get Lumumba out of a military base and into UN hands so he wouldn't be killed. So Kennedy agreed to it and did. So Kennedy's first action was to indicate that he wanted to get Lumumba freed and get him into UN hands. What he didn't know, though, was that the Eisenhower administration had already decided that he should be assassinated. The previous July, the National Security Council, with President Eisenhower as chair, had authorized Allen Dulles to assassinate Patrice Lumumba.

The reason they did that was because Belgium had decided that it wanted to reassert control over its former colony, and Lumumba in order to stop that, he had invited Russian advisers into the Congo to secure the country. At that point, Eisenhower gave the go-ahead to have him assassinated. Either poison him or shoot him. Hammarskjöld calls him and asks him to intercede to save Lumumba, who is in prison on a military base.

Stone: Why was he in prison?

Mahoney: Lumumba had been overthrown the previous summer and Kennedy agrees. So Kennedy, in the lead-up to starting his administration, taking the oath of office as president, is trying to intercede to get Lumumba secure in UN hands and out of prison. So they say in cable traffic: We need to take drastic steps in light of this new man becoming president. And so about forty-eight hours before Kennedy takes the oath of office, Lumumba is sent to Elizabethville and delivered into the hands of his enemies.

During the flight, personnel with CIA cryptonyms are, you know, busy securing him. When they get to Eliizabethville, the secessionist province, he's taken out and shot. Kennedy doesn't know this until a month later, when Hammarskjöld calls the American ambassador to the UN, Adlai Stevenson, and says: Lumumba was executed four weeks ago. Do you want to call President Kennedy or should I? Stevenson says: Mr. Secretary, I think I should. So Adlai Stevenson calls JFK and JFK gets the news and there is a dramatic photo of him, you know, putting his hand to his face and saying, "Oh no, no." at the news of Lumumba's assassination.

Stone: Four weeks after?

Mahoney: Four weeks.

Stone: And the CIA knew that he was dead?

Mahoney: Oh, they knew he was dead. They were in and around the assassination. There's no question.

Stone: So Dulles had no obligation, felt no obligation to tell the incoming president?

Mahoney: None at all. It's clear that two things happened with regard to the Central Intelligence Agency. They moved quickly to execute this man, because John F. Kennedy was coming into the office of the presidency. Once executed, they didn't tell President Kennedy at all. He got the news through the UN through Hammarskjöld.

Stone: We have to talk about the Hammarskjöld killing.

Mahoney: Kennedy supported Hammarskjöld actively. So the Democrats in Congress gave a huge supplementary package for the peacekeeping operation run by the UN in the Congo. And Kennedy backed Hammarskjöld in terms of getting a government of national unity in Leopoldville. To make a long story short, Hammarskjöld himself was assassinated in September of 1961.

Stone: Describe what UN troops are trying to do?

Mahoney: The UN had gone into the Congo to avert civil war and to stop the secession of a mineral-rich province called Katanga. The operation was not supported by the Eisenhower administration. So when Kennedy came in, the United States changed its policy. It decided to back the UN to back Hammarskjöld, to try for a democratic solution to the conflict and to stop the secession of this particular province called Katanga.

Stone: European imperialism is evolving. Describe Katanga with the mineral wealth and the concept of secession—splitting the Congo.

Mahoney: The province secedes from the Congo and announces itself as an independent country supported by British and Belgian imperial interests.

Stone: Didn't Kennedy have to go to the UN a second time in order to keep their UN military forces in Congo?

Mahoney: After Hammarskjöld was killed, Kennedy flew to New York to address the United Nations and to say that in the memory of Dag Hammarskjöld, we need to keep the United Nations in the Congo and finish the job that he started. And so the United States became the leader of the UN mission, the peacekeeping mission in the Congo. And Kennedy came back to the United Nations a year after that to reiterate the fact that the peacekeeping operation is working, we have a democratic government, and we still do not accept Belgium's role in the secession of this province called Katanga.

Stone: So the secession did not succeed?

Mahoney: No, ultimately it did not.

Stone: What happened with Katanga when Kennedy was alive?

Mahoney: Kennedy goes to the UN a year after Hammarskjöld is dead to address the General Assembly and say its working and we need your support. What was working was the peacekeeping operation, with about three thousand troops, was keeping the country together. They had isolated the secessionist province of Katanga and ultimately used Indian troops to overwhelm the Belgian mercenaries who were defending Katanga and bring it back into the Congolese union.

Stone: What a story. Amazing. I remember it. Wasn't there a lot of suspicions around the Dag Hammarskjöld air crash?

Mahoney: Yes. Suspicions were everywhere that there had been foul play. The first person on the scene was the US air attaché. And there were bullets that he said were in the victims including Hammarskjöld. And a close friend of President Kennedy, Edmund Gullion, sent a cable home saying: Contrary to the official explanation for this tragic incident, this was an assassination.

Stone: Wow. So Kennedy got that information from a man he trusted?

Mahoney: It was only his ambassador, Gullion, using his air attaché, doing an investigation, basic forensics, that indicated that there had been an explosion in the wheelhouse of the plane. And that's the reason it crashed. I talked to Ed Gullion, and he said: You know, I think what happened was, after the fact, there may have been two or three of them who were still alive and the squad came in—and you know. The Central Intelligence Agency, to the contrary, stuck to the official story that it was an accident.

Stone: This is big news. We can kill Third World leaders, but now all of a sudden, white leaders are being killed. This is pretty significant if Kennedy realizes that this is a bigger game. Certainly, suspicion has to cross his mind that somebody in the power structure killed Hammarskjöld.

Mahoney: After the Bay of Pigs ... Kennedy wanted Dulles gone. He had to do it properly and he realized that this was a very dangerous agency. Really a rogue elephant. And if he didn't handle this well, he himself might show up in their crosshairs.

Stone: You think he thought that?

Mahoney: Let me give you an example. There was a book being written by Fletcher Knebel, who was a journalist who mostly wrote for *Look*. It came out in the form of a novel called *Seven Days in May*. It was about a military coup in the United States by the Joint Chiefs of Staff. When Knebel talked to Kennedy about the book, he asked Kennedy: Do you think that could really happen? And the response was, Yes.

Stone: What happened after Hammarskjöld's death?

Mahoney: Kennedy really assumed the role of being the leader of the UN peacekeeping operation in the Congo and dedicated himself to getting a democratic government in power. He did that.

Stone: And how quickly and radically after the murder of President Kennedy did President Johnson alter the policy in Congo?

Mahoney: President Johnson did a 180-degree turn in terms of Congo policy. The US, which under Kennedy was a champion of African nationalism and the lead peacekeeper in the Congo, became the agent of white reactionary nationalism and imperialism. Led by the Belgians, and South Africans and, of all things, the anti-Castro Cubans. All of whom intervene in 1964 in the Congo. Belgian paratroopers, South African mercenaries, and anti-Castro Cuban pilots mount this operation to return a reactionary government to power under Joseph Mobutu and to bring Moïse Tshombe, who was the secessionist leader of Katanga, back in as prime minister. It was a 180-degree turn. It was as if the United States had never really had this deep association with African nationalism under President Kennedy.

(Editor's Note: In fairness to LBJ, the pretext for all this was the Simba Rebellion, made up partly of the last of Lumumba's followers. But no author on the subject thinks that Johnson handled this rebellion with any skill or insight. See, for example, the late Jonathan Kwitny's Endless Enemies, *pp. 80–85.)*

Stone: What happened under Mobutu briefly?

Mahoney: As soon as Mobutu takes power, the Belgian commercial and clandestine interests and the Central Intelligence Agency are back in business big time. And for three decades, he brutalizes his country, murders wantonly, profits at an incredible rate and becomes one of the worst dictators in the world.

Stone: From your years of study, what was Kennedy's attitude towards some of his military advisers?

Mahoney: His attitude towards his military advisers was one of unalloyed hostility. He was a guy who wasn't really hostile about very much. But on the subject of the military, and specifically, his Joint Chiefs of Staff, he was very hostile and very suspicious.

Stone: Anything quotable?

Mahoney: Kennedy said: The first thing I'm going to tell my successor is you can't trust the military on anything, including military matters. So he routinely disparaged them. He said for example: You know these guys have it right in the sense that we'll all be dead if we follow their advice.

Robert F. Kennedy Jr.

Robert F. Kennedy Jr. is a best-selling author, chairman of the Children's Health Defense group, and a longtime successful environmental attorney.

Oliver Stone: How did the Alliance for Progress begin as an idea and what was its progress?

Robert F. Kennedy Jr.: My father and uncle had an intense interest in Latin America, particularly vis-à-vis the relationship of those nations with the United States. My uncle and my father were aware that US policies towards Latin America had been anti-democratic and US policy essentially was a policy that was driven by the economic interests of US corporations and the strategic interests of fighting communists wherever they were. So the US was very willing, and the CIA from 1954 began overthrowing governments that threatened US interests and my uncle said at one point, the only thing that a dictator had to do to get US aid showered upon him was to say that he was killing communists.

And they tried to create a formula where we would tie US aid to the democratization of the country, to the disbandment of oligarchies, to land reform, to education reform. Essentially making an effort to have US policy drive at the objective of creating middle classes in these countries that were polarized by wealth. The middle class they believed was critical to the stability of a democracy.

Stone: Was this a—call it a philosophy—that they learned from Franklin Roosevelt, do you think?

Kennedy: I think that they were very much influenced by my grandfather, Joseph Kennedy. My grandfather believed that US policy—he essentially agreed with what Adams and Madison and Jefferson had said, John Quincy Adams particularly. That we should encourage democracy all over the globe. We shouldn't go abroad looking for monsters to destroy. My grandfather believed that America's strength came from a strong economy and from being a model democracy. That we should fortify our shores as a fortress America. We should make ourselves too expensive to invade. But we should not be spreading forces, or acting like a police force around the rest of the globe. He was very anti-communist, but he wasn't anti-communist in the sense that we should go kill communists and beat them up. He thought the system was unworkable, and the only thing holding the system together, international communism together, was US military opposition to it. That the military threat, which was our strategic response to communism, was actually holding the communist world together. And he … made a famous speech in 1946 called fortress America at the University of Virginia where he reiterated that.

Stone: Who did?

Kennedy: My grandfather. He had been against World War I because he thought it would only benefit the bankers and that millions of people would be killed. He lost a tremendous number of friendships. He opposed World War II until Pearl Harbor as did most Americans. He believed that America was an exemplary nation. What that meant was we were actually supposed to make ourselves an example of fairness and democracy. Not that we were supposed to go around the world and force people to do what we wanted them to do at the barrel of a gun.

Stone: Say that again? I'm sorry.

Kennedy: America was the first modern democracy. My father used to talk all the time that we were the first modern democracy and we were really the template. By the Civil War, by 1865, there were six democracies. In 1960, when my uncle became president, the whole world was becoming democratic because the colonial powers were falling apart. I watched, every three or four months, the globe, and I had in my second, third, fourth grades in elementary school, the names of the countries were changing all the time because the colonial world was falling apart. My uncle was on the African subcommittee in the US Senate and because he had an intense interest in watching and encouraging the democratization of Africa and the end to colonization.

(Editor's Note: Senator John Kennedy had become the chairman of that subcommittee in 1958.)

He made a speech about Algeria specifically in 1957, and even today when I go to Africa or the Middle East, people remember it with this extraordinary attitude. People name their kids after my uncle because of that speech. And in that speech, he essentially said Africa should be ruled by the Africans.

That speech garnered him the vitriol not just of Republicans like Nelson Rockefeller and Barry Goldwater, Ronald Reagan, etcetera, but also Democrats like Adlai Stevenson. Because they saw that colonial empire as the only thing that was holding the European economy together. And Europe was the bulwark against communism. So we had to support their colonial aspirations and ambitions in Africa. My uncle said: No, we shouldn't be doing that. That is, in the long run, going to weaken us, and in any event it's against every American Ideal. We should be supporting democracy wherever it pops up in the world.

Stone: Some people have suggested it comes also from the Irish roots. That your grandfather and your uncle and your father, they were Irish and the Irish were always fiercely independent and the British Empire was always a big problem.

Kennedy: I think they were very aware of Irish history. Ireland was the first colony and it was the last colony. It was an eight-hundred-year failed experiment in colonization and they were very conscious of that. You know, all of their grandparents came over in 1848 and 1849 during the famine—which was not a famine—it was an engineered starvation by the British government. And they were aware that in Ireland since 1691, the Irish couldn't own land, they couldn't serve on a jury, they couldn't practice law, they couldn't be elected to a political office. They had lost all of their rights because of colonization.

Stone: And what was your father's reaction to President Johnson's intervention in the Dominican Republic in 1965?

Kennedy: My father was horrified at the US intervention in the Dominican Republic. I was very much aware, we all were, of his trip in 1965 to Latin America. He saw that the Alliance for Progress was being destroyed. It was being deliberately destroyed, and he had this confrontation, Richard Goodwin was there: You mean to tell me that all a political leader has to do is say that he's going to support American business and that he is going to kill some communists and we're going to give them aid? But if they say they're going to help the poor and oppose Standard Oil that we're going to cut them off? Thomas Mann had, in a single stroke, destroyed the Alliance for Progress. He was a Texas businessman who had been involved in the coup in Guatemala. After Jacobo Arbenz had been deposed he helped put in power [Carlos] Castillo Armas. And Castillo Armas admitted that he never made a decision without consulting Thomas Mann.

Stone: By the way, your father did go to Chile, right?

Kennedy: My father actually rode a little sled down on rails into the depths of these copper mines. And he saw the miners working as slave labor at the bottom of the mine. And when he came back up, he said, "If I was working in this mine, I'd be a communist too." It's one of the many things he said in South America that, during that South American tour, that angered pubic officials, that angered Thomas Mann, and the Johnson administration. And it shocked local intellectuals.

At one point he had a meeting with some of the intellectual leaders in Lima, Peru. They asked him what he thought they should do strategically with Anaconda Wire and Cable, and with Standard Oil. He said: If I was you, I would nationalize them. And they said to him: well, what would the United States do? He said: You should nationalize them. You should come up with a process for nationalizing them that's fair and you should do it. And don't worry what the United States is going to do.

Stone: After the Missile Crisis in 1962, wasn't President Kennedy attempting a back channel détente with both Russia and Cuba which your father was aware of?

Kennedy: When my uncle met with Khrushchev at the beginning of his administration, at the summit meeting in Vienna, he had high hopes going into that meeting that he would be able to talk reasonably to a reasonable man. And they would be able to defuse many of the conflict areas like Laos and Vietnam and Berlin particularly. And he came away shocked because Khrushchev at that meeting was posturing, he was bellicose, he was pugnacious and daring. President Kennedy left that meeting very discouraged and feeling like we actually needed to do a military buildup to bring the Soviets to the negotiating table. Subsequently after the Berlin Crisis, I think both of them were changed by that crisis. And they realized not only did they need to trust each other but they could trust each other. Khrushchev had taken a very large risk by withdrawing the tanks from Checkpoint Charlie early. And my uncle realized that he was dealing with the man that he had hoped he was going to deal with in Vienna. And letters began to be exchanged between the two men and the letters were very personal. And they proceeded along a course that ended up with them really talking very seriously about complete demobilization.

Jack had an interest in Cuban history and the history of Latin America. When we talked at our dinner table about the great figures of American history, we talked about Washington and Lincoln and Jefferson. But we also talked about Simón Bolívar....and Jack did as well. Jack was very aware of the corruption of the Batista regime and about our role in Cuba since the Spanish American War. And he believed that Castro had a point. He sent a message to Castro, and he read and admired Castro's declaration in the Sierra Maestras about the liberation of Cuba, and the right of the Cuban people to exercise sovereignty over their nation, over their island.

Stone: Let's continue on. Your father's first-day reaction to the assassination of his brother?

Kennedy: Hoover made two calls. A call to say he had been shot and later he called back and said he was dead. The first call, he was eating lunch at the pool with Bob Morgenthau. Morgenthau at that point was leading my father's anti-Mafia campaign. And my father's first phone call was to the

CIA desk officer at Langley. Later that day, he called Enrique Ruiz, Harry Ruiz, who was one of the Cuban leaders. One of the last Cuban leaders who were kind of loyal and friendly to my family. And he was at a hotel room in Washington, DC, with Haynes Johnson, the journalist who had written a book on the Bay of Pigs. And my father got them on a telephone and asked them whether your people had done this.

Stone: On November 29th, which is only a few days after this, about a week later, he has a meeting with William Walton. A long-term friend of the family before his cultural mission to Moscow. And he asks William Walton to talk to Georgi Bolshakov.

Kennedy: Yes, and to convey to Khrushchev. He had a meeting with Bill Walton. And he asked Walton to convey a message through Georgi Bolshakov to Khrushchev saying that our family knew that the Soviets, the Russians, were not involved in the assassination. That it was a right-wing plot from our country.

He knew how to investigate not only the Mafia, the underworld, but also federal agencies. The day his brother died he lost virtually all the investigative capacity at the Justice Department. Half of them were FBI employees who ostensibly worked for him. In reality, they worked for J. Edgar Hoover. He considered it an affront to his dignity, to his authority, that my father did not allow him to communicate with his brother.

After Jack was killed, he had a direct relationship with Johnson. That was a long-term relationship. And that was mutually beneficial, because he was also spying on my father. During the 1968 campaign….the FBI offered to protect him and he declined that offer because he knew Hoover would just be spying on him.

Stone: Do you think there's a relationship between the assassination of your father and your uncle?

Kennedy: It's very clear from the autopsy reports and the police reports that Sirhan could not have killed my father. The four shots that killed my father all came from behind. According to Thomas Noguchi's autopsy report, they were all contact shots. There's seventy-seven witnesses to Sirhan's shooting and they say he never got within three feet of my father and he was always in front of him. So you know, it's unclear. There are suspects. There was a security guard, Thane Eugene Cesar, who was holding my father, was in the position to shoot him who has a strange background. Who lied repeatedly and who had his gun drawn. So we don't know what happened.

Edwin Lee McGehee

Edwin Lee McGehee is perhaps the last surviving witness to the famous Clinton/Jackson incident. This was the sighting of Oswald 110 miles northeast of New Orleans in East Feliciana Parish. Oswald was first seen by local barber McGehee in Jackson.

(Editor's Note: In this interview we first visited the retired McGehee at his home. He then took us to the location of his barbershop which has been completely renovated, outside and inside. We then journeyed to the home of deceased state representative Reeves Morgan. And we came back to the site of the old Clinton voter registration office, which has also been renovated. We traced the trail that Oswald took in the area prior to handing in an application for a job at East Louisiana State Hospital in Jackson. This very important episode is treated by several authors. [A concise, incisive version is by William Davy in Let Justice Be Done, *pp. 101–18.])*

We begin at the site of his old barbershop.

Jim DiEugenio: So your old barbershop has now been renovated.

Edwin McGehee: Yeah, you can't even tell that it was there.

DiEugenio: Ed, describe how you met Oswald that day in the summer of 1963.

McGehee: Well, 1963, last of August or early September, I had a barbershop in Jackson, Louisiana right here. That was the entrance right there. And one lazy afternoon, very slow, this young man walked into the shop and he said, "A barber shop's a good place for a haircut and information." I said yes it is. Have a seat. He sits down. And he said, "I'm looking for a job." I said, "Well, it's mighty slim pickings, the only place we got is East Louisiana State Hospital. I said, you know that's a mental institution." And he jumped. And he said, "Oh, do they have all kind of jobs, like an electrician?" "Yes" I said, "But you need help getting on." I said, "If you don't have anybody you need help getting on. It's all political." And then I told him how to get to Reeves Morgan's house, our state representative. I said, "He can probably help you." And out the door he went. It's the last I saw of him.

And, then I didn't, until the assassination, and they showed his picture and I told my wife. We were eating lunch at my mother-in-law's, and I said my goodness, I know that fella from somewhere.

(This part of the interview was done in front of Morgan's house.)

DiEugenio: Ed, after you directed Oswald to go to Reeves Morgan's house, that is actually what he did, right?

McGehee: Right. He went straight out here to Reeves Morgan's house, which is not easy to find. And I told him how to get there and then when he got out there on 952 to ask somebody to tell you where the house is, and undoubtedly they did. Because he came here. And Mary and Reeves and Van, his son and daughter, both saw him drive up in the car and get out.

DiEugenio: Now Reeves then directed him to do something the next day?

McGehee: Later on I talked to Reeves and he said he directed him to go to Clinton, to the registered voters office to become a registered voter.

DiEugenio: And was Clinton the county seat?

McGehee: Clinton, Louisiana, the county seat. Undoubtedly he went.

DiEugenio: And that's how Oswald ends up in the voter registration—

McGehee: Right. That's how he was standing in line with the rest of 'em. Long line.

(This part of the interview was done during the drive back to Clinton and then in front of the old Registrar of Voters office, which has also been renovated.)

McGehee: We're going to Clinton.

DiEugenio: We're following Oswald step by step.

McGehee: This would have been the way he come when we left Jackson. He would have come on this road right here and turn on Dawson Road and went to Reeves's house.
(In front of the old courthouse)

McGehee: The judge's chamber was upstairs. That's where they held court upstairs. And then the clerk of court has since moved over to where, next to where the registry of voters were on Main Street. It was, at the time, it was a bank.

DiEugenio: So, Ed, Francis Fruge was an investigator for Jim Garrison.

McGehee: He was a state trooper. He was on loan from John McKeithen, the governor.

DiEugenio: And so what happened when he came to visit you as an investigator for Jim Garrison?

McGehee: Oh, he'd ask all kinds of questions. Just, just, he just kept on digging, digging and asking and wanting to know new leads or some, who, where, who lived where and who did this or who said that. I would assume the Clinton and Jackson area. That's where he stayed every day, every day in my barbershop, I saw him every day.

DiEugenio: Did he keep a diary of his investigation?

McGehee: Yeah, he kept a diary. Every day he would write in his little diary, he'd pull it out and he'd start writing. When Joe West come by and doing his investigation and he asked about Fruge and we looked up his address, and we found it over around Opelousas somewhere all within that area. And Joe West went over there and knocked on the door. His wife come to the door and he introduced himself. She said come on in. And he said, had Fruge kept a diary? She said oh yeah, he kept a diary. And she said it's in his desk back there. So, she went back there to get it and he said can I see it? She said oh yeah. Went back there, pulled the drawer open, and it's gone. They couldn't find it nowhere. It's the same way, it was the same way with me with Corrie Collins. We registered him to vote in August 1963. That was his birthday. He was twenty-one and he was the head of CORE (Congress of Racial Equality) in Clinton. And it showed his birthday and we, we had his file there right in front of us. And I think I went to show it to Fruge, or somebody showed it to somebody, I can't remember who asked about it, and we couldn't, we couldn't find it. It was gone. I said can you believe this?

DiEugenio: Tell us about your meeting with DA Harry Connick, who succeeded Jim Garrison.

McGehee: The registrars of voters had, we have a convention every year somewhere in the state. In 1982 or '83, which one it was, I'd have to look it up, we went to Slidell, Louisiana, and I was talking to Robert Faucheux, the registrar from Ascension Parish. And he was saying, boy, I've never seen this many politicians in one place in all my life. I said well we got them. And he said there is Connick, DA from New Orleans. And I, me, I go over there and shake hands with Connick. So I ask him then I said, how is Jim Garrison. Have you seen him lately? And he said just who are you? I said I'm Edwin Lee McGehee, the registrar from East Louisiana Parish. I was the first witness called in the Clay Shaw trial. And when I said that he started shaking and he was visibly upset. And he said I didn't know that, I didn't know it. And out the door he went. He left. Thought that was strange.

(Editor's Note: Although Henry Palmer was legally the registrar at the time of Oswald's appearance, McGehee had been the registrar prior and would be later. He had a status of registrar emeritus for years on end.)

DiEugenio: And Shaw and Ferrie were seen there, across the street in their car in the black Cadillac. There was even a picture taken.

McGehee: I guess Shaw and Ferrie, they were wondering what the heck was going on.

DiEugenio: How soon after the assassination did you go ahead and talk to Reeves Morgan about seeing Oswald?

McGehee: I think it was a couple of days right after. When they showed his picture on there. Reeves come in the shop. And he said you know that fella? I said Reeves, I said that's the fella I sent out to your house. That's the only fella I ever sent out to your house to see about a job. Reeves thought he was a nice fellow too. You know, he said you know he was above average. And he was, he was nice. But he kept when he was getting his haircut he kept saying things like you have change for a five? [A] haircut back then was a dollar. He said do you have change for a five?

DiEugenio: So very soon after the assassination it got to be kind of common street knowledge that Oswald had been up here.

McGehee: Like you said, when my customers would come get a haircut we talked about it and just like the congressman, I think he was a judge at the time.

(Editor's Note: McGehee is likely talking about John Rarick, who was a judge in 1961 and then a congressman in 1966.)

We, I started to tell him what happened to me and Reeves and then and that, that's when John Wright put it in *The Councilor* and that's when Garrison picked it up, or the House Un-American Committee activity. I can't think of that fellow's name down in Baton Rouge. He picked it up and they gave it to Garrison.

But it was, what amazed me about the whole thing was Reeves told the FBI. He called them and told them that Oswald was up here and they said we are well aware that he is, he was in the area. And so I said, when Reeves and I were talking in the shop, and I say well no need of me saying anything if you told them Reeves. And they never showed up. I thought that was strange.

DiEugenio: Do you recall the first person to get in contact with you from Garrison's office?

McGehee: Probably Sciambra.

DiEugenio: Andrew Sciambra?

McGehee: Yeah. Sciambra. He come with a stenographer.

DiEugenio: So he took your deposition?

McGehee: Right. I always thought this part about the whole thing, if they were thinking that that there was no hanky-panky going on with the assassination, why did they block Garrison so much? I mean when we went up there the day of the, when we went to trial, we went in his office, all of us from Clinton and Jackson. And he said I want to thank you all for your civic duty. He said so many people refused to honor their subpoena. They even left the state and he said I appreciate y'all. And that was, that was it. That's all, that's all it, of course the only time I saw Garrison.

DiEugenio: After you testified for Jim Garrison at the Clay Shaw trial, can you describe the experience you had when you got back home?

McGehee: When I got back home from the trial in New Orleans, it was either that night or the next night, I got a call from the police station in town and he said would you come down here to see if you can identify this guy? I said OK. I went down there and I said what guy you talking about? Said we've got him locked up back there. So I went back there and he grabbed a hold of the bars and he was shaking 'em and he said are you the bagman? Are you the bagman? And I said no, I'm not the bagman. I didn't even know what a bagman was. So I walked back in and I sat back over the corner. About that time a car drives up, door opens up, young man comes in. He said, 'Is my buddy in here?' He said, "Well, if he's the one selling magazines he's locked up back there. We got him.' He said, 'What is his bond?' He says 'Seventy-five dollars.' He said, 'Well, can I make a phone call?' Said yeah. I can't remember how he, whether he dialed collect or what. I can't remember that. I remember saying International Trade Mart building, International Trade Mart. And that guy when, he told him what he wanted, he blasted him out. He, woo, he was screaming and hollering. 'Don't ever call here again! Don't you ever call here again!' That was it.

DiEugenio: So in other words this is supposed to be a prowler who was selling magazines?

McGehee: Right. Right. It was supposed to been. It was, it was illegal to sell magazines door-to-door in Jackson. We had an ordinance.

Debra Conway

Conway is the owner of JFK Lancer Productions and Publications. She has held conferences on the Kennedy assassination for decades and edited and published many books on the subject.

Oliver Stone: How did you know the late John Hunt?

Debra Conway: I met John Hunt at a conference in Washington, DC, many years ago and I realized what type of researcher he was. He was almost, I would call him the mad scientist because he never stopped. There were layers and layers that he would delve into and he wasn't satisfied unless he could get down to that bottom layer.

Stone: Yeah, and what did he do for you? And who are you, by the way?

Conway: Oh, well, I own a company called JFK Lancer and I named it that because the JFK Act had been passed and we were getting materials that we would have never gotten. When the JFK Act was passed is when JFK Lancer came into being as a distributor of information for anyone that needed it. I attended all of the meetings of the JFK Review Board.

Stone: You did? I see, you worked with them?

Conway: Yes. And we began our conferences in 1996 and we called on what we felt were document-oriented speakers that would talk about what we were finding, and then we would release that information to the public.

Stone: So John Hunt came to your attention about what year?

Conway: Well, I would say the early 2000s and then he spoke at our conference in 2006 and 2008 and presented material based on his studies of the Warren Commission that were outstanding. John Hunt proved to be a tenacious investigator in the Warren Report, Warren volumes, the Dallas police files, the FBI files and he practically moved into the National Archives in Washington DC. They allowed him to set up a desk with a computer and his own scanner. And he was able to scan photographs, documents, statements, and so on. And I think he was very unique in that he went there every day. But he was meticulous and the exciting thing about his work is that he stepped out of the way and he presents the evidence. He did not take on a persona of "this is something that I found and you didn't" or. . .

Stone: Right, there was no egotism.

Conway: And he also did something different. He didn't interview policemen and FBI people and he wasn't swayed by their excuses. He went straight to "this is what you told and you signed your name. This was your statement and you signed your name." And so the materials that he was able to get at the archives, back then, right after these materials were released was very exciting.

Stone: You're talking about the Records Review Board.

Conway: Yes, very exciting.

Stone: Well, it was about eight years after, I guess, but at least he got in.

Conway: Yes. And there were other people, I'm not going to say he was the only person you know. I'm saying this to you, John Newman and people like that they had their areas, but he chose to work the crime scene. That was something that he wanted to do.

Stone: Right, so he got some information about 399, the bullet. Can you tell us about how and who?

Conway: Well, he looked into any paperwork that he could find as far as examinations, official examinations either from the Dallas police or the FBI. And he found one paper in particular about the bullet that had, of course, the photos of the people that had signed, they had etched their initials into the bullet showing that they had reviewed it. And then they gave testimony to the Warren Commission and to the FBI and I'm sure the Dallas police. And there was one person in particular that said that he had seen the bullet, and it was the bullet, and that he had initialed it as well, but his initials are not on the bullet.

Stone: To the Warren Commission?

Conway: Yes.

Stone: And the name of that person was?

Conway: Elmer Todd.

Stone: Yes. And John Hunt found that out?

Conway: Yes. And what he did was he took the slides, the photos of the actual bullet in a better level than what we saw in exhibits of the Warren Commission volumes. So you can read the initials. And you know and he would make a joke and say that there is a little notch in the tip of the bullet where they took material for examination and his initials would have had to have been the tiniest ever etched onto a bullet because they're not there.

Stone: So there were other initials on there?

Conway: Yes, there were.

Stone: But nothing that says Elmer Lee Todd?

Conway: No sir.

Stone: OK, so because the initials are not on there, it's fair to say the FBI misrepresented this fact. And what else did John discover about the 399?

Conway: One of the most important things that John found was falsification of the time line of where they had the evidence and when they examined the evidence. Robert Frazier was the expert on the evidence and they had to turn everything over to him. And so Todd gave a different time, that was not possible that he would have turned the bullet over to Mr. Frazier.

Stone: What time was that?

Conway: In Frazier's notes, he writes that he received the bullet at 7:30 when actually Mr. Todd did not get the bullet himself to send to Mr. Frazier and till after 8:00 p.m. Discrepancy there. Yes. So what bullet did Mr. Frazier get that he has in his report? Because he certainly did not get it at 7:30.

Stone: Let's repeat this—Frazier receives a bullet at 7:30. Todd gives a bullet at 8:50. Frazier receives a bullet at 7:30, an hour and twenty minutes earlier? This is bizarre. And John Hunt found this out?

Conway: Yes, in John's work, he found that Mr. Todd has the bullet until 8:50. And that's when he has in his record that he sent it to the FBI. So Mr. Frazier writes in his notes that he got the bullet at 7:30 and began his examination.

Stone: Wow. Was Hunt surprised by this?

Conway: Yes I would say that John was very excited to see this, because it gave a record of the times that this bullet—this all-important bullet—was supposed to have been . . . You would think that they would have handled it, you know, like it would been gold going to the bank, and they let, you know . . . There it is in the record that someone is lying about when they got the bullet.

Stone: It's accurate then to say that neither the Warren Commission nor the House Select Committee did this kind of analysis.

Conway: I don't believe that there were any government agencies that went into the detail that John was able to do.

Stone: Chain of custody is a very important fact in any crime.

Conway: Yes, I feel like there was no chain of custody after looking at what John was able to find in the records.

Stone: What was Tom Alyea's occupation in 1963?

Conway: Tom Alyea was a reporter in 1963 and one that was in Dallas.

Stone: And what did he do?

Conway: Well, he interviewed people, and he also was a photographer.

Stone: He was the first reporter to get the sixth floor, correct?

Conway: Yes.

Stone: And what did he see there?

Conway: Well, he was shown the evidence that was collected on the sixth floor. Tom Alyea was the first reporter that made it up to the sixth floor. Now, surprisingly there was no one that stopped him from going up on the sixth floor and he's there with policemen and detectives there that were looking for evidence because they believed that that's where the shot came from and one of the things that they had been was they found the shells that were ejected from the rifle and they found what looked like someone's lunch.

Stone: OK, the shells were in what position?

Conway: Well, the shells looked as though they were placed in some type of pattern on the floor. They did not look like they had been ejected from a rifle. They were very close together.

Stone: They were side by side?

Conway: Pretty much yes, side by side. Well, he didn't question it at the time. And photos were taken and it wasn't until much later that people started questioning, you know, I've shot a rifle and I couldn't even find my shells. And so when Tom looked into that and saw the photos of. . . the first person that took those photos, you know, what shells was he seeing and who lined them up.

Stone: It became important later, obviously.

Conway: It became important because it looked like the scene was staged.

Stone: So he never suspected anything. He followed the Warren Commission?

Conway: I would say that he was a friend to the Dallas Police because he worked as a photographer on many crime scenes and he probably knew most of these officers that were there.

Dr. Donald Miller

Donald Miller is a professor emeritus at the University of Washington at Seattle. He worked there in the Division of Cardiothoracic Surgery for almost forty years.

Oliver Stone: Let's start with how you knew Malcolm Perry.

Don Miller: When I finished my training in New York, I went to work in Seattle. And Dr. Tom Shires had left Dallas, he'd been chief of surgery at Parkland and he brought an entourage with him which included Dr. Malcolm Perry, Dr. Jim Carrico, and two other surgeons. And in 1975, Dr. Shires hired me on the faculty at the University of Washington in the cardiac surgery division. Malcolm had come with Dr. Shires in 1974 and we developed a professional relationship, and we would operate together on complex cases which were thoracic abdominal aortic aneurysms, where I would remove the chest part of the aneurysm and he removed the abdominal part. And with that connection, we got to be friends, his office was just a couple doors down from mine. So I got to know Malcolm when I joined the faculty. Dr. Shires left and went to Cornell shortly after he hired me in 1975. Malcolm stayed until 1978 and then he joined Dr. Shires in New York. So for several years we operated together and I was particularly interested in Dr. Perry's position with the JFK assassination because he did the tracheotomy on him after he was shot. And I knew as a student of the assassination, beginning in 1967 when the first books came out, that at a news conference Dr. Perry had announced to the world that there was a bullet wound in the neck at necktie level that was a wound of entrance. But in front of the Warren Commission he testified that the wound was consistent with an exit wound. So I was particularly interested now that I had Dr. Perry right there in the same hospital with me—which was the truth? The problem is that Malcolm categorically refused to ever discuss the assassination and he wouldn't answer my questions about that neck wound.

Stone: Well, you were friends with him at this point? You'd have dinner together?

Miller: Yeah. We had operated together for a year or so, and we'd become friends, but he still would categorically say, "I don't want to talk about the assassination." And then one night after we had operated together for many hours on a complex case, we were sitting in the surgeons' lounge alone drinking coffee, and I once again asked him about that neck wound. And this time he said it was an entrance wound, unquestionably an entrance wound. I took that admission as given in confidence. So it was sort of tacitly in confidence, and then when he testified in front of the House Select Committee on Assassinations a year later, he once again said that it was consistent with an exit wound which of course was required if the single-bullet theory would hold water. And then when I read that publicly, once again, in front of the House Select Committee on Assassinations, he agreed that it was an exit wound. I realized that I would keep this in confidence.

Stone: He said it was an exit wound to the House Select Committee?

Miller: Yes.

Stone: He said that.

Miller: Dr. Perry told me it was an entrance wound, and as he put it, unquestionably an entrance wound.

Stone: He told you that at that cafeteria?

Miller: At the surgeons' lounge after we'd done the surgery together. But a year later in front of the House Select Committee on Assassinations, he once again reverted publicly like he did with the Warren Commission and said it was an exit wound. So I didn't say anything about what Malcolm had told me until after he died. He died in 2009.

Stone: Did Dr. Perry ever say he saw the film [*JFK*] in 1991?

Miller: No, I never saw Dr. Perry after 1978 when he moved to New York and then back to Texas. I would have loved to know what he said, but I had no contact with him.

Stone: So he told you this on what date, what year was it?

Miller: 1977.

Stone: That's when he told it to you.

Miller: Yes.

Stone: Was he bothered? Did you see any signals of his attitude about this, his talking to the Warren Commission as he did?

Miller: No. He had an attitude, if you would ask him about all of that he would get exasperated and not want to talk about it. But I did learn in researching it, that the main reason he changed his testimony and publicly agreed it was an exit wound is a Secret Service agent put the pressure on him, and that person was Elmer Moore. It turns out that in 1970, Elmer Moore was the head of the Secret Service office in Seattle, and a graduate student named Jim Gochenaur became friends with him. Jim Gochenaur disappeared for a while but he turns out he's still alive in his seventies living in Milwaukee. And last year, together, we presented a paper at the CAPA meeting in Dallas where he talked about his experience with Elmer Moore.

Stone: You also knew George Burkley, Kennedy's attending physician. Can you tell us how you knew him?

Miller : When I was a teenager, Dr. Burkley and his family of four children and my father and our family of four children shared a duplex, lived together at the Newport Naval Hospital in Newport, Rhode Island where Dr. Burkley MD, was chief of medicine and my father Donald Miller Senior was chief of surgery. And we spent a couple of years together in this duplex, which is still there. I looked on Google Earth and it is still on that compound. And he had a son, George, who was my age, sixteen, and we became buddies and, in fact, one time we sailed his sixteen-foot sailboat up Narragansett Bay and camped out on a small uninhabited island. I lost touch with George after we moved away from Newport, but I looked him up again in 2012, and it turns out he's a retired Marine Corps pilot living in Hawaii. I asked him about his dad and what his dad had told him and his siblings about his role in the Kennedy case. It was interesting. He said [his] Dad was a close hold on his professional life and he wouldn't talk about the assassination. That the only thing that he would say was that he couldn't understand why the Warren Commission never asked him to testify as Kennedy's personal physician.

So I've studied this and read all the relevant research on it, and it turns out the reason he didn't say anything to his children was that he didn't want them to know that he was intimately involved in the cover-up. Dr. Burkley knew perfectly well why he wasn't asked to testify before the Warren Commission, because it would have invalidated, he would have invalidated, the single-bullet theory, because the death certificate which Admiral Burkley filled out showed the bullet wound in the back to be five and a half to six inches below the neck. So in order for that bullet to have come out Kennedy's neck and wounded Governor Connally, shot from the sixth floor behind him, it would have had to turn upward into an acute angle to come out his neck and then turned down to go through Connally. And so basically Dr. Burkley's death certificate makes the single-bullet theory bogus, and the way the Warren Commission dealt with it was they didn't publish the death certificate. They had twenty-six volumes of eighteen thousand pages and they had exhibits like… the one exhibit that I liked the most was Commission Exhibit 53 which had a fragment of Tchaikovsky's opera *The Queen of Spades*. And so there was no death certificate in all these volumes.

And the other thing that the Warren Commission did with regard to Burkley. Dr. Burkley was the only physician who was in the motorcade at Parkland, on Air Force One, and at the autopsy. And the face sheet for the autopsy—where it shows the front and back silhouette of the body where you marked scars and bullet wounds and things—the face sheet showed the bullet wound in the back at the level of thoracic vertebra T3 which is five and a half to six inches below, exactly where Dr. Burkley had it in the death certificate. So that was a problem for the Warren Commission. And the way they handled that was, the face sheet, Dr. Burkley had signed his name and written "verified" on it. But Dr. Burkley's signature and his writing "verified" has been erased. So that way the only person they had to question about it was Commander Boswell. And he said that he made a mistake. The bullet wound was much higher, to lend credence to the single-bullet theory. And they didn't have to question Admiral Burkley about it, because his signature had been erased along with his "verified."

Now I remember Dr. Burkley when I was a teenager when we were living next to each other. He was a pleasant man, a straight-arrow naval officer like my father. And it's evident that he felt guilty about his participation in this cover-up.

And there will be times after the assassination where he would contact an assassination researcher and say he had his lawyer get ahold of Richard Sprague with the House Select Committee on Assassinations to say that there was a conspiracy. But then when Sprague was fired and the cover-up proceeded with the HSCA, Burkley clammed up. And then he talked to another assassination researcher in the early '80s, saying that it was conspiracy but he wouldn't elaborate. He told another one that there was an exit wound and the back of the head was blown out. But when questioned further he wouldn't say anything.

Douglas Horne in his book *Inside the Assassination Records Review Board* makes very clear that Dr. Burkley was quite conflicted and guilty about the cover-up he participated in, and there will be times where he would want to come clean. But then he would back off, fearing for his reputation and the effect on his family. And so it made sense in going through this, that his son, that I caught up with fifty years later, said his dad wouldn't talk about it and couldn't understand why the Warren Commission didn't ask him to testify, when he of course understood perfectly well. And he went along with the cover-up until he died I think in 1991 at the age of eighty-eight.

Dr. Randy Robertson

Randy Robertson is a radiologist from Tennessee who has testified before congress on the JFK case. He is a member of the board of directors of the Assassination Archives and Research Center in Washington.

Randy Robertson: I'm Dr. Randolph Robertson, a diagnostic radiologist who's been interested in the case for about twenty-seven years, about the time the movie *JFK* came out. I originally started investigating before I saw the movie because of all the bad press. I thought I'd look into the thing before I actually saw the movie itself. As a physician I was immediately drawn to the medical aspects of the case and I was lucky enough to gain permission to look at the original autopsy materials held in National Archives. I've done so several times, most recently in 2015, I believe. It was my final time that I really needed to go in and check things over again.

Oliver Stone: Is it tough to get in there?

Robertson: It's fairly tough. Yeah, the deed of gift by the Kennedy family states that you have to have a historical significant thing to go over and you have to have qualifications such as a professor, doctor, some, you know, qualifications which will allow you to assess the material.

Stone: Not anybody can walk into the National Archives.

Robertson: No, it's a very small group of people have been allowed that.

Stone: You went to the archives, about what year was that?

Robertson: I think it was sometime around 1992.

Stone: Right after the film?

Robertson: Yeah. And at that point I had already formulated my idea about the president being shot twice in the head from two different directions based upon the Zapruder film and the X-rays. And I'd attempted to get it published in the medical literature. I actually presented this to the *Journal of Forensic Sciences*, I think it was 1998. They said they could find nothing wrong with my work, but they refused to publish it. Because it wasn't going to change the minds of the people who had made errors in the past.

Stone: When did you see the X-rays, by the way?

Robertson: Initially I looked at the ones had been provided to the public via the HSCA investigation. But the first time I actually saw the X-rays themselves was in the old National Archives in DC, not at College Park. I've viewed them several times at College Park.

Stone: Two directions. OK, keep going.

Robertson: And since then you know I've been involved with different conferences and things like that. And pertinent to what we're talking about today, during the course of my investigations, which I specifically do the medical evidence and Dealey Plaza—I'm not into who did it, why, and all that. That's beyond my capabilities and I realize that. And I put it together and in the course of this—on a Google search… and up pops this article from this obscure, the Office of Medical History in the Bureau of Medicine and Surgery Department of the Navy. And here was James Young's handwritten contemporaneous account of the past 24–30 hours—

It was James Young who wrote that contemporaneously and he still had the piece of paper, as well as some other important documents. And I was astounded, because I'd only heard of him peripherally in *The Death of a President*, one sentence. There is a document where he was present when a piece of skull was brought to Burkley on the 27th of November of '63. And Dr. Boswell said that . . . No, excuse me, Dr. Ebersole the radiologist present that night said it was Dr. Young who invited him to the White House to draw pencil lines on the skull X-rays. As it turns out those were trajectory lines which all the radiologists have failed to recognize as such.

Stone: OK. So let's get to Young then. Can you repeat what you said about Young? He had actually for how many hours you said he took. . .

Robertson: Well, they did, I think, eight sessions—late December 2001, early January 2002, about an hour and a half each session. They covered quite a bit, not all of it which was related to the autopsy. It was quite a wide-ranging interview. But the most spectacular thing that I saw was his mention of this bullet—not only here, he kept himself under the radar. In fact, he was the physician who ordered Chiefs Mills and Martinell, their assistants, to go to the White House and retrieve what they knew were skull fragments in the limousine at that time. Under orders, they retrieve those and they brought back an additional envelope with the bullet with a bent tip, which was totally unexpected to him. And since he was their commanding officer, they brought it immediately to him. So he was the first one at the autopsy to see these materials recovered from the limousine.

Stone: You say he found this bullet. Can you describe what he found?

Robertson: Yeah. He described a bullet, brass-colored with a bent tip, he described as five millimeters in diameter.

Stone: What were the circumstances? How come he's. . .

Robertson: Oh, what brought him to the autopsy was that he had been in the White House that day, he'd actually been in the room, Jerry Behn's office when the open line to Parkland was going on. But later that day he thought he would go out to Bethesda to relieve Dr. Burkley who was sixty-something-years-old at the time. He felt that he might be getting tired during the course of the events of that day. And at that time both Mills and Martinell showed up as well. And subsequently dispatched them to the limousine to retrieve—

Stone: The limousine was in Washington?

Robertson: Yeah, at that time it had come back and it was in the White House garage.

Stone: So Mills and Martinell went to the limousine?

Robertson: Yeah. Mills and Martinell went to the limousine, gathered the materials up—there were three skull fragments which were recovered and this bullet with a bent tip.

Stone: Which no one had seen?

Robertson: At that point, no, because it was the first time that the limousine had been, you know, closely examined.

Stone: Where was the bullet?

Robertson: They said it was in the back seat. They didn't, weren't, real specific.

Stone: In the back seat but not on the ground or in. . .

Robertson: Well it was on the floor of the limousine in the back.

Stone: Relatively undamaged?

Robertson: Except for the bent tip, yeah it was intact.

And the whole thing about this, is that the bullet itself is important, but what's more important is when it struck and where it came from. And previously at 313, when the bullet went forward through JFK's head, a small fragment had cracked the windshield from the inner surface. Later the final shot, was at 328 was when it struck, both times there were flares of reflected light as the glass was deformed from the impacts of one of a fragment and two of a whole bullet and these two events occurred in point nine seconds. So therefore they could not have been shot from the same rifle.

Stone: So what's the most extreme thing that Young said in the interview?

Robertson: The most extreme thing, I think, is just that he had found the bullet. And I think it was his honesty, really, because he had definitely kept himself off the radar, you know. And I think that's fortunate he did because—

Stone: His naivete you mean?

Robertson: Well, I don't know if it's his naivete but I think he just didn't want to get involved with it. But, if you'll remember, when Dr. Burkley approached the HSCA saying that he had knowledge of the president being struck by more than two shooters, they took care of that. You know, instead he comes out with an affidavit afterwards—none of which related to his knowledge of conspiracy.

Stone: And didn't Burkley contact him or anything?

Robertson: No, they actually had . . . there was some tension between them, because Burkley. I guess I can say it now, seen from Young's observations to be somewhat of an incompetent physician.

Stone: Really?

Robertson: Yeah.

Stone: First I've heard of that.

Robertson: Yeah. And he couldn't pass his boards. He was not board certified, whereas Young, at thirty-four years of age, had passed his boards on the first try. And so there was a tension between them, because Burkley's attitude was he just wanted to take care of the president and his close family. Anybody else who showed up, he'd say take two aspirin go to your own doctor. And Dr. Young on the other hand was very conscientious, and he would help out anybody who showed up, because he figured if I'm helping someone at the White House, it's for the whole effort, so everybody will be healthy and can work well. And he said Burkley was getting paranoid because more people were seeking Young out and he thought that maybe Young was trying to position maybe to take his spot away, you know his position to the president.

The most spectacular thing was just his, one his presence, because you know I had no idea prior to this, after reading much, much material in the medical evidence that Young was ever at the autopsy. And second, for him to see a bullet, which at that time, I knew already that a bullet had struck the windshield frame and it was just a matter of at that time determining what happened to it. I initially thought that it had bounced off and gone forward and gone in the dirt somewhere near that manhole cover. But when I saw him say, "Oh yeah, we found this bullet with a bent tip in the back of the limousine," that was, "Aha!" This is where it makes more sense. And Young was a completely believable individual.

In fact if I could give you a quick bio about Dr. Young, he's a fascinating person. He was born in poverty in Massillon, Ohio. He went to high school, was a star football player under the tutelage of Paul Brown, founder of the Cleveland Browns. He then went on to Duke, starred in football there, was offered a contract with the LA Rams to play football, he was so good. He turned it down to pursue medicine.

Well he had given many talks during his life, mainly as his role as a White House physician. But I think, either, I don't know what the impetus was, but he started thinking about this bullet. He initially contacted Professor Robert Gilbert at Northeastern who he told the story about the bullet finally, confided to him. He may have confided in others, maybe his family, immediate family, I don't know. And Gilbert encouraged him to write Ford and in his interviews with the Navy, he claimed that he had written Ford. So I called—

Stone: Which Ford?

Robertson: Gerald R. Ford. Gerald Ford at that time was the last living member of the Warren Commission. That's why he went straight to him. Ford gave him a really quick response saying he had been conscientious in attending the Warren Commission hearings.

Stone: What year is this when he tried to reach Ford?

Robertson: It was on December 27, 2000 that he wrote his letter to Ford.

Stone: Thirty-six years later?

Robertson: I don't know what the impetus was. It may have been. I'm conjecturing possibly, I think. When did the ARRB stop? Was that 1998?

Yes. OK. So it may have been some news about the ARRB and its machinations have kind of aroused his or rearoused his questions, because he had said it bothered him over the years about this bullet that he knew he had seen. In fact, he called up Tom Mills during the course of these interviews with the Navy and said Tom you know—no he didn't do that. It was actually Jan Herman who called Mills up, because Young had contacted Mills during the course of investigation prior to going to the Navy for the interview. And Mills says, "Yeah I remember it. I remember bringing that bullet." And then when he made that claim in the interviews Jan Herman called up Mills and Mills says, "Hey do you remember Dr. Young calling you asking you about this bent bullet?" He says, "Yeah I remember that, him calling me." He remembered it. He says, "Can you shed any light on it?" And he says, "I would rather not talk about that." You know, if I had found this years earlier, I could have interviewed Young and the questions I would have asked would have been much more pointed and different than the ones—

Stone: When did he die?

Robertson: Two thousand eight. And I would have asked a complete a different series of questions, but luckily he brought this subject up about the bullet.

Stone: He goes to Ford in 2001 after the ARRB is closed down.

Robertson: Right. And the ARRB never found him. I'm surprised.

Stone: How did Ford react?

Robertson: Well, Ford just wrote him a short letter saying he was conscientious about attending the hearings, he had never heard of this bullet, and he referred him to two books: *November 22, 1963: You Are the Jury* by David Belin and *Case Closed* by Gerald Posner. And so I think he was unsatisfied with Ford's reaction which is why he followed up with Arlen Specter. He called Arlen Specter up in August of 2001, I believe, and discussed with him.

Stone: What year did you find the Young interview?

Robertson: 2017 is when I initially—This has been hidden for, as I said, he ran under the radar, and he gave the interview in 2001.

Stone: So sixteen years later.

Robertson: And that's the other thing about this is that it was published in November of 2013.

Stone: So it was not published until then?

Robertson: Right. It wasn't because they had to wait—they waited till he died to publish it. I think that's because he hadn't signed the release. Whether that was right or not, I'll let the lawyers decide. But the thing is though, that as of 2017, in this article that had been on the blog since 2013, there had only been one hundred views. Only one hundred people had seen that article.

Stone: And the hundred views, did they understand?

Robertson: Nobody knew what was going on. And even the interviewers, they were unaware of the significance of what this extra bullet.

Stone: The significance of this extra bullet means that there were two shooters.

Robertson: Right. Without a doubt, because you've got two flashes of light, OK? You've got Zapruder reacting to each one of these shots in a predictable manner. Based upon his distance from each shot because they're less than a second apart. And that means two shooters and that means conspiracy.

Stone: Let's go again on that. This new bullet that James Young found proves beyond a doubt that there had to be two shooters?

Robertson: Oh certainly, yeah. Because it wasn't the shot that missed—the supposed shot that missed and hit Tague.

Stone: Right.

Robertson: It wasn't CE 399 and it wasn't the one that fragmented in Kennedy's head because this was an intact bullet with a bent tip. It had only been seen by . . . And this is the incredible part of this story, is that it went from Mills and Martinell to Young to Humes, it disappears. That evening there may have been as little as four people who saw that bullet before it disappeared. And the reason why it's important, which is why I make the point about the Zapruder film, is that this just isn't some guy making up a story because I know the exact frame in which that bullet impacted and why it should have been found in the limo as it was.

Stone: And Mills and Martinell passed?

Robertson: Martinell died many years ago. As of 2017, Mills was still alive. He was in his eighties. In fact, no, it gets better, it gets better because guess what? Mills followed LBJ down to the ranch and LBJ kept him as an employee on his ranch for many years until he retired or until LBJ died.

This is somewhat conjecture, but I think it's pretty interesting. Dr. Burkley, shortly after the assassination, wanted to retire. And so LBJ said, "Hey, I'll make you a three-star admiral." And then Burkley said, "Well, you know, do I have to stick around to get that upgrade pay for my retirement?" And that's on the web—the G.A.O. had to make a special determination and they said "no." Burkley had to work at least two more years as a three-star admiral before he could get his higher retirement pay. As it turned out, by LBJ giving him this three-star admiral, he was higher ranked than the surgeon general. I think LBJ knew the people to keep around him and Burkley was one. Mills was another.

Stone: Now I just want to clarify, because Young made a mistake I gather on the tape where he's referring to the Queen Mary limousine, he found the bullet in the Queen Mary. Can you explain that mistake?

Robertson: Yeah. During his interview he repeatedly misstated that it was the Queen Mary that had been inspected rather than the SX 100X, the presidential limousine. I've been told by some people that it was interchangeable, between the backup car and the presidential limo. But Young's misstatement about the Queen Mary should in no way make people think that it wasn't the present presidential limousine that was examined that evening, from which skull fragments and the extra bullet were found. They were all found in the presidential limousine despite Young's misstatements.

Stone: OK. The only other thing I have is . . . This is probably gonna be a little bit . . . Try to explain it to us who for the people who don't understand this: How did you find out about the neuromuscular reaction that's supposed to explain Kennedy's back and to the left movement? What do you think about the neuromuscular reaction?

Robertson: Well, I don't think much of it because it's never been reported in the medical literature. It was just something made up.

Stone: Well how do you mean? We're talking about frame 313 here?

Robertson: Right. Yeah, exactly. And they said, the HSCA forensic pathology panel put forward two guesstimates as to what happened. One was the reverse jet effect and two was a neuromuscular—every movement of the body is a neuromuscular reaction unless that's acted upon by an outside force. And their conclusion was that somehow this bullet traversing his brain caused a downward rush of stimuli to his body to contract muscles. The only problem is, the only thing that really moves first is his head and you don't see his arms or legs flail. There is no neuromuscular reaction. It's bogus. If you asked one of those people to cite the medical article that a neuromuscular reaction like this was ever tried, you'll never find it. It's not in the medical literature. They made it up. OK. That's just pure garbage.

Stone: Is this Specter again?

Robertson: No, well, this is a forensic pathologist Dr. Michael Baden. You know, Cyril Wecht was on that panel.

Stone: Well, he doesn't agree with that.

Robertson: Oh no, no, he thought it was ridiculous as any well-versed physician would.

Stone: All right. So I just want to review again the chain of possession of this new bullet, this extra bullet, this fourth bullet, or whatever we call it—the one that James Young finds.

Robertson: Right. OK. As I said before, we know where it hit, it had to land somewhere. It was in the car, it traveled with the car, as with the skull fragments. The larger skull fragments were identified in the plane on the way back to Washington DC. They knew there were skull fragments in the car at that time. That's why it was dispatched. Now, it goes from Parkland Hospital, gets on the plane, goes straight to DC, DC to White House garage, it is covered up, the limousine's covered up. Mills and Martinell come, they're the first ones to really go over it, they find the three skull fragments. They find the bullet. They immediately take them straight back to Dr. Young. Dr. Young then gives them to Dr. Humes. And they disappear. Never to be recorded. And you could tell that it was a bit—as I said, there may have been as little as four people who saw that bullet that day. I have the feeling that some of the Secret Service agents at the White House garage probably saw that bullet and maybe they wrote it off just as Young did because there could have been some confusion between CE 399 which had come back from Dallas, as well as this you know, fourth bullet that was later found.

Bibliographic Essay

In the two scripts that are included in this book, the reader can see that many of the sources we used are declassified documents that were made available as a result of the ARRB. But we did use other sources like more recent books, essays, and prior documentaries. As one looks through this bibliography, two things are evident. We do not list any of the classic polemical texts on the case from first-generation critics, e.g. Sylvia Meagher's *Accessories After the Fact* or Harold Weisberg's *Whitewash* series. That is because we tried to use the most *current* critiques of the Commission's evidence. Some of them were made possible only because of the work of the Review Board.

We did this for two reasons. We understood that the general public was not familiar with this new evidence. Even though there have been many programs produced on the JFK case since 1998, virtually none of them utilized the evidence newly available to them. Why that was the case can only be ascertained by talking to the executives at places like Discovery Channel and Creative Differences Productions.

Secondly, we felt that this more recent work added a new dimension to the pioneering efforts of the early critics. Specifically with topics like Commission Exhibit 399, Oswald's alibi, Kennedy's autopsy and the question of the rifle in evidence. This newer work goes further and deeper in a forensic, courtroom sense.

The second trait the reader will recognize is that much of the bibliography does not deal with the forensic side of the Kennedy case since many of those issues were dealt with in primary documents and testimony created by the ARRB.

But another reason is that *JFK Revisited*, especially in the four-hour version, concerns itself not just with Kennedy's assassination, but with Kennedy the man. We deal with his career as both senator and his less than three years in the White House. The Review Board also unveiled interesting things about this aspect of the case, which we deal with in the film. One instance being the Northwoods documents. These were plans proposed by the Joint Chiefs of Staff to create a phony pretext to invade Cuba. One method being by launching a false flag domestic terrorist attack; another being by blowing up a plane in midair. Kennedy refused to countenance these schemes. These papers had not been revealed prior to the existence of the Review Board.

Another quite valuable document that the ARRB declassified was the record of the May 1963 SecDef Conference in Hawaii. As the reader will recall, Oliver Stone and Zachary Sklar—the cowriters of the script for *JFK*—were viciously attacked for maintaining the thesis that Kennedy was withdrawing from Vietnam at the time of his death. The records of that conference prove that this was Kennedy's intent in 1963. Also that Robert McNamara, his Secretary of Defense, knew that and was implementing it at this conference and throughout that year. In the film, we also played a tape that proves that Lyndon Johnson knew Kennedy was withdrawing, disagreed with the policy as vice president, and consciously reversed Kennedy's policy when he entered the White House.

In the long version of the film we show that this was not the only place where this happened. It also occurred in Indonesia, Congo, and the Middle East. All with a deleterious impact on Kennedy's quest for peace, so eloquently expressed at American University. We also prove that his reformist type of foreign policy did not begin in 1963. It stems back to his 1951 visit with diplomat Edmund Gullion in Saigon. There, Kennedy learned from Gullion that the French effort to regain and maintain its colony was doomed. Further, that if the United States tried to continue that attempt on its own, America would suffer the same fate. As Bobby Kennedy noted, this meeting had a very deep impact on Kennedy's thinking. In the long version of the film, we show how that thinking evolved over time into the famous and highly controversial speech promoting Algerian independence that Senator Kennedy made in 1957. That speech met with a withering attack not just from Republicans, but from people in his own party like Dean

Acheson. With that speech, Kennedy had violated the foreign policy norms of both parties.

In this aspect, we did use some of the older biographies of Kennedy. But we coupled those with the newer efforts of more current historians such as John Newman, Robert Rakove, Philip Muehlenbeck and Greg Pouglrain. Once the audience becomes acquainted with those books it is hard not to conclude that the effort to conceal who Kennedy was is probably more rigorous and systematic than the effort to hide the true circumstances of his assassination. So much of this material is relatively recent that today there simply is no adequate biography of John Kennedy. The work of authors like Robert Dallek is so inadequate that it is actually not worth reading. Which is why we had to use more than one interview source and several books about the man.

As the reader can see in *JFK Revisited*, Kennedy was a unique president and an original thinker. Which is why he was essentially managing his own foreign policy through his brother Robert and through back channel sources, like Norman Cousins with the USSR, and William Attwood with Cuba. It is the thesis of both films, and through a multitude of sources that the meeting with Gullion in 1951 gave birth to an intellectual curiosity which attempted to solve a problem: How could America promote nationalism and decolonization in the Third World while competing with the Soviets on the Cold War stage? Kennedy did his best to try and solve a dilemma which both his predecessor and successor all but ignored. He was not allowed to work his way through to a permanent solution. And his policy was not without faults when he was murdered. But perhaps the best way to summarize his singular achievement is to paraphrase Richard Mahoney from his milestone book *JFK: Ordeal in Africa*: His shortcomings derived from the contagion of the times, his virtues were his own.

Bibliography

BOOKS

Bernstein, Irving. *Promises Kept* (New York: Oxford University Press, 1991).

Blight, James, and Janet M. Lang. *The Armageddon Letters* (New York: Rowman & Littlefield, 2012).

Blight, James, Janet M. Lang, and David A. Welch. *Virtual JFK: Vietnam if Kennedy Had Lived* (New York: Rowman & Littlefield, 2009).

Bolden, Abraham. *The Echo from Dealey Plaza* (New York: Crown, 2008).

Cousins, Norman. *The Improbable Triumvirate* (New York: W.W. Norton, 1972).

Crenshaw, Charles. *Trauma Room One* (New York: Paraview, 2001).

Davy, William. *Let Justice be Done* (Reston: Jordan, 1999).

DiEugenio, James. *Destiny Betrayed, Second Edition* (New York: Skyhorse, 2012).

———. *The JFK Assassination: The Evidence Today* (New York: Skyhorse, 2018).

DiEugenio, James, and Lisa Pease, editors. *The Assassinations: Probe Magazine on JFK, MLK, RFK and Malcolm X* (Los Angeles: Feral House, 2003).

Douglass, James. *JFK and the Unspeakable* (Maryknoll: Orbis, 2008).

Ernest, Barry. *The Girl on the Stairs* (Gretna, LA: Pelican, 2013).

Gardner, Lloyd C., and Ted Gittinger. *Vietnam: The Early Decisions* (Austin: University of Texas Press, 2017).

Gill, William J. *The Ordeal of Otto Otepka* (New York: Arlington House, 1969).

Goldstein, Gordon. *Lessons in Disaster* (New York: Times Books, 2008).

Hancock, Larry. *Someone Would Have Talked* (Southlake, TX: JFK Lancer Productions and Publications, 2006).

Hilsman, Roger. *To Move a Nation* (Garden City, NY: Doubleday, 1967).

Hinckle, Warren, and William Turner. *Deadly Secrets* (New York: Thunder's Mouth, 1992).

Horne, Douglas P. *Inside the ARRB Volumes I–V* (Published by the author: 2009).

Hurt, Henry. *Reasonable Doubt* (New York: Henry Holt, 1985).

Kaiser, David. *American Tragedy* (Cambridge, MA: Harvard University Press, 2000).

Kornbluh, Peter, editor. *Bay of Pigs Declassified: The Secret CIA Report on the Invasion of Cuba* (New York: The New Press, 1998).

Kwitny, Jonathan. *Endless Enemies: The Making of an Unfriendly World* (New York: Penguin, 1987).

LaFeber, Walter. *Inevitable Revolutions: The United States in Central America* (New York: W.W. Norton, 1984).

Law, William Matson. *In the Eye of History* (Southlake, TX: JFK Lancer Productions and Publications, 2005; Revised Second Edition by Trine Day: Walterville, Oregon, 2015).

Logevall, Fredrik. *Choosing War* (Berkeley, University of California Press, 1999).

Mahoney, Richard. *JFK: Ordeal in Africa* (New York: Oxford University Press, 1983).

Mantik, David. *John F. Kennedy's Head Wounds* (Self-published Kindle Edition, 2015).

Mattson, Roger. *Stealing the Atom Bomb* (CreateSpace Independent Publishing Platform, 2016).

May, Ernest, and Philip Zelikow. *The Kennedy Tapes* (Cambridge, MA: Harvard University Press, 1997).

Moise, Edwin. *Tonkin Gulf and the Escalation of the Vietnam War* (Chapel Hill: University of North Carolina Press, 1996).

McKnight, Gerald. *Breach of Trust* (Lawrence: University Press of Kansas, 2005).

Mellen, Joan. *Our Man in Haiti* (Walterville, OR: Trine Day, 2012).

Morley, Jefferson. *The Ghost: The Secret Life of CIA Spymaster James Angleton* (New York: St. Martin's Press, 2017).

Muehlenbeck, Philip. *Betting on the Africans* (New York: Oxford University Press 2012).

Newman, John. *JFK and Vietnam*, Second Edition (CreateSpace Independent Publishing Platform, 2016).

———. *Oswald and the CIA* (New York: Skyhorse, 2008).

———. *Countdown to Darkness* (CreateSpace independent Publishing Platform, 2017).

———. *Into the Storm* (CreateSpace Independent Publishing Platform, 2019).

Pease, Lisa. *A Lie Too Big to Fail* (Port Townsend, WA: Feral House, 2018).

Poulgrain, Greg. *JFK vs. Allen Dulles: Battle Ground Indonesia* (New York: Skyhorse, 2020).

Powers, David, and Kenneth O'Donnell. *Johnny We Hardly Knew Ye* (Boston: Little, Brown, 1972).

Prados, John. *Operation Vulture: America's Dien Bien Phu* (New York: Diversion, 2014).

Rakove, Robert. *Kennedy, Johnson, and the Nonaligned World* (Cambridge, UK: Cambridge University Press, 2013).

Russell, Dick. *The Man Who Knew Too Much* (New York: Carroll & Graf, 2003).

Schlesinger, Arthur. *A Thousand Days* (Boston: Houghton Mifflin, 1965).

———. *Robert Kennedy and His Times: Volumes 1 and 2* (Boston: Houghton Mifflin, 1978)

Simpson, Bradley. *Economists with Guns* (Palo Alto: Stanford University Press, 2008).

Sorenson, Theodore. *Kennedy* (New York: Harper & Row, 1966).

Talbot, David. *Brothers: The Hidden History of the Kennedy Years* (New York: Free Press, 2007).

———. *The Devil's Chessboard* (New York: HarperCollins, 2015).

Thomas, Donald Byron. *Hear No Evil* (New York: Skyhorse, 2010).

Williams, Kenneth, editor. *LeMay on Vietnam* (Washington, DC: Air Force History and Museums Program, 2017).

Williams, Susan. *Who Killed Hammarskjöld?* (Oxford: Oxford University Press, 2014).

FILMS

Crisis: Behind a Presidential Commitment, directed by Robert Drew,1963.

JFK: A President Betrayed, directed by Cory Taylor, 2014.

Reasonable Doubt: The Single-Bullet Theory, directed by Chip Selby, 1995

PERIODICALS AND ESSAYS

Adamczyk, Mark, "JFK Records Release: Why the Redactions?," October 27, 2019 at *Kennedysandking.com*

Aguilar, Gary, and Josiah Thompson, "The Magic Bullet: Even More Magical Than We Knew?" at history-matters.com.

Black, Edwin, "The Plot to Kill JFK in Chicago: November 2, 1963," *Chicago Independent*, November 1975.

Bleau, Paul, "Exposing the FPCC Parts 1 and 2", August 7 and 11, 2021 at *Kenndysandking.com*.

Cranor, Milicent, "Navy Doctor: Bullet Found in JFK's Limousine and Never Reported," October 6, 2017, at *WhoWhatWhy*.

Daniel, Jean, "When Castro Heard the News," *The New Republic*, December 7, 1963.

DiEugenio, James, "The Ordeal of Malcolm Perry," May 24,2021 at *Kennedysanking .com*.

———, "How CBS News Aided the JFK Cover Up" at *Consortium News*, April 22, 2016.

Galbraith, James and Heather Purcell, "Did the U.S. Military Plan a Nuclear First Strike for 1963?" *American Prospect*, Fall 1994.

Gibson, Donald, "The Creation of the Warren Commission," *Probe* magazine, vol. 3, no. 4, May–June 1996.

Hardway, Dan. "Dan Hardway rebuts Shenon's assertion that RFK put Allen Dulles on the Warren Commission," at *Real History Blog*, October 18, 2015.

Hunt, John, "Phantom Identification of the Magic Bullet" and "The Mystery of the 7:30 Bullet," at *JFK Lancer* website.

"The Missing Physician," unsigned essay at Mary Ferrell Foundation website.

Newman, John, "The Molehunt and LHO's Defection," at Newman's website *JN, Publications and Books by John M. Newman.*

Norwood, James, "Edmund Gullion, JFK and the Shaping of a Foreign Policy in Vietnam," at *Kennedysandking.com*, May 8, 2018.

Parker, Richard, "Galbraith and Vietnam." *The Nation*, February 24, 2005.

THESIS

Dani E. Biancolli, *The First Dissenter*, College of William and Mary, 2002.

Index

A

Acheson, Dean, 134, 240
Adamczyk, Mark, 118
Adams, Vicki, 37, 114–117, 225, 241–244
Alsop, Joseph, 2, 90
Alyea, Tom, 145, 146, 226, 425, 426
American Rifleman, 35, 142, 143, 255
American Tragedy (Kaiser), 11
Anderson, Jack, 357
Angleton, James, 62–64, 192–195, 278, 343, 356, 363
Arbenz, Jacobo, 410
Armas, Castillo, 410
Assassination Records Review Board (ARRB), 4, 5, 7, 24, 291, 440, 441
  formation of, 8, 24, 87
  Gloria Knudsen interview, 50, 166
  Humes and Boswell interview, 120, 125
  media coverage, 112
  Moore and, 124, 205
  records destruction referenced in, 67, 201
  Seibert and O'Neil interview, 48, 127
autopsy
  Boswell, 44, 120
  brain, 49, 50, 52–54, 160, 161, 163, 164, 225, 290, 293, 298, 310–311
  brain weight, 53, 160, 161
  destroyed autopsy notes, 47, 162, 268
  face sheet, 56
  Finck, 44, 120
  Humes, 44, 120
  missing bone, 300
  missing photographs, 302, 303
  photographer, 49–51
  photos, 43, 48, 49, 168, 269, 270, 283, 284, 323, 324
  report of brain, 286, 290
  report titled "Clinical Summary," 189

team, 18, 26
witnesses, 283

B

Baden, Michael, 283, 445
Bagley, "Pete" Tennent, 194
Ball, George, 211
Banister, Guy, 61, 196, 197, 226, 228
Barnett, Ross, 208
Batista, Fulgencio, 97
Belcher, Carl, 168, 302
Belin, David, 38, 116, 225, 241, 242, 256, 441
Bell, Audrey, 41, 122, 309
Biden, Joseph, 6, 118
Bissell, Richard, 75, 99, 275
Blakey, Bob, 66, 199, 235
Blakey, Robert, 140, 199, 200, 235, 283
Blunt, Malcolm, 194
Boggs, Hale, 3, 21, 33, 102
Bolden, Abraham, 69, 70, 204, 205, 323
Bolshakov, Georgi, 206, 218, 412
Booth, John Wilkes, 279, 321, 322
Boswell, J. Thornton, 44–46, 120, 121, 125, 157, 159, 168, 174, 175, 189, 261, 282, 284, 300–302, 305, 313, 436
Bowles, Chester, 399
Bringuier, Carlos, 60, 198, 233, 234
Brothers (Talbot), 87–89
Brown, Walt, 3, 9, 100
Bundy, McGeorge, 78, 79, 180, 187, 212, 214, 251, 318, 337, 338
Burkley, George, 52, 54–56, 122, 155–157, 167, 170, 173, 266, 303, 304, 431–433, 436, 437, 439, 443
Burris, Howard, 177, 182, 317, 318
Bush, George H. W., 8, 107, 111, 348

C

Canning, Thomas, 223, 288
Carrico, Jim, 40, 126, 158, 429
Carter, Cliff, 92
Castro, Fidel, 92, 185, 196, 199, 206, 234, 411
CIA plots to assassinate, 22, 75, 89, 100, 107, 180, 357
Kennedy's death news, 81, 218
land reform law, 97
CBS, 2, 9, 33, 93, 94, 96
CE 399, 3, 5, 26, 28, 140, 141, 147–149, 170, 175, 223, 224, 231, 262, 369, 443, 445
Cesar, Thane Eugene, 413
Chamberlain, Neville, 184
Chesser, Michael, 169, 269, 292–298
Church, Frank, 22, 107, 355–357
Church Committee, 9, 22, 59, 74, 107, 108, 124, 153, 191, 324, 325, 328–330, 332, 333, 345, 357
CIA
attempt to overthrow Sukarno, 135, 352, 354
Colby and, 107
connections with Mafia, 88, 89, 108, 357

and Cuban Student Directorate, 199, 233, 234
Dulles and, 3, 21, 72, 83, 92, 98, 99, 274
Ferrie and, 60
firing sequence by, 138
FPCC and, 203
Lumumba and, 22, 74, 89, 107, 276, 277
Oswald and, 64, 68, 192–195, 202, 343, 358
and Otepka's request, 62, 63, 192
plots to assassinate Castro, 22, 75, 89, 100, 107–108, 180, 357
role in JFK assassination, 66, 357
Shaw and, 64, 65
tapping operation, 356
Clark, Kemp, 39, 40, 121, 158, 294, 295
Clark, Ramsey, 267, 283
Clinton, Bill, 8, 111, 348, 385
Colby, William, 107, 356
Connally, John, 1, 16, 23, 26, 30–32, 44, 47, 101, 102, 120, 138–141, 175, 223, 224, 262, 265, 288, 432
Connick, Harry, 344, 385, 386, 417, 418
Conspiracy of Silence (Crenshaw), 43, 124, 281
Cooke, Alistair, 399
Cooper, John Sherman, 3, 20, 30, 31, 33, 102
Cousins, Norman, 15, 207
"crackpot realism," 238–240
Crenshaw, Charles, 43, 123, 281, 309
Cronkite, Walter, 33, 96

D

d'Estaing, Valery Giscard, 3, 57, 176
de Gaulle, Charles, 73, 99, 100, 135, 182, 275, 276, 364
Devlin, Larry, 277
Dillon, Douglas, 356
Dobrynin, Anatoly, 185
Dolce, Joseph, 30, 140, 170, 223
Dorman, Elsie, 117, 243
Dudman, Richard, 172
Dulles, Allen, 3, 21, 22, 274–278, 332, 354, 359, 360, 391, 392, 401
appointment to Warren Commission, 83, 91, 92
fired by Kennedy, 111, 205, 278
JFK letter to, 131
Mafia connection, 108
and Non-Aligned Movement, 135
Dulles, John Foster, 75, 130–132, 135, 239, 246, 352, 381, 391, 392
Dwyer, Dan, 328, 330

E

Ebersole, John, 168, 266, 296, 302–304
Edwards, Brian, 27, 224, 252–258
Eisenhower, Dwight, 20, 73–75, 97, 103, 130, 132–135, 196, 227, 239, 332, 353, 360, 379–381, 391, 400
Ellis, Stavis, 172

Ernest, Barry, 2, 9, 114–117, 225, 241–244

F

Fair Play for Cuba Committee (FPCC), 59, 60, 69, 196–198, 203, 233, 344, 372, 374
Feinman, Roger, 33, 96
Ferrie, David, 60, 61, 195, 196, 198, 228, 418
Finck, Pierre, 44, 45, 47, 120, 162–164, 173, 189, 282, 300, 302
Fisher, Russell, 260, 262
Ford, Gerald, 3, 21, 57, 107, 175, 440, 441
Ford, Gerry, 92
Frazier, Robert, 27, 28, 35, 142, 147, 148, 424, 425
Freedom of Information Act, 5, 87, 342, 384
Freeman, H. R., 172
Fritz, Will, 150

G

Galbraith, John Kenneth, 77, 183, 185–186, 334, 395
Garner, Dorothy, 38, 39, 117, 225, 243
Garrison, Jim, 1, 7, 64, 227, 228, 344, 357, 385, 416, 418–420
Gayton, Carver, 327–329
Gheesling, Marvin, 65, 201
Gilbert, Robert, 440
Girl on the Stairs, The (Ernest), 39, 115–117, 225
Glanges, Evalea, 172
Gochenaur, Jim, 42, 124, 320–330
Goldstein, Gordon, 11
Good Night America program, 23, 109
Graham, Fred, 260
Gray, Gordon, 333
Gribkov, Anatoly, 184
Groden, Robert, 108, 109
Guinn, Vincent, 140
Gullion, Edmund, 105, 129, 130, 238, 239, 358, 359, 376, 403
Gunn, Jeremy, 9, 10, 49, 161, 164, 167, 168, 305, 306, 308, 310, 311, 313

H

Halberstam, David, 11
Hammarskjöld, Dag, 74, 75, 104, 105, 399–403
Harper, Billy, 128, 271
Harper, Jack, 271
Harper's Magazine, 72, 98, 274
Hart, Gary, 22, 107
Harvey, William, 89
Helms, Dick, 66, 199, 234
Helms, Richard, 63, 211, 278, 362
Helpern, Milton, 119, 366
Hill, Clint, 126
Holmes, Chuck, 187
Holmes, Harry, 150, 253
Hoover, J. Edgar, 22, 25, 31, 89, 92, 93, 101, 108, 151, 254, 362, 412
Horne, Douglas, 4, 9, 10, 163, 166, 225, 268, 299–314, 433
Hosty, James, 1, 150, 328, 329

House Select Committee on Assassinations (HSCA), 4, 8–10, 23, 27, 55, 66, 109, 110, 123, 140, 156, 223, 235, 283, 288, 343, 345, 350, 430, 433
Humes, James, 47, 120, 158, 159, 162, 261, 268, 289, 300, 302, 304, 305, 443, 445
Hunt, John, 27, 28, 147, 148, 224, 422, 425
Hurt, Henry, 55, 145, 156

I

Indonesian Communist Party, 136, 246, 249–251

J

Jenkins, James, 303
Jenkins, Marion, 294
JFK (1991 film), 4, 7–8, 24, 43, 86, 110, 124, 169, 227, 269, 281, 339, 357
JFK Records Collection Act, 7, 8, 24, 76, 111, 181, 220, 422
JFK Revisited documentary, 2, 4, 5, 8, 10
JFK's Alliance for Progress, 211
Joannides, George, 66, 199, 200, 226, 234, 235, 349, 350
Johnson, Haynes, 412
Johnson, Lyndon B.
  alterations to NSAM 273, 79, 215, 216, 338
  Burkley and, 157
  Congo policy, 210, 404
  foreign policy, 210
  intervention in Dominican Republic, 409, 410
  reversal of Kennedy's policies, 3, 209, 215, 227, 404
  Tonkin Gulf, 217
  Vietnam war, 3, 10, 79, 227, 396
  Warren commission, 2, 3, 20, 91, 93, 387
Johnson, Richard, 27, 147
Johnson, Robert, 332
Jones, Howard, 11
Journal of the American Medical Association (JAMA), 281, 287, 289

K

Kaiser, David, 11, 216
Katzenbach, Nicholas, 31, 89, 90, 101, 151
Kavanaugh, Brett, 235, 236
Kelley, Thomas, 150
Kennedy Half Century, The (Sabato), 83, 220
Kennedy, Jackie, 17, 18, 52, 159, 160, 260, 286
Kennedy, John F.
  Algeria speech, 363, 378, 398, 409
  antinuclear plans, 207
  approach to Indonesia, 352
  assassination, 1, 3, 8, 16, 23, 107, 285, 367
  Bay of Pigs operation, 274, 275
  brain photos, 10
  Burkley comments, 156

Chicago plot, 68–70, 202, 203
civil rights speech, 209
death, 17, 218–220
death certificate, 55, 155, 266, 432
Dobrynin and, 185
Dulles and, 176–177
failed plots, 371–374
fiftieth anniversary, 8
Finck autopsy, 47
foreign aid bill, 394
foreign policy, 4, 136, 178
Gullion and, 129, 130
Humes and Boswell autopsy, 44–47
Khrushchev and, 185, 206
LeMay's disagreements, 188
Nasser and, 178, 179, 391
Non-Aligned Movement, 135
opposed to nuclear proliferation, 179–180
opposition to Vulture, 132
peace speech, 15, 208, 221, 277
plans for Indonesia, 212
prior plots to kill, 67, 201
problems with Lemnitzer, 181, 182
Saigon trip, 376
Sukarno and, 247–248, 355
threat sheets, 200
tracheotomy, 40, 121
UN speech, 105, 106
Vietnam withdrawal plan, 4, 186–187, 317–319, 334, 336
world trips, 69, 129, 358, 359
X-ray of skull, 267, 269
Kennedy, Joseph, 134, 407–413
Kennedy, Robert, 88, 90, 185, 275, 303, 318, 319, 362
assassination, 221
foreign policy adviser, 205
meeting with Gullion, 238, 239
reactions to JFK death, 82, 87, 89
Sukarno and, 353, 355
Khrushchev, Nikita, 15, 81, 92, 182, 183, 185, 206, 207, 218, 394, 411, 412
Kilduff, Malcolm, 40, 121
Kirkpatrick, Lyman, 274, 275
Knebel, Fletcher, 403
Knudsen, Gloria, 166, 270, 312
Knudsen, Robert, 10, 50, 165, 166, 269, 270, 303, 311, 312
Krulak, Victor, 336
Kurtz, Michael, 56, 156

L

Lane, Mark, 2, 3, 7, 9, 58, 139, 153, 254
Lansdale, Edward, 180, 334, 335
Latona, Sebastian, 36, 144, 145, 226, 257
Leavelle, Jim, 253
LeMay, Curtis, 184, 185, 187, 188, 190, 228, 313
Lemnitzer, Lyman, 176, 181, 182, 333–335
Leon, Richard, 235
Lewis, Anthony, 94, 286, 287
Liebeler, Wesley, 113
Limited Test Ban Treaty, 207

Lipsey, Richard, 305
Lopez, Gilberto Policarpo, 69, 203, 373, 374
Lovelady, Billy, 115, 116, 242, 243
Luce, Henry, 237, 240
Luciano, Lucky, 88
Lumumba, Patrice, 22, 73, 74, 103, 104, 107, 210, 275–277, 332, 333, 399–400

M

MacArthur, Douglas, 182
MacMillan, Harold, 106
magic bullet, 3, 26–29, 140, 146–148, 174–175, 265
Mann, Thomas, 410
Mantik, David, 231, 264–272
Marlowe, Vaughn, 372
Martinell, William, 170, 171, 437, 443, 445
Marwell, David, 306, 308
Mboya, Tom, 136, 137
McCarthy, Eugene, 318, 319
McClelland, Robert, 128, 158, 160, 270
McCloy, Ellen, 33
McCloy, John, 21, 33, 96, 278
McCone, John, 138, 278
McDonnell, Gerald, 272
McKeithen, John, 416
McNamara, Robert, 76–80, 176–177, 181, 186, 187, 215, 317, 335–336, 338–340, 388
Mills, C. Wright, 238
Mills, Thomas, 170–171, 437, 441, 443, 445
Mobutu, Joseph, 74, 104, 210, 404
Moore, Elmer, 42, 123, 204, 205, 321–326, 328, 329, 431
Morgan, Reeves, 414, 415, 418
Morgenthau, Bob, 411
Moyers, Bill, 90, 91

N

Nasser, 359, 378–382
Nasser, Gamal Abdel, 391
National Archives, 70, 111
  brain pictures, 5, 49, 54, 163, 164, 168, 225
  different versions of Adams's testimony, 116
  Hunt bullet information from, 147, 148
  Stroud document, 38, 117
  X-rays and photos missing, 168, 344
  X-rays of Kennedy's skull, 169
  Zapruder film, 113
National Security Action Memorandum (NSAM)
  NSAM 111, 76, 183
  NSAM 263, 78, 79, 187, 214, 216, 336, 337
  NSAM 273, 214–216, 338
National Security Agency (NSA), 250
NBC, 2, 9, 33, 93, 94, 96, 152, 227
Nehru, Jawaharlal, 378, 379, 394, 395

Neutron Activation Analysis, 140, 141, 262
New York Times, 2, 4, 33, 50, 94–96, 107, 112, 152, 165, 260, 281, 286–287, 337, 356, 360, 377
Newman, John, 4, 10, 331–340, 423
Nichols, John, 266, 282
Nitze, Paul, 240
Nixon, Richard, 131, 132, 137
Nkrumah, Kwame, 363
Noguchi, Thomas, 412
Non-Aligned Movement, 135, 246
Noteboom, Gerard, 271

O

O'Connor, Paul, 189, 190, 303
O'Donnell, Kenny, 82, 87
O'Neill, Frank, 10, 48, 49, 52, 56, 126, 127, 160, 161, 167, 173, 189, 304, 307
Odum, Bardwell, 29, 148, 224
On the Trail of the Assassins (Garrison), 1
Operation Celeste, 105, 106
Operation Grand Slam, 106
Operation Mongoose, 180
Operation Northwoods, 75, 180
Operation Underworld, 88
Operation Vulture, 131, 239
Oswald, Lee Harvey
- 201 file, 193, 343
- Andrews and, 64, 197, 198
- Banister and, 61, 196
- CIA and, 64–66, 68, 192, 194, 202, 343
- communist, 60, 62, 195, 233
- in Cuban exile training, 61, 195
- denying charges, 18, 19, 151
- earnings record, 194, 308–309
- FBI and, 65, 101, 149, 196, 197, 201
- FBI informant, 202
- Ferrie and, 60, 61, 195, 228
- FPCC and, 59, 60, 197, 233
- funeral, 59
- Lane and, 2, 58, 153, 254
- Marine Corps, 59, 193, 194, 308
- in Mexico City, 1, 93, 361, 362, 374
- Otepka and, 62, 191, 192
- rifle, 34, 35, 142–144, 255
- tape of, 361, 362

Oswald, Marina, 35, 143, 144
Otepka, Otto, 62, 63, 191, 192, 194, 358

P

Pearson, Drew, 357
Perry, Malcolm
- on bullet wounds, 121, 122, 281, 304, 429, 430
- Moore and, 42, 124, 322
- testimony changed, 42, 123, 322
- testimony on Warren Commission, 41–42, 123, 429

Phillips, David, 198, 199, 361
Pike, Otis, 356, 357
Pope, Alan, 136, 247, 352, 353
Popkin, Richard, 7
Posner, Gerald, 9, 441
Powers, Dave, 82, 87, 182, 385

Prouty, Fletcher, 4, 227, 334
Purdy, Andy, 283

R

Ramsey Clark panel, 260, 267, 283, 285, 293
Rankin, J. Lee, 38, 57, 58, 90, 108, 117, 126, 153, 172, 192
Reagan, Ronald, 134, 356
Riebe, Floyd, 164, 289
Rivera, Geraldo, 23, 109
Robert Kennedy and His Times (Schlesinger), 90
Robinson, Tom, 160, 161, 189, 309
Rockefeller, Nelson, 107, 134
Roosevelt, Franklin, 130, 131, 393, 407
Rose, Earl, 39, 119, 120
Roselli, Johnny, 89
Rostow, Eugene, 90
Rostow, Walt, 77, 177, 182, 183, 316, 318
Rowley, James, 27, 28, 40, 147, 172
Ruby, Jack, 326
  FBI informant, 22, 108
  Mafia connections, 153
  Oswald murder, 1, 20, 93, 151, 152
Rusk, Dean, 177, 179, 352, 395
Russell, Richard, 3, 20, 31, 32, 92, 100–102
Rydberg, Harold, 125, 261, 267, 295

S

Sabato, Larry, 9, 83, 220
Salant, Richard, 33, 96
Salisbury, Harrison, 286
Saslaw, Leonard, 47, 163
Schlesinger, Arthur, 90, 97, 178, 206, 275
Schweiker, Richard, 9, 10, 22, 59, 107, 108, 191, 328
Seven Days in May (Knebel), 403
Shaw, Clay, 45, 64, 65, 173, 189, 197, 198, 228, 282, 344, 363, 385, 386, 418, 420
Sheehan, Neil, 11
Shelley, William, 115, 116, 242, 243
Shenon, Philip, 9
Shires, Tom, 41, 123, 429
Sibert, James, 10, 48, 56, 57, 126, 127, 173, 189, 304, 307, 309
Simpson, Bradley, 4, 135, 212–214, 245–251
single-bullet theory, 26, 30, 31, 47, 48, 56, 101, 102, 123, 126, 138, 139, 141, 157, 173–175, 223, 284, 307, 430, 432
Sirhan, 412, 413
Six Seconds in Dallas (Thompson), 27, 46, 139, 149, 224, 265
Sklar, Zachary, 4, 10
Specter, Arlen, 140, 300, 324, 441
  interview of Sibert and O'Neill, 126, 173, 307
  interview of Tomlinson, 224
  meeting with Humes and Boswell, 125
  seven-wound trajectory, 223
  single-bullet theory, 26, 47, 48, 139, 174, 223

Spencer, Saundra, 10, 51, 52, 166, 167, 226, 270, 271, 309, 312
Sprague, Richard, 55, 156, 433
Stevenson, Adlai, 74, 104, 106, 132, 134, 240, 277, 392, 399, 400, 409
Stokes, Louis, 10, 306, 345
Stringer, John, 49–52, 163–166, 168, 225, 269, 290, 302, 310–312
Stroud, Martha Jo, 38, 39, 117
Student Revolutionary Directorate (DRE), 60, 198–200, 233, 234
Styles, Sandra, 38, 39, 116, 117, 225, 243, 244
Suharto, 213, 214, 251
Sukarno, 135, 136, 212, 213, 246–250, 252, 352–355, 381
Sullivan, William, 187, 336
Symington, Stuart, 176

T

Tague, James, 25, 31, 138, 150, 172, 443
Talbot, David, 72, 73, 82, 87–90, 273–279
Tanenbaum, Robert, 58, 59, 154, 198
Taylor, Charles, 172
Taylor, Maxwell, 77, 78, 182, 183, 185–187, 216, 275, 316, 335, 336, 338
Thompson, Doug, 32
Thompson, Josiah, 27, 29, 46, 139, 140, 149, 175, 224, 225, 265
Thousand Days (Schlesinger), 97, 178
Tippit, J. D., 1, 5, 19
Tito, Josip Broz, 393
Todd, Elmer Lee, 27, 28, 147, 148, 224, 231, 424, 425
Tomlinson, Darrell, 45, 46, 174, 224, 265
Tonkin Gulf, 79, 80, 216, 217
Truman, Harry, 130, 238
Trump, Donald, 5, 6, 8, 118, 220, 236, 347, 389
Tshombe, Moïse, 210, 404
Tunheim, John, 4, 5, 307, 341–350

U

Ugly American, The (Burdick), 360, 377

V

Vallee, Thomas Arthur, 68, 70, 202, 204, 372, 373

W

Wallach, Paul, 324, 325, 328, 330
Walton, Bill, 218, 412
Warner, Roger, 42, 322
Warren Commission
  Adams testimony, 37–38, 115–117
  Brennan testimony, 114
  conclusion about Ruby, 152–153
  Connally testimony, 32, 101
  creation of, 2
  Dolce's work on, 30
  Dulles and, 108, 111
  Dulles's appointment to, 83, 91
  evidence destroyed, 37, 116, 243
  eyewitness testimony, 158
  firing sequence, 138

Hill testimony, 126
Hoover and, 108, 254
Humes testimony, 125, 164
Lane testimony, 9
Latona testimony, 36, 144, 145
major findings, 21, 93
McClelland testimony, 160
members of, 20–21
Perry testimony, 41–42, 123, 429
release of evidence and testimony, 5, 94, 287
role of Elmer Moore in, 42
shooting sequences, 26, 114
single-bullet theory, 47
Specter and, 125, 223
Stroud document, 39, 117
wound drawings, 125
Warren Omission, The (Brown), 3, 9, 100
Warren, Earl, 20, 90, 92, 100, 325
Washington Post, 50, 90, 165, 311, 337
Wecht, Cyril, 7, 26, 222, 259–263, 283, 445
Wegmann, Edward, 344
Weldon, Doug, 172
Whitaker, George, 172
Whitten, John, 192
Who Killed Hammarskjöld? (Williams), 75
Williams, Harry Ruiz, 89
Williams, Susan, 75, 105, 106
Wilson, Rob, 6, 227, 230, 231
wound
back wound, 26, 46, 56, 150, 173, 174, 261, 266, 282, 283
diagrams, 48, 125, 127, 309
entrance wound, 40–42, 121–123, 164, 281, 301
exit wound, 40–42, 56, 121–123, 156, 175, 294, 302, 429–431, 433
neck wound, 26, 40, 42, 122, 123, 173, 266, 322, 429
Wright, O. P., 149, 224, 225, 265

X

X-rays, 272, 436
alteration, 272
evidence, 170, 284
fragment trial, 169, 293
of Kennedy's skull, 169, 267, 269, 436
missing, 168, 260
original, 296

Y

Young, James, 170, 171, 436, 438–445

Z

Zapruder film, 10, 23, 52, 108–109, 113, 139, 171, 225, 263, 267, 282, 285, 286, 289, 295, 313, 327, 368, 443
Zapruder, Abraham, 21, 23, 109